THE CAMBRIDGE COMPANION TO
EPICUREANISM

This *Companion* presents both an introduction to the history of the ancient philosophical school of Epicureanism and also a critical account of the major areas of its philosophical interest. Chapters span the school's history from the early Hellenistic Garden to the Roman Empire and its later reception in the early modern period, introducing the reader to the Epicureans' contributions in physics, metaphysics, epistemology, psychology, ethics and politics. The international team of contributors includes scholars who have produced innovative and original research in various areas of Epicurean thought and they have produced essays which are accessible and of interest to philosophers, classicists, and anyone concerned with the diversity and preoccupations of Epicurean philosophy and the current state of academic research in this field. The volume emphasizes the interrelation of the different areas of the Epicureans' philosophical interests while also drawing attention to points of interpretative difficulty and controversy.

JAMES WARREN is a Senior Lecturer in the Faculty of Classics, University of Cambridge. Previous books include *Facing Death: Epicurus and his Critics* (2004) and *Epicurus and Democritean Ethics: an Archaeology of Ataraxia* (2002).

The Cambridge Companion to

EPICUREANISM

Edited by James Warren
University of Cambridge

CAMBRIDGE UNIVERSITY PRESS
Cambridge, New York, Melbourne, Madrid, Cape Town, Singapore, São Paulo, Delhi, Dubai, Tokyo, Mexico City

Cambridge University Press
The Edinburgh Building, Cambridge CB2 8RU, UK

Published in the United States of America by Cambridge University Press, New York

www.cambridge.org
Information on this title: www.cambridge.org/9780521695305

First published 2009
Reprinted 2010

Printed in the United Kingdom at the University Press, Cambridge

A catalogue record for this publication is available from the British Library

Library of Congress Cataloguing in Publication data
The Cambridge companion to epicureanism / edited by James Warren.
p. cm.
Includes bibliographical references and index.
ISBN 978-0-521-87347-5 (hardback) – ISBN 978-0-521-69530-5 (paperback)
1. Epicureans (Greek philosophy) I. Warren, James, 1974– II. Title.
B512.C35 2009
187–dc22

2009008249

ISBN 978-0-521-87347-5 Hardback
ISBN 978-0-521-69530-5 Paperback

CONTENTS

CONTRIBUTORS

ELIZABETH ASMIS is Professor of Classics at the University of Chicago. She is the author of *Epicurus' Scientific Method* and has written articles on Greek and Roman Stoicism, Hellenistic aesthetics, Philodemus, Lucretius, and Cicero's political thought.

CATHERINE ATHERTON teaches Classics and Philosophy at UCLA. She is the author of *The Stoics on Ambiguity* and is currently working on an edition of Chrysippus' *Logical Questions* (*PHerc.* 307) and on various topics in Stoic logic and in Epicurean philosophy of language.

DAVID BLANK is Professor of Classics at UCLA. He has written on various topics in ancient philosophy and the study of language in antiquity, including a translation and commentary on *Sextus Empiricus, Against the Grammarians*. He is currently editing several books of Philodemus' *On Rhetoric*.

ERIC BROWN, Associate Professor of Philosophy at Washington University in St Louis, is the author of several articles on Greek and Roman philosophy and of *Stoic Cosmopolitanism*.

DISKIN CLAY is Distinguished Professor Emeritus of Classical Studies at Duke University in Durham, North Carolina. He has recently written a chapter on the Epicurean movement for the collection *Lire Épicure* and a chapter on 'Plato Philomythos' for the *Cambridge Companion to Greek Mythology*.

MICHAL ERLER is Professor Ordinarius in Classics at the University of Würzburg. He is the author of *Epikur-Die Schule Epikurs-Lukrez* (Überweg series) and *Römische Philosophie*, editor of *Epikureismus in der späten Republik und der Kaiserzeit*, and has published various articles on Plato, Platonism, Epicurus, Epicureanism and Greek drama.

CHRISTOPHER GILL is Professor of Ancient Thought at the University of Exeter. He is the author of *Personality in Greek Epic, Tragedy, and Philosophy: The Self in Dialogue*; *The Structured Self in Hellenistic and Roman Thought*; and *Naturalistic Psychology in Galen and Stoicism*. He has edited or co-edited a number of volumes of essays on ancient philosophy and is currently co-editor of the journal *Phronesis*.

PIERRE-MARIE MOREL is Professor of Ancient Philosophy at the École Normale Supérieure de Lettres et Sciences Humaines in Lyon. His books include: *Démocrite et la recherche des causes*; *De la matière à l'action: Aristote et le problème du vivant*. He is also the co-editor of the collective volumes *Lire Épicure et les Épicuriens* and *Democritus: Science, the Arts and the Care of the Soul*. He has published various articles on ancient atomism and on Aristotle's psychology.

TIM O'KEEFE is an Associate Professor of Philosophy at Georgia State University. He is the author of *Epicurus on Freedom*, as well as articles on topics such as Epicurean friendship, Cyrenaic ethics, Aristotelian cosmology, and Platonic *spuria*.

DAVID SEDLEY is Laurence Professor of Ancient Philosophy in the University of Cambridge, where he is also a Fellow of Christ's College. His books include: *The Hellenistic Philosophers* (with A. A. Long); *Lucretius and the Transformation of Greek Wisdom*; and *Creationism and Its Critics in Antiquity*. He was editor of *Classical Quarterly* 1986–92, and of *Oxford Studies in Ancient Philosophy* 1998–2007.

LIBA TAUB is a Reader in History and Philosophy of Science and Director of the Whipple Museum of the History of Science at the University of Cambridge, and a Fellow of Newnham College. She is the author of *Ptolemy's Universe: The Natural Philosophical and Ethical Foundations of Ptolemy's Astronomy*, *Ancient Meteorology* and *Aetna and the Moon: Explaining Nature in Ancient Greece and Rome*, as well as numerous articles on ancient Greek and Roman – as well as later – science.

VOULA TSOUNA is Professor of Philosophy at the University of California, Santa Barbara. She is co-author of *[Philodemus] [On Choices and Avoidances]*, author of *The Epistemology of the Cyrenaic School*, *The Ethics of Philodemus*, and numerous articles on Plato and Hellenistic and Roman Philosophy. She is currently writing a monograph on Plato's *Charmides* and a series of articles on Hellenistic theories of concept-formation.

JAMES WARREN is a Senior Lecturer in Classics at the University of Cambridge and Fellow and Director of Studies in Philosophy at Corpus Christi College. He is the author of *Epicurus and Democritean Ethics: An Archaeology of Ataraxia*, *Facing Death: Epicurus and his Critics*, and *Presocratics*, as well as various articles on Epicureanism and other topics in ancient philosophy.

CATHERINE WILSON is Distinguished Professor of Philosophy at The Graduate Center, City University of New York. She is the author of *Epicureanism at the Origins of Modernity* and of *The Invisible World: Philosophy and the Invention of the Microscope*, as well as other books and articles on metaphysics and natural science in the seventeenth century.

RAPHAEL WOOLF is Reader in Philosophy at King's College London. He has translated Cicero's *De Finibus* ('On Moral Ends') for the series *Cambridge Texts in the History of Philosophy*, and written on Plato, Aristotle and Hellenistic philosophy.

JAMES WARREN

Introduction

> Philosophy, as long as a drop of blood shall pulse in its world-subduing and absolutely free heart, will never grow tired of answering its adversaries with the cry of Epicurus: 'The truly impious man is not he who denies the gods worshipped by the multitude, but he who affirms of the gods what the multitude believes about them'.
>
> Karl Marx, Foreword to his 1841 Doctoral dissertation[1]

> As you say of yourself, I TOO AM AN EPICUREAN. I consider the genuine (not the imputed) doctrines of Epicurus as containing everything rational in moral philosophy which Greece and Rome have left us.
>
> Thomas Jefferson, Letter to William Short, 31 October 1819

> In addition to removing all hope of help and favours from the gods, as we said, Epicurus blinds the part of our understanding that loves learning and the part of our practical reason that loves honour. He packs them tightly into a narrow vessel and removes any pure pleasure from body and soul. He degrades our nature, as if there were no greater good than the avoidance of evil.
>
> Plutarch, *Non posse* 1107C

Epicurean philosophy has always tended to provoke strong reactions. Its account of the universe in terms of the motions and interactions of atoms in the void combines with its account of the good life being the

[1] For a translation with notes of *The Difference Between the Democritean and Epicurean Philosophy of Nature with an Appendix*, see the online version at the Karl Marx Internet Archive: www.marxists.org/archive/marx/works/1841/dr-theses/index.htm.

life of pleasure and freedom from mental pain to form an overall outlook on things which has always generated impassioned responses, whether approving or critical. For some, Epicureanism offers a liberating account of the universe which frees humanity to work out for itself its own natural goals without supernatural authority and influence.[2] For others, and in fact for most ancient commentators, Epicureanism is founded on a dangerous combination of the twin follies of materialism and hedonism, encouraging humanity either to think of itself as too powerful – the ultimate masters of our own destiny and heedless of any divine commands – or else to think of humans merely as beasts like all the other creatures around us, pandering only to our basest physical natures and needs. In particular, the Epicureans' insistence that the gods take no part in and have no care for us and our world has been thought of either as a rallying cry for humanity and philosophy against stifling religious strictures (Marx's view) or as tantamount to atheism and a rejection of the requirements of proper piety and the proper conception of human nature (Plutarch's view).

Of course, neither of these partisan views can do justice to the full range of detailed argument and philosophical interest to be found in Epicurean texts. It is hoped that the various chapters in this volume might serve as a stimulating introduction to the school and an attempt to offer a more rounded appraisal of its philosophical and historical importance together with a sense of the ongoing interpretative controversies and open questions which drive current scholarship. This volume takes its place in a trio of *Cambridge Companions* dealing with the major philosophical movements which can trace their origins to the Hellenistic period of Antiquity.[3] Yet, while these three volumes share a similar approach and will deal with some similar methodological problems, there are some aspects of the study of Epicureanism which mark it out as interestingly different from other areas of research into philosophy of this general period.

[2] For an interesting example of this kind of positive appraisal in modern scholarship see Farrington 1939, who makes Epicureanism into a populist anti-aristocratic movement. See the important review by Momigliano 1941 and the angrily critical review by Guthrie 1940. Farrington's later work is no less enthusiastic: see e.g. the final chapter of Farrington 1967.

[3] For the Stoics see Inwood 2003. For the Hellenistic sceptics see some of the chapters in Bett (forthcoming).

In comparison with students of Stoicism, for example, who need to rely on very fragmentary or second-hand material for information about the earliest phases of the school, those working on Epicureanism have a rich abundance of primary source material written by committed and informed Epicureans. Some complete works by Epicurus himself, the *Letters to Herodotus*, *Pythocles* and *Menoeceus*, have survived through quotation by Diogenes Laërtius in the final book of his *Lives and sayings of the eminent philosophers*. In addition, we have the great Latin hexameter poem *On the nature of things* (*De rerum natura*) by the Epicurean Lucretius. And more and more Epicurean texts in various states of preservation are being edited, re-edited and published. A scholar of Epicureanism has plenty of primary material to work with, even before turning to the various other discussions of Epicureanism found in philosophical and other writers from Antiquity.

A particularly striking aspect of the study of Epicureanism which contributes to its ongoing interest and presents its own set of challenges, is the survival in a variety of different forms of various pieces of textual evidence for Epicurean views. Not only do we have Epicurean texts, such as Epicurus' *Letters* and Lucretius' poem, which were transmitted along with the corpus of ancient literature and thought via the Middle Ages and Renaissance, but we also have Epicurean works which have been preserved in such a way that they survive directly from Antiquity unaffected by the familiar forces which took their toll on many ancient texts. That is not to say, however, that these other works have survived their journey entirely unscathed and their method of preservation requires the use of additional sets of technical skills to generate useful information. This makes the study of Epicureanism rather unusual in ancient philosophy since there is a steady flow of new texts, new readings and new material to be integrated into our overall understanding of the school. I have in mind, of course, two particularly remarkable sets of evidence. First, a library of Epicurean works was preserved by the eruption of Vesuvius in AD 79 in the ruined villa of L. Calpurnius Piso just outside Herculaneum and rediscovered in the eighteenth century.[4] These often fragmentary texts, which require considerable care to

[4] For a good introduction to the library and the methods used in deciphering the texts see Gigante 1995 and Sider 2005. The Friends of Herculaneum Society maintains a

unroll, decipher, reconstruct and then interpret, continue to increase our knowledge of Epicureanism both in its earlier Hellenistic phase and also as it developed through to the first century BC and later. Increasingly sophisticated methods of electronic imaging coupled with the best standards of papyrological and philological scholarship have allowed us to make great advances in reading these texts. Otherwise lost works revealed by these methods written by Epicurus himself, as well as by other Epicureans such as Demetrius Lacon, Polystratus and Philodemus, have done a great deal to enhance our knowledge of Epicurean philosophy as well as offer a new perspective on the various methods of scholarship, differences of opinion and range of interests demonstrated by various committed Epicurean writers. The library also allows us a glimpse into the world of a group of Epicureans in the late Roman Republic and early Empire, their interests, what they were reading and, perhaps, what aspects of Epicureanism they were most interested in.

The second peculiar but fortunate survival from Antiquity is the long monumental Epicurean inscription from Oinoanda in Lycia, Asia Minor (modern Turkey), paid for and partly written by a second century AD Epicurean philanthropist, Diogenes. Parts of it survive and the fragments can be pieced together and reconstructed in ways very like those used to put together the Herculanean texts. The combination of close epigraphical work and detailed philological and philosophical analysis has allowed this curious monument once again to enhance our knowledge of Epicureanism in general and also offers a window on the continuation of Epicureanism as a way of life in later Antiquity.[5]

From all this material emerges a philosophical movement and world-view which is in many ways refreshingly unlike the dominant trends of ancient thought. Unlike much of Greek and later philosophy, the Epicureans resolutely resist tracing their origins back to Socrates or to the various Socratic thinkers who came afterwards. The relationship between Epicurus and the two giants of classical

very useful website listing the various works from the library together with a bibliography and a guide to recent editions. (See: www.herculaneum.ox.ac.uk/papyri.html.) *Cronache Ercolanesi*, the journal of the Centro Internazionale per lo Studio dei Papiri Ercolanesi (CISPE see: www.cispegigante.it) contains articles discussing the villa, the history of scholarship on it and its papyri, and the most recent editions of various texts.

[5] For more discussion, see Erler, ch. 3, this volume.

philosophy – Plato and Aristotle – is complicated; there is, for example, good reason to suspect that Epicurus and certainly later Epicureans were relatively avid readers of Plato, at least – but unlike the Stoics and the Academics the Epicureans saw nothing in Plato and Socrates that they wished to claim as their inspiration. Indeed, in the broadest terms the Epicurean view of things is opposed to this alternative tradition in nearly all matters of substantive philosophical importance. The Epicureans saw our world, or *kosmos*, as just one among indefinitely many which are generated and destroyed in the infinite and everlasting universe simply as a result of the unceasing motion of atoms in a void. Our world is not the product of any form of rational design, nor are any of its constituents or inhabitants as they are because of some kind of natural teleology.[6] The Epicureans saw humans, as a consequence, as free to seek their own natural well-being, fitted as a result of natural processes of selection with the faculties of perception and reason which allow them to acquire reliable knowledge of the world about them and with the means to live a good and fulfilling life free from the constraints of any external divine authority. Although Epicureanism was known since the foundation of the school for the combination of a robustly materialist outlook on the world and the promotion of hedonism as the recipe for the good life, both of these characteristics – while obviously true – require careful qualification and consideration. Their materialism is far from brutish or unreflective; their general metaphysical outlook is in fact rather complex. And their hedonism too does not advocate a simple-minded abandon; the Epicurean good life turns out to be a relatively sober affair, founded on the proper understanding of human nature and human needs but with room for both friendship and the enjoyment of intellectual pursuits.

The articles presented here fall into two major groups. The first, comprising the pieces by Diskin Clay, David Sedley, Michael Erler and Catherine Wilson, takes a diachronic view, tracing the history of the school from its roots in Hellenistic Athens, through the Roman Republic and Empire, and on to later Antiquity, the Christian era, and beyond. Epicureanism was a developing philosophy which was able to respond as well as contribute to the developing cultures of Antiquity. Together, these chapters serve as an introduction to the

[6] For an account of ancient teleology and the atomist tradition see Sedley 2007.

major episodes in the school's history, its prominent members and the general atmosphere in which the various surviving Epicurean texts were created, read and discussed. The emphasis here is on the school as a historical movement, its organization and influence.

The influence of Epicureanism on the development of modern thought before the eighteenth century was exerted without the aid of these new sources of information from Herculaneum and Oinoanda. However, Epicurus' own writings transmitted by Diogenes Laërtius, together with Lucretius' poem and works by non-Epicureans such as Cicero and Plutarch, managed to paint a picture of a materialist and hedonist philosophy which repelled and attracted different kinds of readers. The story of the reception of Epicurean philosophy is not much discussed in this *Companion*, although Catherine Wilson's contribution sets much of the scene for the early modern period. In the main, this is a deliberate decision because much of the story can be found already discussed in some detail in the *Cambridge Companion to Lucretius*, which is in many ways a 'companion' *Companion* to this volume, and also in Catherine Wilson's own larger-scale monograph on the topic.[7] That omission, forgivable I hope, allows more space for a detailed discussion and analysis of ancient Epicureanism and the content of Epicurean philosophy itself.

The second group of contributions focuses to a larger extent on the presentation, analysis and criticism of Epicureanism in terms of its philosophical content, divided into its major subject areas: physics and metaphysics (chapters by Pierre-Marie Morel, Christopher Gill, Tim O'Keefe and Liba Taub), epistemology (Elizabeth Asmis), philosophy of language (Catherine Atherton), aesthetics (David Blank), and ethics and politics (Raphael Woolf, Eric Brown, Voula Tsouna and James Warren). Of course, these discrete areas of interests were all meant to combine to produce a satisfying and systematic whole, and therefore where appropriate the contributors note areas of overlap and interrelation. They also note cases in which the school's attitude may have changed over time or where there are potential disagreements between members of the school.[8] However, the approach in

[7] See Gillespie and Hardie (eds.) 2007 and Wilson 2008. See also Jones 1989.

[8] See, for example, the discussion of the Epicurean justification of friendship in Brown, ch. 10, this volume.

these chapters is generally philosophical: the emphasis is on Epicureanism as a set of arguments and conclusions to which the reader is invited to respond critically. It should be clear that, beyond broad areas of agreement, the interpretation and evaluation of Epicurean philosophy is still in many ways a matter of serious disagreement. This volume therefore makes no excuse for the fact that the respective authors have been asked not to offer a mere survey of the evidence and of different possible views. Rather, each has undertaken to produce what they take to be the best account of a given area of Epicurean thought, sometimes in explicit disagreement with other current interpretations. Also, since some topics of discussion are relevant to more than one chapter, no uniform interpretation has been imposed on what are genuinely disputed subjects. See, for example, the different discussions of the difficult matter of Epicurean *prolēpseis* in the chapters by Asmis and Atherton or the different discussions of the metaphysical relationship between an object's constituent atoms and its various perceptible and causal properties in the chapters by Morel, Gill and O'Keefe. It is hoped that in this way the reader will be introduced not only to what the Epicureans had to say but also to good examples of what current scholarship and research on Epicureanism is like and what its concerns and ongoing controversies are.

The cover image shows part of a mosaic from a Roman villa at Autun, in central France, now in the Musée Rolin. It depicts the Epicurean philosopher Metrodorus contemplating the wisdom of *Vatican Saying* 14, which is repeated around the sitting figure: 'We have been born just the once; it is impossible to be born twice and it is necessary eternally to be no longer. But you, though you are not master of tomorrow, throw away enjoyment. Life is worn out by procrastination and each and every one of us dies without time on our hands.'[9] It seems an appropriate image for the volume for two reasons. First, it is a second- or third-century AD Roman mosaic from France repeating a late fourth- or early third-century BC Greek idea, a good example of the continuity of the ancient tradition of Epicureanism and its reach across ancient Europe and across the span of Antiquity. Second, it is a good example of the characteristically

[9] The text of this *Vatican Saying* is disputed. For further discussion see Warren 2000a: 237 n. 17.

direct and positive pedagogical intent of much of Epicurean philosophy. Its message is clear. Life is indeed short but it can be enjoyed to the full. And for those who are fortunate to be right-minded about what matters, there is no reason not to think that it can be fulfilling and good.

As editor, my thanks go to all the contributors for their work and patience during the volume's rather slow process of coming-to-be. Throughout, Michael Sharp was a helpful and robust commissioning editor for the Press and Sarah Newton was a swift and understanding copy-editor. I would also like to record thanks to the Musée Rolin, for permission to use their photograph for the cover image, and to Martin Ferguson Smith, for permission to reprint his reconstruction of Diogenes of Oinoanda's inscription (Fig. 1, p. 55). Thanks are also due, as always, to Sara Owen, who put up with me as I put the volume together.

DISKIN CLAY

1 The Athenian Garden

Fair Quiet, I have found you here.
. . .
Mistaken long, I sought you then
In busie Companies of Men.
Your sacred Plants, if here below,
Only among the Plants will grow.
Society is all but rude,
To this delicious Solitude.

Andrew Marvell, *The Garden*

Epicurus' Garden was once located outside the walls of Athens and its Dipylon Gate. It has come to seem a metaphor for the retiring and non-political character of his philosophy. According to Seneca, who thought that Epicurus secluded himself outside Athens to avoid notice, there was an inscription at the entrance to his suburban garden. It read: 'Stranger, your time will be pleasant here. Here the highest good is pleasure.' (In Seneca's Latin: *hospes hic bene manebis hic summum bonum voluptas est*, *Ep.* 79.15.) Epicurus' Garden would seem to be the prototype of Rabelais' Abbaye de Thélème. The inscription must be an invention, but it stands in pointed contrast to the inscription that led into the garden and groves of Plato's Academy, which was also located outside the walls of Athens: 'Let no one unversed in geometry enter here.' In his move to Athens from the Greek East in 307/306 BC Epicurus acquired this garden located not far from Plato's Academy. The sum seems large: 80 minae (or 8,000 drachmae, DL 10.10), but his sworn enemy Timocrates of Lampsacus claimed that he spent a mina a day on food (DL 10.7). By contrast to Epicurus' Garden, Aristotle's Lyceum was located in a public gymnasium just inside the walls of Athens to the south east. Zeno established his 'school' of philosophy in the *Stoa Poikilē* adjacent to the political centre of Athens, the Agora.[1]

Evidently Epicurus, who was from the Attic deme of Gargettos (and styled Gargettius),[2] also owned a house and small garden within the walls of Athens in the deme of Melite near the Hill of the Nymphs.[3] But neither garden was ever a *hortus deliciarum*, although the word garden (*kēpos*) became a term of abuse.[4] The austere life of Epicurus and his fellow philosophers attracted the attention of Seneca, but Epicurus never led a life completely removed from the society in which he lived. His association with the powerful is evident in his earlier career in Mytilene on Lesbos and at Lampsacus and his many years in Athens.[5] His injunctions 'Die as if you had never lived' and 'Do not involve yourself in political life' were observed by the minor infractions of Epicurus and his fellow philosophers.

1 A revealing sketch of the location of the four Hellenistic schools of philosophy by Candace H. Smith is displayed in Long and Sedley 1987: vol. 1, p. 4. This clear picture is now muddled by the expansion of modern Athens and sporadic excavations. For what little is known of the excavations see Dontas 1971.

2 By Statius in *Silv.* 2.2.113.

3 Epicurus' garden in Melite was to become the residence of his successor, Hermarchus (DL 10.17). There is a dispute over where the garden of Epicurus was actually located. As did Judeich 1931: 364 and 391, I see no problem in Epicurus, who was a man of some means, having a small urban house and garden (*hortulus*) in Melite (*in ipsa urbe*, Pliny *NH* 19.50) and a suburban garden (*hortus*) as well. Seneca (*Ep.* 33.4) seems to imply that Epicurus' garden was located outside of Athens, and texts of both Cicero (*Fin.* 5.1–5) and Heliodorus (*Aethiopica* 1.16.5) make it clear that the Garden proper was outside the Dipylon Gate and on the road to the Academy. This road followed the course of the Demosiosema or the public burial area of the Keremikos. Along this road the Stoics, Zeno and Chrysippus were given honourable burial (Paus. 1.30.15). Wycherley (1959) argued that Epicurus' house and garden in Melite were located outside the Dipylon Gate, but this implausible hypothesis has been shown wrong by Dontas 1971, Clarke 1973 and Lalonde's recent study (2006).

4 It seems to be derogatory in Cicero (*ND* 1.93). It is clearly abusive in Heraclitus, *Homeric Problems* 4.2.

5 Momigliano 1935 makes plausible connections between the early Epicurus and the successors of Alexander of Macedon (Antigonus Monophthalmos, his son Demetrius Poliorcetes and Lysimachus) and in his Athenian phase with the Syrian Mithres, the finance minister of Lysimachus. It is clear that his early associate in his period in Lampsacus, Idomeneus, was involved in the politics of the successors to Alexander of Macedon (Seneca *Ep.* 21.3–4 = fr. 13 Angeli) and Plutarch *Adv. Col.* 1127D.

THE BEGINNINGS OF A PHILOSOPHICAL COMMUNITY IN THE GREEK EAST

'Epikouros' (the transliterated form of the Latinized 'Epicurus') is uncommon as a Greek proper name. Metrodorus, one of Epicurus' earliest associates, named his son after him, as did Leonteus and Themista. All are associates from Epicurus' stay in Lampsacus (DL 10.19 and 27). The name Epikouros is also a speaking name, meaning someone who comes to another's aid. In Plato's *Republic* the *epikouroi* come to be subordinated to the true guardians of Socrates' ideal city as Socrates introduces the myth of the metals and golden, silver and bronze citizens (415a). For most ancient and modern students of ancient philosophy, Epicurus would rank as a member of the silver race of philosophers and Plato as golden; so Epicurus called Plato derisively (DL 10.8). But for his followers over the ages he was a saviour and a god. Lucretius praised him as a god for the good he had done for humankind (*deus ille fuit, deus*: *DRN* 5.7), and, in the last chapter of the history of Epicureanism in Antiquity, he is called 'the herald who saved us'.[6] Diogenes of Oinoanda reflects his appreciation of the meaning of Epicurus' name and evangelical mission when he uses the verb *epikourein* to describe his own apostolic mission in the Greek East in the second century AD.[7]

Epicurus was an Athenian, but, unlike Plato, he was not born in Athens; neither were the founders of what we regard as two of the four major schools of Greek philosophy, the Lyceum and the Stoa. Aristotle came from Stagira in Macedonia and Zeno from Citium on Cyprus. Epicurus was born on the island of Samos in 341 of Athenian parents who migrated there when the island had fallen once again under Athenian control. At the age of 18 he came over to Athens for two years of military service as an ephebe (323–322).[8] It is likely that he was forced to leave the island for Lesbos on his return in 322, when the Athenian colonists were expelled by Perdiccas after the death of Alexander of Macedon. He then established himself as a teacher for a short and seemingly tumultuous time in Mytilene where he

[6] Diog. Oin. 125.IV.3 Smith. Cf. Erler, ch. 3, this volume.

[7] Diog. Oin. 2.V.7 Smith.

[8] Strabo speaks of Epicurus' father, Neocles, as one of the 2,000 Athenian cleruchs sent to Samos (around 352), *Geography* 14.1.18; he adds that as an ephebe Epicurus served with the comic poet Menander. Diodorus Siculus 18.18.9 is our source for the expulsion of the Athenian settlers from Samos.

converted Hermarchus, who would become his successor in Athens, to philosophy. Epicurus then moved on to Lampsacus on the Hellespont where he made friends who were to remain faithful to him and his philosophy to the end of his or their life: Metrodorus, Leonteus and his wife Themista, Polyaenus and Idomeneus. In 306 Epicurus left the Greek East and lived in Athens for some thirty-five years. He died there in 270 after he had made dispositions for the survival of his writings and the philosophical community he had gathered about him. Diogenes writing in the third century AD speaks of the survival of his school after almost all others had died out (DL 10.9). He goes on to give an almost biblical list of the successors, including Apollodorus, the 'tyrant of the garden'.[9]

We know very little about Epicurus as an independent philosopher before he arrived in Athens sometime during the archonship of Anaxicrates in 307/306. There circulated a number of ancient lives of Epicurus and a fair number of biographical anecdotes survive. The biography in Diogenes Laërtius' *Lives and sayings of the eminent philosophers* draws on many of these and is our fullest source for Epicurus' life. Diogenes also provides a long list of the titles of his works.[10] His *Life* also contains some brief mention of Epicurus' students or, better, 'fellow philosophers' (*sumphilosophountes*) and a catalogue of the writings of Metrodorus and Hermarchus.[11] Some of these works are now hardly more than titles, but the collection of the titles of the writings of these early associates are revealing about the polemical character of the early members of Epicurus' community who were called by later generations of Epicureans 'those who led the way' (*kathēgemones*).

After he left Samos, Epicurus accompanied his father to Asia Minor and was active it seems as a school-teacher (*grammatodidaskalos*) in Colophon (DL 10.2). 'School-teacher' is a term Epicurus employed to abuse his older contemporary, Nausiphanes of Teos (DL 10.8). Later he attracted associates such as Hermarchus of Mytilene and Idomeneus,

[9] DL 10.25–6. The successors listed by Diogenes and those named in the entry of Epicurus in the Suda do not extend beyond the date of the death of Caesar in 44 BC, as Usener 1887: 373 calculated.

[10] DL 10.1–13, 27–8. What little is known about these biographies is set out by Goulet 2000: 158–160.

[11] The evidence for the organization of the 'school' of Epicurus to be discovered in the papyri from Herculaneum is set out by Longo 1978.

Metrodorus, Polyaenus, Pythocles and Colotes of Lampsacus. What doctrine or what manner of life attracted these life-long 'fellow philosophers' we do not know, although an anecdote deriving from a letter of Epicurus to Colotes attests to the power of his discourse on what was then described as *physiologia* (the philosophy of nature). Plutarch, who records the scene, would have paid a great deal for a painting of Colotes embracing the knees of the master as if he were a god (*Adv. Col.* 1117B–C). Epicurus' ancient biographies associate him naturally enough with the atomism of Democritus of Abdera, the hedonism of Aristippus of Cyrene, and strangely Nausiphanes of Teos, whom Epicurus abused not only as a school-teacher but a 'jellyfish' (*pleumōn*). We can say next to nothing about his serious attitude towards Aristippus. It now appears that there is more to say about Epicurus' relation to Nausiphanes, and we can recognize clear signs of Epicurus' debt to the ethical theory of Democritus.[12] But there is impressive evidence for Epicurus' critical attitude to Democritus and his doctrine of the mechanical necessity created by the ballistics of atoms moving blindly in space.[13] In a telling anecdote, it is reported that he turned to philosophy in disgust at the inability of teachers to explain Hesiod's Chaos, an anecdote that evinces an early interest in cosmology and the earliest conception of the void (*Theogony* 116; DL 10.2). In his philosophical inscription of the second century AD, Diogenes of Oinoanda preserves a precious early document – a letter Epicurus wrote to his mother after he had left Samos. This letter reveals that following the lead of Democritus the young Epicurus had already developed a theory of vision and dream visions. He had also adopted an austere and autonomous manner of life and a conception of himself as 'equal to a god'.[14] In another early letter he wrote to Hermarchus of Mytilene, where he first established himself as a

[12] Warren 2002a has explored Epicurus' relation to Democritean ethics and the ideal of *ataraxia* and also his relation to Nausiphanes. Kahn 1985 has clearly demonstrated the influence of Democritus' ethical maxims on the maxims (the *Kyriai Doxai* and *Sententiae Vaticanae*) of Epicurus.

[13] Evident in the formulation of *SV* 40 and what has been identified as Book 25 of Epicurus' *On Nature*. A papyrus from Herculaneum mentions a letter or package (of Epicurus?) that included some books of Democritus (see Philod. *Ad contubernales*, *PHerc.* 1005 fr. 111 Angeli = 113 Arr.). In his *Adv. Col.* Plutarch makes it clear that Epicurus professed a debt to Democritus, despite having called him *Lērokritos* ('nonsense monger', DL 10.8), *Adv. Col.* 1108E.

[14] Diog. Oin. 125 Smith.

philosopher, Epicurus urges Hermarchus to 'steer clear of the speeches' of the orators, knock on the doors of philosophy, and enter 'our gathering.' This too is preserved on the wall of Diogenes' stoa in Lycia. We know of Hermarchus' early interest in rhetoric from Diogenes Laërtius.[15] Metrodorus' renegade brother Timocrates would characterize the exclusive character of the society Epicurus established in Mytilene as 'a coven of initiates', perhaps not unfairly (DL 10.6).

Even when he was firmly established in Athens Epicurus maintained contact with his friends in Mytilene and Lampsacus, especially with Idomeneus, the aristocrat who seems to have served as the protector of the Epicureans in Lampsacus.[16] Strabo could speak of Epicurus as 'in a way a citizen of Lampsacus'.[17] In one of his letters preserved on Diogenes' stoa in Oinoanda, Epicurus describes a shipwreck he survived sailing to Lampsacus and in a letter to a child he speaks of a trip to Lampsacus with Hermarchus and Ctesippus.[18] The last letter he wrote from Athens was addressed to Idomeneus in Lampsacus; in it he speaks of the suffering of his last illness and the comfort of remembering their conversations of the past. These conversations go back to the time he spent in Lampsacus forty years earlier. Unless our Latin sources have simply confused the name of the addressees, he wrote a similar letter to Hermarchus, the associate he named as his successor in the Garden.[19]

THE FIRST GENERATION OF THE EPICUREAN SCHOOL IN ATHENS

There were four established 'schools' in Athens. They attracted students from throughout the Greek world. First founded was Plato's Academy outside the walls of Athens to the north west; next came

[15] DL 10.23; cf. Diog. Oin. 127 Smith.

[16] For the role of Idomeneus and Leonteus in Lampsacus, see Angeli 1981: 46–61.

[17] *Geography* 13.1.19.

[18] Diog. Oin. 72 Smith. This letter is cited in a letter Diogenes himself wrote to Epicureans on Rhodes on the disaster that befell a friend by the name of Niceratus. For this argument see Clay 1998: ch. 12. The letter to a child is found at *PHerc*. 176 fr. 5 XXIII Vogliano (176 Us., 261 Arr.). For the most recent edition of this papyrus see Angeli 1988b, esp. 50–1 for this section and various possibilities about its authorship; cf. Militello 1997: 49–56.

[19] DL 10.22; 52 Arr. (fr. 5 Longo Auricchio). The letter to Hermarchus is cited by Cicero *Fin*. 2.96 and is paraphrased admiringly by Marcus Aurelius in *Meditations* 9.41.

the Lyceum of Aristotle outside the walls to the east; then came Epicurus' Garden, which was a neighbour to the Academy; last came the school of Zeno in the Painted Stoa (*Stoa Poikilē*). What attracted Epicurus' followers first in the Greek East and then to his Garden outside the walls of Athens we do not know, but it is clear that he attracted fellow philosophers during the time he spent first in Mytilene and then in Lampsacus. Some of these moved to join him in Athens. His successor (*diadochos*), Hermarchus, was one of these. In his last will and testament Epicurus speaks of him as having 'grown old with him in philosophy'. By 'philosophy' Epicurus means a philosophical way of life and not only a set of doctrines.[20]

There is much in Epicurus' developed philosophy that most Greeks would have found repugnant (and Romans more so). The Epicurean gods are remote from humankind and can neither be provoked to anger at human failings nor influenced by human propitiation. There can be no such thing as divine providence or divination. There is, therefore, no justification for an attempt to propitiate the gods, although, as we shall see, there is a good reason for the Epicurean philosopher to participate in the cults of his city.[21] There is no personal survival after death and, therefore, there can be no cult of the dead. Yet the cults of the first generation of Epicurus' Garden offer the greatest – or seemingly greatest – example of his philosophy contradicted by his practice. The world in which we live is not the product of a divine and philanthropic design; it is part of an infinite universe in which worlds form and dissolve in autonomous combinations of atoms in an infinite void.[22] Marcus Aurelius would characterize the gap between his own philanthropic teleology and atomism in the stark alternatives: 'either Providence or atoms'.[23] And philosophers involved in political and religious life such as Cicero, Seneca and Plutarch were offended by Epicurus' withdrawal from the political life of Athens.[24]

But then there is the appeal of the intimacy of the small society of friends (*philoi*) who gathered about Epicurus. In Greek *philoi* can designate family members. Epicurus' three brothers, Neocles,

[20] DL 10.20. The strict meaning of philosophy not as a set of doctrines to be mastered and defended but a way of life is exemplified in DL 10.17.

[21] See Warren, ch. 13, this volume. [22] See Taub, ch. 6, this volume.

[23] *Meditations* 4.3.2; cf. 4.27. [24] See Erler, ch. 3 and Brown, ch. 10, this volume.

Chairedemus and Aristobulus were early members of his philosophical community. They and Epicurus' parents figure in the paradoxical cults that Epicurus sought to perpetuate in his last will and testament (DL 10.18). *Philoi*, as the term was used by Epicurus himself, Trajan's widow Plotina in a letter to Hadrian of 121 AD, Diogenes of Oinoanda and Diogenes Laërtius, means members of Epicurus' philosophical 'family'.[25]

For his Garden in Athens Epicurus did not accept the principle that the possessions of friends should be held in common (a Pythagorean principle fundamental to Plato's *Republic*). In a letter Epicurus wrote to Metrodorus (in 291/290) he boasted that he could live on less than (in Latin translation) a copper coin (*as*) a day, but he reminded his correspondent, Polyaenus, that Metrodorus had not yet made this progress.[26] Support for the austere life of Epicurus and the friends came from many sources, including, evidently, Epicurus' own family wealth and property, voluntary contributions from Lampsacus and assessments.[27] One of Epicurus' main injunctions was 'do not get involved in political life' (*mē politeuesthai*). Throughout the history of the Epicurean school there is very little evidence of Epicureans involved in political office, although there is some striking evidence of some Epicureans being involved in the religious life of their communities and, as we shall see, Cicero's contemporary, Phaedrus, had a statue dedicated to him on the

[25] Some examples: Epicurus' letter to a child = *PHerc.* 176 fr. 5 XXIII Vogliano (176 Us., 261 Arr.); Plotina, *IG* II^2 1099; Diog. Oin., letter to Antipater, 62.II.2–5 Smith; and DL 10.9. Philodemus *De Epicuro, PHerc.* 1232, XXVIII Tepedino Guerra, preserves a letter of invitation to a feast in which Epicurus speaks of 'those who belong to the household', translated on p. 24 below.

[26] Seneca *Ep.* 18.9. The paltry value of the Roman *as* is well illustrated in Catullus 5.5.

[27] We discover a few indications of the financial backing of the Garden in the provisions of Epicurus' last will and testament (DL 10.16–21). The extreme frugality of the community is reflected in documents such as: the letter to Idomeneus discussed by Seneca at *Ep.* 22.5 (56 Arr.); the letter to Polyaenus discussed by Seneca at *Ep.* 18.9 (83 Arr.); the anecdote in Plutarch's *Life of Demetrius* 34.2; and the letters to Mithres, the finance minister of Lysimachus, discussed in Philodemus *Pragmateiai* XXVIII–XXXVI Militello. All contradict the slander of Timocrates and are telling of the truth of Epicurus' admonition that wealth comes from the elimination of unnecessary desires (cf. his letter to Idomeneus on Pythocles, cited at Stob. 3.17.23 (53 Arr.)). The other evidence for the assessments (*syntaxeis*) supporting the Epicurean community in Athens is well summarized in Erler 1994: 70.

Athenian acropolis. Epicurus seems to have endorsed the practice of the philosopher participating in civic cult.[28]

EPICUREAN POLEMIC: MAKING FRIENDS BY HAVING ENEMIES

The polemics of Epicurus have caused some shock among ancients and moderns but, beyond their affirmation of Epicurean truth against the errors of earlier and contemporary philosophers, Epicurus' polemics had another purpose than the refutation of all heresy. They helped defend and define the Epicurean philosopher against the errors of other philosophers. Now only a few traces remain of what was a significant feature of the writings of the first generation of the Epicureans 'who showed the way' (the *kathēgemones*). These *kathēgemones* were Epicurus first, the early associate Epicurus named as his successor, Hermarchus, and then Metrodorus and Polyaenus. The mild Polyaenus alone seems to have refrained from polemics.[29]

Diogenes lists six titles of polemical works of Epicurus (the first of which is his epitome of his objections to the philosophers of nature), but the fact that only some are titled *Against* ... (*pros*) someone is no guarantee that other works like the thirty-seven books of his *On Nature* or the three letters preserved by Diogenes with his *Kyriai Doxai* do not contain anonymous polemic; they do. Metrodorus also produced polemical tracts. One was directed against his brother, Timocrates, who reviled Epicurus in a polemical pamphlet. In this he followed the lead of Epicurus' *Against Timocrates* (in three books). Hermarchus wrote a series of letters against Empedocles.[30] Perhaps the most extravagant piece of Epicurean polemic was that of Colotes of Lampsacus with the modest title *On the Fact that according to the Teachings of the other Philosophers it is not even possible to live* (probably dedicated to Ptolemy II and thus written after 268). This polemic attracted the ire of Plutarch and provoked his *Against Colotes*. It also inspired the title of Plutarch's tract against

[28] DL 10.120 and Philod. *De pietate* 790–819 and 867–95 Obbink.

[29] His generous character is reflected in DL 10.24.

[30] In addition to his *Epitome of Objections to the Philosophers of Nature*, there are polemics *Against the Megarians*, *On Emotions against Timocrates* as well as the *Timocrates* (listed in DL 10.27–8). Metrodorus produced tracts *Against Doctors*,

Epicurus' ethics, *According to the Doctrines of Epicurus the Life of Pleasure is not even possible.*[31]

Epicurus had an unfortunate reputation as a polemicist, as did his devout follower Colotes. But Epicurus' polemics do not represent, as John Rist claimed, a nadir of philosophical discourse.[32] Their philosophical importance is beyond doubt (but now only faintly visible). The function of Epicurean polemic in asserting the identity and assuring the allegiance of the Epicurean philosopher is more apparent. A longish section of Diogenes' life of Epicurus (10.3–8) is devoted to the scurrilous attacks on Epicurus' dissolute personal life (reflecting a caricature of his ethics of pleasure). It is followed by a section culling quotations of Epicurus' curt dismissal of earlier philosophers and some of his contemporaries (10.8). This paragraph has led to the bizarre conclusion that these barbs derive from a forged letter foisted on Epicurus, but David Sedley has shown that they derive in fact from two letters of Epicurus: one *On Occupations in Life*, another *To the Philosophers in Mytilene.*[33] The fact that these sharp barbs come from letters of Epicurus shows, if anything, his care in writing to 'fellow philosophers' for promoting the self-definition of the Epicurean against other and erroneous ways of thinking and living.

'THE ACTS OF THE EPISTLE'

The letters Epicurus addressed to an individual were in fact encyclical, that is, they were meant to be read by the person to whom they were addressed and to be circulated among the friends. Epicurus

Against the Dialecticians, *Against the Sophists* (in 9 books), and *Against Democritus* (DL 10.24). Hermarchus wrote a series of letters hostile to Empedocles (frs. 27–34 Longo Auricchio). This polemic against Empedocles, Plato and the belief in metempsychosis continues in Diog. Oin. 41 and 42 Smith.

31 Colotes seems to have violently disliked Platonic dialogues. He wrote against Plato's *Lysis*, *Euthydemus*, *Gorgias* and, as we know from Plutarch's *Adv. Col.*, the *Republic*.

32 Rist's language is worth recording: Epicurus 'himself set a depth of polemic hitherto unplumbed among ancient philosophers, and reserved some of his bitterest contempt for those from whom he learned the most' (1972: ix). In Epicurus' abuse of Nausiphanes (the 'jellyfish'), Sedley 1976: 135 discovers the sole instance of Epicurus captured 'in a truly vitriolic mood'; on this abuse the comments of Warren 2002a: 189–92 are worth recalling. By contrast the frequent polemics of Epicurus' *On Nature* are all anonymous.

33 Sedley 1976.

makes this clear when he says that one of his letters was meant to be read both by an individual and others of the community (*PHerc.* 176 fr. 5 Col. xv Vogliano = 59 Arr.). Once Epicurus had established himself in Athens, letters were a means to maintaining the cohesion of the 'fellow philosophers' abroad and they are more numerous than the letters of any other ancient philosopher save Seneca. Oddly, we have dates for some of Epicurus' letters by Athenian archon years. The first of these dates a letter of Epicurus to the archonship of Nicias (296/295), ten years after Epicurus' arrival in Athens. The last dates a letter to Mithres to the archonship of Pytharatus (271/270), the year of Epicurus' death.[34] It was to Mithres that Epicurus addressed his treatise on disease and its aetiology (DL 10.28). Even when his associates were absent he kept in contact with them by a remarkable epistolary corpus, copies of which must have been preserved in Athens and circulated widely as we can judge by the frequency with which they were cited by Philodemus, Seneca and Plutarch. Even Marcus Aurelius cites one of the letters Epicurus wrote at the end of his life, keeping not to the letter but to the thought which he had made his own.[35]

In his sardonic comments on the role Epicurus and Metrodorus played in the liberation of Mithres imprisoned by Craterus in the Peiraeus after the death of Lysimachus (in 281) Plutarch mocks the letters Epicurus dispatched to all and sundry, men and women alike. He derides his encyclical letters as flagrant violations of his principle 'Die as if you had never lived': 'Epicurus, let us begin: Do not write letters to your friends in Asia or recruit disciples in Egypt or cultivate the young men of Lampsacus or circulate pamphlets to all and sundry, men and women alike, to advertise your own wisdom or make

[34] Dorandi 1990b has compiled a list of Epicurean works cited by Athenian archon year. These include the dates to be found in the writings of Philodemus of Gadara. The series ends with the archonship of Nicetes (84/83). I have argued that the dating of Epicurus' writings by Athenian archon year is evidence that he deposited his letters and the 37 books of his *On Nature* (for which we have two dates) in the Metroön or State Archive of Athens: Clay 1998: ch. 3. He was the first to deposit a private document (his will) in these Archives (DL 10.16–18).

[35] Marcus Aurelius *Meditations* 9.41. The fact that Seneca dates a letter of Epicurus by the archon year in which it was written (*Charino magistratu, Ep.* 18.9 (83 Arr.)) must mean that he knew the letters from an official collection. Plutarch makes it clear that he possessed a collection of Epicurus' letters (*Non posse* 1101B).

arrangements for your funeral.'[36] We will return to this last strange detail of Epicurus' 'funeral'.

The last of Epicurus' works listed by Diogenes has the title *Letters*.[37] The letters of Epicurus to the three other *kathēgemones* also circulated in epitomes.[38] Diogenes Laërtius cited the letters to Herodotus, Pythocles and Menoeceus as 'epitomes' of Epicurus' entire philosophy. The Epicurean practice of what can irreverently be called 'the acts of the epistle' prepared for the epistles of St Paul and the early Christians and it continued until the age of Diogenes of Oinoanda. Diogenes' letter to Antipater (directed to Athens) on the infinite universe is clearly encyclical. In it he attests the widespread Epicurean communities of Athens, and Chalcis and Thebes in Boeotia.[39]

PARADOSIS AND SURVIVAL

Epicurus' last will and testament provides our best evidence of how, at the end of his life, he devised to transmit his property to assure the survival of the Epicurean community in Athens and we will examine it for the private cults he provides for. He bequeathed his books to Hermarchus; but how could Epicurus, 'the most prolific of philosophers' (DL 10.26), assure the survival of his *philosophy*? According to legend, Epicurus' last words to his disciples were 'remember my doctrines' (DL 10.16). Epicurus also expected his disciples to *memorize* his *writings*.

Anyone who has attempted to decipher the papyri of his *On Nature* preserved in the library of the Villa dei Papiri in

[36] *Lat. viv.* 1128F–1129A, cf. *Non posse* 1101B.

[37] DL 10.28. Usener divided the letters into three groups, as did Arrighetti: those directed to a recipient who can be identified; those to a group; and those to an unknown readership. Yet it is clear that Epicurus meant his letters to be read both by the individual to whom they were addressed and to a larger group. The evidence for his epistolary habit has increased with the discoveries in Oinoanda: 125 Smith (Epicurus to his mother), 127 Smith (to Hermarchus), 128 Smith (to Dositheus and Pyrson), 126 and 130 Smith (to unknown recipients). Epicurus' letter describing a shipwreck he survived on his way to Lampsacus (72 Smith) is quoted in a letter of Diogenes himself directed to friends on Rhodes (70–1 Smith). For this letter of Diogenes see Clay 1998: chs. 11 and 12; Clay 1973 and 1984.

[38] Hermarchus fr. 40 Longo Auricchio; DL 10.28–9. Seneca quotes (in Greek) a letter of Metrodorus to his sister as coming from 'the letters of Metrodorus' (*Ep.* 99.25).

[39] Written from Rhodes, 62–7 Smith.

Herculaneum will realize at once that it would be impossible for anyone, including Epicurus himself, to memorize its thirty-seven books. The *On Nature* was very much a work in progress. Despite his insistence on keeping in mind the primary meaning of words (*Ep. Hdt.* 38), Epicurus deploys a technical vocabulary that would be incomprehensible to anyone save his closest associates. A ready example of what Epicurus presupposes of his readers comes from Book 28, which is cast as a dialogue between Epicurus and Metrodorus on problems of inference, argument and the proper use of language. Its frequent evocations of Epicurus' methods (*tropoi*) of reasoning were evidently familiar to his small and immediate audience, but they are now obscure to us. The dialogue concludes with an address to Epicurus' readers: 'And now I think that I have finished prattling to you (plural) this twenty-eighth installment of our continuous lecture course' (fr. 13 XIII.6–10 Sedley, his translation). Amazingly, Epicurus expects his addressees to memorize (or keep in mind) the doctrines of this book. Epicurus then promises the next book that will be read (aloud to the group) in sequel (fr. 13 XIII.1–6 Sedley). The technical language of another book of his *On Nature* provoked Graziano Arrighetti to speak of it as 'truly a text for the initiate'.[40] Timocrates criticized Epicurus' *On Nature* for its repetitions and polemics (DL 10.7), but at least one reader seems to have appreciated his concision and comprehensiveness in speaking of the soul (*PHerc.* 998 fr. 11, 32 Arr. and see Arrighetti 1973: 709).

Perhaps late in his career, Epicurus realized that for his thought to survive him he would have to reduce it to a comprehensible and memorable form. The three letters and his *Kyriai Doxai* preserved in Diogenes Laërtius represent, as Diogenes says, epitomes of his doctrines (DL 10.21). The *Letter to Herodotus* was designed to recall Epicurus' essential doctrines for those who had already made some progress in his system of the physical world (*Ep. Hdt.* 35–6); the *Letter to Pythocles* on meteorology was in response to Pythocles' complaint that his doctrines 'were hard to remember' (*Ep. Pyth.* 84); in the *Letter to Menoeceus* Epicurus sets out his major ethical doctrines and expands on many of the precepts abbreviated in the forty *Kyriai Doxai* that Diogenes reproduces as 'colophon' of his *Lives and*

[40] Arrighetti 1973: 626. He is describing the language of *Nat.* 25. See the recent edition by Laursen 1995 and 1997.

sayings of the eminent philosophers and 'the beginning of a life of happiness' (DL 10.138). Epicurus concludes his *Letter to Menoeceus* with the injunction: 'Study these doctrines and those germane to them day and night, reading them both to yourself and to someone like yourself, and never, either awake or dreaming, will you be disturbed, but you will live as a god among mortals in possession of immortal goods' (*Ep. Men.* 135).

These epitomes assured the survival of the essentials of Epicurus' philosophy and, since they are preserved in Diogenes, they survive until the Renaissance, when Diogenes was translated into Latin by the Camaldolese monk, Ambrogio Traversari (in 1433), at the urging of Cosimo de' Medici the Elder and much to Traversari's distaste. Book 10 preserved Epicurus' philosophy in its essential formulations in Greek long after his library had been dispersed in Athens and the library of the Villa dei Papiri had been overwhelmed (and partially preserved) in the eruption of Vesuvius in 79 AD. The importance of Epicurus' organized and elementary presentation of his physics and ethics can be seen by the fact that many of his 'elementary propositions' (*stoicheiōmata*) were translated and developed by Lucretius as the philosophical armature of the *De rerum natura*.[41]

THE CULTS OF EPICURUS

The other means Epicurus devised of perpetuating the community he had gathered about him in Athens were the cults he refers to and perpetuates in his last will and testament (quoted in DL 10.16–20). The religious language Epicurus and his followers used to describe one another offended many non-Epicureans, but it is not mere hyperbole or hypocrisy. Rather it is the expression of the new conception of the serenity and tranquillity of the philosopher who had come to resemble the Epicurean gods. Epicurus writes to his mother as if he were a god; he writes to his disciple Colotes as if they were both

[41] The Greek texts and Lucretius' Latin translations of them are set out in Appendix 1 of Clay 1983a. Epicurus' motives and method of reducing his philosophy in clear and concise formulations and his demand that his students memorize these formulations are presented in Clay 1998: ch. 1. The extreme reduction of the four main doctrines of the letter to Menoeceus and the first four of the *Master Sayings* was known as the 'Fourfold Remedy' (*tetrapharmakos*): Diano 1974.

divine, and writes of the expected arrival of Pythocles as if the young man were divine.[42]

Epicurus' last will and testament and evidence from other sources make it clear that, as he prepared for death and survival, he meant to perpetuate five cults he had founded in the Garden (set out in DL 10.18). First, he provided for the continuation of the annual commemorative offerings (*enagismata*) to his father, mother, and three brothers; then for the annual gathering of the group to celebrate his birthday on the tenth of Gamelion (in January). Provisions follow for the joint cult of Epicurus and Metrodorus on the twentieth of each month and a cult during the month of Poseideon (in December) to commemorate his brothers, and, last, a cult for Polyaenus in the month of Metageitnion (July). It was common Greek practice to commemorate the dead by celebrations on the day (*hēmera*) of their birth. We know of celebrations held on the birthdays of Socrates and Plato.[43] As we have seen, what is paradoxical about the cults of Epicurus is that they seem to fly in the face of two of his most important ethical injunctions: 'Die as if you had never been born' and 'Death is nothing to us.'

Alert and hostile readers of the strange provisions of Epicurus' will pounced on the contradiction of his precept and practice. And here we discover the explanation of Plutarch's remark about Epicurus' concern for his funeral. Plutarch continues: 'What is the meaning of these common meals (literally 'tables', *trapezai*)? Of the gatherings of your associates and the fair? Of the tens of thousands of lines written in honor of Metrodorus, Aristobulus, and Chairedemus – lines painstakingly composed so that not even in death they should be forgotten' (*Lat. viv.* 1129A). Both Cicero (who knew the text of Epicurus' will) and Pliny note the contradiction of Epicurean precept and practice.[44] And Aelian, the sworn enemy of Epicureanism, complains about the gluttony of these commemorative meals and asserts that Epicurus

[42] Epicurus, in the *Letter to Mother* preserved in Diog. Oin. 125 IV.1–8 Smith; Colotes in Plut. *Adv. Col.* 1117B (65 Arr.); Pythocles in DL 10.5 (88 Arr.); Menoeceus, in the *Letter to Menoeceus* 135; and, for the general practice among Epicureans, Plut. *Non posse* 1091B–C.

[43] Socrates on the sixth of Thargelion and Plato on the seventh, Plut. *Quaest. conv.* 717B. There seems to have been an annual cult for Arcesilaus on the day of his birth, DL 4.67.

[44] Cicero *Fin.* 2.101, Pliny *NH* 35.3.

arranged to have a table placed over his grave (fr. 39, 218 Us.). If there was a table placed at Epicurus' grave it was surely a 'sacred table' to receive offerings to the god Epicurus.[45]

In Philodemus' treatise *On Epicurus* we have a remarkable record of an invitation to an Epicurean feast. It comes from a letter of Epicurus himself and reads:

> ... as concerns those who experience turmoil and difficulty in their conceptions of natures that are best and most blessed. [But Epicurus says] that he invites these very people to join in a feast, just as he invites others – all those who are members of his household and he asks them to exclude none of the 'outsiders' who are well disposed to him and his friends. In doing this [he says], they will not be engaged in gathering the masses, something which is a form of meaningless 'demagogy' and unworthy of the natural philosopher; rather, in practising what is congenial to their nature, they will remember all those who are well disposed to us so that on their blessed day they can join in making sacred offerings that are fitting. Of the friends ...[46]

There are two other striking features about Epicurus' will: the first is that his community in the Garden honoured him during his lifetime; the second is that both he and Metrodorus received honours on the twentieth day of each *month*. A yearly cult to the dead is a familiar practice in Greece. A monthly cult was reserved for divinities: Artemis had a cult on the sixth day of a month and Apollo on the seventh. Apollo, the god sacred to Socrates and Plato, also had a cult on the twentieth of the month. The Epicureans came to be known as Members of the Cult of the Twentieth (*Eikadistai*). We learn from an inscription from Athens of a group organized around the cult of the hero Eikadeus in the worship of Apollo Parnessios (of Parnassos, *IG* II^2 1258). The Epicurean cult of the twentieth was, therefore, conceived of as a cult to Epicurus and Metrodorus as divinities. Their votaries were known as *eikadistai*. As Epicurus' opponents noticed, these cults and the memorial literature that was read during these celebrations of the heroic dead seem to contradict two fundamental doctrines of Epicurean philosophy. A true Epicurean could not hope to become a member of 'the grateful dead' or pleased in death by the

[45] The function of cult tables is well set out by Obbink 1996 in his commentary to Philod. *De pietate* 840–5.

[46] Philod. *De Epicuro*, *PHerc.* 1232, XXVIII Tepedino Guerra. The text and translation here are based on Clay 1998: 80–2 (= Clay 1986) where the text is cited as fr. 8 col. 1.

worship of successive generations of his 'fellow philosophers'. But Epicurus understood the wisdom of his own maxim: 'Piety is a great benefit to the pious' (*SV* 32). It is the worshipper who benefits from his worship not the object of his worship.

The purpose of any Greek hero cult was to foster in the worshipper a sense of communal identity. Being founded as a religious organization (or *thiasos*) was not necessary for a philosophical association to be recognized by the state of Athens, but it surely was the means to its cohesion during the lifetime of its founder and survival after Epicurus' death.[47] These days of communal cult and commemoration therefore served for the Epicureans of Athens (and later in Herculaneum)[48] the purpose for which they were established.

In a remarkable passage in his *Rhetoric* Aristotle described the traditional Greek conception of honour (*timē*): 'The elements of honour are sacrifices, memorials in verse and prose, special marks of distinction, sanctuaries, front-row seating, public funerals, images and maintenance at public expense' (*Rhet.* 1361a33–6). Epicurus claimed posthumously the special marks of distinction of being treated as a *hērōs* (in the religious sense of this word), saviour, herald and god by later generations of his followers. His life was commemorated by an extensive memorial literature even as he himself had written memorials in praise of his associate Metrodorus and at least two of his brothers. He also claimed sacrifices. It is very likely that a statue of him stood on the grounds of his Garden. There is a tradition that Socrates was honoured by the Athenians after his death by a statue (DL 2.43); just so, his native Samos honoured Epicurus by a bronze statue (DL 10.9).[49] His funeral was a private affair, certainly, unlike

[47] The evidence for the cults of Epicurus is set out in Clay 1998: ch. 5; Clay 1986 for the quasi-religious character of the philosophical founder of a school, see Sedley 1989.

[48] As shown by Philod. *Epigram* 27 Sider.

[49] Dontas 1971 has identified two of the four statues found in what he takes to be the area of Epicurus' Garden (C and D) as copies of a well-known statue of Epicurus from 280–270 BC. He dates them to the age of Marcus Aurelius or the Severans (161–235 AD). Remarkably, later Epicureans (Phaedrus and Titus Pomponius Atticus) were honoured by statues in sanctuaries. Atticus dedicated a statue of Phaedrus on the acropolis and Phaedrus and Lucius Appius Saufeius were honoured by statues in the Eleusinion of the Athenian agora (Raubitschek 1949). Frischer 1982 offers the most extensive and challenging treatment of the function of the statues of Epicurus and his closest associates in the task of recruitment. A brief survey of the images of Epicurus can be found in Richter 1984: 116–19.

the huge public funeral of Theophrastus of Eresus (described in DL 5.41). Other philosophers wrote wills that happen to have been recorded. They are interested in disposing of their property, funerals and memorials, the altars and statues established on the grounds of their properties, and manumitting their slaves.[50] Only Epicurus is concerned with the preservation of the private cults of the community of his Garden.

THE 'SCHOOL' OF EPICURUS

Epicurus' Garden was not a school. Seneca had it right when he commented: 'it was not the school of Epicurus that made Metrodorus, Hermarchus and Polyaenus great men but their shared life' (*Ep.* 1.6.6). *Non schola sed contubernium.* (The word *contubernium* means a shared tent.)[51] In Greek one of the meanings of *scholē* is a lecture and what we would call a school (*diatribē*) is a place where the adept spends his time. Only later did the Garden become known as a sect (*hairesis*).[52] Unlike the Academy under the direction of Plato, the Peripatos under the direction of Aristotle, Theophrastus and Strato, the community of mathematicians settled in Cyzicus contemporary with Epicurus' stay in Lampsacus, and, indeed, unlike the 'Think Tank' (*Phrontisterion*) of the 'Socrates' pilloried by Aristophanes in the *Clouds*, there was no scientific or historical research conducted in Epicurus' Garden.

The community of 'fellow philosophers' that gathered about Epicurus in his Garden during the last thirty-five years of his life is remarkable for including Epicurus' three brothers and perhaps his parents. More women are associated with Epicurus' Garden than are recorded for any other 'school'. They can be named in alphabetical order: Batis, Boidion, Demetria, Hedeia, Leontion, Nikidion and

[50] The wills are collected by Diogenes Laërtius. The will of Epicurus is remarkable for having been deposited in the State Records Office of Athens, the Metroön (DL 10.16–17). The will of the Academic Arcesilaus is cited in DL 4.43–4. The wills of the Peripatetic Theophrastus are cited in 5.51–4; of Strato of Lampsacus in 5.61–4; of Lyco in 5.69–74. It is an interesting coincidence that the private Garden of Theophrastus which Demetrius of Phaleron obtained for him after the death of Aristotle (in 322 BC) is mentioned by Diogenes. His Garden he willed to his fellow philosophers (DL 5.37 and 52).

[51] The status of our conception of the Garden as a philosophical 'school' is properly challenged by Dorandi 1999.

[52] This term and related terms are exhaustively studied by Glucker 1978: 159–225.

Themista. The name Hedeia (Pleasure) suggests that she and likely others were prostitutes. Epicurus provides for the children of his community in his will and for his philosophical slave Mus (Mouse), whom he frees on his death. Children and a slave were also important members of his community. Later Epicureans looked on the most prominent members of the Athenian Garden as 'those who led the way' (*kathēgemones*). In the period of Zeno of Sidon a distinction was made between those who were being prepared for a life of philosophy (the *kataskeuazomenoi*) and their older directors, but no diplomas were granted to those who reached the end of the path of philosophy.

Epicurus himself went through distinct stages in his career: at 18 he came to Athens to serve as an ephebe; he then became a teacher. In Lampsacus he continued to gather disciples; by the time he returned to Athens he had become, with Hermarchus, Metrodorus and Polyaenus a Leader (*kathēgemon* or later *kathēgetēs*). In death he became a *hērōs*, a herald, a saviour and a god.

THE END OF THE GARDEN

The conversation of the last book of Cicero's *De Finibus* is set in the Academy. Cicero recalls a day (in 79 BC) when he, his cousin Lucius, Pupius Piso and Titus Pomponius Atticus left the gymnasium called the Ptolemaeum and the lectures of the last member of the Academy, Antiochus of Ascalon, in the agora of Athens. They left the city and made for the quiet of the Academy a mile and a half from the Dipylon Gate. There the company was moved by the memory of Plato and his successors. On their way to the Academy they had passed Epicurus' Garden, which brought to the mind of the Epicurean, Atticus, the time he and the Epicurean Phaedrus had spent there. The young Cicero gives no hint of Sulla's destruction of these gardens of two very different schools of philosophers in 86.[53] Epicurus was then still remembered not only in portrait paintings but his image on cups and rings.[54]

Years after his philosophical stay in Athens Cicero wrote (in 51 BC) to Gaius Memmius (the addressee of Lucretius' *De rerum natura*) on

[53] Recorded in Plutarch *Sulla* 12.3 and Appian *Mithridatic Wars* 30.

[54] *Fin.* 5.1–3. Pliny attests to the practice of Roman Epicureans displaying images of Epicurus on the celebrations of the twentieth of the month in Rome, *NH* 35.5.

behalf of Patro, then the head of the Epicurean school in Athens who had followed Phaedrus. Cicero's purpose was to dissuade Memmius from pulling down the ruins of Epicurus' house in Melite within the city walls. He sent a copy of this letter to Atticus to reinforce his plea.[55] Epicurus' house and small garden near the Hill of the Nymphs were in ruins by the time Cicero wrote to Memmius and Atticus, but the school and Patro's feelings of reverence and duty to Epicurus and his fellow Epicureans in Athens is evident from Cicero's letter to Memmius.[56]

As for the fate of Epicurus' Garden on the road from the Dipylon Gate to the Academy and down to the Peiraeus, we hear from Heliodorus' *Aethiopica* of a woman who planned to meet the husband of her mistress at a place 'where the monument of the Epicureans is'.[57] When Pausanias visited the nearby Academy in the middle of the second century AD, he noticed a 'monument of Plato'.[58] At the time of Pausanias' visit this monument to Plato was a desolate funerary monument. It has now vanished. As for Heliodorus' 'monument of the Epicureans' it is likely that in the fourth century and after the Herulian invasion of 267 AD no Epicurean still occupied Epicurus' Garden, yet it was still remembered in a context of pleasure. Epicurus' suburban Garden is now, however, a part of the industrial zone that has also enveloped the Academy.[59]

[55] *Fam.* 13.1; *Ad Att.* 5.19.

[56] Cicero speaks eloquently of 'Patro's honour, duty, the legal standing of Epicurus' will, the prestige of Epicurus, and the pleas of Phaedrus' (*honorem, officium, testamentorum ius, Epicuri auctoritatem, Phaedri obtestationem*): *Fam.* 13.1.5.

[57] *Aethiopica* 1.16.5.

[58] *Description of Greece* 1.30.3.

[59] The site is described by Dontas 1971.

DAVID SEDLEY

2 Epicureanism in the Roman Republic

Any account of philosophy in the Roman Republic must start from the events of 155 BC. The city of Athens, appealing to the Roman senate against a fine levied for its sack of Oropus, sent as ambassadors the current heads of three leading philosophy schools – the Academy, Stoa and Peripatos. The excitement generated by these philosophers during their stay in Rome was sufficient to ignite the long Roman love affair with philosophy. Roman patronage became in time a factor that few Greek philosophers could afford to ignore. Many Romans travelled, or sent their sons, to Athens to study in the metropolitan schools. But, conversely, many of the philosophers migrated towards the new centre of power, typically joining the entourage of a powerful Roman. By the mid first century BC, Rome itself had become one of the leading philosophical centres. This shift of the centre of gravity away from Athens was a gradual one, but was intensified by Sulla's crippling siege of Athens during the Mithridatic War, 88–86 BC, a critical period which, for example, saw both contenders for the headship of the Academy move the scene of their operations elsewhere – Philo of Larissa to Rome, Antiochus to Alexandria. The leading Stoic of the first century BC, Posidonius, who was frequently to be found in Rome, did not succeed to the headship of the Stoa in Athens, but eventually set up a school on the island of Rhodes.

By this gradual process of decentralization,[1] each philosophical movement loosened its links to its original Athenian home, and

[1] Philosophical change in the period: P. Hadot 1987; Frede 1999; Sedley 2003. Events of 155 BC: Ferrary 2007.

relocated itself in a diaspora of smaller schools, spanning much of the Mediterranean world. The same process brought in its wake a partial refocusing of philosophical activity. Membership of one of the Athenian schools had meant belonging to an unbroken living tradition stemming from the founder. In the new decentralized philosophical world that same adherence came typically to take the form of reverent study of the school's canonical texts. Thus it was that from the end of the Roman Republic through until the end of Antiquity textual commentary was one of the leading forms of philosophical activity.

Finally, it is important to note that this was an era of philosophical syncretism. As each philosophical movement rethought its heritage in this newly decentralized world, it became increasingly natural to look not only to the school's founder, but also to other traditions whose affinity was sufficient to make them allies. Stoics became increasingly engaged in the study of Plato, for example. Aenesidemus, who refounded Pyrrhonist scepticism in the early first century BC, found Heraclitus a valuable recruit to his cause. And Antiochus, who competed for leadership of the Academy, brought Aristotle and to some extent the Stoics in under the Platonist umbrella.

How far does any of the above apply to Epicureanism?[2] The first thing to notice is that the philosopher-ambassadors of 155 BC did not include the head of the Epicurean school. It was common enough for philosophers to be called on for ambassadorial duty, including, in those cities where they had earned sufficient respect, even Epicureans (Philonides, on whom see further below, and probably a certain Apollophanes, as recorded in an inscription at Pergamum). It is therefore not unlikely that the omission of an Epicurean from the embassy of 155 was deliberate, and reflected the not always unjustified perception of Epicureans as politically unengaged (more on this below). It may also be no coincidence that just a few years later two Epicureans, Alcius and Philiscus, were for unrecorded reasons expelled from Rome.[3] Epicureans often enough found themselves at the civic margins, not only for their political minimalism but also because of the suspicion of atheism.

[2] The best comprehensive guide to individual Epicureans in this period is Erler 1994.

[3] Ferrary 1988: 354–6; Benferhat 2005: 59–60.

However, one region in particular provides an instructive contrast. In Syria,[4] Epicureanism not only flourished but exercised considerable political influence. Philonides of Laodicea-on-Sea – whose own philosophical education appears to have been local although he later made two extended visits to the Athenian Garden – had converted Antiochus IV to Epicureanism, and remained as court philosopher under Antiochus' successor Demetrius I (162–150).[5] Some leading figures in the Athenian Garden during the following generations hailed from Syria, including (see below) Zeno of Sidon and Philodemus of Gadara, as had its fifth scholarch Basilides of Tyre, appointed 205 BC. It seems then that already during the third century BC Syria had become a major regional centre for the movement, reminding us that even in Epicurus' own day Epicurean communities had flourished outside Athens. We may infer that the Epicurean school's Athenocentric focus had all along been less pronounced than that of other major schools, making its eventual migration into the Roman world that much less traumatic.

However, there is no reason to doubt that the Athenian Garden remained the school's headquarters throughout at least the greater part of this period. After Basilides' death *c.* 175 – whether immediately or not is uncertain – Apollodorus became scholarch, to be succeeded in turn by Zeno of Sidon (scholarch *c.* 100–*c.* 75), Phaedrus (*c.* 75–*c.* 70) and Patro (from *c.* 70 until at least the late 50s).[6] Apollodorus was a prolific author, but little is now known of his work. Zeno, Phaedrus and Patro were all well-known figures who earned considerable respect among Romans, Epicurean and non-Epicurean alike. One particularly influential contemporary of Zeno in the Garden, who, however, did not become school head, was Demetrius of Laconia. Some of his works have survived fragmentarily on papyrus at Herculaneum (see further below), and he was known for his meticulously lucid analyses and defences of Epicurus, which were later drawn on by Sextus Empiricus.

Despite the continued eminence of the Athenian school, the effects of growing regionalization can already be seen by the end of Zeno's

[4] Crönert 1907; Smith 1996. For non-Athenian Epicurean communities see also Clay, ch. 1, this volume.

[5] Gallo 1980: 21–166; Benferhat 2005: 48–51; Haake 2007: 148–59.

[6] Chronology: Dorandi 1999: 43–54.

headship. The high standing of the Epicurean scholarch in Roman circles was not replicated in the eastern Aegean. There was by this date an Epicurean school in Rhodes, whose members also taught on nearby Cos. Philodemus (*Rhetoric* 2) reports news of a conversation between members of this school and other Epicureans recently returned from the Garden. The former flatly denied that any kind of rhetoric was considered a genuine art by Epicurean theory. The latter reported that according to the Athenian school 'sophistic' (i.e. display) rhetoric was an exception to this disapproval, although they had only the vaguest recall of what the verbatim support from the school's canonical texts was supposed to be. Neither party appeared to pay close attention to the current scholarch, Zeno, who as Philodemus despairingly remarks 'lives in Athens, not in Persia'.[7]

It is high time to give Philodemus his formal introduction.[8] We would know very little about him were it not for the 79 AD eruption of Vesuvius. It buried just outside Herculaneum a library which, when from the 1750s onwards it was recovered and made partly legible, proved to consist largely of Philodemus' works. It is therefore widely assumed to have originated as his own collection, especially as it includes works by Epicurus and other Epicureans, and variant drafts of some of Philodemus' own treatises. By a further well-founded conjecture, the magnificent villa which housed the library is widely held to have belonged to L. Calpurnius Piso Caesoninus, who, in addition to being the father-in-law of Julius Caesar, was Philodemus' Roman patron. The presence of Philodemus' library there further suggests that the villa had been the location of his school.

Philodemus was born in Gadara in the late second century. At some point in his life he was in Alexandria, and it may have been there that he formed a lifelong friendship with the Academic Antiochus, as also with some of Antiochus' pupils.[9] He studied Epicureanism in the Athenian

[7] On this episode: Sedley 1989. For Philodemus on rhetoric see Blank, ch. 12, this volume.

[8] Of the large literature on Philodemus, see esp. Sider 1997 for biography; Asmis 1990b for a philosophical synopsis; and more widely Erler 1994: 289–362; Gigante 1995; Obbink 1995; Auvray-Assayas and Delattre 2001; Fitzgerald, Obbink and Holland 2004; Tsouna 2007a and 2007b; and Delattre 2007.

[9] This relies on a new reading of Philodemus' *Index Academicorum* (*PHerc.* 1021 and 164) by David Blank (Blank 2007).

Garden during Zeno of Sidon's headship, *c.* 100–*c.* 75. And before finally settling at Herculaneum he seems to have taught at Himera in Sicily, until he was exiled for causing religious offence. This sequence of moves, whatever its precise order may have been, by the late 70s BC had led him to Southern Italy. There he is thought to have remained until his death, probably in the 30s.

Philodemus' new standing in Italy enabled him to create his own Epicurean circle at Herculaneum, and to exert his influence on aspiring young literary figures like Horace and Virgil. A contemporary Greek Epicurean, Siro, taught at or just outside the nearby Greek city of Naples, but Herculaneum was in a primarily Roman area, and although Philodemus wrote – and presumably taught – in Greek he is likely to have geared his teaching more to a Roman patrician clientele. His *On the good king according to Homer* (*PHerc.* 1507) is a good example: addressed to Piso, it sets out to extract the lessons about good and moderate government that can be gleaned from Homer despite the many abuses of power that he also portrays.

One might have thought that the accident of Vesuvius' eruption had preserved for us the remnants of an unexceptional local philosophical school, perhaps one of a great many scattered around Italy, and that this very ordinariness was what made the find so illuminating about philosophical practice in the period. But this does not in fact seem to be so. When Cicero's Epicurean spokesman Torquatus (*De Finibus* 2.19) cites the authorities on whom he himself relies, he picks out Siro and Philodemus, with Cicero's own express approval. We do not know of any other Greek Epicureans of comparable standing working in Italy at this date. Moreover Philodemus is, both intellectually and stylistically, a more significant writer than his reputation has generally conceded. Most of his works have to be recovered from badly damaged papyri, and the strained texts that confront readers are often the result of unsatisfactory editorial conjecture. Those passages which have been more or less fully preserved are in general lucid, not inelegant, and philosophically competent; and the best modern editions of his works – of which we may hope for more in the future – reach that same standard.[10]

[10] The high scholarly standards now being attained, supported by improved methods of decipherment and fragment-alignment, are well exemplified by Obbink 1996, Janko 2000 and Delattre 2007.

With the growth of Roman domination, some other Epicureans had migrated eastwards from Athens, away from the new centre of power: Demetrius of Laconia, for instance, had set up school at or near Miletus.[11] Philodemus instead chose to move towards the new centre, where patronage and political influence could best be won. In settling on the Bay of Naples, rather than at Rome itself, he was not banishing himself to an obscure existence in the provinces, but working right at the intersection of the Greek and Roman worlds, where, as the example of Piso's villa illustrates, the ear of a wealthy and powerful Roman elite might easily be won.

Thanks to the rediscovery of Philodemus' library, we have access to parts (especially the relatively undamaged closing parts, at the centre of the scrolls) of many of his Epicurean treatises. Since the 1970s in particular, intensive new work on the badly damaged papyri has steadily improved our access to these. A broad, if selective, overview of Philodemus' known and probable works will give some idea of their range:

Philosophical history: *On Epicurus*; *Studies* [*Pragmateiai*] *of documents concerning Epicurus and some others*; a biography of Philonides; a polemical work on the Stoics; a history of the Academy; a history of the Stoa. At least these last two are likely to come from his *Compendium of the philosophers*, in ten or more books.

Aesthetics: *On poems* (at least five books); *On music* (at least 4 books); *On Rhetoric* (approximately ten books).

Ethics: *On the good king according to Homer*; *On characters and lives* (a multi-volume work, including *On frank speech*, *On conversation*, *On gratitude*, *On wealth*); *On vices and the opposed virtues* (another multi-volume work, including Book 7 *On flattery*, Book 9 *On household management*, Book 10 *On arrogance*, and an unidentified book *On greed*); *On anger*; *On envy*; *On death* (at least four books); *[On choices and avoidances]*; *On piety*.

Theology: *On the gods* (at least two books); *On the way of life of the gods* (at least three books). Cf. above, *On piety*.

[11] Puglia 1988: 41–8.

Epistemology: *On [...] and sign-inferences* (commonly known as *On signs*; at least four books); *[On perception]*.

Epigrams (around thirty, preserved not at Herculaneum but in the *Greek Anthology*).

Not without justification, we tend to think of Epicureanism as a brand of atomism. Atomist physics had after all been a centrepiece of Epicurus' own writings, and the subject of his major work, the thirty-seven books *On Nature*. The most striking feature of Philodemus' oeuvre is the total absence of works on physics, except in so far as 'canonic' (epistemology) and theology were regarded as falling under this heading. So pronounced a disregard for physics on the part of Philodemus may reflect the cultural tastes of his Roman milieu. Compare his contemporary Cicero, who near the end of Philodemus' lifetime set out to represent in Latin the main Greek philosophical canon, Epicureanism included: his only philosophical works bearing on physics are again epistemological (the *Academica*) and theological (*On the nature of the gods*). Philodemus possessed in his own book collection multiple copies of Epicurus' *On Nature*, and cited them frequently in his *On piety* in so far as they touched on theological matters. But we may conjecture that the overall thematic balance of his writings, which again closely resembles Cicero's, reflects the tastes and priorities of a powerful Roman elite educated in the liberal arts.

It may be significant that Philodemus' teacher Zeno, working in an Athenian environment, albeit with an influx of Roman pupils, *had* still been writing on physics (fr. 12 Angeli–Colaizzo). In doing so he was maintaining the school's earlier tradition, already well represented in this regard by Philonides. But one more particular motive driving Epicureans of the two or three generations previous to Philodemus' own was their engagement in debate about the specifically mathematical aspects of physics. Epicurus and his disciple Polyaenus had used their theory of a mathematically smallest magnitude to reject conventional geometry as misconceived, a stance which caused some outrage in the Greek intellectual world. Philonides (himself a recognized mathematician), Zeno of Sidon and Demetrius of Laconia had all been deeply embroiled in a debate about this, one which in its most recent phase had drawn in the great Stoic physicist and mathematician Posidonius on the opposition side.

Interest in Greek mathematical theory had not, on the other hand, yet penetrated far into the Roman cultural world, and shows up neither in Philodemus nor, once again, in Cicero. Hence differing cultural contexts may in this narrower way too help account for Philodemus' downplaying of physics.

A further question of some importance is whether the full range of Philodemus' works circulated in the public domain, and therefore simply happen not to have survived through the medieval tradition. The epigrams (not found at Herculaneum) did so survive. His *Compendium of the philosophers* is cited by Diogenes Laërtius (10.3), so it too will have been in circulation. It may be significant that the two Philodemean papyri most likely to belong to it, histories of the Academy and the Stoa respectively, are to all appearances written from a philosophically neutral perspective, without a visible Epicurean bias. This is in keeping with an age in which, perhaps for the first time – again as reflected in Cicero's philosophical oeuvre – a rounded philosophical education was expected to include a basic training in all the major schools. Philodemus' own pupils would have expected no less. The work's non-partisan stance may however at the same time have made it the more suitable for public dissemination.

At the other extreme, *On frank speech*, has a subscript to its title which announces it as in effect Philodemus' own record of Zeno's classes in Athens. There are traces of a similar subscript in two other papyri, and his *On anger* has also been plausibly argued to share such an origin. Furthermore, *On signs* is, at least in its surviving part, a report of debates Zeno had with a probably Stoic opponent called Dionysius. In addition to his own notes on Zeno's lectures, Philodemus adds for good measure those taken by his fellow-student Bromius, who he makes it clear had attended Zeno's course on a different occasion, and finally a very similar account of the same debate written up by Demetrius of Laconia. Texts like this, which are essentially records of teaching in the Athenian Garden, may well – perhaps not unlike the school treatises of Aristotle – have been intended for in-school use rather than for public dissemination.

A case has been made for seeing Philodemus' *On piety* as the source for Cicero, *On the nature of the gods* 1.25–41. But even if that were accepted, it would remain an open question whether it testified to the public availability of Philodemus' treatise, or merely confirmed Cicero's implication (*Fin* 2.119, see above) that he turned to Philodemus as his own private Epicurean consultant.

A general survey of Philodemus' work would exceed the limits of this chapter. Other chapters will to some extent fill the gap, since Philodemus is our major Epicurean source on emotional therapy and on rhetoric and poetics, as well as a vital supplementary source on developments in epistemology.[12] What can be offered here instead is a characterization of the working methods and priorities of Greek Epicureans during the period.

I noted at the outset that in the philosophical diaspora the study of foundational texts became increasingly important as a way of maintaining one's school identity. This tendency is more pronounced in the Epicurean school than in any other before the Roman imperial age (when textual commentary was to become the very life-blood of Platonism). For Philodemus himself it shows through above all in his – very probably original, and perhaps pioneering – biographical researches on early Epicureans, based especially on their collected correspondence. The *Pragmateiai* is a particular striking specimen of such prosopography.

In addition, it is instructive to see how Epicureans at this date lean on the school's canonical texts. Philodemus may be fiercely loyal to his teacher Zeno, but Zeno does not have the status of an authority. Four ultimate authorities are recognized: Epicurus himself, and his three leading pupils Metrodorus, Hermarchus and Polyaenus. They are known collectively as *hoi andres*, literally 'the Men', although 'the Great Men' better captures the term's flavour. When Philodemus enters a debate with contemporary Epicureans on some point of doctrine (cf. above on rhetoric), it is common ground to both parties that the correct interpretation must be backed by appeal to the writings of these founding figures. To contradict them, says Philodemus, would be close to parricide (*Rhet.* 1 VII.18–28 Longo Auricchio).

It has become common in modern studies to present Philodemus as an Epicurean loyalist who, when appealing to the canonical texts, is fighting off 'dissident' Epicurean rivals. This contrast is a misleading artefact of the accident that it is his rather than their writings that

[12] See discussion of these topics in, respectively, Tsouna, ch. 14, Blank, ch. 12, and Asmis, ch. 5, this volume.

Vesuvius preserved. Naturally the rivals saw it precisely the other way round: they were the true loyalists, the correct interpreters of the school's canon, while Philodemus was the heretic. Philodemus' one advantage here lay in his agreement with the current school-head, Zeno. But the weakened standing of the metropolitan school in his day (see p. 32 above) makes it doubtful whether that was enough to mark the difference between loyalism and dissidence, especially as Philodemus himself repeatedly locates his rivals' heresy in their alleged departure from the word of the founders, not from that of Zeno.

The need for canonical textual support is likely to underlie two practices which, while not so characteristic of Philodemus, were prominent in the Athenian Garden when he studied there. One, attributed to his teacher Zeno, is the athetization of allegedly inauthentic works passing under the names of the four founders.[13] This expulsion of apocrypha from the Epicurean canon may well have been put at the service of doctrinal debate, either to outlaw unwelcome doctrines or to eliminate apparent contradictions between the four founders. The second practice, this time associated especially with Demetrius of Laconia,[14] is the emendation of the canonical texts, sometimes based on the collation of manuscripts and choice between competing readings. Some of these repairs may have been intended to protect Epicurus from critics outside the school, who often extracted verbatim quotations from his works in order to portray him as a sensualist or immoralist. But there can be little doubt that they also played their part in the school's internal debates about canonical doctrine.

My opening characterization of philosophy in the era of philosophical decentralization included mention of a tendency to syncretism, the creative integration of teachings from other schools. In general this is not a pronounced feature of Philodemus' work. Debate with rival schools, such as Stoics and Peripatetics, is ubiquitous, and extraneous technical concepts (for example Stoic ones in *On anger* and *On signs*) are freely used when adapting the school's position to its contemporary philosophical context. But we may interpret this

[13] Notably Zeno fr. 25 Angeli–Colaizzo 1979; Snyder 2000: 50–2.
[14] Puglia 1988, Snyder 2000: 52–3.

more as a symptom of the era's burgeoning philosophical *lingua franca* than as genuinely syncretistic in spirit.

Philodemus is not averse to recruiting a non-Epicurean ally, as he does in *On arrogance*, whose closing section is, with due acknowledgement, borrowed wholesale from one Ariston (whether the Peripatetic Ariston of Ceos or the Stoic Ariston of Chios is disputed). And even in *On household management*, where he quotes rival philosophers in order to criticize them, he adds the following reflection: 'If we have conceded that some of the ideas stemming from Xenophon and Theophrastus were not unconvincing even to philosophers, we must adopt those too, being more ashamed to omit something useful than to borrow from others' (XXVII.12–20). If this echoes the syncretistic spirit of the age, it does so weakly. Philodemus adopts a pluralistic voice only where there is no risk of compromising the integrity of Epicurean doctrine. There is, for example, no anticipation of the non-Epicurean cosmopolitanism which the second-century AD Epicurean Diogenes of Oinoanda was to incorporate into his philosophy.

So far our focus has been on the Greek Epicurean tradition of the Athenian Garden, as developed and defended both in Athens itself and in the Campanian circle of its alumnus Philodemus. But in the very same period a native Italian Epicurean movement is visible, conducted in Latin. The normal practice of educated Romans was to discuss philosophy either in Greek or at any rate with the use of Greek loan-words, and when Cicero near the end of his life (45–44 BC) set out to create a Latin philosophical vocabulary, that still had a strong air of cultural innovation. The Italian Epicureans are, if so, a notable exception. They represent by far the earliest recorded efforts to translate any Greek philosophy into the Latin language. Their literary efforts at Latinizing Epicurean technical terminology are derided by Cicero and his associates, but Cicero concedes the popularity of their writings: 'They have taken over the whole of Italy' (*Tusc.* 4.7). We know the names of three leading figures in this movement: Amafinius, Rabirius and Catius Insuber. Their dating is controversial, other than that Catius died in 45 BC, but it is reasonable to think of them as Philodemus' older contemporaries, perhaps starting in the late second century BC.

Another distinctive feature of this Italian movement is that, unlike the work of Philodemus, it retained alongside its ethical teaching the focal concern with physics that had marked the early phase of the school. Whatever cultural factors had in Philodemus' circle turned the spotlight away from physics onto ethics, politics and aesthetics had not fully exerted the same influence here. The Athenian Garden's early disparagement of the liberal arts had in the more recent phase represented by Philodemus been subtly re-orientated so as to acknowledge a modest degree of positive value in each of them. But it probably survived unmodified in the Italian Epicurean movement, whose intellectual boorishness Cicero does not hesitate to denounce (*Acad.* 1.5), by contrast with the cultural refinement of his close friend Atticus (*Fam.* 13.1.5), a devotee of the contemporary Athenian Garden.

This brings us to the second towering figure in the Epicureanism of the late Republic, alongside Philodemus: Titus Lucretius Carus. Lucretius[15] has two largely unconnected claims on our attention. First, he is among the greatest of all Roman poets. Second, thanks to the loss of other texts, he is today our major informant on large parts of Epicurean doctrine, especially physics, for which he will be extensively plundered as a source elsewhere in this volume. For his one surviving poem, *De rerum natura* (*On the nature of things* or *On the nature of the universe*) is a six-book versification of Epicurus' physics.

Born in 94 BC, and dying in the mid-to-late 50s, Lucretius is a contemporary of Philodemus and Cicero. We have virtually no further reliable data on his life, beyond whatever can be inferred from the poem itself. The sole contemporary or near contemporary reference to him is found in a letter, written in 54 BC (*Ad Q. fr.* 2.9.4), in which Cicero briefly agrees with his brother about the 'flashes of genius' and 'craftsmanship' that characterize Lucretius' poetry.

There is no doubt of Lucretius' influence on the next generation of Roman poets, especially Virgil, who admired not just his poetic genius but also his philosophical message: 'Happy he who was able to know the causes of things (*felix qui potuit rerum cognoscere causas*), and who trampled beneath his feet all fears, inexorable fate, and the roar of devouring hell' (*Georgics* 2.490–2). (On the vexed question whether it was unorthodox for an Epicurean to use

15 Most relevant aspects of Lucretius are addressed in Gillespie and Hardie eds. 2007, along with extensive further bibliography.

verse as a medium for philosophy, see Blank, ch. 12, this volume.) The specific poetic tradition in which Lucretius unmistakably places himself is that of Empedocles, the fifth-century BC Sicilian philosopher-poet.

Whether Lucretius can be treated as a representative voice of contemporary Epicureanism is a harder question. His poem is centrally on physics, as the title proclaims, and its ethical passages, although among its justly celebrated highlights, are strictly prefatory to or consequent upon the physical arguments. This degree of emphasis on physics, along with his declared ambition to make Epicureanism available in Latin, suggests that we might associate him with the Italian tradition represented by Amafinius more than with the school of Philodemus. So far as Philodemus is concerned, no significant philosophical links between him and Lucretius have yet been discovered. Although small fragments of Lucretius' poem have been purportedly recognized among the remains of Philodemus' library, the identification, even if it were finally authenticated, would not prove any direct link between the two.[16] But also when it comes to the Italian Epicureans, although Lucretius' profile resembles theirs much more closely, his emphasis on the novelty of his task in Latinizing Epicureanism (e.g. 5.335–7) is an obstacle to seeing him as part of a tradition which had already been Latinizing the Garden's philosophy for decades. Add to this his lack of detectable engagement with contemporary developments in other schools, especially the Stoa, and it starts to look safer to view him as operating outside established philosophical circles.[17] It is easier to imagine his cultural milieu as primarily a poetic one.

Lucretius certainly consulted one or more Greek Epicurean sources. He himself declares that it is Epicurus' writings alone that he follows (3.1–13), with no gesture towards the others among the canonical four founders to whom Philodemus repeatedly defers, or for that matter towards a living teacher. Given this, plus the difficulty of

[16] The identification of parts of *PHerc.* 1829 and 1831 as containing scraps of Lucretian verses was proposed by Kleve 1989. For a strong critical reaction to this proposal see Capasso 2003 and the response by Delattre 2003. Most recently, Kleve's proposal has been supported by Obbink 2007.

[17] For Lucretius' lack of engagement with Stoicism and other recent systems: Furley 1966, Sedley 1998a: ch. 3; against, Schrijvers 1999; evaluation of the two sides: Warren 2007b.

identifying any references to developments in the school after Epicurus, the best hypothesis is that he is working directly from Epicurus' *On Nature*, specifically its first fifteen books, whose order of contents he can be seen to be following much of the time.[18]

The brilliant ethical diatribes at the end of Book 3, against the fear of death, and 4, against sexual passion, may be predominantly original Lucretian compositions, or at any rate based on Greek Epicurean material ranging beyond *On Nature*. The proems to the six books likewise give every appearance of being independent creations, and even contain (1 and 5) theological material which has proved hard to reconcile fully with Epicurean doctrine, including the much-debated opening hymn to Venus. When it comes to the main physical arguments, on the other hand, there is very little reason to doubt their Epicurean authenticity. Some are known, albeit in more condensed form, from independent sources; others would be all but lost to us but for the survival of Lucretius' poem. Probably the most celebrated in the latter class is the defence of the atomic 'swerve' (2.216–93),[19] which is among the most widely discussed of all Epicurean arguments, but which we could barely have begun to reconstruct from our other sources.

It is widely, though controversially, held that Lucretius died before the poem was fully finalized. However, its six-book structure is itself at any rate clearly a meticulously planned one, achieved by a modest number of adjustments to the order of topics bequeathed by Epicurus. The poem falls into three matching pairs of books:[20]

1. The permanent constituents of the universe: atoms and void
2. How atoms explain phenomena
3. The nature and mortality of the soul
4. Phenomena of the soul
5. The cosmos and its mortality
6. Cosmic phenomena.

The first pair of books deals with the microscopic world of atoms, the second moves up the scale to the level of human beings, the third to the cosmos as a whole. Within each pair of books, the first explains

[18] For *On Nature* as Lucretius' source: Sedley 1998a: chs. 4–5. For a more complex alternative, see Clay 1983a.

[19] See O'Keefe, ch. 8, this volume. [20] See also Farrell 2007.

the basic nature of the entities in question, the second goes on to examine a range of individual phenomena associated with them. Mortality is a further theme that links the odd-numbered books: Book 1 stresses from the outset the indestructibility of the basic elements, while 3 and 5 in pointed contrast give matching prominence to the perishability and transience of, respectively, the soul and the cosmos. In addition, the poem falls into two balanced halves, orchestrated by the themes of life and death. It opens with a hymn to Venus as the force inspiring birth and life. The first half closes, at the end of 3, with Lucretius' eloquent denunciation of the fear of death. And book 6 returns in its finale to the theme of death, with a grim passage on the great Athenian plague: whether or not this, as we have it, is in its finished form, there can be little doubt that its location at the close represents the author's own architectonic plan, especially as it closes a book which has opened with a hymn of praise to Athens as the cradle of civilization.

This two-edged portrayal of Athenian civilization brings us, finally and briefly, to the theme of Epicureans in politics.[21] Lucretius' opening proem expresses anxiety about the current troubles of the Roman Republic, albeit without any indication of his own political allegiance, if indeed he had one. A large number of other politically engaged Romans more or less contemporary with him were Epicureans. These included not only Torquatus, whom Cicero chooses as his Epicurean spokesman in *De Finibus*, but also and more famously Cassius, the co-assassin of Caesar. Yet a number of other Roman Epicureans are known to have taken Caesar's side. In this period no simple correlation between philosophical and political allegiance is evident. In fact, in so far as any pattern has been detected among Epicureans, it follows class divisions: aristocrats tended to oppose Caesar, *equites* to support him.

None of this should surprise us, because Epicureanism lacked a formal political agenda. The school's declared political minimalism had from the start led it to a pragmatic preference for whatever regime could provide local conditions conducive to an Epicurean community's tranquil independence. If Epicurus approved in principle, and

[21] Politically engaged Roman Epicureans: Momigliano 1941; Castner 1988; Griffin 1989; Benferhat 2005.

Epicureans such as Philonides took up in practice, the role of court philosopher to a Hellenistic monarch, that too was a practical expedient, not an expression of any preference for monarchy as such. The lack of an Epicurean political agenda is once again confirmed.

What has caused most debate is the readiness with which, in the final crisis of the Republic, Roman Epicureans apparently contravened Epicurus' injunctions 'Stay out of politics' and 'Live unnoticed', invoking a clause reported to have allowed the prohibition to be set aside in a time of emergency. In this political context a distinctive feature of Epicureanism was that it offered its adherents a reasoned choice between political engagement and voluntary withdrawal, and both options had their takers. Atticus, Cicero's great friend despite the latter's distaste for his Epicureanism, maintained the school's traditional political quietism during the final crisis of the Republic. Cassius on the other hand wavered on this very point, withdrawing from politics in 48 BC, which is probably the date of his conversion to Epicureanism, and returning to the struggle in 44, when, without renouncing his Epicureanism, he joined the Academic Brutus in fomenting the conspiracy against Caesar.

The chief significance of Epicurean political engagement during the late Republic lies elsewhere. In the Hellenistic world, Epicurean communities had easily appeared to be offering an alternative to political society – a self-marginalization which invited a matching degree of distrust from the local authorities. Philonides, in successfully wooing the local regime, had to all appearances been untypical. Against such a backdrop, the age of Cicero is remarkable, and probably unique, for the degree of sheer civic respectability that Epicureanism had acquired. In an environment in which it was commonplace for members of the Roman elite to adopt a Greek philosophical allegiance, Epicureanism had come to be as widely and unabashedly espoused as any other creed.

This chapter of Epicurean history ends on a note of historical irony. Lucretius' Epicurean poem is dedicated to the Roman aristocrat Gaius Memmius, whose conversion to the school's philosophy is Lucretius' declared ambition. His failure to achieve that goal colours certain events of the late 50s BC, in the immediate aftermath of the poem's publication. In Athens, Memmius had come into possession of a derelict house that had once been Epicurus' own, and was planning to redevelop the site. The Epicurean school's head, Patro, along with Cicero's Epicurean friend Atticus, recruited Cicero to help beg Memmius to spare the building. It is unclear whether the redevelopment was in fact abandoned, but Cicero's letter to Memmius (*Fam.* 13.1) gives clear signals of the latter's contempt, not only for the reverence felt by many Romans towards hallowed philosophical relics, but also for Epicureanism itself. Lucretius' poem is the most illustrious monument of Epicureanism in the Roman Republican era, but whether it did anything to promote the cause in its own day remains open to serious question.

MICHAEL ERLER

3 Epicureanism in the Roman Empire

Descriptions of Epicureanism in Rome often end with Lucretius in the first century BC.[1] No innovations are expected of Epicureanism under the Principate[2] and, in fact, anyone expecting to widen our knowledge of Epicureanism through the study of Imperial sources will often be disappointed, since Epicureans in this period mostly pronounce the familiar doctrines, while anti-Epicurean polemics, from pagan and Christian camps, are content to draw on the arsenal of well-rehearsed arguments, almost always aimed at Epicurus' materialism, his rejection of providence, his denial of the immortality of the soul and his hedonism. Certainly, Epicurus' teachings were not particularly favoured under the Principate. Throughout the first two centuries down to the time of Marcus Aurelius, Hellenistic philosophy, by comparison with resurgent Platonism and Christianity, was indeed favourably viewed; but even then Epicurus' teachings stayed in the background in comparison with Stoicism. His philosophy was eventually to lose all significant influence when, in Late Antiquity, Platonism and Christianity became dominant. One reason for the growing neglect might have been the alleged atheism of Epicurean doctrines.[3]

Nevertheless, Epicureanism crops up in a variety of contexts. We find traces of his teachings in authors as diverse as Seneca, Plutarch,

Translated from the original German by Annemarie Künzl-Snodgrass (with thanks to Anthony Snodgrass)

[1] Fundamental: W. Schmid 1962; useful: Jones 1986; Ferguson and Hershbell 1990: 2260. The contributions in Erler 2000 illustrate different aspect of Epicureanism at this time.

[2] For Epicurean orthodoxy cf. Clay 1983b; Erler 1992 stresses flexibility.

[3] Cic. *ND* 1.123; SE *M* 9.58. Cf. Winiarczyk 1990; Obbink 1996.

Lucian, the Alexandrine Church Fathers, Augustine and the Late Antique commentators on Plato, whose attitudes are mostly critically distant, or even dismissive. There are also, however, authors like Lucian, Diogenianus or Celsus,[4] who are more sympathetic. In Diogenes of Oinoanda in Asia Minor, we even meet a fervent admirer of Epicurean teachings, who erected a monumental inscription, the content of which is enriching our knowledge of Epicurean teachings. But the critical reception of Epicurus is also of great interest. The various ways in which Epicurean teachings were received are instructive for how we deal, not only with Epicurus, but with Greek pagan philosophy generally, in a changing context.[5]

The use of Epicurean arguments in philosophical disputes, for instance on the question of whether the world was created,[6] the adaptation by Seneca of Epicurean concepts to his own, Stoic ideas,[7] or the integration of Epicurean teachings through re-labelling – for example by the Platonist Marinus, who praises Proclus' 'life out of the public eye' and explains the widely criticized maxims of the Epicurean way of life as Pythagorean teaching[8] – are just some of the reasons why it is worthwhile to examine the reception of Epicurean teachings under the Principate. In addition, they attain an almost paradigmatic character for the further history of the reception of Epicurus during Medieval, Renaissance and modern times. The picture already beginning to emerge during the first century BC becomes clear during the Principate:[9] Epicurus' practical ethics, his range of techniques for a life accompanied by the principles of reason, were appreciated even by those who sharply rejected his materialistic physics and theology. Clearly the Epicurean understanding of philosophy as therapy (*philosophia medicans*), assisting in the practical management of life and the acquisition of knowledge, suited the Romans' practical understanding of philosophy and the rather worldly atmosphere of the beginning of the Principate. It also retained its significance later, in the curriculum of Neo-Platonist philosophy, more concerned with life after death, as a stepping-stone in the mental and personal preparation for philosophical instruction proper (*praeparatio philosophica*).[10]

[4] For Celsus see Clay 1992. [5] Schmid 1962: 761ff. [6] Baltes 2000.
[7] I. Hadot 1969 and Schmid 1955. [8] Marinus *Life of Proclus* 15.29–32.
[9] Gigante 1975: 53ff.; Nussbaum 1986: 31ff. [10] Erler 1999: 119–22.

CONTINUITY AND DISCONTINUITY

Diogenes Laërtius attests that, unlike the Academy and the Peripatetics, the Epicurean community survived down to his own lifetime, into the late second and third centuries AD.[11] To be sure, Diogenes enumerates leaders of the Garden only down to the first century AD and it is uncertain whether the institution of the *Kēpos* continued in Athens itself. Numenius, however, confirms there was continuity of the Epicurean community.[12] Epigraphical evidence from the time of Hadrian proves the existence of 'Diadochi' known to us by name, Popilius Theotimus and, in Heliodorus, even a *peregrinus*.[13] Even if they were not successors as heads of the *Kēpos*, but of a private 'Epicurean' school,[14] their existence speaks for the continuity and vitality of the Epicurean tradition, which in addition enjoyed goodwill at the highest level. After Trajan's death, his widow Plotina won an assurance from Hadrian that the Epicurean community be allowed to choose its own leaders and even to consider non-citizens as candidates.[15] The Emperor Marcus Aurelius initiated the setting-up of a chair of Epicurean philosophy in Athens.[16]

Further, interest in Epicurus' philosophy was widespread in the Empire. We meet Epicureans not just in Athens, where they were amongst Paul's audiences,[17] but we also come across Epicurean communities in the West, in Herculaneum or Sorrento, in the East, on Rhodes and Cos, in Pergamon, Lycian Oinoanda, Syrian Apameia, in remote southern Lycian Rhodiapolis or in Amastris in Bithynia on the Black Sea.[18] In the first two centuries AD, Epicurus' teachings were obviously also attractive for many of those who belonged to the city elites. A glance through the writings of Plutarch shows that quite a number of his own friends, though Epicureans, were still happily

[11] Cf. DL 10.9–10; see Erler 1994.

[12] Numenius fr. 24 Des Places, for helpful chronology: Glucker 1978: 368f.; Ferrary 1988: 460f.; Dorandi 1991a: 43ff.

[13] *CIL* 3, 12283. 14203, 15 = Dessau 7784; cf. Oliver 1938. Dorandi 2000: 147f.

[14] Glucker 1978: 366; for the importance of the first century BC for the Epicurean tradition see Sedley 2003: 31–41 and ch. 2, this volume.

[15] For the positive answer by Hadrian see *IG* II² 1097.

[16] Philostr. *Vitae soph.* 2.2; Lucian *Eun.* 3.

[17] *Apost.* 17, 18.

[18] Luc. *Alex.* 25; for Epicureans in Syria see Smith 1996: 125–7.

tolerated in his circle.[19] This fact alone disproves as groundless the common notion that Epicurus was successful only with the lower classes, because of the populist appeal to human weakness of his teachings.[20]

The reasons for this lay not least in the fact that Epicurus' teachings could be tapped according to need for the planning of one's own life, without having to enrol in a philosophical system. This attitude, already put into practice to some extent by Cicero and Horace, and to be found in the Christian context in Clement of Alexandria, supported the circulation of Epicurean thought, and leaves its traces in some surprising contexts.[21] Further, Epicurus' own way of life lent authenticity to his teachings, in particular to his ethics, and impressed followers and opponents alike. Diogenes Laërtius dedicated his massive history of philosophy to a lady with Platonist ambitions. But this did not prevent him from rounding off his work by placing at its end the description and praise of Epicurus' teachings and life and making Epicurus' *Kyriai Doxai* the colophon of his work, in the conviction of thus making 'the end (sc. of his work) coincide with the beginnings of happiness'.[22]

EPICURUS, OPPONENTS AND INITIATORS

In the first century, Seneca appropriates Epicurean ideas for his own aims, above all in the area of practical ethics, despite significant reservations. Although a Stoic, he does not unconditionally surrender to the authority of that school.[23] Rather, he sees himself as a 'scout' in a foreign philosophical camp. He lays claim to a personal approach, citing as justification that truth has no master. His writings, his letters in particular, show that Seneca is extremely familiar with Epicurus' writings and possibly also with those of Philodemus.[24] Of all philosophers Seneca, in his letters, quotes Epicurus most frequently, after Lucretius.[25] It is no coincidence that the first thirty letters to Lucilius finish with Epicurean maxims whose content Seneca, with a view to the addressee, seeks to bring into line with

[19] Hershbell 1992: 3355f.; Timpe 2000: 60f. [20] Lact. *Inst.* 3.17.7 (553 Us.).
[21] Hor. *Ep.* 1.1.14; Cic. *Tusc.* 4.7. [22] DL 10.138; Gigante 1992: 4302–7.
[23] Sen. *De otio* 3.1.
[24] Sen. *Ep.* 33.4ff.; Gigante 2000 sees Philodemean influence in Seneca.
[25] Lana 1991: 263.

fundamental Stoic concepts. He rejects populist Epicurean polemics – for example, the teaching of hedonism – but he is ready to agree with Epicurus in points where he thinks he can recognize convergences with his own views.[26]

The aim of Seneca's philosophy is a happy life, based on security and greatness of the soul. Like Epicurus, Seneca sees in philosophy a therapeutic model for dealing with life; like Epicurus before him and Marcus Aurelius after him, Seneca sees himself as a leader of souls.[27] It is therefore not surprising that Seneca reconnoitres Epicurus' camp and directs his search above all at Epicurus' practical ethics.

Of course, divergences in important questions of doctrine cannot be overlooked; but neither are they concealed. Seneca disapproves of Epicurus' banning of the gods from the state, and equally of his reticence over political engagement. If Seneca demands that the individual engage with politics, since no-one should live outside the state, then this pragmatic evaluation is not as far from that of Epicurus as the latter's call for a 'life out of the public eye' seems to suggest. In Seneca's opinion, the difference lies rather in the degree of intensity of the engagement: whereas the Stoic sage engages when nothing hinders him, the Epicurean, by contrast, engages only when it is absolutely necessary.[28]

In the Greek-speaking world, the first–second century Platonist Plutarch is much less open-minded and positive about Epicurus' teachings.[29] Like Seneca, Plutarch is very knowledgeable about Epicurean teachings; his view of Epicurus can certainly claim to be taken seriously. But Plutarch's dispute with Epicurus also shows that their points of view are, on most issues, irreconcilable. Here it should be recognized that Plutarch does not only criticize Epicurus from his own point of view, but intermittently takes the viewpoint of Epicurus and then tries to show this to be self-contradictory.[30] Plutarch's arguments are hardly original, but come from the arsenal of traditional polemics. He criticizes sundry precepts of Epicurus, for example the maxim 'Live out of the public eye' (*De latenter vivendo*), or the

[26] Sen. *De vita beata* 12.4; *Ep.* 12.11. [27] Sen. *De vita beata* 13.4.

[28] Sen. *Ep.* 90.35; about different views of political involvement cf. Sen. *Ep.* 68.2; *De otio* 3.6. Roskam 2007.

[29] Boulogne 2003. [30] Well stressed by Roskam 2005.

writings of influential Epicureans such as Epicurus' pupil Colotes, whose work *That it is impossible even to live according to other philosophers' precepts*, he tried to answer with his own work *Against Colotes* (*Adversus Colotem*) and also echoes in his *That it is impossible to live pleasantly following Epicurus* (*Non posse suaviter vivi secundum Epicurum*).[31] These writings further illustrate that a shared reading of Epicurean writings, and a critical discussion of them, was part of the activity of Plutarch's circle. Indeed, in his anti-Epicurean writings, he quite often lets followers of Epicurus from his own circle of friends hold the stage.

Much as Plutarch criticizes Epicurus' view of religion, his physics or his hedonism, he still knows how to distinguish between Epicurus the person and Epicurus the philosopher, and to see positive features in Epicurus the person – this, too, is a strategy which is known not least from the reception of Lucretius: 'If they (sc. the Epicureans) were completely wrong in their opinions ... and in their statement that no-one wiser than Epicurus existed, yet someone who attracted such affection is to be admired.'[32] However much Plutarch criticizes the fundamental principles of Epicureanism, agreements in the area of practical ethics can nevertheless be observed, particularly in his discussions of emotions, such as anger (in the *De cohibenda ira*), or garrulousness (in *De garrulitate*), and of how to deal with them in a methodical fashion. When, for example, in *De cohibenda ira*, Plutarch recommends a method for controlling and appropriately handling the emotions, which he calls *epilogismos*, the rules he prescribes are much like Philodemus' recommendations.[33] Plutarch's strict anti-Epicureanism does not exclude borrowing from Epicurus in other areas when it seems opportune to him.[34]

In any case, Plutarch's extensive and detailed discourse with Epicurean teachings demonstrates his belief that he is dealing with a living philosophy, one to which he evidently conceded real political influence and which he apparently saw as a threat for the practitioners of traditional religion, such as those at oracle shrines.[35]

[31] Westmann 1955; Zacher 1982. [32] Plut. *Frat. am.* 487D.
[33] On Plutarch's use of this method cf. Ingenkamp 1971; Erler 2003: 147–62.
[34] Plut. *Cons. ad ux.* 609D–611A, despite 611D.
[35] Plut. *Pyth. or.* 398B; *Def. orac.* 434D.

EPICURUS THE SAVIOUR

In the second century, we also meet authors who engage with the positions of other schools from an Epicurean point of view, or who profess open allegiance to Epicurus and propagate his teachings.

Diogenianus may serve as an example of the former group.[36] For a long time, he was placed in the Academic–Peripatetic tradition but now it seems probable that Diogenianus argues from an Epicurean position.[37] We can conclude from the texts preserved by Eusebius that Diogenianus takes issue with Chrysippus' teachings on fate, and also argues against the Stoic view of oracles. To Chrysippus' claim that Homer already supported a deterministic view of the world, since in Homer human actions were governed by the Gods and were, as such, predetermined, Diogenianus responds by pointing out Homeric passages which show him as an advocate of the freedom of human action. Diogenianus speaks against using such a self-contradictory author as Homer as a basis for philosophical discussion. In addition, his emphasis on the central role that chance plays in human life is apparently also based on Epicurean ideas. Further, he argues that the existence of chance deprives oracles of any serious scientific basis. If events happen to turn out as predicted, this is just coincidence. And even if sound prescience existed, it would have no purpose, for the predestined events are inevitable. Further, if the events are bad, the suffering will be made greater through prescience. With his observations, Diogenianus intervenes in a lively contemporary debate about questions of providence and self-determination from an Epicurean point of view.[38]

Despite all other differences, Epicurus' rejection of all forms of religious superstition turned the Epicureans into welcome allies of the Early Christians where the struggle against the growing obscurantism of the second and third centuries was concerned. In particular, the rise in the misuse of oracles led to passionate and often brutally conducted disputes. Thus the Epicurean Euphronius, who dared to prefer the human art of medicine to that of the god Asclepius, had to be told by a priest in a dream that there was salvation for him only if

[36] Testimonies collected by Gercke 1885: 691–704, 705–48. [37] Isnardi Parente 1990.

[38] On chance in Epicureanism: Isnardi Parente 1990: 2441ff.; traditional arguments (Cic. *Div.* 2.20–259) are used by Epicureans (Schol. Aesch. 624 = fr. 395 Us.).

he burned Epicurus' books, mixed the ashes with liquid wax and then spread this medicine on his chest.[39]

Such disputes with contemporary religious zealotry form the everyday background to the writings of Lucian, where there is no lack of criticism of Epicurus' teachings, but where his person and his teachings are often sympathetically depicted, or even become the addressees of the treatise.[40] Epicurus is particularly favourably portrayed in the treatise *Alexander or the false prophet*, which introduces him as a philosopher who wishes to protect people from the impositions and excesses of religious zealotry and, through an enlightened attitude, lead them to a quiet, tranquil, and happy life. Epicurus is occasionally described as a saviour (*sōtēr*) or messenger (*kēryx*), terms which are also used by Epicureans themselves and are reminiscent of Old Testament expressions.[41] Perhaps such a choice of words was intended as a kind of 'competitive offer' to the blossoming Christianity. Lucian's *Alexander* seeks to put up a monument to Epicurus the 'saviour', 'for this in the truest sense holy and divine man, the only one actually to recognize that which is true and good and, through its dissemination, to become a liberator and benefactor of his disciples'.[42]

In the *Alexander* a dramatic debate is described over a serpent-oracle of Glykon or Asclepius, founded by the same Alexander.[43] Lucian tells us how the Epicureans – unlike the Platonists, Pythagoreans or Stoics but together with the Christians – unmask this oracle as a fraud and, in doing so, face hostility from Alexander's followers. The sad culmination of this struggle is a public burning of Epicurus' main precepts, 'as though it were the author himself', on a pyre in the city of Abonuteichos. Lucian himself took sides in this dispute, supporting Epicurus' teaching, 'since it liberates the soul from all fear of imagined fantasies and supernatural things, as well as from all vain hopes and desires and, in return, furnishes it with reason and true concepts'.[44] In Amastris, before the Roman Legate in Bithynia and Pontus, L. Hedius Rufus Lollianus Avitus, Lucian brought an action against

39 T 99 Edelstein and Edelstein 1945. 40 Clay 1992.

41 Cf. for instance Luc. *Alex.* 61 (or Diog. Oin. 72.III.12–14 Smith); see also Clay 1989: 243 n. 41 and Clay 1992.

42 Luc. *Alex.* 61.

43 To put Lucian's story in its place see Robert 1980: 393–421; Jones 1986: 133–48.

44 Luc. *Alex.* 25, 38, 47.

Alexander, saying that he had plotted to kill him on his journey from Abonuteichos to Amastris.[45]

EPICURUS AS BENEFACTOR OF MANKIND: DIOGENES OF OINOANDA

At about this same time, Diogenes of Oinoanda,[46] a place in Lycia near the river Xanthus, had a monumental Epicurean inscription erected in a public place.[47] He seeks to help people from all over the world to achieve true happiness with the help of Epicurus' teachings.[48] Two hundred and twenty-three fragments of this inscription have been discovered and read since 1883. We can infer that the inscription was over 80 metres long, that the overall height of the sections of the text was 3.5 metres, and that so far only 30 per cent of it has been found.[49]

Everything that we know about Diogenes is derived from this inscription. Diogenes was already old (3.II.7–8 Smith) and ill when he had the inscription made. We hear of a network of Epicureans with whom he was in contact, and that he was planning a journey to Athens, Chalcis and Thebes in Boeotia (fr. 69 Smith) in order to meet friends such as Antipater. Diogenes must have been a well-to-do citizen to afford to have such a monumental inscription put up in a public place of his home town.[50]

Along with the papyri from Herculaneum, the inscription is one of the most important later sources for Epicurean philosophy and enriches the corpus of Epicurean writings by new testimonies, by four hitherto unknown letters of Epicurus, by new aphorisms of the school's founder and, not least, by extensive discussions of Epicurean teachings by Diogenes himself.[51]

The precise original arrangement of the text is controversial. It is nevertheless generally agreed to consist of seven horizontal rows of

[45] Luc. *Alex.* 57. [46] Text and commentary: Smith 1993 and 2003a.

[47] 3.V.12–VI.2 Smith; the localization of the inscription is debated as is the date; much can be said in favour of the first half of the second century AD, see Smith 1993: 35ff.; 2003a: 48ff.

[48] Fr. 3.III.3ff. Smith. [49] Smith 2003b: 270. [50] Smith 1993: 35ff.; 2003a.

[51] Smith 1993: 86ff.

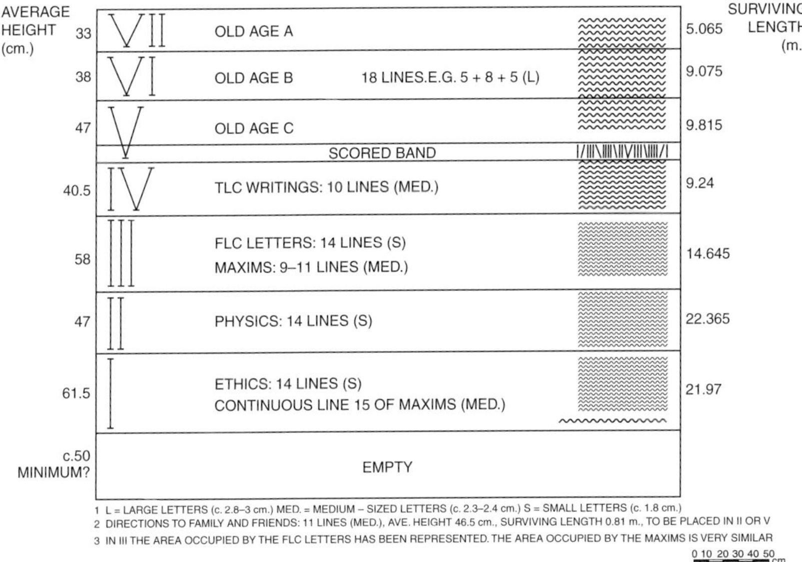

Figure 1. The Philosophical Inscription of Diogenes of Oinoanda. Reconstruction from Smith 1993, fig. 6.

script with numerous sections, which are arranged one above the other.[52] (See Figures 1 and 2.)

Diogenes addresses his inscription to open-minded novices in Epicurean philosophy (3.III.4ff. Smith), citizens of Oinoanda, people from all over the world and future readers. Like Epicurus, Diogenes sees philosophy as a *vade mecum* for his fellow citizens and for passers-by from all over the world, seeing himself as a cosmopolitan. 'Although various kinds of people live in various parts of the world, the whole world provides one land to all people, namely the entire earth, and there is a common house, the world' (30.II.3–11 Smith).

Diogenes' view is that most people are afflicted by the pestilence of false opinion about the true nature of things (3.IV.4ff. Smith), by the

[52] For discussion of the various arrangements see Clay 1990 and Smith 1993, especially 92 n.60. Since 1993 new discoveries have altered the surviving lengths of the various sections. For details see Smith 2003a: 58–9.

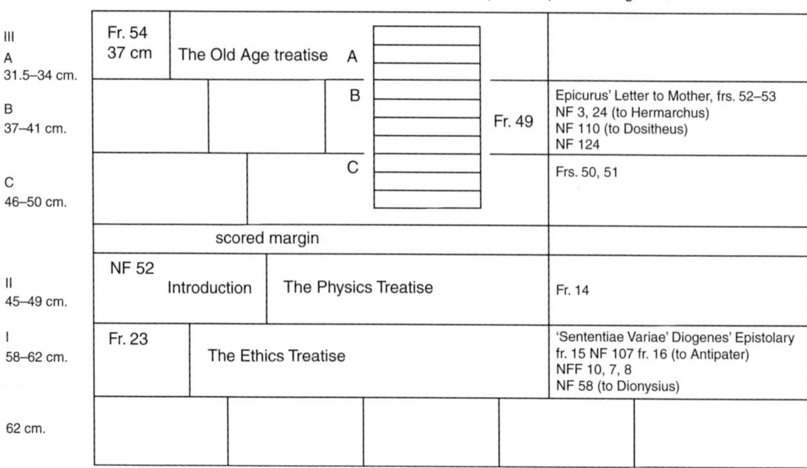

Figure 2. The Philosophical Inscription of Diogenes of Oinoanda. Reconstruction from Clay 1990. Clay's reconstruction uses Chilton's numbering of the fragments and later discovered 'New Fragments' (NF) numbers. For a concordance see Smith 1993.

fear of the gods, by death and generally by all that is foreign. By his inscription Diogenes seeks to offer his readers an aid to remedies for their lives, and to help them to help themselves.

For this purpose the texts should be read and learned, in accordance with Epicurean tradition, in a certain order: the treatise on physics (II) is conceived as an introduction for the whole inscription (2–3 Smith); then the texts on ethics (I), the letters (III), Epicurus' guiding principles (basis), then the further texts until the treatise on old age is reached. This didactic intention is emphasized by the design of the inscription as if it were an open papyrus roll. Each section is written in columns, with strict rules of syllabification. This is a way of offering to the reader, in a public place, something akin to an open book with a curriculum of Epicurean doctrines. The reader is to appropriate the advice offered in a quasi-meditative way, as is hinted in the fragment of a letter from the inscription (74 Smith).

This very public display may be seen as conflicting with Epicurus' maxim, that Epicureans were to live a reclusive life (*lathe biōsas*). But Diogenes himself, by implication, takes up a position in relation to this by describing his observations as a special kind of politics (3.1.5ff. Smith), which sees itself as a therapy for the souls of his fellow citizens.[53]

Diogenes proves that he has a profound knowledge of Epicurean teachings and even includes in his inscription writings by Epicurus himself that have not otherwise survived. For example, the remains of a hitherto unknown letter by the obviously still relatively young Epicurus to his mother (125–6) are particularly impressive. In addition, Diogenes is keen to show that he knows his way around the Greek philosophical tradition – the Presocratics, Pythagoras and Empedocles, Diagoras, Theodorus, Protagoras, Socrates, Plato and Aristotle (to whom Diogenes strangely attributes the view that nothing is scientifically knowable because of universal flux),[54] and above all, Democritus.

In his treatise on physics he tries to refute those who, like Socrates in Plato's dialogue *Phaedo*, think that physiology is useless (frs. 1–27 Smith). He critically discusses Heraclitus and Democritus, the role of perception, the origin of human life and the emergence of civilization and culture. In doing so, he touches on problems of astronomy, meteorology, religion and theology and supports the thesis that it was not the Epicureans, but philosophers such as Protagoras, who were to be seen as the atheists.

In his tract on ethics (28–61 Smith) Diogenes reminds us specially that happiness (*eudaimonia*) is the aim of all human endeavour. This kind of *eudaimonia*, however, is gained not by virtue, but by pleasure. The fear of the gods, of death or of pain is a particular obstacle to happiness and Diogenes warns of the dangers of unfettered desires. Ideas such as metempsychosis are critically discussed and the problem of divination is treated in the context of human liberty and self-determination.

Particularly remarkable is a fragment in which Diogenes announces a 'Golden Age': if everyone were an Epicurean, friendship and justice would rule, laws and fortresses would be superfluous (56 Smith). This emphasis echoes other contemporary second-century ideas,[55] and while it follows logically from some of Epicurus' own teachings there is no sign of this ideal in the early Hellenistic Epicurean texts; its presence here may be Diogenes' own innovation.[56]

[53] Roskam 2007: 131ff. [54] Diog. Oin. fr. 5 Smith and Smith 1993: 128–9.
[55] Gordon 1996. [56] Long 1986: 314ff. See also Brown, ch. 10, this volume.

In the section on old age (137–79 Smith) Diogenes speaks out against the prejudices that young people have against the old. Contrary to the opinions of many, Diogenes is convinced that the human mind stays active also in old age. As a proof, Diogenes cites Homer who tells us that old men too can still be good orators. Old people, he says, may be slow as elephants, but similar to them in intelligence (146.I.2–6 Smith). Likewise, Diogenes sees no disadvantage in the decrease of sensual desires.

The remains of some of Diogenes' letters to his friends are also interesting. The *Letter to Antipater* (62–7 Smith) recalls, in its form and content, Epicurus' *Letter to Pythocles* and discusses the infinite number of worlds in the universe. Further letters are concerned with epistemology, ethics or biography. In one, Epicurus is called a messenger, who brought complete salvation (72.III.13 Smith). We even hear of Epicurus being saved in an accident at sea, a shipwreck.[57]

Of further interest are two theological fragments, found and published only recently by Martin Smith. They argue that belief in the gods in no way guarantees justice among men, as is so often claimed. For, so the argument runs, people who do not respect justice will not be deterred from injustice by the fear of the gods. Sages, on the other hand, are men of justice not because they fear the gods, but because their actions are governed by reason. Finally, ordinary people will in the end be willingly law-abiding. As proof, Diogenes points to the Jews and Egyptians, who in his view are problematic peoples in terms of their morality, although they are governed by superstition.[58] Finally, in another important fragment (19.II.6ff. Smith) Diogenes demands that the statues of the gods should smile in order to create an appropriately serene mood in the viewer.[59]

Diogenes does not present himself as an original thinker. Even if occasional convergences with contemporary views of the Second Sophistic can be suspected, Diogenes' reflections can all be described as orthodox Epicurean. In every respect, his inscription copies his master Epicurus, in both form and content. But this lack in originality should in no way be used as a reproach; on the contrary, it is the aim of all Epicureans to be faithful exegetes of their master.[60] Diogenes succeeded in this in a remarkable way. To him we owe

[57] Fr. 72 Smith. See also Clay, ch. 1, this volume. [58] Smith 2000: 69f.
[59] Clay 2000: 98ff. [60] On Epicurean exegesis of the master see Erler 1993: 281–303.

new information and the confirmation that Epicureanism was still a lively force in the second century AD, and that such reports as we find, for example, in Lucian are therefore to be taken seriously.

'HEAVY BIRDS': THE RECEPTION OF EPICURUS IN LATE ANTIQUITY

Although Epicurus' teachings enjoyed a renewed blossoming in the second and third century,[61] they did finally recede into the background with the rise of Neo-Platonism in Late Antiquity. The Emperor Julian even thought that most of Epicurus' writings had been destroyed by the gods, and Augustine asserts in a letter of AD 410 that Stoics and Epicureans would no longer play any part in the schools of rhetoric.[62]

Such remarks may be exaggerated or driven by wishful thinking. At any rate, we can observe that Epicurus' teachings left their mark even in the difficult circumstances created by the now dominant Platonism. The Neo-Platonists proved their great aptitude for integration,[63] even when it came to Epicurus. For this, however, we need to look carefully. For when Epicurean ideas were to be integrated, we find that they were often wrapped in a Platonist cloak, to the point where their provenance became almost unrecognizable. Epicurean empiricism, hedonism and atomism, however, were irreconcilable with Neo-Platonist intellectualism, teleology and Platonist ethics, which aim for assimilation at the highest level of principle. Plotinus finds a nice image for this when, with the Epicurean orientation towards this world not least in mind, he complains about 'heavy birds, which have taken over too much of the earth – and are incapable of flying high'.[64] Even so, in Plotinus' view the Epicureans were on the right track to finding the good life, although they had stopped half way there. Yet this deters neither Plotinus nor other Neo-Platonists from making use of certain ideas of those 'heavy birds', above all in matters of practical philosophy.[65] Pleasure, for example, plays a part in Plotinus' work, but only in moderate form and as an accompaniment

[61] Schmid 1962: 769; but cf. Timpe 2000: 44.
[62] Jul. fr. 89b (1, 2, 141, 24 Bid.=301c Spanh.); August. *Ep.* 118.21 CSEL 34, 684, 23; cf. fr. 317 Us.
[63] O'Meara 1999: 83. [64] Plotin. 5.9.1. [65] O'Meara 2000: 249.

to all that is good. For Damascius, too, every natural activity is accompanied by moderate pleasure. Thus Epicurean ethical ideas are not rejected completely by the Platonists, because they in no way attribute to Epicurus that coarse hedonism, which traditional polemic is bent on finding in his ideas. Porphyry does not shrink from bringing Epicurean, as well as Platonic, ideas into a letter in which he invites his mother Marcella to study philosophy.[66] Proclus solves a problem in the Platonic theory of prayer which had already been pointed out by the Epicurean Hermocrates – does one have to pray to be able to pray properly? – by using Epicurean ideas of prayer as meditation, when the good is not a result generated from outside, but consists in the act of the prayer itself and, consequently, in looking after the self.[67] Even late Neo-Platonists like Damascius or Simplicius were apparently well informed about Epicurus; here, too, Epicurean reminiscences are often given a Neo-Platonist colouring.[68] To be sure, in Late Antique Neo-Platonism there is no longer a lively debate over Epicureanism. But even then those two strands in the reception of Epicurus which were characteristic for the reception of Epicurean teachings during the Principate can be observed: rejection of fundamental Epicurean doctrines in conjunction with a positive appreciation of practical elements of Epicurean ethics.

CONVERGENCES AND DIVERGENCES WITH THE CHRISTIANS

The relationship between early Christianity and pagan philosophy has been discussed mostly in relation to the Stoics and Plato. Epicurus, by contrast, is often perceived only as a target for Christian polemics.[69] For some of the Church Fathers, Epicurus was seen as an atheist who questioned the world order and providence.[70] However, it is Epicureans, not Stoics or Platonists, whom we find as allies of the Christians, in resisting false prophets and oracle fakers like Alexander of Abonuteichos. Not by chance was Alexander's demand 'Out with the Christians!' complemented by the cry of his followers 'Out with the Epicureans!'[71] Christians and Epicureans were linked by their aversion

[66] Ferguson and Hershbell 1990: 2309f.

[67] Procl. *in Tim.* 1. 216. 18ff. Diehl = Hermarchus fr. 48 Longo Auricchio and Erler 2001b.

[68] O'Meara 1999: 89. [69] Schmid 1962: 774–814.

[70] See Justin *Apol.* 1.4; see also Althoff 1999: 218–30. [71] Luc. *Alex.* 17, 25, 38, 61.

to pagan superstition, although they were guided by different reasons: the Epicureans were driven by their battle against any form of religious enthusiasm, while the Christians were led by their conviction that they alone had access to the true faith and, of course, a blessed state in the next world. A further instance of convergences with different motivations lay in the fact that Christians and Epicureans alike offered an alternative way of life with their communities, and wished to provide, respectively, for happiness in this world and a blessed state in the next. Both groups opened themselves up equally to the reproach that they refused to engage in public life and with the community.[72] In addition, despite all divergences and all polemics, Epicurus himself as a person was positively held in esteem by the Christians on grounds of the restraint attributed to his way of life, and the occasional Epicurean idea was found to be acceptable. An ambivalent attitude can already be seen in Clement of Alexandria. Certainly, he rejects Epicurus and his teachings as godless, but this does not deter him, however, from finding certain doctrines acceptable (such as the idea of *prolēpsis*), or from invoking the beginning of Epicurus' *Letter to Menoeceus* with its invitation to practise philosophy.[73] At times, Clement illustrates his own philosophical ideas with the help of Epicurean citations, without however signalling them as such.[74] By comparison, Origen is much more radical; he takes issue with Epicurus, referring comparatively often to his teachings and using Epicurus as a weapon in the struggle within the Church.[75] The Alexandrine theologians occasionally mix vehement polemics against Epicurus' teachings with respect for his person. It is remarkable how well informed and at times differentiated the criticism is. A very good example is the dispute of Dionysius of Alexandria, bishop and pupil of Origen, with Epicurean atomism in a treatise *De natura*, in the form of a letter to his son Timotheus.[76] Dionysius critically discusses questions of atomism, directing his fire mainly at Democritus, without losing sight of Epicurus' teachings, where, for example, the theory of the spontaneous deviation of atoms is concerned. In another fragment, arguments are offered against the thesis that the world is the product of chance. Even if Dionysius is credited with little first-hand

[72] Jones 1986: 113; Eckstein 2004: 308ff. [73] Clem. *Strom.* 2.16.3, 4.6.9.
[74] Clem. *Strom.* 6.104.3. [75] Markschies 2000: 192.
[76] Feltroe 1904; Bienert 1978, 1981 and 1985; Markschies 2000: 209.

reading of Epicurus, the remnants of his works prove that Epicurus' teachings were noted and taken seriously in Christian circles.

Epicurean concepts tend to be used to underpin one's own position or to combat opponents' views.[77] Occasionally Epicurean ideas are also used to paint the dark aspects of one's own view of the world in even gloomier tones. When Philo of Alexandria tells us about the snake in Paradise, he does this with a conscious recourse to Epicurean ideas.[78] Finally, it is another favoured tactic to project Epicurean concepts on to opponents in order to make them more vulnerable.[79]

The comparison of Epicurean memoirs with the role that the *Acts of the Apostles* or the saints' *Vitae* played in early Christianity has resulted in some interesting results. The search for parallels, agreements or convergences, however, demands extreme caution. For agreements are often found only on the surface and are conditioned by traditions which run in parallel, especially since in the early Principate pagans and hellenized Christians increasingly spoke the same language and often used the same forms of argumentation characteristic of the shared educational milieu. Differences between the Epicurean and Pauline views on community, therefore, as well as in the function of the letters, should not be overlooked. The addressee of Paul's letters is the community (*koinōnia*) itself as an element in salvation;[80] for Epicurus, community serves the individual's happiness.

Despite all the differences it is often possible to identify Epicurean dogmas in the Church Fathers, as a starting point for their own deliberations, though without their provenance being acknowledged. Tertullian uses Epicurus' classification of the desires – into the natural and necessary, the natural and unnecessary, and the neither natural nor necessary – to prove that the natural need to eat was ordained by God, and to separate it from the sexual instinct.[81] Arnobius who, because of his apparently good knowledge of Epicurus' writings, was occasionally treated as a lapsed Epicurean, made use of Lucretius'

[77] Baltes 2000: 99ff.

[78] Booth 1994: 159–72; on Philo and Epicureanism see Lévy 2000: 122–36.

[79] Ferguson and Hershbell 1990: 2302.

[80] On Paul and Epicureanism see Glad 1995; Eckstein 2004; Fitzgerald, Obbink and Holland 2004.

[81] Tert. *De an.* 38.3; see also DL 10.27; Cic. *Fin.* 1.40.

account of the development of civilization, in order to remove from Christianity the stigma which clung to it as a 'new religion'.[82]

In this context, Augustine is particularly interesting. For Augustine himself confesses an initial affinity with Epicurean ideas.[83] After his detachment from the Manichaeans and before turning to Platonism, Epicurus' teachings apparently played a role in his search for theological certainty, in the context of dealing with this life. Only his own imprecisely based conviction of the immortality of the soul had kept him from handing over the palm of victory to Epicurus: 'Talking to my friends Alypius and Nebridius, I declared that in my heart I would have had to hand the palm to Epicurus, when it came to matters of the greatest good and the greatest evil, but for my own belief in the eternal life of the soul after death and in the continuing rewards of merit and demerit, in which Epicurus simply did not want to believe.'[84]

The main source of Augustine's knowledge of Epicurus is Cicero, above all the *De Natura Deorum*, *Tusculan Disputations* and *De Finibus*. He was familiar with Lucretius, as is shown by allusions, expressions of approval or examples. Epicurus' teachings belong in the educational canon, even if they are a typical example of a world-view to which revelation is denied.[85]

Epicurus' teachings become the main target of Augustine's critique of ancient philosophy (*Util. Cred.* 10; *CD* 5.20). The leading theme is his reproach that Epicurus turns the virtues into the slaves of carnal desire (*Serm.* 348.3). Other points are directed at Epicurus' materialism or his theology. With all these differences, however, Augustine's attitude long remains ambivalent. He is impressed, like others before him, by Epicurus' ethics and his manner of life.[86] He will concede that Epicurus can help in the correct way of dealing with the things of this world and its contents. In Augustine we still see those two strands which can be observed right through the Principate, in the positive appreciation of the Epicurean art of living and the negative evaluation of his other teachings.

[82] Föllinger 1999: 18ff. [83] Erler 2001a.

[84] August. *Conf.* 6.26; on Epicureanism in the *Confessions* see Simpson 1985: 39–48; Fuhrer 2000.

[85] Erler 2001b: 858f. [86] August. *Util. Cred.* 10.

It is this ambivalent, by no means altogether negative, evaluation of Epicurus which is found not only in pagan and Christian Late Antiquity, but accompanies Epicurus' teachings through the Middle Ages and can be observed in, for example, Petrarch, Boccaccio and Dante. Dante, too, bans Epicurus, as a philosopher of this world, into the Sixth Circle of the Inferno. Epicurus the practitioner of practical ethics, on the other hand, he reveres in the *Convivio*, together with the Peripatetics and the Academy, as one of the three women at Christ's empty grave, who have found not truth, but practical worldly wisdom,[87] a point of view which has played an important role in the further reception of Epicurus, despite all other hostile treatments. In the Renaissance, rehabilitation of Epicurean ideas can even occur, on occasion, with the support of the Christian idea of the resurrection of the body.[88]

[87] Dante, *Commedia, inf.* 10.13–15.

[88] Lorenzo Valla, *De Vero Bono* and Erler 2004. See also Wilson, ch. 15, this volume.

PIERRE-MARIE MOREL

4 Epicurean atomism

INTRODUCTION

Epicurean physics is fundamentally atomist. This means that it rests on two principal theses. The first is: 'All bodies are either indivisible small bodies or else are composed of indivisible small bodies.' The Greek adjective *'atomos'* means 'indivisible, what cannot be divided'.[1] When made into a noun, or when a noun is understood, usually it is translated as 'atom' or 'atoms'. Let us call this thesis the 'Atomist Thesis'. Epicurus sets it out in a canonical form at the beginning of his inquiry into physics at *Letter to Herodotus* 40: 'Amongst bodies, some are composites (*sunkriseis*); others are those from which the composites are made. These latter are indivisible (*atoma*) and unalterable ...' Lucretius reprises the argument in the first book of the *De rerum natura* (*DRN*), calling the atoms 'principles' (*principia*) or 'the first elements of things' (*primordia rerum*).[2] The 'composites' are rendered as *concilia*. It appears that Epicurus used this argument on various occasions, at least if we believe the scholion which accompanies this passage in the *Letter to Herodotus*: 'He also says this in the first book of *On Nature* and in books XIV and XV, as well as in the *Great Epitome*'. In short, for Epicurus, atoms are principles (*archai*) in the sense that they

Translated from the original French by James Warren.

[1] So we can talk of indivisible 'bodies' (*sōmata*), e.g. Epic. *Ep. Hdt.* 42, or indivisible 'natures' (*phuseis*), e.g. Diog. Oin. 6.II.10–11 Smith.

[2] *DRN* 1.483–4. Cf. Philodemus *De pietate* 37–41 Obbink, where the argument is cited by the opponents of Epicurean theology. According to the reconstruction of *On Nature* in Sedley 1998a it seems that the argument played a role in Books I and II, then in XIV et XV, devoted to arguments against the opponents of atomism (Sedley 1998a: 123–6). It is possible that it was repeated in the *Summary of arguments offered against the natural philosophers* mentioned in DL 10.27, if we agree, following Sedley 1998a: 123, that this refers to a summary of *On Nature* XIV and XV.

constitute the nature of bodies: 'the indivisible principles are necessarily the nature of bodies' (*Ep. Hdt.* 41).

The second thesis is that the first thesis concerns not only a single aspect or single part of physics, but its essential core on which all others depend in various ways: the Atomist Thesis is the principal argument of Epicurean physics. This means that the Atomist Thesis offers a law which all natural phenomena obey and is the central claim in a set of propositions which constitute the theoretical core of natural philosophy. These are the essential or elementary theses which Epicurus sets out at the beginning of the *Letter to Herodotus* 39–44, in what he calls an 'adequate outline', designed so that we can keep the principles in mind (*Ep. Hdt.* 45). This outline can be expressed as follows:

1. Nothing comes from what is not nor disappears into what is not (§ 38–9).
2. The all is made of bodies and void, which are the only complete natures / *per se* existents (§ 39–40).
3. Amongst bodies, some are composites; other are those from which composites are made (§ 40–1).
4. The all is unlimited or infinite both in the number of atoms and the extent of void (§ 41–2).
5. The number of different atomic shapes cannot be conceived (§ 42–3).
6. The atoms move constantly and endlessly because of the existence of void (§ 43–4).

So, Epicurean physics rests on a restricted number of fundamental propositions which can be considered to be interdependent. We can also see, in the light of these six propositions, that the area of physics which deals with the composition of matter is, by inference, the starting point for every other assertion concerning nature.[3] By way of comparison, the Aristotelian theory of matter is an essential part of Aristotle's physics, but it is in no way the starting point for every other claim about nature. For this reason, Epicurean philosophy can rightly be called 'materialist'.

Further, if we concentrate on the fact that this version of physics differs from other 'materialisms' in being 'atomist', proposition 3

[3] On the inferential structure of *Ep. Hdt.* see Sedley 1996, esp. 313–16. See also Betegh 2006.

takes on a significant function because it expresses explicitly the essential claim: atoms are the ultimate constituents of the things which physics studies, namely bodies. It is therefore a central thesis of the core of Epicurean physics in so far as it is a theory of composition. It answers the question: What are physical bodies made of?

Nevertheless, we must make a number of remarks about this view, both in terms of ontology and epistemology. First, ontology. The fact that the word 'atomism' directly evokes the term 'atom', should not make us forget that the atoms are not the only existents. The Atomist Thesis itself shows that bodies are divided into two categories: atoms (indivisible bodies) and composites. The fact that Epicurus initially refers to 'bodies' (*sōmata* at *Hdt.* 39) and that 'atoms' are mentioned only later (at 41) is not insignificant. We will come back to this, but for now note the essential point that Epicurus does not reserve bodily existence only for the atoms, because composite bodies are perfectly legitimate existents also. One might go on to ask how the properties of composites – for example, colours, complex forms and states such as life, perception and thought – are to be classified alongside the atoms. In other words: should we interpret Epicurean physics as strictly reductionist or should we accept that composite bodies have specific properties over and above their elementary composition?[4] For these purposes, let us understand 'reductionism' as the thesis according to which (i) the properties of composites or macroscopic bodies are explicable in terms of the properties (both intrinsic and relative) of the atoms and (ii) composite bodies have only the causal powers given by the atoms by which they are constituted.[5] This question is central to the notion of action and responsibility: if all properties are reducible in this way to atomic properties, it must be agreed that all causes are derivable from the atoms themselves and it is not clear if a moral agent can be the true cause of his own actions and dispositions.[6]

[4] In support of anti-reductionism see the pioneering article by Sedley 1988, according to which the Epicurean theory of properties, and mental properties in particular, forms a doctrine of 'emergence' which would offer a 'top-down' theory in contrast to the 'bottom-up' theory characteristic of Democritus. For a recent criticism of the anti-reductionist reading see O'Keefe 2005: esp. 65–109, which insists that the emergence of properties, mental faculties included, is not incompatible with reductionism. I return to this below.

[5] Cf. O'Keefe 2005: 68–9.

[6] Epicurus himself poses this question in *On Nature* xxv. See also O'Keefe, ch. 8, in this volume and Masi 2006.

Next, note that the argument does not say that only bodies exist. In fact, atoms are separated by an incorporeal medium, the void (*kenon*), without which they could not move (*Ep. Hdt.* 67). It is important that at the beginning of the exposition of physics summarized by the *Letter to Herodotus*, Epicurus affirms jointly the existence of body and void (proposition 2 above). So we can call Epicurean physics 'materialist' provided we remember to specify that immaterial void is one of the complete or *per se* existents alongside the bodies. Epicurus adds, furthermore, at *Ep. Hdt.* 44 that both the atoms *and the void* are 'causes'.[7]

Second, epistemology. The first formulation of the Atomist Thesis might wrongly suggest that Epicurean physics is purely atomist in the sense that the Atomist Thesis and its corollaries would suffice to construct the entirety of natural philosophy. On the contrary, it appears that according to Epicurean epistemology the observation of the world, empirical acquaintance, is not merely legitimate but, rather, necessary. Epicurean natural philosophy (*physiologia*) as presented in the *Letter to Herodotus*, is a résumé of theoretical elements, a view reduced to an outline or schema (*tupos*: *Ep. Hdt.* 35, 36, 45, 68) and not a completely realized total physical account. It is important to keep this in mind when we consider its form. It is not certain whether the pages, now lost, of Epicurus' *On Nature* which were dedicated to the presentation of atomist physics would have given the same impression. And, even in the specific context of the *Letter to Herodotus*, empirical evidence is called upon on numerous occasions, not only to illustrate some theoretical point or other, but also in order to offer confirmation, direct or indirect. For example: 'no observation undermines' the view that the images (*eidōla*) are extremely fine (*Ep. Hdt.* 47).[8]

Finally, taken literally, the Atomist Thesis does not say how – in particular by which movements – the composites are formed. This question is more sensitive for atomism at Epicurus' time since, as we shall see, it is one of the most vigorous points of attack made by Aristotle on the earlier atomists, Democritus and Leucippus. Without doubt, one of the most significant challenges Epicurus had

[7] Following the manuscripts and rejecting Gassendi's emendation of *aidiōn* for *aitiōn*.

[8] See Asmis, ch. 5, this volume, and for the use of this principle in cosmology see Taub, ch. 6, this volume.

to face was how to 'save the phenomena' by showing that atomism was perfectly capable of explaining not only the *composition* but also the *generation* of bodies and, what is related, their cohesion and persistence. That is a crucial question even for the definition of Epicurean physics: in what way can the Atomist Thesis ground not only a theory of *composition* but also one of *generation*?

ATOMISM AS A THEORY OF COMPOSITION

Epicurus and the Democritean heritage

The principles of Epicurean physics which announce the opening argument of the *Letter to Herodotus* are, in their essentials, taken from the physics first elaborated by Democritus, who had subscribed to the following: reality is composed of bodies and void; bodies are either indivisible, i.e. atoms, or are composed of atoms; the atoms are unlimited in number and the void, in which they move, is also unlimited. We can also now add a cosmological claim which follows logically from these principles: there is an unlimited number of worlds.[9]

This influence is attested by various ancient sources, notably Cicero, Sextus Empiricus and Clement of Alexandria. Diogenes Laërtius (10.2) even reports that Epicurus embarked on philosophy when he discovered the books of Democritus. Whatever the truth of this, it points to Epicurus' essential Democritean heritage, probably via the intermediary of Nausiphanes. It was generally agreed throughout Antiquity that Epicurus shamelessly stole Democritus' physics.[10] But he nevertheless formulated various criticisms of the true founder of atomism, whom he nicknamed 'Lerocritus' which probably means 'someone interested in – or concerned with – foolish things'. Epicurus set out both to appropriate and also to criticize Democritean physics.

This paradoxical form of defence is probably rooted in Aristotle's anti-atomist polemic. Although Epicurus' precise knowledge of Aristotle has been and continues to be the subject of debate, it is

[9] See Taub, ch. 6, this volume.

[10] See esp. Cic. *ND* 1.73, Plut. *Adv. Col.* 1108E. On Epicurus' debt and ambivalent attitude to Democritus see Morel 1996: 249–54 and Warren 2002a: 193–200.

quite likely that he wanted to save the doctrine from the criticisms, notably by Aristotle, offered against the first generation of atomists: Democritus and Leucippus.[11] It is clear, in any case, that Epicurus wished to keep the doctrinal core of atomism, which he shared with Democritus, in the face of criticism from those who preferred to think of matter as continuous, of whom Aristotle is a leading example. As we shall see, Epicurus did not remain content merely to restate wholesale Democritus' view. If he is Democritus' heir, he is so in the sense that he takes up a number of *problems* and offers his own original response. The difficulties produced by Aristotle against the idea of reducing bodies to atoms play an evidently central role in this process. In this light, we may suppose that the first historical impetus for Epicurean physics was the preservation of and support for a discontinuous conception of material composition: to identify the primary material elements and affirm that these atoms are the ultimate indivisible components of matter. However, Aristotle was not content in his attack on Democritus merely to reject atoms in favour of the continuum; he also denounced the general explanation of phenomena which – in his eyes – could not properly account for generation. For Aristotle, on the one hand, the first atomists explained neither the motion nor the organization of matter since they knew only the 'material cause' and not the 'efficient', 'formal' and 'final' causes. On the other hand, their notion of matter, because it consists in juxtaposed existents incapable of intermingling, makes it impossible to understand how a higher-level unity might be produced. It is in effect impossible to understand, according to Aristotle, how a genuine unity can be produced from a plurality of elements, such as the atoms, which cannot cause one another to alter and cannot therefore produce change. Generation, after all, is a kind of change. And unity thus produced is merely apparent.[12] It is possible that the atomists, or Democritus at least, had candidly admitted that the generation of composites was merely apparent since their components – the atoms – was absolutely unalterable. However, as we shall see, that

[11] For a summary of the debate and bibliography on Epicurus' relation to Aristotle see Gigante 1999: 33–50. On Epicurus' reaction to Aristotle's criticisms of Democritus see Furley 1967.

[12] Cf. *De caelo* 303a6–7, 305b1–5; *Metaph.* 1039a3–10; *Gen. et corr.* 325a34–6, 325b29–326a6. On this polemic and the solutions the atomists offer to the problem of generation see Morel 1996: 83–92.

could not have been Epicurus' view, for whom the composites have a genuine unity. As a result, if Epicurus was aware of this polemic, it is logical that he tried to give an explanation not only of the problem of composition, but also of generation. To that latter end, he had to reform the atomist view of composition.

The shapes of atoms

The Epicurean reform turns principally on three issues: the number of different shapes of atoms, the structure of the atoms, and the variety of atomic movement. The Epicureans set themselves apart from Democritean physics also on a more fundamental level which goes beyond simple reform. By ascribing to Democritus an 'eliminativist' position, according to which the atoms are the only truly existing bodies, certain Epicurean texts give evidence of a radical change of perspective. I will return to this point in the last section. But let us begin with the first two points. Democritus had asserted not only the infinity of the number of atoms, but also of their shapes. So all phenomena, events, and all physical arrangements are equally possible and in principle explicable thanks to an unlimited combination of shapes, playing a role equivalent to a principle of sufficient reason.[13] The thesis of infinite atomic shapes therefore plays an essential role in the economy and power of the Democritean theory of atoms and void. However, according to some reports, Democritus had even allowed this infinity of shapes to imply an infinity of sizes: it follows that it is possible for an atom to be the size of a world.[14] It is hard to attribute to Democritus himself a position which would oblige him simultaneously to claim that an atom is by nature imperceptible and that there can be enormous atoms. But in any case, whatever the authenticity of this thesis, the Epicureans saw that it could not be maintained: it would be necessary to suppose, as Lucretius says, that certain atoms might attain a 'monstrous' size (*DRN* 2.498). For his part, Epicurus decided that atomic shapes were 'not absolutely infinite, but only

[13] See esp. Simpl. *In Phys.* 28.15ff. (DK 68 A38). See also Makin 1993: 62–5, who argues that the argument applies equally to worlds and leads Democritus to suppose an infinity of them also.

[14] See Aët. 1.12.6 (DK 68 A47), Eus. *Praep. Ev.* 14.23.2–3 (DK 68 A43).

inconceivable' in number (*Ep. Hdt.* 42–3), though there are infinite atoms of each shape (*Ep. Hdt.* 42–3, 55–6; Lucr. *DRN* 2.479–521). (That is proposition 5 in the list above.) We must set a limit on the infinite or, better, 'indefinite' number of atomic shapes in order to avoid having to accept an infinity of atomic sizes.

This opposition is no mere detail: it reveals the essential difference between Democritus and Epicurus. The latter makes clear at *Letter to Herodotus* 56 that it is not 'useful' in explaining the differences between sensible qualities that all sizes of atoms should be possible. He therefore privileges a particularly economical method, taking as a principle that we should retain the least extravagant explanation. The theoretical cost here is a criterion of discrimination between competing explanations. And, to assess the cost, Epicurus invokes the evidence of sensory experience which prevents us from admitting atoms so big that they might be perceptible. To this extent, his criticism has in its sights not only Democritus' physics, but also his theory of knowledge which is in fact quite critical of sensory experience which, for this reason, cannot corroborate the hypothesis of the principles: atoms and void.[15] For the Epicureans, atomism is answerable to sensory experience, which means – at the very least – that it must not be undermined by it. Lucretius shows elsewhere that the Democritean thesis of the absolute infinity of atomic shapes would have as a consequence an infinite variety of sensible qualities. In that case, it would be impossible to discern the boundaries between them and we would perceive nothing distinct: sensory impressions would be infinitely variable. But this is not the case: by the simple fact of perception we distinguish between different temperatures, colours, smells, and tastes (*DRN* 2.500–21). We will see below that this first correction of Democritean doctrine also has direct implications for cosmogony: the atoms' ability to generate worlds.

[15] On Democritus' theory of knowledge and its critical and sometimes sceptical aspects see esp. Aët. 4.9.8 (DK 67 A32); DL 9.72 (DK 68 B117); Galen *El. Hippoc.* 1.2 (DK 68 A49); Sextus Empiricus *M.* 7.135 (DK 68 B9). This seems to offer a genuine problem to Democritus: he imagines a dialogue in which the senses undermine reason's attempt to condemn the appearances. Galen *On medical experience* 15 (ed. Walzer–Frede) (DK 68 B125). On the problems of Democritean epistemology see Morel 1998.

The structure of the atom

The reform of atomism also looks at the very structure of the atom. According to Democritus, the atom, although three-dimensional, is indivisible because of its smallness and solidity. If we set aside a report by Simplicius that attributes to Democritus the idea of atomic parts, we have no reason to question the consensus that a Democritean atom has no parts.[16] Aristotle objected, however, that because of the continuity of motion, the atom cannot escape mathematical division (*Phys.* 240b8–241a6). Even if we suppose with the atomists that it is *physically* indivisible, no extended body can as a whole instantaneously cross a spatial limit. We ought, therefore, to be able to distinguish those parts of the atom which have moved past a certain point and those which have not. For that reason, according to Aristotle, an indivisible 'cannot move nor change in any way' (*Phys.* 240b31). Everything which moves is necessarily divisible, except those accidentally in movement as part of a larger body which is itself in movement.

This is a strong objection: the early atomists make the existence of movement – at least of atomic movement – an unquestionable principle. So Aristotle dismantles the very basis of their physics. It is true that Aristotle conceives of locomotion as the traversal of a spatial medium, while the first atomists seem not to have given a clear account of the status of the space in which it takes place. Their void is essentially the negative interval which separates atoms, not the place *in which* atoms move. But Epicurean void does play the role of an empty space. It is the empty space (*chōra*) in which atoms move.[17] That is why, in order to think of movement, we have to make the (strictly false) supposition that there is a 'top' and a 'bottom' even though the universe is infinite (*Ep. Hdt.* 60).

Yet this is an insufficient reply to Aristotle's argument for the divisibility of anything mobile. And it is likely that in order to respond to it, Epicurus decided that the atom, while physically indivisible, has parts. The tidying of the first atomists' view is clearly presented by Simplicius as a reply to Aristotle: 'While agreeing with the doctrine of Leucippus and Democritus about the first bodies, he

[16] Simpl. *In Phys.* 82.1–3. [17] Epic. *Ep. Hdt.* 40; Lucr. *DRN* 1.444. See Sedley 1982.

[i.e. Epicurus] kept their impassivity but took away their property of partlessness, trying in this way to reply to Aristotle'.[18] The atom therefore has ultimate parts – what Lucretius calls *minimae partes* – which are unities with extension but which are inseparable from what they constitute and, as a result, unable themselves to produce movements and combinations. They are conceived as analogous to the smallest point perceptible by the senses.[19] We can therefore see in this view a reply to Aristotle's objection in *Physics* Book 6, if we think of the *minimae partes* as being in motion only accidentally, since they are inseparable from the atom.

This does not mean that Aristotle's criticisms had, in the eyes of Epicurus, an absolutely constraining force, nor that the Epicurean doctrine of minimal parts had as its only inspiration the concern to reply to Aristotle.[20] It is true, though, that it had as its object the preservation of a discontinuous view of matter against the objections of continuum-theorists like Aristotle. In any case, the theory probably had a greater end in view. If it were merely an attempt to set a limit to division, it is difficult to see how it avoids an infinite regress: one might have to suppose in turn some parts of these ultimate parts, and so on. Moreover, we might doubt whether Epicurus had wanted to suggest some useful or effective 'measure' of atoms. More likely, the thesis of atomic parts was justified by the concern to think of the variations of atomic sizes as simple multiples of the smallest atomic size.[21] Supposing that there are parts of atoms does not require that we are able to count them; neither Epicurus nor Lucretius imagines any such operation. The Epicureans' goal becomes clearer if we pay attention to the comparison between atoms and perceptible bodies. As in the case of the smallest perceptible thing, beyond which anything smaller cannot be perceived, we must imagine a material minimum beyond which there is nothing. All unities corresponding to this minimum are necessarily equal (*Ep. Hdt.* 58). And atoms are not all of the same size. There must, therefore, be 'limits', the

[18] Simpl. *In Phys.* 925.19–22: this text considerably undermines the idea, found also in Simplicius, that the Democritean atom has parts.

[19] Epic. *Ep. Hdt.* 59; Lucr. *DRN* 1.599–634. [20] Cf. Laks 1991.

[21] Vlastos 1965. We can also note how this view has important geometrical consequences, since it implies that all extensions are commensurable. That said, there is no reason to think it was originally a geometrical view, later applied to physics.

ultimate parts of atoms, which correspond to units of size (*Ep. Hdt.* 59). These 'limits' are not incorporeal separations between bodies – like the limit between two books shelved together in a library – but irreducible parts, limits placed on any division. This does not answer, of course, every difficulty we might raise against atomic minima: are they in contact and therefore separated by a spatial minimum smaller than them? (In this case they would not be the minima of *every* extension, only of bodily extension: which would be paradoxical.) Or, if they have three-dimensional extension, like a sphere, are they not again divisible as a sphere can be divided into two hemispheres? Finally, we might imagine (though this supposition does not provide a direct solution) that the Epicureans did not feel forced to reply to every difficulty faced by atomic minima, on the basis that it simply had to be accepted as a necessary consequence of other atomic properties.

THE MOVEMENT OF ATOMS

The principles of movement

The existence of movement is an axiom in the whole atomist tradition: the reality of motion is an immediate given.[22] We should also suppose that motion never ceases and that in more closely packed composites there remains always a small motion, albeit only the vibration of the component atoms. In fact, atoms are always separated by void, and when there is void, there must also be atomic motions, since there is nothing to impede them (*Ep. Hdt.* 43–4). That is proposition 6 above.

Nature is sufficiently constituted, and in this sense ontologically complete, once we posit an infinity of atoms and their motions, ordered or not. In addition, motion is eternal and without beginning (*Ep. Hdt.* 44). Further, in so far as it is shown by empirical evidence, the existence of motion does not have to be proven. However, the explanation and the varieties of motion seem to have been understood differently by Democritus and Epicurus. The Epicurean texts make some important corrections: atoms move in the void at an equal speed, whatever their weight, since nothing impedes them;

[22] Sextus Empiricus *M* 7.214.

atomic blows simply alter their directions (*Ep. Hdt.* 61–2; Lucr. *DRN* 2.238–9). An atom's weight causes its movement downwards (*Ep. Hdt.* 61; Lucr. *DRN* 2.190). According to Cicero, the Epicureans differ from Democritus on this point: for Democritus, blows were the only cause of atomic motion.[23]

The atomic swerve

The Epicurean doctrine of atomic 'swerve' (*clinamen* in Latin, *parenklisis* in Greek) constitutes not merely a tidying but a decisive innovation in comparison with earlier atomism. According to Diogenes of Oinoanda, it is aimed directly against Democritus. He, in making all things subordinate to Necessity, overlooks the fact that there is a 'free motion in the atoms', a swerve, revealed – according to Diogenes – by Epicurus, and without which we could not conceive of moral responsibility.[24] To justify the introduction of this odd motion, Lucretius, in whose poem we find the only authentic Epicurean account of this matter, imagines the following situation: if weight were the only original principle of motion, would the atoms not have to fall downwards in the infinite void like raindrops?[25] How could they in that case collide with one another and how in that case could nature produce anything? We should therefore suppose that a minimal deviation affects the original motion of the atoms in order to understand the spontaneous generation of bodily combinations and the formation of worlds. The swerve, even if theoretically posterior, is therefore as primary in physical terms as the relationship between weight and downwards atomic motion.

This theory also has an ethical dimension, to the extent that in Lucretius as in Diogenes of Oinoanda, it grounds the possibility of free or deliberate action.[26] When Cicero mentions it in the *De Fato* it is in a context which is both physical and ethical: he opposes and sets side by side Stoic fatalism and the Epicurean swerve, which he

[23] Cic. *Fat.* 46. It is possible that in his attempt to explain an atom's motion independent of blows, Epicurus agrees with Aristotle's criticisms of Democritus' view. See Furley 1989: 90 and all of ch. 7.

[24] Diog. Oin. fr. 54 Smith.

[25] See Lucr. *DRN* 2.216–93, esp. 221–4. There are other references to the swerve: Cic. *ND* 1.69, 73; *Fat.* 22–3; *Fin.* 1.19, 28; Aët. 1.12.5, 1.23.3; Philod. *De signis* LIV.

[26] See O'Keefe, ch. 8, this volume.

considers 'an uncaused motion' which cannot guarantee freedom. Is the doctrine of the swerve primarily ethical or physical? It has, certainly, a central role in Lucretius' poem, beyond its specific contribution to physics, but poses various significant interpretative problems. In particular, we do not have Epicurus' own demonstration, which Cicero and Diogenes of Oinoanda both mention. The modern interpretative options are in general terms as follows: some think Epicurus came up with the theory of the swerve rather late, which is why it is not in the *Letter to Herodotus*; some think that the letter is incomplete, and would have mentioned the swerve at the outset; others doubt that Epicurus was its author.[27] We can nevertheless ask if Epicurus had a genuine need for the swerve and whether he ought to have resolved the problems for which it is proposed as a solution by other means. We will come back to the question of cosmogony: in this case, as it is found in Lucretius, the theory is perhaps born from a concern to reply to attacks from other schools, notably the Stoics.

It is nevertheless hard to give a positive account of the swerve and, furthermore, to explain the relationship between the swerve and voluntary action solely in the light of the passage in Lucretius. The *clinamen*, because of its relative indeterminacy, allows one to think of a break in the necessary mechanical chain of physical causation (*DRN* 2.251–93). But it does not *explain* the process of volition itself. Also, the Lucretian text does not make clear whether the *clinamen* is a motion necessary for voluntary action or whether it intervenes after the decision as a response to a stimulus. Also, is the swerve rare, or is it implicit in every action as a condition of desire or volition needed by every living thing?[28] Perhaps the text's imprecision is deliberate: it invites us not to overestimate the causal function of the swerve. It is merely a simple necessary condition of the possibility and not a true cause of free or voluntary action.[29] By introducing a break in the causal mechanical chain, whatever the modalities of this break, it secures, *in principle*, a certain autonomy of behaviour and saves freedom from determinist accounts. That does not give a positive explanation of how we perform free actions. We can also ask if free action does not depend on causes besides those which are specifically

[27] For a recent account of the debate see O'Keefe 2005. [28] Cf. Englert 1987.
[29] Cf. Gigandet 2001: 35; O'Keefe 2005.

atomic, and if psychological states might have a certain kind of independence from atomic motions.[30] We can equally ask, as a passage in Lucretius suggests, whether the relationship between the *clinamen* and the free movement of the agent is not a simple one of inference by analogy: just as atoms have in themselves a certain motor force besides weight and blows, so we have the capacity to withstand, to some degree, the necessity of external forces and the internal necessity of our own passive dispositions (*DRN* 2.284–93). The point of this inference would be very general: contra the views of Democritus or the Stoics, there is necessity in nature, but it is neither all-powerful nor all-controlling.

ATOMISM AS A THEORY OF GENERATION

Atoms and compounds

As we have seen, one of the physical justifications for Lucretius' doctrine of the swerve is the explanation of the formation of composite bodies. For Lucretius, the *clinamen* is a necessary condition of the coming to be of any arrangement: without it 'nature would have created nothing' (*DRN* 2.224). In other words, it is not sufficient to posit an infinite number of atoms of varied forms and sizes in order to explain the generation of composite bodies and worlds. It is not sufficient, therefore, to define matter merely by its composition: we need equally to describe it by specifying the dynamic conditions of its generation.

The spontaneous dynamism of atomic matter is strongly emphasized in Lucretius' poetry, to the extent that the poet sometimes appears to make large concessions to a providential teleology which he elsewhere denies and which Epicurus had ruled out from the outset.[31] Lucretius gives in effect an allegorical description of nature which makes it in some sense the organizing principle of the world. Nature is a 'creator' (*natura creatrix*)[32] or 'ruler' (*natura gubernans*).[33] It 'compels' (*natura cogit*). It forms agreements and compacts, the *foedera naturae*, which ensure the relative permanence of

[30] Cf. Sedley 1983, 1988. [31] Cf. *DRN* 2.167–83, 4.825–57, 5.156–234.
[32] E.g. *DRN* 1.629, 2.1117. [33] E.g. *DRN* 5.77.

phenomena such as, for example, the stability of natural species. In fact, there is no need to see in such expressions any concession to a form of deliberative teleology or providentialism. Nature has no creative power beyond that enacted blindly by the atoms themselves. Atoms do not deliberate or make decisions, not only because they are inanimate and without any mental properties, but also because they have no need to: arrangements emerge spontaneously from a limitless set of attempts which end with the realization of viable stable structures (*DRN* 1.1023–30). That is how nature 'accomplishes all, spontaneously, without any divine assistance' (*DRN* 2.1092).

Lucretius' descriptions of the atoms make this perfectly clear: atoms are not only 'matter' (*materies* or *materia*); they are also the 'first principles of things' (*primordia rerum*), the 'first bodies' (*corpora prima*), the 'seeds of things' (*semina rerum*) or the 'generators of things' (*genitalia rerum*). Their totality constitutes a 'generative matter' (*genitalis materies*). All these terms refer to atoms but also denote the composites the atoms create.[34] By nature, the atoms are both physically independent and also apt to combine to form bodies. Hence the properties of atoms presuppose the existence of composites. That is the strong implication of the *Letter to Herodotus*, whose argument mentions 'bodies' before 'atoms' and which considers the latter alongside the former: 'Amongst bodies, some are composites and others are those from which composites are made' (40–1). There is therefore no ontological rift between atoms and compounds, but rather a functional distinction between constituents and composites, within the class of 'body'. The fundamental category of matter in Epicurean physics is 'body' and not 'atom'.

The continuity, both physical and epistemological, between atoms and composites has important ontological implications. When he considers the status of properties (*sumbebēkota*), Epicurus distinguishes between permanent properties and accidents (*sumptōmata*).[35] Permanent properties, no doubt because they correspond to constant relations between the atoms which compose a body, give that body an existence or permanent 'nature' of its own (*Ep. Hdt.* 69).

[34] See Sedley 1998a: 38.

[35] Epic. *Ep. Hdt.* 68–71. In Lucretius, *coniuncta* are essential properties and *eventa* are accidental properties (1.449–50).

No property exists *per se*, but neither the permanent properties nor accidents can be reduced to non-being (*Ep. Hdt.* 71). So, the motion or rest of a composite body (the atoms are never at rest) is an impermanent property, but a real property nevertheless. This is certainly implied by the examples Lucretius gives at *DRN* 1.451–8: he gives examples of *coniuncta* (the weight of rock, heat of fire, liquidity of water) and *eventa* (slavery, poverty and wealth, freedom, war, concord). The difference between the two classes points to the fact that the loss of the first class entails the destruction of the subject, while the loss of the second 'leaves the nature intact'. But Lucretius certainly does not suggest that slavery or poverty, war or peace, are nothing but mental projections. On this point the Epicureans distinguish themselves from Democritus, according to whom sensible qualities, perhaps even the composites, have merely a conventional existence, dependent on our beliefs.[36] It is possible, then, that it was via this new theory of properties, rather than via a direct reply to Aristotle about the indivisibility of the atom, that Epicurus wished to ensure the cohesion of composite bodies and, in this way, retain the phenomena.

Whatever position the Epicureans adopted towards 'reductionism', it is clear that the status of the composites' properties is an important point of debate.[37] Unfortunately, the section of Epicurus' *Letter to Herodotus* devoted to properties (68–71) is frustratingly silent about causal matters.[38] In the most general terms, there appear to be at least two arguments worth offering against an anti-reductionist reading. First, it is likely that we should make distinctions between properties: psychological processes, such as judgements or movements of volition, to the extent to which they depend on us, seem to resist strongly a 'bottom-up' explanation. On the other hand, states such as a composite's colour or weight can easily be conceived as the secondary effect of the sizes, shapes and quantity of atoms in the composite. Even so, the fact that colour, for example, depends on atomic

[36] See the criticism of Democritus by the Epicurean Colotes cited by Plutarch *Adv. Col.* 1110F.

[37] On reductionism see above p. 67.

[38] One might say the same about the Lucretian discussion of *coniuncta* and *eventa*. For more on Epicurus' view of properties, see also Gill, ch. 7, and O'Keefe, ch. 8, this volume, in their discussions of these properties *at work*, particularly those which treat questions of psychology and the problem of responsibility.

properties does not mean that for Epicurus or Lucretius colour is not 'real', as Democritus perhaps maintained. Second, even the psychological processes which depend on us do not necessarily undermine a reductionist thesis. Indeed such properties do not exist *per se*; hence they are reducible to – even if not strictly identical to – the underlying group of atoms and their mutual inter-relations. We can therefore imagine that their causal efficacy, in the case of processes such as the exercise of psychological or organic faculties, is secondary to the atoms. Mental states and acts, in this sense, are not causes *per se*, but rather *secondary causes*, dependent on other – strictly atomic – causes. Similarly, even the composites are reducible to atoms, without being for that reason entirely identical to the atoms and without having to be eliminated as bodies, which would be the Democritean eliminativist position explicitly rejected by Epicurus. So, we can happily assert that the soul itself has a causal power, provided it is recognized to be an atomic complex, that is: a structure defined by a *certain type of relation between certain atoms*, and not merely by the simple fact that it is made up of *atoms* without any further qualification.

From atoms to worlds

It is possible to object that the Epicureans beg the question, by asserting the generative power of atoms without demonstrating it. In this way, Aristotle's objections remain strong. It is certainly undeniable in any case that the Epicureans intended to go beyond a simple view of composition, by showing that the atoms should be the only genuine components and, simultaneously, were committed to their having a certain organizing and generative power. To understand this, we must suppose that atomic causation is more complicated than the simple relation between constituent and composite.

Epicurus gives an interesting hint in describing the formation of the infinity of worlds. At *Letter to Herodotus* 45, he suggests that the atoms have a double causal role: 'It is not possible that the atoms I have just described, *out of which* (*ex hōn*) a world might arise, or *by which* (*huph' hōn*) a world might be formed, should be exhausted in just one or in a limited number of worlds.' Is the difference between the prepositional constructions here italicized a mere stylistic lexical variation? The economical style of the *Letter* suggests not. The use of the prepositions *ex* and *hupo* gives reason to think that the atoms, in their constant motion, are not only the constituents ('those out of which') but also genuine spontaneous agents or immediate motor principles ('by which') of the formation of a world. It is possible that the Lucretian *clinamen* is simply a later explanation of this principle.

Even so, that does not tell us *how* it is that atoms are not merely constituents, but also generative principles. The positive account of the generation and arrangement of worlds can perhaps offer a solution. According to the *Letter to Pythocles*, as in Democritus, there is an infinity of worlds which take various forms. But Epicurus offers an important correction: it is not enough to invoke, as Democritus did, an initial 'whirl' (*dinē*) of any kind of atoms to explain the formation of a cosmic structure. Rather, we must posit the presence of 'appropriate seeds (*spermata*)' (*Ep. Pyth.* 89–90). Although this is controversial, it is likely that these 'seeds' are atoms.[39] A world can come to be only when there are atoms 'appropriate' or 'fit' (*epitēdeia*) for its formation. As such, in contrast to what we find in Democritus, it is not the infinity of atoms and their combination which explains, in principle and in fact, the existence of worlds, but a sort of spontaneous selection within this infinity. Probably, that is why worlds can take only certain forms (*Ep. Hdt.* 74).

If atoms are not only constituents but also the generative principles of worlds, that is not in virtue of their *individual* properties attributable to each in isolation; rather it is in virtue of the indefinite sum of atoms in motion, within which a spontaneous principle of selection can take hold. In other words, it seems that atoms are generative principles in so far as they form a plurality within which atomic shapes and size take on a functional character within a purely mechanical process of selection. If we see in this principle the roots of Lucretius' *natura* and its powers of spontaneous selection, we might construct a theory relevant to both the formation of worlds and of other composites.[40] Atomism does not thereby cease to be a theory of

[39] See, contra, Sedley 1998a: 193 n. 6. I give a more detailed defence of my view in Morel 2003.

[40] For worlds see *DRN* 5.416–508 and for living creatures see *DRN* 5.837–924. In the case of composite bodies, on each occasion there is no production of a new structure, as is the case in cosmogony: living things reproduce in virtue of a principle of selection which occurs at the outset once for this species and then recurs for each new individual member.

composition, but it does turn out to be a theory of selective composition.

Successful or not, Epicurean atomism is more than a simple theory of material composition. It wants to be a full-blooded natural philosophy, that is: a cosmology, an account of motion and a theory of the generation and maintenance of natural beings. It is not merely content to offer a theory of discontinuity and reduction; it wants also to explain how worlds are put together – and come apart – within the universe, and of how bodies, animate and inanimate, come to be and perish, take on or lose their cohesion. If we accept that atoms are not only the constituents but also the generative principles of composites, then the Atomist Thesis is indeed the central thesis of Epicurean physics.

ELIZABETH ASMIS

5 Epicurean empiricism

The Epicureans held that perceptions serve as a foundation of scientific inference and, further, that all perceptions are true. This is a unique position among ancient philosophers, and it provoked vigorous attacks. Lucretius defended the Epicurean position with an image: just as a building will collapse if the initial measuring rod is crooked, so reason will collapse if it starts out with false perceptions (*DRN* 4.513–21).

This chapter considers perceptions within the context of Epicurus' methodology as a whole. Epicurus proposed two basic rules of investigation: a demand for initial concepts as a means of formulating problems; and a demand for perceptions and feelings as a means of inferring what is not observed. He discussed the rules in a book called *Kanōn*, literally, a 'straight rod' or 'measuring stick'. The subject, called 'canonic', was considered by the Epicureans to be an adjunct of physics rather than a separate part of philosophy.[1] Canonic is tied to physics in two ways: first, the rules of investigation serve as a preface (or 'approach', DL 10.30) to the physics, and, second, the rules are defended on the basis of the ensuing theory. The Epicurean spokesman in Cicero's *De Finibus* (1.64) sums up this procedure: 'Unless the nature of things is recognized, we shall not be able in any way to defend the judgments of the senses.'

Our sources tend to mingle the pre-theoretical understanding of the rules with their subsequent justification. It is important, however, to keep the two kinds of understanding separate. The initial rules are stipulative; and although they may be cleared up by explanation, they must be applicable without the benefit of theory. After the

[1] See the sources collected at Us. 242.

theory has been developed, it is necessary to check the rules by reference to the theory. At a minimum, the theory must be compatible with the initial assumptions; otherwise, to use Lucretius' image, the whole theoretical edifice crumbles. More than that, the Epicureans held that the theory justifies the initial rules.

Most of this chapter will consist of separating out the initial rules from the theory. I shall argue that Epicurus proposed to anchor his theory in the clarity or 'evidence', called *enargeia*, of sensory observations. What distinguishes *enargeia* is the immediate presence of an object of awareness, stripped of any additional beliefs. Initial concepts are 'evident' (*enargeis*) because they are derived from the 'evidence' of sensory observations. In sum, the basis of scientific inference consists of the 'phenomena', understood as the uninterpreted information supplied by sensory experience.

The theory developed on this basis poses a crucial challenge to the initial assumptions. For it reveals that the objects known directly by perception are appearances produced in us by an influx of atoms. This truth threatens to dissolve the foundation of inquiry into subjective judgements. What we took initially to be real features of the world turn out to be momentary impressions.

Epicurus confronted the problem, I suggest, by proposing that the atomic influx often preserves a continuity with an enduring, objectively existing source. In these cases, what we perceive corresponds not just to the immediate impact of atoms but to objective reality. The initial, pre-theoretical reliance on perception is saved in this way by the theory. All perceptions are true in that they correspond to something from the outside; in addition, we are able to perceive enduring external objects. By relying on perceptions that are common to all, we obtain theories that are based on a recognition of objective reality. By testing our foundation subsequently in the light of our theories, we confirm that it is sound.[2]

Epicurus summarizes the initial rules of investigation in the *Letter to Herodotus* prior to setting out his physical theories. I quote the first rule (37–8):

[2] This essay supplements my remarks in Asmis 1984, esp. 153–4 and 1999, esp. 284–5. Among the many contributions to the topic, I am especially indebted to the studies of Striker 1977 and 1996a; Glidden 1985; and Everson 1990.

First ... it is necessary to have grasped what is subordinate to our utterances so that we may have the means to judge what is believed or sought or perplexing by referring to this, and so that everything will not <be> unjudged by us as we demonstrate to infinity or we have empty utterances. For it is necessary that the first concept in accordance with each utterance be seen and not require demonstration, if we are to have a [standard of] reference for what is sought or perplexing and believed.

As his first rule, Epicurus demands standards by which we judge our beliefs and inquiries. This standard is the 'first concept' corresponding to an utterance, and it is something that is 'seen'. The technical term for this type of concept is *prolēpsis*, 'preconception'. Coined by Epicurus, the term *prolēpsis* signifies that the concept has been 'grasped prior' to the pursuit of an inquiry. Without such a grasp, we would either keep demonstrating to infinity or have empty utterances.[3]

Epicurus' highly condensed statement needs some words of explanation in order to provide sufficient guidance to the beginning investigator. What is needed is clarification, drawing on the investigator's own experience, not an appeal to theory that is yet to be established. Diogenes Laërtius (10.33) supplies details of this kind. His main point is that preconceptions are 'evident' (*enargeis*). Epicurus made the same point by stating that the first concept must be 'seen'. As an example, Diogenes cites the preconception of 'human being': as soon as 'human being' is uttered, we have a concept consisting of an 'outline' (*tupos*). To illustrate how a preconception works in an inquiry, he asks: is the thing standing in the distance a horse or a cow? To make the inquiry, we need to know beforehand the 'shape' (*morphē*) of a horse or a cow. In addition, Diogenes explains that all preconceptions are the result of 'preceding perceptions'. They are 'something like an apprehension or correct opinion or a conception or a stored general thought, that is, a memory of what has often appeared from outside'.

Other sources tell us that preconceptions take the place of definitions.[4] Since there is a clear awareness, there is no need for definition to make the thing clear; in fact, the use of a definition would simply obscure what is already clear. In place of a definition, Epicurus made

[3] See also Atherton, ch. 11, this volume, for another discussion of this passage.
[4] See Asmis 1984: 39–47.

free use of a verbal 'sketch' (*hupographē*): this merely calls to mind the preconception by stating its salient features. For example, we have a preconception of god as an 'indestructible, blessed living being' (*Ep. Men.* 123). This formulation is not a definition, but a 'sketch' of a clear awareness of god.

By starting out with concepts given directly by perception, Epicurus aims to remove anything doubtful or conjectural from the foundation of our investigation. In a discussion of events in the heavens (*Ep. Pyth.* 86), Epicurus writes 'one must investigate nature not according to empty axioms (*axiōmata*) and conventions (*nomothesiai*) but as the phenomena (*phainomena*) demand'. To start with Platonic Forms (a different kind of 'outline'), or definitions, or any agreements other than what is given directly by sensory experience – the 'phenomena' – would found the entire scientific enterprise on arbitrary assumptions.

This is a very ambitious aim. Among numerous difficulties, I would like to focus on two main problems. Both concern Diogenes' claim that a preconception is 'a memory of what has often appeared from outside'. The first problem is: If a preconception is nothing more than a memory, what does the mind contribute to the concept? Does the mind add an element of interpretation that exceeds the information provided by the appearances? The second problem is: If a preconception is a response to appearances, what sort of object do we think of? Does it exist independently of our thinking or is it merely an appearance?

In response to the first problem, it is useful to distinguish a range of preconceptions. At the most basic level, there are preconceptions of sensory qualities such as red, round, square, bitter, sweet. More complex are preconceptions of individuals such as 'Plato' and of general kinds such as 'human being,' 'cow', 'horse', 'body'. Finally, preconceptions of the 'goodness of a poem', 'good household manager', 'justice', 'cause', and 'god' seem to be among the most complex.[5] The mind forms a preconception by gathering similar appearances; and this

[5] Diogenes Laërtius 10.33 mentions 'human being', 'cow' and 'horse'. Philodemus mentions 'human being' and 'body' at *De signis* xxxiv.5–11. 'Goodness of a poem' occurs at Philodemus *De poem.* 5 xxxiii.34–6 Mangoni; 'good household manager' at Philodemus *De oec.* xx.8–32; and 'Justice' in *KD* 36–8; and 'cause' in Epicurus *Nat.* 28, Sedley 1983: 19. Sextus Empiricus' discussion at *M* 7.208–15 implies preconceptions of 'Plato', 'round' and 'square'. The preconception of god is discussed by Epicurus at *Ep. Men.* 123–4, as well as in Cicero's *ND* 1.43–6.

process seems increasingly complex. To sort out the salient features of 'cow', for example, the mind gathers a selected number of perceived similarities into a single conception. In the last group, the mind draws connections involving several preconceptions. The preconception of 'justice', for example, is 'what is beneficial in communal dealings with one another'; and this is an evaluative judgement involving at least the preconceptions of benefit and community.

The Epicureans themselves addressed the issue of complexity in their treatment of the preconceptions of 'human being' and 'god'. According to Sextus Empiricus, Epicurus explained 'human being' ostensively as 'this kind of shape with soul in it'.[6] This appears to be a response to Aristotle's claim that a human being must be alive and is essentially a soul. Epicurus accepts the first part of this claim, while rejecting the second. In his view, to have soul is a perceptually evident attribute, which can be shown by pointing, just like having a certain configuration of limbs. Epicurus' more elaborate version is compatible with Diogenes' simple claim that a preconception is an 'outline'; for he, too, views the human being as a kind of outline, differing from other outlines by certain kinds of observed movement.

In the first century BC, Philodemus (following his teacher, Zeno of Sidon) took a new turn by arguing that a preconception or 'proper account' (*idios logos*) is obtained by a method of inference (*sēmeiōsis*) called 'transition by similarity' (*kath' homoiotēta metabasis*) or simply 'the method of similarity'. According to Philodemus, this is the only valid method of inference. It consists of examining many perceptible instances and concluding, on the basis of regularly observed similarities and differences, that certain conjunctions hold by necessity. In making this examination, we use *epilogismos*, 'calculation' that is directed at the phenomena.[7] Preconceptions are one of four ways of determining that one thing is necessarily joined to another *qua* itself; for example, 'body as body has mass and resistance, and human being as human being is a rational living being'.

Philodemus' interpretation raises a serious difficulty. If a preconception is a type of inference involving calculation, how accurate is it to call it a memory? Is the preconception of a human being as a

[6] SE *PH* 2.25.

[7] On *epilogismos*, see Sedley 1973: 27–33; Asmis 1984: 177–78 and 204–6; and Schofield 1996.

'rational living being' merely an empirical variant of 'this kind of shape with soul in it', or is it fundamentally different?

Other writers assign some element of inference to the preconception of god. There is much controversy on how to interpret the claim in Cicero's *On the nature of the gods* (1.105) that we obtain the preconception of god by 'similarity and transition' (*similitudine et transitione*). I agree that Cicero is here translating *kath' homoiotēta metabasis* and referring to the method of similarity set out by Philodemus.[8] In his account of how humans came to think of gods, Lucretius does not mention the method of similarity but he also suggests a process of reflecting upon the appearances; for example, humans came to think of the gods as indestructible as a result of seeing them forever unchanged in shape and undiminished in strength (5.1169–79). Sextus (*M* 9.45–6) reports that the preconception of god as indestructible and perfectly happy was formed by 'transition' (*metabasis*) from human beings by heightening qualities found in humans.

It appears, then, that some preconceptions at least involve some rational analysis of the appearances. Aristotle and the Stoics distinguished memory from concept formation as a prior stage of cognition. According to them, memory precedes experience (*empeiria*), which consists of a multitude of memories of the same type, and experience in turn precedes the formation of a single, universal concept out of this multitude of memories.[9] Do Epicurean preconceptions likewise require some element of insight that is not simply a memory of appearances? Diogenes' identification of a memory as a concept seems to be a rather spectacular leap.

The apparent leap can be defended, however, as a deliberately empirical move. On the Epicurean view, the mind remembers not just many similarities of the same type, but complex relationships of similarity and difference; and this awareness results in the formation of a single concept. For example, the many memories a person has of Socrates, Plato and others, all having the same animated shape, result in a single memory, or preconception, of a human being as an animated shape. Likewise, the conception of a human being as a rational living being is an empirical judgement, consisting of a memory of many living beings whose behaviour is observably rational, by

[8] Asmis 1984: 75 cites a range of views; see also Purinton 2001.

[9] Aristotle *Metaph.* 980b28–81a12 and *APo.* 100a3–9. For the Stoics, see *SVF* 2.83.

contrast with the behaviour of other living beings. In the case of the gods, the preconception involves a comparison with human beings, but this can be explained similarly as the result of a sorting process by which certain observed features are grouped together in contrast with the observed behaviour of human beings.

In this process, the mind is not simply passive. Although it does not add any information to what appears from outside, it responds by an act of attention. As Clement explains, a preconception is an 'application (*epibolē*) to something evident (*enarges*)'.[10] An application is a kind of 'thrust' (-*bolē*) toward an object of awareness. Cicero (*ND* 1.105) provides an illustration: the mind obtains a preconception of god by 'focusing' (*intenta*) on what comes from outside. The act of *epilogismos*, 'calculation' of the phenomena, it turns out, is nothing other than the act of attending to the differences and similarities among the appearances. It consists of taking account of what appears from outside, just as a calculator or computer or accountant would do. There is an act of inference; but it consists of simply recognizing connections that are given.[11]

If this is right, all preconceptions, even the most complex, are a record of appearances from outside, free of any added element of interpretation. We come, then, to the second problem: Does a preconception show what exists externally to us or is the object of thought merely an appearance, having no existence except as an object of thought?

To address this problem, I shall draw two more kinds of distinction. First, appearances from outside are of two kinds: what appears to the five senses; and what appears to the mind. The only attested preconception of the latter kind is the preconception of god: it is a response to appearances that occur to the mind in sleep or in a waking state.[12] In recent years, there has been much debate whether we have a preconception of the gods as they really exist or whether the gods are merely objects of thought.[13] One reason for doubting their

[10] Clem. *Strom.* 2.4 (Us. 255).

[11] Cf. Asmis 1984: 79 and Glidden 1985: 195–6 and 203–7. On *epibolē* see also Morel 2007: 39–41.

[12] Lucretius 5.1169-71 and Cicero *ND* 1.46.

[13] That gods are mental constructs is argued by Long and Sedley 1987: vol. 1, pp. 145–9 and Sedley (forthcoming); their view is opposed by Mansfeld 1993 and Schiebe 2003. Cf. Warren, ch. 13, this volume.

existence is that we also have mental appearances of Centaurs, of flying horses, of Furies.[14] How do the appearances of the gods differ from these apparitions? The problem, however, is not confined to mental appearances; it also applies to the five senses. Suppose I have never seen oars except as partially submerged in water. What is to prevent me from developing a preconception of oars as objects that are bent? Never having seen real-life elephants, I might develop a preconception of elephants as products of an artist's imagination.

Second, preconceptions are either common – that is, held by all humans – or held only by some. We have two explicit cxamples of common preconceptions. Epicurus calls the preconception of god a 'common notion' (*koinē noēsis, Ep. Men.* 123); and Philodemus appeals to the 'common' preconception of a good poem.[15] In general, we may suppose, there are common preconceptions for every feature that humans experience in common, such as 'human being' and 'body'. By contrast, different natural or social environments will result in preconceptions that are not shared by all. Only some humans, for example, will have a preconception of a tiger or an elephant as a living animal. Epicurus (*KD* 32) indicates that humans who did not make compacts not to hurt each other did not develop a preconception of justice.

There is some evidence that common preconceptions may be relied upon to show objective existence. In the *Letter to Menoeceus* (123), Epicurus demands that one must think of god just as is shown by the 'common notion'. One must preserve this conception without adding incompatible attributes; 'for gods exist; for knowledge of them is evident (*enargēs*)'. It seems implausible to take 'exist' in anything but the ordinary sense of 'exist' – that is, the gods exist not just in our minds, but objectively; and this is how Cicero's Epicurean spokesman, Velleius, takes it in his exegesis of Epicurus' theology in *On the nature of the gods* (1.43–5). Velleius asserts, first, that Epicurus alone 'saw that there are gods since nature itself imprinted a conception of them in the minds of all'. After calling this a 'preconception' (*prolēpsis*), Velleius puts Epicurus' insight in the form of a syllogism (1.44):

[14] Cf. Cicero's objection at *ND* 1.105 and 108.

[15] See n. 5 above. For a different view of what makes the preconception of god 'common', see Rist 1972: 26 and Obbink 1992: 200–1 and 227.

Since the opinion has not been established by some convention or custom or law and there abides a firm agreement by everyone, it must be understood that there are gods, since we have implanted or rather inborn (*innatas*) concepts of them. Moreover, that on which the nature of all agrees must be true. Therefore it must be admitted that there are gods.

Although there is some imprecision in the articulation of the argument, it appears that the conclusion that there are gods follows from two main premises: first, the 'nature of all' agrees that there are gods; second, what all are naturally agreed on is true. In addition, Velleius explains what it is for the 'nature' of humans to agree: the opinion is not established by convention, but is 'inborn' in humans. Preconceptions are 'inborn', I take it, in the sense of 'having grown in' us from the beginning of their development, thus developing entirely within us, as opposed to being imposed on us by others and so being accepted by convention.[16]

As Velleius' opponent points out (*On the nature of the gods* 1.64), the appeal to universally held beliefs was a strategy used also by other philosophers. Velleius has cast his argument in the form of a syllogism that is intended to persuade other philosophers. There is no reason, however, to suppose that he is not explicating Epicurus' own thinking. Like Epicurus, he appeals to the common preconception of god as proof that the gods exist. Non-common preconceptions, too, may show what exists objectively; but only common preconceptions offer a guarantee of objective existence. The reason appears only as a result of investigating the causes of perception. As we will see, the investigation reveals that many (though not all) appearances correspond to objective reality. It reveals at the same time, I suggest, that the common experience of humans, sorting out a vast number of appearances into a single common conception, can be relied on to show what is objectively real.

Importantly, Epicurus does not demand in his first rule of investigation that we use only common preconceptions. To discriminate among preconceptions in this way would be to make an arbitrary choice. Instead, we must use all preconceptions alike. As it turns out, however, we use common preconceptions in order to obtain a theory that all can agree on. Suppose that Epicurus or anyone else uses

[16] See also Konstan (forthcoming). For a different view, see Sedley (forthcoming), cf. Long and Sedley 1987: vol. 2, p. 148.

preconceptions that others do not share. Some will have a standard by which to settle an inquiry; others will not. Having no standard of their own, the latter would need to rely on the authority of others; and this would be an arbitrary starting-point. The investigation can command assent only on the basis of shared assumptions; and this is how Epicurus, in fact, proceeds. Subsequently, the theory reveals the reason why the consent of all provides a guarantee of objective existence.

Let us, then, turn to the second rule of investigation. Epicurus summarizes it in the *Letter to Herodotus* (38) immediately following his first rule:

> Next, it is necessary to observe all things in accordance with the perceptions, and simply the present applications of the mind or any of the criteria, and similarly [in accordance with] the feelings that occur, so that we may have the means to infer both what is waiting [to be observed] and what is non-apparent.

In sum, the second rule is: it is necessary to use perceptions (*aisthēseis*) and feelings (*pathē*), just as they are present to one's awareness without any added element of interpretation, as signs of what is not yet observed and what cannot be observed at all. There are two kinds of signs: perceptions, consisting of acts of attention by either the mind or the five senses; and feelings. There are two kinds of inferences: inferences about what is 'waiting' to be observed (*to prosmenon*), and inferences about what cannot be observed (what is 'non-apparent', *to adēlon*).

The structure of the sentence is complicated by the parenthetical explanation 'and simply the present applications (*epibolai*) of the mind or any of the criteria'. This insertion is intended to make clear what is understood by 'perceptions': the mind has 'perceptions' just like the five senses, consisting of present acts of attention. The mind and senses are 'criteria' in the sense of 'instruments of judgement'. Using the term 'criteria' in a different sense to signify 'standards of judgement', Diogenes (10.31) tells us that Epicurus recognized three 'criteria of truth' – preconceptions, perceptions and feelings – and that his followers added the 'presentational (*phantastikai*) applications of the mind' as a fourth. It is plausible to suppose that Epicurus included the 'presentational applications of the mind' among 'perceptions' and that his followers, heeding the usual sense of 'perception' to refer only to the five senses, separated them out as a fourth standard. The term 'presentational' signifies that the mind attends to an appearance ('presentation', *phantasia*) from outside.

We have already encountered the term 'application' (*epibolē*) in reference to preconceptions. In the case of perceptions too, the mind or sense organ attends to what is presented from outside, without any added element of interpretation. This sense is underscored by the terms 'present' and 'that obtain': the recognition is restricted to what is presently perceived, thus excluding what might be perceived in the future or cannot be perceived at all.

The perceptions and feelings complement each other: we 'perceive' what is presented from outside, such as colour, shape, sounds; and we 'feel' inner conditions, in particular, pleasure and pain.[17] The beginning investigator can rely on ordinary experience to make these distinctions. Ordinary experience also prompts the question: how reliable are the 'present applications of the mind'? For the mind views not only what we ordinarily think of as real or true, but also dreams and other apparitions that we ordinarily do not accept as true. The problem, moreover, extends more widely; for we ordinarily suppose that the senses, too, can be deceptive. We noted the same problem in the case of the preconceptions.

Epicurus responded with the famous doctrine that there is no error in sense perception. As later sources put it, the senses never lie; all perceptions and all presentations are 'true', and all perceptibles are 'true and existent'.[18] There has been much discussion about Epicurus' position.[19] I suggest that he offered two basic arguments. The first is that unless one accepts all the perceptions, stripped of any added opinion, as a basis of judgement, there is no way of settling, or

[17] In what follows, I shall omit discussion of the feelings. Diogenes (10.34) states that the two kinds of feeling, pleasure and pain, serve as a criterion of 'choice and avoidance'. As I have argued (1984: 96–9 and 169–70), they also serve as a basis of scientific inference, notably in inferences about the nature of the soul.

[18] Us. 243–54, including Sextus' claim that perceptibles are 'true and existent' (*alēthē kai onta*) at *M* 8.9 and Lucretius 4.379–521.

[19] Bailey 1928: 257 proposed that 'by the truth of a sensation Epicurus meant and could only mean its truth to the external object which it represented' and that his followers altered his position. Against this interpretation, Rist 1972: 19–20 argued that Epicurus meant that 'a real event takes place in the act of sensing'. Others, with whom I agree, have argued that what makes a perception true is a correspondence between the appearance and the influx of atoms; so Furley 1971: 616; Long 1971: 117; and Everson 1990: 172–80. See also Striker 1977 and Taylor 1980.

indeed conducting, any enquiry. The second is that whatever appears in perception corresponds to something that enters us from outside; in every case, therefore, we perceive something from the outside as it really is. The second argument depends on knowing the atomic causes of perception. The first argument is used to get the investigation started, and it requires only the ability to distinguish between a present object of sensory awareness and the addition of an opinion.

Epicurus presents the first argument in *KD* 24. Focusing on opinions about what is 'waiting' to be observed (*to prosmenon*), he presents a dilemma: 'if you simply throw out a perception', you will throw the remaining perceptions into confusion; and if you affirm everything that is 'waiting' in your opinions, you will admit error and preserve every dispute. The key to escaping the dilemma is to distinguish between a present object of awareness and an added opinion, so as to accept every sensory presentation as free from error and test every opinion by reference to this standard. In the *Letter to Herodotus* (50–2), Epicurus extends the dilemma to opinions about what is non-apparent (*to adēlon*). He also explains that we add an opinion when 'we take another movement within ourselves', which is 'attached' to the perceptual presentation but 'has a distinction'. The opinion admits of error, but the perception does not. If we fail to make this distinction, either 'the criteria in accordance with evidence (*enargeia*)' will be eliminated, or the affirmation of error will throw everything into confusion. The 'criteria', it appears, are the five senses and the mind, presenting to us what is 'evident', as opposed to the addition of opinion from within.

Epicurus' distinction between perception and opinion, we might object, simply sweeps the problem under the rug. If we must treat all perceptions alike, why not simply throw out all alike as unreliable? The sceptic accepts this consequence. Why, then, does Epicurus choose to accept all perceptions alike as a basis of judgement? He makes the choice initially, I suggest, as a rule of investigation. Setting up a method to guide the investigation, Epicurus stipulates, without proof, that we must accept the phenomena – whatever appears directly in sensory awareness – as a basis of judging what there is besides the phenomena. He offers no proof that the phenomena are a reliable guide; he merely demands that we use them as a basis of judgement – otherwise the investigation cannot proceed. He will offer a justification for his demand subsequently on the basis of his theory.

In setting up his rules, however, he simply puts a choice to the would-be investigator: either accept all perceptions alike as a basis of judgement, or there is no path of enquiry.

Against this interpretation, many scholars have held that Epicurus distinguished between perceptions that are 'evident' or 'clear' and those that are not; the former show what exists objectively, the others do not.[20] This distinction is contradicted directly by Sextus, who reports (*M* 7.203) that Epicurus called a presentation (*phantasia*) an *enargeia*, and by Plutarch, who claims (*Adv. Col.* 1121D–E) that, on the Epicurean view, no presentation or perception is more 'evident' than another. Still, there is an important problem: how sound is a foundation that consists of all perceptions alike, whether or not they show objective reality?

A closer look at opinions about what is 'waiting' (*to prosmenon*) will make clear what is at stake. We may note at the outset that the meaning of the term is not at all transparent: what is it that 'awaits' ('expects') and what is it waiting for? Diogenes (10.34) offers just a little help: 'to wait and come close to the tower and learn how it appears up close'. Diogenes' wording suggests that what is waiting is the observer. Epicurus' usage suggests that what is waiting is what is expected. The two meanings may be taken to coincide: an expectation consists of something that is expected. The tower was a favourite example among the Epicureans: it appears roundish from a distance (Lucretius 4.353–63); we add an opinion, and it is confirmed or not when we come close.[21]

Epicurus held that opinions of this kind 'become' true if there is 'witnessing' (*epimarturēsis*) and false if there is 'no witnessing' (*ouk epimarturēsis*). On the other hand, opinions about what is non-apparent 'become' true if there is 'no counterwitnessing' (*ouk antimarturēsis*) and false if there is 'counterwitnessing' (*antimarturēsis*).[22] The term 'become' indicates that the opinion is initially neither true nor false; it becomes true or false as the result of a method of testing. Sextus illustrates the first method as follows. Suppose I see a figure from a distance and form the opinion that it is Plato. When he has come close, this opinion is 'witnessed' by 'evidence' (*enargeia*); or the opinion is 'not witnessed' if, when the distance has been eliminated,

[20] So Bailey 1928: 242–3 and 254–7; Long 1971: 117–18; and Jürss 1991: 122.

[21] SE *M* 7.208–9 and Plutarch *Adv. Col.* 1121C.

[22] *Ep. Hdt.* 51, and SE *M* 7.211–16.

we learn through 'evidence' that it is not Plato. According to Sextus, then, what makes the expectation false is not merely the absence of an appropriate presentation, but the occurrence of an incompatible presentation. After discussing the second method, which concerns what is non-apparent (and which we will consider later), Sextus concludes: *enargeia* is the 'base and foundation' of everything.

It is widely held, then, that the observer first has an unclear view from a distance and then, upon coming close, obtains a clear view, called *enargeia*, which shows the expected thing as it really is. As I have suggested, by contrast, all presentations are equally 'evident'. It does not matter that one lacks the details shown by the other; all are 'evident' insofar as they show something. The crucial difference is between what appears and what does not appear, or between what is present in perception and what is added by opinion. It follows that an opinion about what is 'waiting' becomes true whenever the feature that has been added by opinion becomes evident, whether or not this feature exists objectively. Against this view, one may object that this is to turn the notion of 'true opinion' on its head; for the truth of an opinion will be entirely relative to the observer. How can we 'learn' it is Plato, as Sextus says, unless the presentation shows what is objectively true? The reliance on a close view, moreover, has a basis in Epicurean theory. Epicurus held that the influx of atoms that produces a perception is more likely to correspond to its external source when the distance is short. In general, it would seem perverse to accept all presentations as a basis of judgement when only some correspond to objectively existing reality.

We can sharpen the problem by considering a criticism by Plutarch. Plutarch objects that the Epicureans unwittingly agreed with the Cyrenaics that all we can know by perception is our own subjective impressions, not objectively existing reality. In response to this objection, he constructs the following reply by a hypothetical Epicurean (*Adv. Col.* 1121C): 'But, by Zeus, I will go up to the tower and touch the oar, so as to declare that the oar is straight and the tower polygonal, but he [the Cyrenaic] will agree only to opinion and appearance, nothing more, even if he comes close'. Plutarch retorts: you don't see what follows from your own position; the Cyrenaic does.

Did the Epicureans, then, hold that a close view shows what exists objectively and that, in general, all opinions about what is 'waiting' (*prosmenon*) are opinions about what exists objectively? Plutarch, I suggest, is confusing two positions. First, any opinion about what is 'waiting' is an expectation about what will appear, not an opinion about what exists objectively. The expectation becomes true when the expected thing appears, and it becomes false when it fails to appear. Second, as will be discussed in the next section, a perception often corresponds to an enduring, objectively existing object. Perception itself, however, cannot reveal whether or not it shows such an object. This type of judgement is outside the competence of the senses: as 'instruments of judgement' (*kritēria*), they judge only what is present to one's awareness. As Lucretius (4.384–5) insists, the eyes cannot 'know the nature of things'; this must be discerned by the 'reason of the mind'. Likewise, Epicurus drew a distinction between 'what is relative to us' (*to pros hēmas*), which is just as it appears, and 'a thing in itself' (*to kath' hauto*), which may be the same as what appears or different.[23] What we perceive is relative to us; what a thing is in itself, or its nature, is ascertained by reason. Plutarch fails to distinguish between the immediate evidence of sense perception and conclusions that are obtained by a rational examination of the phenomena. What the Epicureans in fact said, but Plutarch garbled, is: going up close to the tower, or touching the oar, is one way, among numerous others, of testing, through the use of reason, what exists objectively.

If this is right, Epicurus demanded that we accept all perceptions alike as a basis of judgement. Corresponding to the two rules of investigation, we start out with two kinds of true belief: preconceptions, which are correct opinions (as Diogenes calls them at 10.33) about general features of our sensory experience; and correct opinions about particular sensory events. What makes both kinds of opinion correct is that they do not affirm anything but what appears directly in sensory experience.

Just like preconceptions, perceptions may be common or not, as Epicurus indicates in this summary of his second rule (*Ep. Hdt.* 82): 'We must attend to the present feelings and the perceptions – those that are common in accordance with what is common, and those that are individual in accordance with what is individual – and to all the present evidence (*enargeia*) in accordance with each of the criteria.'

[23] At *Ep. Pyth.* 91, Epicurus writes that the size of the sun and remaining stars 'is just as it appears relatively to us, but in itself is larger or a little smaller or just as it is seen'.

Perceptions that are common to all observers do not differ intrinsically from those that are not; both kinds alike show what is 'evident'. In the course of our investigation, however, we necessarily use common perceptions to obtain conclusions that all can agree to. The result is that our theory is based on perceptions (along with preconceptions) that show objective reality.

Equipped with the two rules, the investigator is ready to explore what cannot be observed (*to adēlon*). I shall briefly consider the first few theories of Epicurean physics in order to illustrate the method of investigation, then turn to its vindication by the theory of perception. The first two doctrines are: nothing comes to be from non-being, and nothing is destroyed into non-being (*Ep. Hdt.* 38–9). After concluding that the universe is always the same, Epicurus adds another doctrine: the universe consists of bodies and void (*Ep. Hdt.* 39–40). The doctrines are proved by reference to preconceptions, including those of 'non-being', 'coming-to-be', 'being destroyed', 'body', and 'void', and by the use of perceptions as signs of what is non-apparent.

The first two doctrines, as well as the existence of void, are proved by the method of 'no counterwitnessing' (*ouk antimarturēsis*). More specifically, they are proved by the 'counterwitnessing' (*antimarturēsis*) of the negation of the thesis. To prove the first doctrine, Epicurus claims: if it were not the case that nothing comes to be from non-being, 'everything would come to be from everything, without requiring seeds'. As Lucretius (1.159–214) proves with a string of arguments, the world would be a topsy-turvy place, with everything coming to be out of everything, at every time, growing to every size, and so on. Since we do not observe this, the negation of the thesis is false and the thesis is true. As Sextus explains (*M* 7.213–14), '"counterwitnessing" is the "elimination" of a phenomenon by what is proposed, whereas "no counterwitnessing" is the "consequence" (*akolouthia*) of a thesis upon a phenomenon'. To illustrate, he uses Epicurus' argument for the existence of void: if void did not exist, there would not be motion as it 'appears' (*phainetai, Ep. Hdt.* 40). The opinion is true because the existence of void follows on the phenomenon of motion; the contradictory is false because the non-existence of void is eliminated by the phenomenon.

All three doctrines appear to rely on common perceptions and preconceptions. Epicurus mentions that 'perception witnesses (*marturei*) in all cases that there are bodies' (*Ep. Hdt.* 39). This is an example of the method of 'witnessing' (*epimarturēsis*). Epicurus, moreover, seems to appeal to the perceptions of all humans as proof that bodies exist objectively. Likewise, we may suppose, all persons perceive that not everything comes to be from everything, and so on. It is entirely possible, for example, that some people lack the preconception of a rose (as cited by Lucretius at 1.174) or fail to observe that roses bloom in spring; but this deficiency is made up by other observations, resulting in the common belief that not everything grows at every time. Even if some people, on some occasions, see their friends turning into wolves (or Furies), all alike observe regular patterns of change.

As noted earlier, Philodemus argued that inference by similarity is the only method of proving what cannot be observed. To make his point, he recasts the argument for the existence of void as follows: we prove that there is void by observing that movement never occurs without void and concluding, on the basis of a rational examination of the phenomena, which offer no counterindication, that it is impossible for movement to occur without void.[24] In Epicurus' own writings, inference by similarity occurs most frequently as a method of formulating multiple explanations about events in the heavens; but it is also prominent in his theory of perception.[25] Although it is not clear to what extent Epicurus anticipated Philodemus' view, the following statement suggests that he came close to it (*Ep. Hdt.* 80): 'We must give explanations about the events in the heavens and everything that is non-apparent by comparing in how many ways a similar thing happens in our experience.' Sextus does not mention inferences by similarity in his account of 'no counterwitnessing'. However, his explanation of it as a relation of 'consequence' agrees with Philodemus' contention that the method of similarity, no less than the method of 'elimination', shows what follows on our observations. Sextus' brief analysis is compatible with a more extensive discussion along the lines that Philodemus proposed.

We come, then, to the test of the method. How does the theory of perception agree with the reliance on the phenomena that Epicurus demanded from the beginning? Epicurus answers with a detailed analysis of sight and mental perception. He begins with the basic

[24] *De signis* VIII.26–IX.3 and XXXV.36–XXXVI.2 De Lacy and De Lacy.

[25] See also Taub, ch. 6, this volume.

claim that there are 'outlines' (*tupoi*) that are similar in shape to the 'solids' from which they are detached (*Ep. Hdt.* 46). 'None of the phenomena counterwitnesses (*antimarturei*)' that these outlines, called 'eidols' (*eidōla*), have 'unsurpassed fineness' (47). The continuous flow of eidols from a solid 'preserves the position and arrangement of the atoms for a long time, although it is sometimes in a state of confusion'. Eidols may also be formed suddenly in our surroundings and in some other ways. None of these ways of conveying 'evidence' (*enargeia*), as well as preserving a 'sympathy with external things', 'is counterwitnessed by the perceptions' (48). We see or think of an external object when outlines that are similar in colour and shape enter us. In these cases, the 'unitary continuity' of the outlines with the underlying solid 'produces a presentation and preserves a sympathy with the underlying object' that extends deep within the reverberation of atoms inside the solid (49–50).

The first thing to notice is that Epicurus bridges the gap between perceptual experience and objective reality by the method of comparing what happens in our experience or, in the words of Philodemus, the 'method of similarity'. In his theory of perception, 'no counterwitnessing' consists of the method of showing that certain similarities extend from our experience to what is non-apparent. As Lucretius illustrates (4.54–97), we observe fine emissions, such as smoke from fire, skins shed by snakes and colour cast by awnings; we must suppose, therefore, that there are especially fine images coming from the surface of things. Further (4.129–42), just as clouds gather with ever shifting shapes in the sky, so images gather in midair. By indicating that there are various ways of eidol formation, including the formation of streams that preserve an unaltered continuity with a solid, the phenomena provide an explanation of why some perceptions are what we ordinarily call 'deceptive', whereas others are what is ordinarily call 'true'.

The theory as a whole rests on a distinction between objectively existing 'solids' and fine outlines, or 'eidols'. There are two main kinds of situation: either the outlines form a continuum with an underlying solid, or they do not. The first type of situation admits of two possibilities in turn: either the outlines preserve the position and arrangement of atoms on the solid, so as to yield a presentation that corresponds to the colour and shape of the solid; or they become confused, so as to represent the shape or colour of the solid in a confused way. Sextus (*M* 7.207–9) discusses these two possibilities. He explains that we do not see the whole solid; instead, we see only the colour, and this is partly on the solid and partly outside it. When eidols flow from a solid, their arrangement either is preserved, as happens at a close or moderate distance, or becomes disturbed, as happens at a long distance. In the first case, we see the colour on the solid; in the second, we see the colour that is outside the solid.

In all of these cases, what is presented by the eidols does not admit of error. As Epicurus points out, dreams and the apparitions of madmen, too, are free from error; for they too are things that we 'encounter' (*Ep. Hdt.* 51). As Sextus explains (*M* 8.63), Orestes' vision of Furies is true because it is moved by underlying eidols. In general, all perceptions are true because the presented object is just as it is presented by its cause, the influx of atoms. We are not, however, restricted to perceiving only the immediate objects of our encounter. The stream of atoms allows us to extend our cognitive reach beyond what we immediately encounter. Whenever the stream is continuous with an underlying solid but has been disturbed, we obtain a grasp of what exists between us and the solid. Whenever the stream of atoms is unaltered, our awareness extends to the underlying solid. The solid itself has colour and shape – or indeed solidity – only insofar as it is perceived; but we are able to perceive its colour and shape exactly as it is produced by the atoms at its surface.

The distinction between an immediate encounter and an underlying source applies to all the senses. Like sight, hearing and smell occur at a distance from the source. Analogously to sight, hearing is produced by a stream of atoms that may be continuous with an external source. If it is, the stream produces 'for the most part' a perception that is 'on' the source; otherwise, it makes clear only what is 'outside' it (*Ep. Hdt.* 52–3). In the case of taste and touch, where there is no distance, there is a distinction between the external surface, which we encounter directly, and the inner substance, which we may perceive through this encounter. When we touch a stone, Lucretius (4.265–8) tells us, we encounter the surface of the stone, but feel the hardness deep within. In all cases of perception, moreover, what we perceive corresponds to impacts from outside, but how we receive the impacts depends on the condition of the sensory organ. If it is in disarray, it may introduce further confusion; if it is properly adjusted to the incoming stream, it preserves the continuity that comes from outside.

In many cases of perception, then, we perceive what exists objectively, or things 'in themselves'. We might object, in the first place, that we perceive qualities, such as the shape or colour of a solid, smell, sound, and so on, that the atoms, which constitute all things, do not possess. In response, Epicurus assigns perceptual qualities to external objects on the ground that this is how we perceive their nature as atomic complexes.

A further problem is: how can we know whether what we perceive exists objectively? Perception cannot reveal by itself whether or not an object exists objectively. For this, we must make a rational examination of the phenomena, inferring by the use of reason what is unobserved. By accepting all perceptions as true, we learn to discriminate between situations in which the continuity with an external object is preserved and those in which it is not. There is no possibility of verifying judgements of this kind by the direct testimony of the senses, or 'witnessing' (*epimarturēsis*); but we can verify them by the method of 'no counterwitnessing' (*ouk antimarturēsis*). Upon a thorough examination of the phenomena, we conclude that since nothing contradicts our opinion, it is true.

Finally, how sound is the foundation of our theory? If we accept all phenomena alike as true, what prevents us from basing our conclusions about the nature of things on a distorted view of the outside world? Only subsequent testing in the light of our theory can tell us whether or not our initial assumptions correspond to objective reality. Such testing indicates that by relying on common preconceptions and perceptions from the beginning, we have made sure that our theory is based on a recognition of objective reality.

Epicurus proposed in this way, I suggest, to escape Democritus' dilemma: 'by convention (*nomōi*) sweet, by convention bitter, by convention warm, by convention cold, by convention colour, but in truth atoms and void'.[26] On Epicurus' view, sweet, bitter, and so on, exist by nature, not convention, as the effect of atoms that enter us from our environment. This environment is not a random fog, as it were, of atoms and void, but contains enduring objects that are joined to us by continuous streams of atoms and may be perceived just as they are. Democritus staged a contest in which the perceptions

[26] DK 68 B9. On Epicurean ontology see also Morel, ch. 4 and O'Keefe, ch. 8, this volume.

accuse the mind: 'Miserable mind, after taking your proofs from us, you overthrow us: that overthrow is your downfall.'[27] Epicurus responded: the mind saves the perceptions by proving that they correspond to our environment, including enduring objects, just as it is.

[27] DK 68 B125.

LIBA TAUB

6 Cosmology and meteorology

A goal of Epicurean philosophy was the achievement of calm and freedom from anxiety. Epicurus believed that if people can be freed from fear – including fears relating to the actions of gods – they can then achieve *ataraxia* ('being undisturbed'). Epicurean cosmology and meteorology were motivated by the desire to alleviate fear of gods.[1] While Epicurus recognized the existence of gods, he denied the possibility that they have any cosmic influence. He developed a strict materialist philosophy, designed to offer natural explanations of phenomena that were often seen as due to activities of gods. Questions about the origin and order of the world, its possible beginning and end, are potentially disturbing: violent natural phenomena, particularly thunder, lightning, hail and earthquakes, can be terrifying and destructive. If such phenomena are not due to gods, there is no reason to fear the gods' involvement in our world. Epicurean meteorology explained the *meteōra* (the phenomena of the sky, and earthquakes); cosmology focused on the nature of our local cosmos (*kosmos*), while acknowledging the existence of an infinite number of *kosmoi* (worlds). The Greek word *kosmos* carried a range of meanings; its use in natural philosophy was coloured by the worldview of the user.

In the *Letter to Pythocles* (88), Epicurus defines a *kosmos* as follows: 'a *kosmos* is a circumscribed portion of *to pan* ('the universe', 'the all' or 'entirety'), which contains stars and earth and all other visible things, cut off from the infinite, and terminating in an exterior

I am grateful to David Sedley and James Warren for their comments on an earlier version of this chapter.

[1] See Wasserstein 1978 on the reliance of Epicurean ethics on scientific doctrine.

which may either revolve or be at rest, and be round or triangular or of any shape whatever'.[2] Defining *to pan* by the modern English word 'universe' must be done cautiously. So, for example, the principal modern definition of 'universe' offered in the *Oxford English Dictionary* refers to notions of 'systematic', 'creation' and 'Divine power', descriptors that Epicurus would not have used. A definition of 'universe' more suitable for understanding Epicurus' sense of *to pan* would be: 'the sum total of the entire infinity of bodies and space, within which ours is just one of infinitely many worlds'. Here, the word 'universe' will be used in the Epicurean sense of 'the all', the sum total of everything; '*kosmos*' will refer to a 'world', a particular part of the universe.

Modern astronomers and astrophysicists may work on cosmology, but in Antiquity, cosmology and astronomy were two completely different approaches applied to the study of the universe and the celestial bodies. Cosmology was part of the study of nature – of physics – as is indicated by its place in Aristotle's extant writings, including *De caelo* (*On the heavens*).[3] Astronomy, on the other hand, was clearly understood to be a branch of mathematics. Epicurus makes it clear that he does not value astronomy (*Ep. Hdt.* 79), but he regarded both cosmology and meteorology as useful to his broader philosophical programme. Here, cosmology should be understood as referring to the understanding of *kosmoi* (worlds); meteorology is the study of the *meteōra*, which include those phenomena that today are regarded as meteorological, as well as other phenomena now referred to as astronomical (for example, comets) or seismological (such as earthquakes).

Our knowledge of Epicurean meteorology and cosmology comes principally from three texts. Two of these are didactic letters, the *Letter to Herodotus* and *Letter to Pythocles*, attributed to Epicurus and preserved in their entirety in the biography of Epicurus written by Diogenes Laërtius (*c.* 300 AD) in his *Lives and of sayings of the*

[2] Epicurus' letters are preserved by Diogenes Laërtius, in his *Lives and sayings of the eminent philosophers*, Book 10. Unless otherwise noted, translations here of Epicurus' letters are by R.D. Hicks, in the Loeb edition, with occasional slight modifications.

[3] So, for example, at the beginning of *De caelo* (268a1–7) Aristotle outlines what knowledge of nature is concerned with: bodies and magnitudes, their changing properties and motions, and the causes of those beings.

eminent philosophers.[4] The third key text is the Latin poem *On the nature of the universe* (*De rerum natura*) by Lucretius (*c*. 94–55 or 51 BC). Several of the six books of Lucretius' work are particularly relevant for understanding Epicurean meteorology and cosmology (Books 2, 5 and 6).[5] The motion of the atoms in the void is explained in the second book. The origin of the world and the growth of human society are treated in Book 5; in the final book (which may be unfinished), Lucretius treats meteorology.[6]

The consideration here of Epicurean cosmology and meteorology will focus on the evidence contained in these writings. The letters of Epicurus are rather brief, intended to serve as *aides-mémoire* for his followers; the poem of Lucretius is more elaborate, offering vivid examples and, in some cases, providing fuller arguments to support Epicurean positions. In addition to these texts, fragments of a massive Greek inscription (about 80 metres long) erected by Diogenes of Oinoanda (probably second century AD) also provide information on Epicurean teachings; portions of the inscription dealt with Epicurean ideas about physics and astronomy. While some other authors, including Cicero and Plutarch, offer accounts and criticisms of Epicurean ideas, the focus here will be on Epicurus' letters and Lucretius' poem.[7]

One intriguing aspect of the surviving Epicurean texts is that each of the various formats – letter, poem, inscription – used to convey Epicurean teaching was intended to be accessible to a broad but literate audience, not only to individuals with highly developed interests. In Antiquity, Epicurean ideas were communicated in Latin as well as Greek, and were presented within different cultural contexts. The desire to speak to a broad range of people was an important aspect of Epicurus' school in Athens, the Garden, which included women and slaves as members.[8]

4 I adopt the term 'didactic' letter from Mansfeld 1999: 5.

5 As Furley 1999: 419 notes, it should not be assumed without argument that Lucretius follows Epicurus completely. Nevertheless, Furley 1966 himself regards Lucretius as a close follower of Epicurus. See also Clay 1983a and Sedley 1998a.

6 The poem is unusual in its length; furthermore, it is not clear whether the poem was completed. Most earlier ancient didactic epics consisted of only a single book, however the *Georgics* of Virgil (70–19 BC), a near contemporary of Lucretius, was composed in four books.

7 So, for example, see Cicero *ND* 1.18–23, 1.52–3; Plutarch *Adv. Col.* 1109C–E.

8 See Clay, in this volume, on the Epicurean use of letters.

The intention to communicate widely is clear from the formats of the surviving texts and from explicit statements contained within those texts. The surviving Epicurean texts are not presented with specialist readers in mind, as detailed treatises aimed at the expert or even the advanced student. Epicurus makes it clear that his aim in the *Letter to Herodotus* is to offer the chief doctrines of his physics in the form of a summary (82–3): 'so that, if this statement be accurately retained and take effect, a man will, no doubt, be incomparably better equipped than his fellows, even if he should never go into all the exact details'.

Epicurus indicates that he had himself worked out the details of his views more fully; nonetheless, in the *Letter to Herodotus* he clearly intends that 'the summary itself, if borne in mind, will be of constant service'. Similarly, the *Letter to Pythocles* is presented as an *aide-mémoire*; Epicurus responds to Pythocles' request (84): 'To aid your memory you ask me for a clear and concise statement respecting meteorological phenomena; for what we have written on this subject elsewhere is, you tell me, hard to remember, although you have my books constantly with you.' While Epicurus at several points in these letters voices the idea that more detailed explanations are not automatically more helpful (and, regrettably, may be anxiety producing), he does not exclude those who are more learned in these subjects from the benefit of his letters. These two Epicurean aims, to communicate broadly and to alleviate anxiety, are at the forefront of their cosmological and meteorological explanations. In this way, Epicureans offered ways to achieve *ataraxia* with regard to a number of potential fears.

EPICUREAN APPROACHES TO EXPLANATION

In order to be happy, it is necessary to have the right kind of explanations (*Ep. Pyth.* 84). For the Epicureans, there is only one explanation of the nature of the universe: it is composed of atoms and the void. The acceptance of atomic theory contributes to happiness. But it is not necessary to look for a single 'true' cause of various phenomena, including those of the night sky, as well as weather. In order to alleviate anxiety, it is sufficient to be able to offer a number of possible explanations for these phenomena. Epicurus rejects divine agency as a possible cause. Epicurean cosmology and physics have often been described as 'mechanistic';[9] the Epicurean worldview argues against any notion of divine providence or teleology: the idea that things occur for a particular purpose or goal (*telos*).

So that we can comprehend that, in principle, potentially worrying phenomena can be accounted for naturally, without recourse to the gods, it is particularly useful to be able to rely on ordinary experience; this reliance on the mundane, and the 'natural', precludes the necessity of invoking any special or 'supernatural' causes as explanations. In attempting to understand the world, our ordinary, everyday experiences can serve us well. At the beginning of the *Letter to Herodotus* (37–8), Epicurus offers a summary of his views regarding the appropriate method for studying physics. He emphasizes the importance of understanding the terminology used to describe and explain phenomena: we must understand what it is we are talking about. As part of developing an explanation, reliance on sense experience – to help determine what requires confirmation and what is unclear – is crucial.[10] Information obtained through observation is vital, and analogies to common, everyday experiences can also be useful to understand things that are far away, including meteorological phenomena, such as clouds. In principle, sufficient understanding of cosmology and meteorology are available to ordinary people to alleviate their anxieties, simply by using common everyday techniques, involving using clear language, observations, and analogies to what is already familiar.

In fact, Epicurus warns against gaining excessively detailed knowledge about phenomena: such knowledge may lead to further anxiety and contribute little to peace of mind. He explains: 'when we come to subjects for special inquiry, there is nothing in the knowledge of risings and settings and solstices and eclipses and all kindred subjects that contributes to our happiness'. He argues that

> those who are well-informed about such matters and yet are ignorant what the heavenly bodies really are, and what are the most important causes of phenomena, feel quite as much fear as those who have no such special information – perhaps even greater fear, when the curiosity excited by this

[9] Cf., for example, Long and Sedley 1987: vol. 1, p. 63.

[10] See Mansfeld 1994: 34–8 on the 'methodological introduction' to the *Letter to Pythocles*. See also Asmis, ch. 5, this volume, on epistemology.

additional knowledge cannot find a solution or understand the subordination of these phenomena to the highest causes. (*Ep. Hdt.* 79)

Astronomical knowledge, in Epicurus' view, cannot contribute to one's happiness; accordingly, he does not advocate the detailed mathematical study of the motions of the heavenly bodies.

The explanations offered by Epicurus and his followers for astronomical and meteorological phenomena were not intended to be definitive; rather, they were offered as possible, even plausible, explanations. Epicurus (*Ep. Hdt.* 80) notes that 'if then we think that an event could happen in one or other particular way out of several, we shall be as tranquil when we recognize that it actually comes about in more ways than one as if we know that it happens in this particular way'. In many cases, Epicurus provided several possible explanations for phenomena, without favouring a particular one. He is of the view that, with regard to celestial phenomena, 'if we discover more than one cause that may account for solstices, settings and risings, eclipses and the like ... we must not suppose that our treatment of these matters fails of accuracy, so far as it is needful to ensure our tranquillity and happiness'.

The hypothesis of multiple possible causes is a hallmark of Epicurus' approach in his *Letter to Pythocles*, in which he presents his explanations of the *meteōra*. Even some questions that might be regarded as cosmological – for example, the existence of other worlds – are considered in this letter. Epicurus makes it clear (86) that explanation of the *meteōra* requires an approach particular to the subject matter, arguing that it is not the case, for meteorological phenomena, that only one explanation is possible; rather, these phenomena 'admit of manifold causes for their occurrence and manifold accounts'.

Epicurus is concerned with epistemology, and how we gain what we consider to be knowledge. He recognizes limits to our ability to know, and justifies his advocacy of multiple causation by explaining that, according to his teaching, 'we do not seek to wrest by force what is impossible, nor to understand all matters equally well, nor make our treatment always as clear as when we discuss human life or explain the principles of physics in general' (*Ep. Pyth.* 85–6). In Epicurus' view, meteorology requires a set of methodological procedures different from those applied to general physical questions or to human life. He cautions against becoming too attached to one dogmatic explanation which, he claims, is a superstitious trap into which others have fallen: 'when we pick and choose among [causes], rejecting one equally consistent with the phenomena, we clearly fall away from the study of nature altogether and tumble into myth' (86–7; 94). For Epicurus, a single conclusive explanation of a given phenomenon is not necessary for the achievement of *ataraxia*. By advocating a number of possible causes for meteorological phenomena, it is likely that Epicurus was building on the work of Aristotle's pupil Theophrastus (born *c.* 371, died *c.* 287 BC), who held the view that, for some meteorological phenomena, a number of different causes exist; Theophrastus specifies which causes are responsible for particular phenomena, often presenting a list of possibilities.[11]

More generally, Epicurus strongly advocated the use of empirical observation. Regarding meteorological phenomena, Epicurus emphasizes that the causes proposed and accounts offered must not contradict experience. For Epicurus, agreement with the phenomena is imperative; even though meteorological phenomena may be explained by a number of causes, none of these may contradict sensory perception. He advocates that 'in the study of nature we must not conform to empty assumptions and arbitrary laws, but follow the promptings of the phenomena' (86–7). Furthermore, he is adamant that no divine cause can be offered for the phenomena: 'the divine nature must not on any account be adduced to explain, but must be kept free from the task and in perfect bliss', and not saddled with 'burdensome tasks' (97; cf. 113–14).

EPICUREAN COSMOLOGY

Epicurus' philosophical commitment to the usefulness of the phenomena – sensory experience – in theory development and validation is indicated by his statement that: 'all these alternative [explanations] are possible: they are contradicted by none of the phenomena in this

[11] Theophrastus' relevant work is referred to as the *Metarsiology* by some scholars (including Mansfeld 1992) and the *Meteorology* by others (e.g. Daiber 1992, who published the first full edition and English translation of the work). See also Sedley 1998a: 179–82 and Taub 2003: 115–26.

world, in which an extremity can nowhere be discerned'; if an explanation is not contradicted by what is observed, it is acceptable.

THE INFINITE UNIVERSE (*TO PAN*)

Epicurus (*Ep. Hdt.* 39) states that *to pan* (the whole or entirety of being) always was as it is now, and will remain so: 'the sum total of things [*to pan*] was always such as it is now, and such it will ever remain. For there is nothing into which it can change. For outside the sum of things [*to pan*] there is nothing which could enter into it and bring about the change'.[12] The whole of being (*to pan*) consists of bodies (atoms) and space (the void), and is without limit; that is, it is infinite.

The infinite universe is composed of an infinite number of atoms in the infinite void; for Epicurus, both matter and space are infinite (*Ep. Hdt.* 42). This must be the case, because if the void were infinite but the bodies were finite, the material bodies would be so thinly dispersed through the infinite void as never to be able to congregate; if the void were finite, there would not be enough room for the bodies of matter.[13] Since there is no extremity (*akron*), there is no boundary (*peras*), and since there is no boundary *to pan* must be unlimited or infinite (41).

Lucretius offers a more detailed account in Book 1 (958–64), including the statement that there is nothing beyond the universe; it, therefore, has no boundary, in the sense of a margin at which it borders into something else. He enlarges the discussion, by incorporating a further argument, presumably based on the 'thought-experiment' posed by the Pythagorean Archytas (fl. *c.* 400–350 BC) regarding the determination of the limits of the universe, and reported by Eudemus (later fourth century BC). Archytas argued against the idea that the universe is limited: if the universe has a limit, and I walk to the outermost edge of the heaven, could I extend my hand or staff into what is outside the heaven or not? According to the Archytan argument, it would be paradoxical not to be able to extend one's hand. But if it is possible to extend it further, then a new limit will be reached; this can be repeated, each time to a new limit. There will always be something

[12] Brunschwig 1994a provides a detailed consideration of this passage.

[13] Epicurus states that while the number of atoms is infinite, the number of their shapes is not infinite, even though it is indefinitely large (*Ep. Hdt.* 42).

else into which a staff can be extended; that something must then be unlimited.[14] Lucretius' version of the argument involves hurling a javelin beyond the alleged edge of the universe, providing an elaborated version of the Archytan thought-experiment to counter the idea of a finite universe. He provides other arguments as well, including the suggestion (1.984–97) that if the universe were limited, by now everything in it would have sunk to the bottom; if this were the case, neither the night sky or the sun's light would exist, because everything would be lying in a heap.

DIRECTION OF MOTION WITHIN THE UNIVERSE

The question of the direction of motion of matter in the universe – and the idea that everything could be at the 'bottom' – is significant for Epicurean cosmology: Epicurus stated that atoms are in continual motion (*Ep. Hdt.* 43) and move with equal speed, regardless of their weight (61). Atoms move downwards, because of their weight; upward or sideways motion is due to atoms colliding. While the 'swerve' (*parenklisis*; Latin *clinamen*) is not discussed by Epicurus in his surviving writings, in the context of his treatment Lucretius (2.216) explained that atoms are generally carried downwards in a straight line through the void by their weight.[15]

Epicurean atoms naturally move downwards through the void, but Epicurus thought it necessary to question and clarify the terminology used to describe direction in the void, in order to make his own views clear. He argued (*Ep. Hdt.* 60) that 'of the infinite it is necessary that one not use the expressions "up" or "down" in the sense of "highest" and "lowest"'. Having already cautioned Herodotus at the beginning of the letter that it is crucial to understand the way words are used (37–8), Epicurus launches into an attack on the use of certain direction terminology. Epicurus argues:

> For certainly, while it is possible to produce [a line] to infinity in the direction overhead from wherever we may be standing, [it is necessary] that this [view] never seem right to us, or that the lower part of the [line], imagined to infinity, be at the same time up and down with respect to the same thing. For this is

[14] On Archytas' thought experiment, see Huffman 2005: 540–50.
[15] Cf. Wasserstein 1978: 485. See Morel, ch. 4 and O'Keefe ch. 8, in this volume.

impossible to conceive. Therefore one may assume one upward course imagined to infinity and one downward, even if something moving from us toward the feet of those above us should arrive ten thousand times at the places over our heads, or something moving downward from us at the heads of those below. For the whole course is nonetheless imagined to infinity as one [direction] opposed to the other.[16]

Epicurus' argument seems to be directed against the Aristotelian tenet that 'downwards' motion is directed towards the centre of the (spherical) *kosmos*, while motion 'upwards' is towards the periphery.[17]

The Aristotelian conception of a spherical *kosmos* was rejected by the Epicureans. Because the Aristotelian *kosmos* is spherical, motion 'downwards' would be towards its centre. An infinite Epicurean universe, in contrast, cannot have a centre; the idea of motion towards the centre being 'downwards' is absurd to the Epicurean, for whom an absolute, and natural, 'up' and 'down' in the universe is unproblematic. Indeed, Lucretius objected (1.1052–3) to the idea that 'all things press towards the centre of the whole' as part of his larger argument against the idea of a spherical (and bounded) *kosmos* and in favour of an infinite universe. Furthermore, Lucretius argues directly against the idea that the Earth itself is spherical, pointing to what he regards as the absurd consequences of this notion:[18]

> That all the heavy things below the earth
> Press upwards and rest upside down upon it,
> Like images of things reflected in water.

He ridicules the adherents of the idea of a spherical Earth, complaining:

> And likewise they contend that animals
> Wander about head downwards and cannot fall
> Off from the earth into the sky below
> Any more than our bodies of themselves can fly
> Upwards into the regions of the sky.[19] (1.1058–64)

Lucretius evidently attacks the theory of the spherical Earth, but there is surprisingly no explicit statement that the Earth is flat in surviving Epicurean texts.[20] Nevertheless, Epicurean ideas regarding the weight of bodies and the direction taken by falling bodies

[16] Tr. Konstan 1972: 270. [17] See also Konstan 1972. [18] See Furley 1996.
[19] Translations here of Lucretius are by R. Melville 1997, unless otherwise noted.
[20] Cf. Conroy 1976: 110.

(cf. Lucretius 2.217–18: 'bodies move by their own weight straight down through the empty void') strongly suggest that they held a 'flat Earth' view.[21]

OUR *KOSMOS*, ONE OF AN INFINITE NUMBER

Our *kosmos* is only one of the infinite number of *kosmoi* (*Ep. Hdt.* 45; *Ep. Pyth.* 89). These worlds have arisen from the infinite (*Ep. Hdt.* 73; cf. Lucr. 2.1018–89). Epicurus (*Ep. Hdt.* 45) uses the principle of indifference – the assumption that there is no reason to suppose a difference – to argue that because the atoms that can constitute a *kosmos* are not used up in making one *kosmos* or even a finite number of *kosmoi*, there is nothing to prevent the existence of an infinite number of *kosmoi*.The different *kosmoi*, or worlds, cannot be assumed to be all the same shape (*Ep. Hdt.* 74); in the definition of a *kosmos* offered in the *Letter to Pythocles* 88 (quoted above), Epicurus asserts that a *kosmos* may 'be round or triangular or of any shape whatever'.[22]

The existence of an infinite number of *kosmoi* has further consequences with regard to the various explanations of phenomena on offer, and the Epicurean commitment to positing multiple possible causes. Relying on Epicurean modal theory, Lucretius explains that it is difficult to know which specific cause operates in our *kosmos*, but it must be one of the many possible causes (5.526–33). Because there is an infinite number of *kosmoi* in which a particular cause may apply, each possible cause must actually operate in some *kosmos*; what is 'possible' is 'true in one or more (actual) worlds', whereas 'necessary' is 'true in all (actual) worlds'.[23]

Focusing on our own *kosmos*, Lucretius (5.534–49) explains that the Earth is a part of the *kosmos*. It rests in the middle region of the *kosmos*, but is not a burden to the air, because it is part of a whole. He draws an analogy to the human body, to explain the way the Earth does not fall:

21 See, for example, Furley 1999: 420–1 and Conroy 1976 on this subject.

22 This type of indifference reasoning is characteristic of Epicurean argumentation; see Asmis 1984: 265, 310–11, 319, 335; see also 249, 306–7. Asmis considers the use of the principle of indifference with regard to discussions of atomic shapes at 271–2.

23 Sedley 2004; see also Warren 2004b, particularly 359ff.

A man's limbs have no weight that he can feel,
The head's no burden to the neck, nor body
For all its size weighs heavy on our feet.

Lucretius explains that the analogy is especially apt, because:

... earth was not suddenly
Imposed on air as something alien,
Or from outside thrust in on alien air,
But from the first beginning of the world
It was conceived and grew together with it,
A fixed part of it, as limbs are of our body.

Although the Earth rests in the middle region of our *kosmos*, this location does not have the same meaning within Epicurean cosmology as it does within Aristotelian physics; the Earth does not act as the centre of the universe, as the 'natural place' to which heavy bodies move.

COSMOGONY: THE ORIGIN OF *KOSMOI*, AND THEIR GROWTH AND DECLINE

Epicurus touches only very briefly on the question of cosmogony, the origin of the *kosmoi*. Both he and Lucretius emphasize that many worlds have come to be. In the *Letter to Herodotus* 73, Epicurus states that all *kosmoi*, both small and large, have arisen from the infinite, having been 'separated off from special [or particular] conglomerations of atoms'. Furthermore, all of these will be 'dissolved': 'some faster, some slower, some through the action of one set of causes, others through the action of another'. Lucretius also emphasizes that our world is not the only one:

It must be deemed in high degree unlikely
That this earth, this sky, alone have been created,
And all those bodies of matter outside do nothing. (2.1056–7)
...
Wherefore again and again I say you must admit
That in other places other combinations
Of matter exist such as this world of ours .... (2.1064–6)

These passages in Epicurus and Lucretius are replete with analogies to living things – seeds, irrigation, creation and extinction.

Epicurus asserts (*Ep. Pyth.* 89) that it is possible for a world (*kosmos*) to arise in a world, or in one of the *metakosmia* (the so-called *intermundia*); he explains that by this term he means 'the spaces, or interstices' between worlds. He describes the flowing of certain appropriate 'seeds' from a single world, or from several, which 'undergo gradual additions or articulations or changes of place ... waterings from appropriate sources, until they are matured and firmly settled in so far as the foundations laid can receive them' (cf. Lucretius 2.1122–74). Epicurus' cosmology is sometimes described as 'mechanistic' but, as David Furley has pointed out, even though the text has difficulties and is vague, the language – incorporating words such as 'seeds' and 'irrigations' – serves to underpin a 'biological' model for the growth of *kosmoi*.[24] The use of language suggestive of generation and corruption, and the analogies to living things are conspicuous; the language of seeds, irrigation, settling in and maturing is evocative of horticulture.

Epicurus was not concerned solely with our *kosmos*; his description concerns many possible worlds. Lucretius (2.1070–6) emphasizes the possibility (indeed, great likelihood) of life in other worlds:

> And if there exists so great a store of atoms [seeds]
> As all the years of life on earth could never number,
> And if the same great force of nature stands
> Ready to throw the seeds of things together
> In the same way as they have here combined,
> Then of necessity you must accept
> That other earths exist, in other places,
> With varied tribes of men and breeds of beasts.[25]

Following Epicurus, he also describes, at some length, the end of the life cycle of our *kosmos*, once again invoking analogies to living organisms (2.1105–74). The passage is lengthy and beautiful, offering a sober end to Book 2. Having used language that evokes biological functions and processes, emphasizing growth, nourishment and decay, Lucretius closes his discussion of the cosmic 'life-cycle'

[24] Furley 1999: 425. The Stoic-influenced poet Marcus Manilius (early first century AD), who may have written his poem in part as a response to Lucretius, describes the world (*mundus*) as a living creature. See also Schrijvers 2007.

[25] Although Melville uses the word 'atoms' in the first line, a more literal translation would be 'seeds'.

bemoaning the current state of the earth and of agriculture, which no longer produces food in abundance as it once did (2.1164–74).

In Book 5 (5.416–70) Lucretius offers a lengthier account of the origin of our world, in which deliberate design played no role, but rather the world was created by the chance coming together of atoms. Turning to the heavenly bodies, he describes the motions of the sun and moon again using analogies to living bodies:

> Next the beginnings came of sun and moon,
> Whose globes revolve in middle course on high.
> Them neither earth nor mighty ether claimed,
> Being not so heavy as to sink and lie
> Nor light enough to rise through highest heaven,
> But in between they turn as living bodies
> And take their place as parts of all the world;
> As in our bodies too some limbs may stay
> At rest, while others yet are moving. (5.471–9)

The processes of the *kosmos* are similar to those of a living organism with a fixed life-cycle, being subject to growth and decline. Our *kosmos* – as well as the other *kosmoi* – is not immortal and everlasting, but will cease to exist. Like living beings, *kosmoi* grow, decline, and finally come to an end.[26] The mortality of the Epicurean *kosmoi* is in sharp contrast to the immortal and unchanging nature of, for example, the Aristotelian *kosmos*.[27]

EPICUREAN METEOROLOGY[28]

In the *Letter to Pythocles*, Epicurus offers explanations of the *meteōra*, writing to a certain Pythocles, who has asked for a summary of his views. In considering meteorological phenomena and their causes, Epicurus' stated aim is to contribute to peace of mind (*ataraxia*), through eliminating fear of potentially frightening phenomena. He asserts that 'knowledge of meteorological phenomena, whether taken along with other things or in isolation, has no other end in view

[26] See Solmsen 1953: 50 citing fr. 305 Us. (=Aëtius 2.4). Asmis 1984: 314–15 comments briefly on the idea that the growth and decline of worlds is analogous to the growth and decline of living beings. See also Schrijvers 2007: 272–3.

[27] See Solmsen 1953: 50 n. 62.

[28] Some of the topics treated here are discussed at greater length in Taub 2003: chs. 3–4.

than peace of mind and firm conviction' (85). In seeking *ataraxia*, Epicurus recommends the rejection of traditional ways of explaining weather, including those that affirm divine intervention.

Keeping in mind the fundamental point that the *meteōra* are not the work of gods, Epicurus argues that the occurrence of weather signs can be explained in more than one way. While he does not give any examples of weather signs, we can assume that he was referring to an ancient equivalent to such maxims as 'red sky at night, shepherds' delight'. He explains that it may be the case that the various signs in the sky indicating future weather are due simply to the succession of the seasons, as is the case with the signs that are indicated by animals. Or, it may be the case that weather signs are caused by changes and alterations in the air. Neither explanation is in conflict with the observations and it is not possible to know whether the effect is due to one or the other cause (*Ep. Pyth.* 98–9).

Traditionally, within the polytheistic cultural context of the Greco-Roman world, many natural – particularly meteorological – phenomena were associated with and thought to be due to activities of the gods. So, for example, Zeus was often depicted holding the thunder-bolt he was presumed to wield. In Epicurean cosmology and meteorology, the gods play no causative role. Epicurus rejects the use of weather signs as indicative of the gods' activities, for this would violate his theology. He argues that

> the fact that the weather is sometimes foretold from the behaviour of certain animals is a mere coincidence in time. For the animals offer no necessary reason why a storm should be produced; and no divine being sits observing when these animals go out and afterwards fulfilling the signs which they have given. For such folly as this would not possess the most ordinary being if ever so little enlightened, much less one who enjoys perfect felicity. (*Ep. Pyth.* 115–16)

The Epicurean gods are too busy being blissful to bother with human concerns, including the weather.

Turning to astronomical phenomena, Epicurus focuses above all on those associated with the sun and moon, particularly eclipses, night and day. Addressing the regularity of the orbits of celestial bodies, Epicurus asserts that these must 'be explained in the same way as certain ordinary incidents within our own experience' (*Ep. Pyth.* 97); this appeal to common, everyday experience – including the use of what we see and explaining things through analogies to the familiar – is advocated throughout the *Letter to Pythocles*.

Many of the points made briefly by Epicurus are discussed at length by Lucretius. For example, Epicurus (91) states that the size of the sun and stars, relative to us, is as great as it appears, but that the sizes may be slightly larger, or smaller, or even exactly as they seem to be, drawing an analogy to fires seen at a distance.[29] Lucretius (5.564–91) asserts that their sizes cannot be much smaller or larger than they seem to our senses. Concerning astronomical phenomena, Epicurus had quite a bit to say about their study in the *Letter to Herodotus* 76–82, but he also made it clear that he thought it possible to get too carried away thinking about astronomy. Lucretius offers several possible causes of such phenomena, stating that

> Which of these causes operates in this world
> It is difficult to say beyond all doubt. (5.526–7)

While we may be uncertain which is the actual cause, Lucretius states that there is only one explanation of astronomical motions in our world, but others possible for other worlds (5.509–33).[30]

As Epicurus turns to what we regard as meteorological phenomena, he straightforwardly acknowledges the difficulty of explaining them. In the case of distant ones, for example those that occur high above us, he advocates the use of analogy to everyday experience (*Ep. Hdt.* 80; *Ep. Pyth.* 87). Epicurus discusses various meteorological phenomena: clouds, rain, thunder, lightning, thunderbolts, waterspouts (or whirlwinds),[31] earthquakes, wind, hail, snow, dew, frost, ice, rainbow, halo, comets and falling stars, but his treatment of specific phenomena tends to be very brief. Nevertheless, he incorporates his hallmark explanatory tactics of drawing analogies to everyday experience and suggesting a number of possible causes. As an example, 'thunder may be due to the rolling of wind in the hollow parts of the clouds, as it is sometimes imprisoned in vessels which we use; or to the roaring of fire in them when blown by a wind, or to the rending and disruption of clouds, or to the friction and splitting up of

[29] Cf. Asmis 1984: 313; Barnes 1989; and Furley 1999: 428–9.

[30] On the apparent motions of the astronomical bodies, cf. Lucretius 5.508–770; cf. Asmis 1984: 325; Furley 1999: 430–1.

[31] The meaning of the term used by Epicurus (*prēstēr*) is not straightforward; see Taub 2003: 207 n. 28.

clouds when they have become as firm as ice' (100). Throughout, he emphasizes the multiplicity of possible causes, noting that the phenomena encourage us to give a plurality of explanations. The use of analogies to familiar situations is an important part of his overall method, and he suggests that it is easy to see that lightning may occur in any number of ways 'so long as we hold fast to the phenomena and take a general view of what is similar to them' (102). The analogies offered must fit with what we observe. Common, everyday experience is useful in explaining things that are distant, or hidden. He goes on to explain that 'exclusion of myth is the sole condition necessary; and it will be excluded, if one properly attends to the facts and hence draws inferences to interpret what is obscure' (104).

Curiously, Epicurus' treatment of ice is markedly different from that of other meteorological phenomena. He refers to atomic theory and uses geometrical language ('circular','scalene', 'acute-angled') to describe the possible shapes of ice atoms:

> Ice is formed by the expulsion from the water of the circular, and the compression of the scalene and acute-angled atoms contained in it; further by the accretion of such atoms from without, which being driven together cause the water to solidify after the expulsion of a certain number of round atoms. (*Ep. Pyth.* 109)

The use of technical terms to describe ice contrasts with the language of everyday experience used to describe most other phenomena, for example, the description of wind trapped in a jar. Atomic theory is also important in Epicurus' explanations of the rainbow; he characteristically offers several possibilities, and cites (110) the aggregation of the atoms as one possible cause. Lucretius' (6.527–34) discussion of ice is rather different; for example, he does not use geometrical terms. In considering the forms of matter that originate, grow and condense in clouds – namely, snow, wind, hail and frost – Lucretius asserts that it is easy to discover and form a mental picture of how things come into being or are created once you have understood the elements, but offers no further explanation.

The relationship of Epicurus' views and methods to those of his predecessors is unclear, and is debated. However, Theophrastus appears to have an important influence on him, and through him, on Lucretius. This may be seen in certain styles of explanation adopted by both Epicurus and Lucretius, notably the use of multiple causes and analogy. The positing of a number of possible causes may also owe something to the doxographical style of collecting and presenting the opinions of others.[32]

Nevertheless, there are some noticeable differences between Epicurus' approach and that of Theophrastus; the latter offers multiple causes as explanations only when it appears that he cannot decide on only one. This may be the case either because of the cause itself or because he cannot find sufficient evidence to make a determination; at times, Theophrastus' suggestions for further research only make sense if further evidence would help decide between different possible causes. In contrast, Epicurus and Lucretius seem happy to entertain plural causes on each and every occasion (in terms of aetiology), because they regard their role as providing at least some natural cause, in order to encourage peace of mind.[33]

While Epicurus advocated the use of analogies with everyday experience in the explanation of meteorological phenomena, he only provided sketchy examples in the *Letter to Pythocles*, such as the analogy between thunder being due to the rolling of wind in the hollows of clouds and wind being trapped in ordinary vessels (100). In Book 6 of *On the nature of things*, Lucretius offers natural and rational explanations for those phenomena that humans most commonly attribute to supernatural causes, including thunder, lightning, thunderbolts, waterspouts, earthquakes, volcanoes, the flooding of the Nile and magnets. The list of phenomena discussed is similar to that covered by Epicurus in the *Letter to Pythocles*, but the order is different.[34]

Lucretius provides more detailed analogies than Epicurus. So, for example, in his explanation of thunder being caused by the power of wind splitting a cloud with a terrible crash, he explains that this is no wonder, since even a small bladder filled with air makes a noise when

[32] Sedley 1998a, particularly 125–6, 145–6, 157, 182–5, has argued that Epicurus used Theophrastus' *Physical opinions* as his source for earlier views, providing examples of possible explanations to be suggested. See also Mansfeld 1992, and Asmis 1984: 328–9. Epicurus did not agree with everything that Theophrastus had to say; Epicurus also wrote a work *Against Theophrastus*.

[33] I am grateful to Geoffrey Lloyd for having helped me think through the differences here. See also Hankinson 1998: 221–3; Allen 2001: 197.

[34] Sedley 1998a: 157–60 points to Epicurus' *On Nature* (Book 13) as Lucretius' source; cf. also 135–44. See also Fowler and Fowler 1997: xxvi–xxvii for a brief discussion of the possible sources of Lucretius' poem.

it bursts suddenly (6.121–31). Lucretius offers several explanations of thunder, including descriptions of the noise that sometimes accompanies lightning (6.145–55). He uses another detailed analogy to common experience to explain why we see lightning before we hear the thunderclap (6.164–72):

> Things always come more slowly to the ears
> Than to the eyes; as this example shows:
> If in the distance you observe a man
> Felling a tall tree with twin-bladed axe
> You see the stroke before the sound of it
> Reaches your ears; so also we see lightning
> Before we hear the thunder, which is produced
> At the same time as the fire, and by the same cause,
> Born of the same collision of the clouds.

The poetic medium makes the analogies suggested by Epicurus more immediate and, possibly, the explanations more comprehensible.[35]

Lucretius also uses an analogy to explain how multiple explanations can apply to those phenomena that are remote (6.703–11). He describes seeing a corpse from a distance, whose cause of death is unknown:

> For though you could not prove that steel or cold
> Had caused his death, or disease perhaps, or poison,
> We know quite well that what has happened to him
> Is something of this kind.

Through this, Lucretius argues that distant phenomena can only be sufficiently observed to be identified as examples of possible, but not conclusive, explanations; it is impossible to get close enough to gain further information. All possible explanations should be cited in order to include the one relevant to the particular instance. All of the explanations are potentially true, even though only one is true for each particular event.[36]

Like Epicurus, Lucretius rejects the possibility that meteorological phenomena are instances of the gods at work, for example punishing humans for their shortcomings. He asks (6.387–92):

[35] See also Schiesaro 1990 on Lucretius' use of analogy. [36] Cf. Asmis 1984: 324.

> If Jupiter and other gods, my friend,
> Shake with appalling din the realms of heaven,
> And shoot their fire where each one wants to aim,
> Why do they not arrange that when a man
> Is guilty of some abominable crime
> He's struck, and from his breast transfixed breathes out
> Hot flames, a bitter lesson to mankind?

The gods are not interested in the activities of human beings; frightening weather events are not due to divine retribution. The Epicureans' aim was to demonstrate that the universe and various distant phenomena can be explained without reference to anything outside of nature, or extraordinary. It was the elimination of fear and anxiety (particularly about the intervention of the gods in the world) that motivated Epicurus and Lucretius to present their views on cosmology and meteorology, and to argue that ordinary experience is invaluable in helping us to understand the universe as natural.

CHRISTOPHER GILL

7 Psychology

I. INTRODUCTION

Although 'psychology' does not constitute a distinct sub-division of Epicurean theory, the term can be used to refer to a number of well-marked topics in their philosophical framework. These include (1) the bodily nature of the psyche,[1] (2) the atomic composition of the psyche, and (3) links between psychological functions and the structure of the body. These topics fall, broadly, under 'physics' in Epicurean philosophy. However, the bodily and atomic nature of the psyche also has implications for Epicurean ethics, implications that can also be seen as part of their thinking about psychology. These implications include (4) the capacity of the psyche, in human beings, for the development of agency and responsibility, and (5) the mortal nature of the psyche. Also relevant is (6) Epicurean use of psychological language in ethical contexts, often without explicit reference to the bodily or atomic nature of the psyche, and (7) the psychological assumptions underlying the Epicurean therapy of beliefs and emotions. The focus here is on the first four topics, illustrated by reference to certain key sources, and on the issue of how to understand the theory of psyche–body relations implied in these ideas (Sections II–V). However, there is briefer comment on the latter three topics, indicating how the conception of psychology involved in those topics depends on, or is at least compatible with, Epicurean thinking about the psyche as bodily (Section VI).[2]

[1] 'Psyche', (*psuchē*) in Greek, *anima* in Latin, is treated here as a naturalized English term and is not normally transliterated. The modern terms often used to translate psyche ('soul', 'mind', 'personality') are all in various ways inappropriate as equivalents.

[2] For fuller treatment of topic (4), see O'Keefe, ch. 8, this volume; for topic (5), see Warren, ch. 13, this volume; for topic (6), see Woolf, ch. 9, this volume; and for topic (7), see Tsouna, ch. 14, this volume.

There is some discussion here of how to analyse, in modern terms, Epicurean thinking about psyche–body relations. But the emphasis falls on locating psychology within the Epicurean theoretical framework set out in this *Companion* as a whole. More broadly, the aim is to show how Epicurean ideas about psychology reflect their larger philosophical outlook. In epistemology, the Epicurean approach is empirical, rather than idealist. Their world-view is materialist (rather than idealist, again) and mechanical (rather than teleological). For some ancient critics of Epicureanism, this meant that their philosophy could not provide a credible psychological account of human beings as rational agents capable of virtue and happiness. As I hope to bring out, this criticism is not well founded for several reasons. One important factor is that Epicureanism combines an account of the psyche as bodily, and atomic, with a conception of human beings as coherent and complex wholes, capable of advanced psychological and ethical functions.

II. THE PSYCHE AS BODILY

In the *Letter to Herodotus*, summarizing the key principles of his physics, Epicurus sets out the main points of his idea of psyche (63–8). The psyche is a part of the body; and its distinctive functions, such as sensation, are the result of conjunction with the rest of the body. When the body as a whole is injured or disintegrates in death, this conjunction ends, and so do the psychological functions. In Epicurus' own words:

> The psyche is a fine-structured body (*sōma*) diffused through the whole aggregate (*athroisma*) [i.e. the rest of the body], most strongly resembling wind with a certain blending of heat, and resembling wind in some respects but heat in others. But [psyche] is the part [of the whole aggregate] which differs greatly also from wind and heat themselves in its fineness of structure, a fact which makes it the more liable to co-affection (*sumpathes*) with the rest of the aggregate. All this is shown by the psyche's capacities, experiences, ease of motion and thought processes, and by those features of it whose loss marks our death. We must grasp too that the psyche has the major share of responsibility for sensation. On the other hand, it would not be in possession of this if it were not contained in some way by the rest of the aggregate. (Epic. *Ep. Hdt.* 63–4, tr. Long and Sedley, with modifications[3])

[3] Passages cited below use the translations in Long and Sedley 1987 unless otherwise stated. For alternative translations of this difficult passage, see Inwood and Gerson 1997: 13, von Staden 2000: 81.

Despite Epicurus' (typically) awkward style of writing, the salient points come out clearly. The psyche is bodily, its distinctive make-up being explained by partial resemblance to other fine and mobile forms of body (wind and heat). Accordingly, Epicurus replaces the traditional (at least, Platonic and Aristotelian) contrast between psyche and body with that between the psyche (one part of the body) and the rest of the aggregate (the total bodily complex). Psychological functions such as sensation and thought, and indeed life itself, depend on the conjunction and co-operation of the psychic part and the rest of the body, which is disrupted by illness and ended by death.[4]

How does this account of the psyche relate to Epicurus' philosophy more generally? The most obvious links are with Epicurus' thinking on the nature of reality, or, in his terms, 'things that exist in themselves'. According to Epicurus, there are only two types of independently existing things, body and void.[5] Epicurus assumes that the psyche falls into the class of things that exist in themselves, and argues that the psyche must be a body, since it is capable of acting and being acted upon, causal properties which belong only to bodies. Epicurus thus rejects, implicitly at least, one of the main competing ancient ideas, that the psyche is non-bodily, an idea put forward, for instance, in Plato's *Phaedo*. Epicurus argues that, if the psyche were non-bodily, it would have to be void, but that this is impossible since the psyche (unlike void) can act and be acted on.[6] A second link is with Epicurean thinking on epistemology and the correct methodology of natural enquiry. Epicurus maintains that knowledge must be based on the evidence of the senses. A correct picture of the world is to be formed by drawing inferences from what is 'evident' (based on sensation) to what is 'non-evident', rather than by an independent, non-empirical, process of reasoning or thought.[7] In Book 3 of

[4] In more technical terms, the capacity for sensation and other psychological functions are accidental properties of the psyche which depend on the conjunction with the (rest of) the body. See Epic. *Ep. Hdt.* 63–7 (also 68–73), and von Staden 2000: 85–6.

[5] See Epic. *Ep. Hdt.* 39–40; see further Sedley 1999: 366-9, and Morel, ch. 4, this volume.

[6] See Epic. *Ep. Hdt.* 67. The idea that the capacity to act and be acted on is a criterion of independent existence (which Epicurus adopts) goes back at least to Pl. *Soph.* 247d–e. Epicurus does not refer to the Aristotelian idea of psyche as the actualization (or essence) of a natural body potentially capable of life (*De an.* 2.1).

[7] More precisely, the criteria of truth are sensations, preconceptions and feelings (DL 10.31); see further, Asmis 1999 and ch. 5, this volume.

Lucretius' *On the nature of things* (a poem that seems to be based closely on Epicurus' main work on physics, *On Nature*),[8] Lucretius argues at length that the bodily nature of the psyche can be demonstrated by reference to perceptible evidence and to the general account of reality that can reasonably be based on this evidence.[9] Epicurus also indicates that his account of the psyche is based on this kind of method.[10] So the Epicurean account of psyche is not simply assumed or asserted but is argued for, on the basis of a considered methodology of natural enquiry and the principles based on this methodology.

III. THE PSYCHE AS ATOMIC

In his account of the core principles of reality, after identifying body and void as the only things that exist in themselves, Epicurus analyses body in terms of atomic ('uncuttable') units. He then sets out to explain the nature of the universe, both objects and events, as the result of the unplanned collisions of an innumerable set of atoms moving in infinite space.[11] The only fundamental properties of atoms are resistance, size, shape and weight. In principle, it would seem, *all* phenomena are taken to be explicable by reference to atomic structure and interaction, by deploying one of two types of explanation. In the first type, distinctive features of phenomena are explained by corresponding features at the atomic level. In the second type, although there is not a one-for-one equivalence between atomic and phenomenal properties, the rearrangement of atoms is held to explain properties that only exist at the phenomenal level, such as colour and flavour.[12]

In general, the first type of explanation seems to be more prominent in Epicurus' analysis of the bodily nature of the psyche. For instance, the distinctive features of psychological functions are

[8] On the relationship between the two works, see Sedley 1998a: esp. chs. 4–5.

[9] See e.g. Lucr. 3.460–547, for repeated appeals to the evidence of the senses.

[10] See Epic. *Ep. Hdt.* 63, 68, linking the claims made with the evidence of sensations and feelings.

[11] Epic. *Ep. Hdt.* 40–3; also Sedley 1999: 372–9, and Morel, ch. 4, this volume.

[12] LS 12; also Hankinson 1999: 498–503, Sedley 1999: 379–82. On Epicurus' thinking about atomism and psychology, see further Section V below.

explained by reference to a distinctive type of atomic structure, namely a combination of four exceptionally fine and mobile types of atom.

Epicurus [said that the psyche is] a blend consisting of four things, of which one is fire-like, one air-like, one wind-like, while the fourth is something which lacks a name ... The wind ... produces movement in us, the air produces rest, the hot one produces the evident heat of the body, and the unnamed one produces sensation in us.[13]

In a comparable move, Lucretius explains the character traits of different animal species, and the traits of different human individuals, by reference to the dominance of certain types of atoms in their physical make-up:

But there is more heat in those with fierce hearts and angry minds which easily boil over in anger. A prime example is the lion, which regularly bursts its chest with roaring and groaning and cannot contain the billows of rage in its chest ... The nature of cattle, on the other hand, is characterised more by calm air ... Likewise the human race. Even though education may produce individuals equally well turned out, it still leaves those original traces of each mind's nature. And we must not suppose that faults can be completely eradicated, so that one man will not plunge too hastily into bitter anger, another not be assailed too readily by fear, or the third type not be over-indulgent in tolerating certain things.[14]

The suggestion is that the dominance of fire-like, wind-like or air-like atoms in the psychic make-up results in animal or human character-types that are relatively angry, frightened or placid.

The first type of explanation (made in terms of one-for-one correspondence between atomic and phenomenal properties) is sometimes seen as less theoretically sophisticated than the second type, which does not assume this correspondence.[15] However, this type is sometimes worked out in a way that is quite complex and that comes close to the second type of explanation, as indicated in these comments by Lucretius:

[13] Aëtius 4.3.11, translation by Long and Sedley, slightly modified. See also Epic. *Ep. Hdt.* 63–4, cited in Section II above.
[14] Lucr. 3.294–8, 302, 307–13.
[15] See e.g. Hankinson 1999: 501; Warren 2002a: 69–71.

The primary particles of the elements so interpenetrate each other in their motions that no one element can be distinguished and no capacity spatially separated, but they exist as multiple powers of a single body (*unius corporis*) ... heat, air and the unseen force of wind when mixed form a single nature (*unam naturam*), along with that mobile power [the unnamed fourth element] which transmits the beginning of motion from itself to them, the origins of sense-bearing motions through the flesh.[16]

Two features of this passage are worth noting. One is that the distinctive characteristics of the psyche are explained not just by the special features of the component types of atom but also by the exceptionally complete blend of their qualities, making up what Lucretius calls a single body or nature. When taken with the conjunction and co-operation of psychological with (other) bodily operations, this helps to explain the occurrence of complex and subtle functions such as the discrimination of qualities involved in sensation.[17] Producing this blend of qualities is the special role of the (unnamed) fourth type of psychic atoms, which seems to have been introduced to provide an explanation at the atomic level for this exceptionally complete blend. Just as the psyche as a whole pervades and animates the (rest of the) body, so the fourth type of atom permeates and unifies the blend of psychic atoms and is in this sense described as the 'psyche of the psyche' (*anima animae*).[18] A second relevant point worth noting is that the completeness of the atomic blend means that 'no one element can be distinguished and no capacity spatially separated'. Similarly, as Lucretius comments later, he cannot specify the many different forms of atomic compound underlying the variations in human individual characters.[19] Although it is still assumed that there is an atomic basis for psychological features, it is not claimed that these can be precisely correlated on a one-for-one basis.[20]

[16] Lucr. 3.262–5, 268–72, cf. 282–7.
[17] On the co-operation of psychological and other bodily functions, see Section II above; on Epicurean thinking on sensation, see LS 14.
[18] Lucr. 3.273–81, esp. 275; on the fourth nature, and its consistency with Epicurus' physicalist approach to psychology, see Annas 1992: 139–40.
[19] Lucr. 3.263–4, cited above, and 315–18.
[20] See further, on the atomic explanation of psychological capacities, Section V below.

IV. THE PSYCHE AND BODILY STRUCTURE

Since the psyche is seen as part of the body, how do its functions fit into the body as a whole? The psyche as a whole seems to have been subdivided into (in Latin) *animus* ('mind') and *anima* ('spirit'), characterized in one (Greek) source as 'rational' and 'non-rational' parts.[21] Lucretius presents their operation in this way:

> The mind and spirit are firmly interlinked and constitute a single nature (*unam naturam*), but the deliberative part which we call the mind is, as it were, the chief, and holds sway throughout the body. It is firmly located in the central part of the chest. For that is where fear and dread leap up, and where joys caress; therefore it is where the mind is. The remaining part of the psyche [i.e. the spirit], which is distributed throughout the body, obeys the mind and moves at its beck and call.[22]

Although Lucretius goes on to explain that the mind sometimes has thoughts or emotions that do not affect the spirit or the body,[23] he stresses that mind and spirit typically function as an interconnected pair and that their operations are closely integrated with the rest of the body. For instance, when the mind feels intense fear, the spirit 'shares the feeling' and produces related bodily effects such as simultaneous pallor and sweating. On the other hand, both mind and spirit are affected by things that happen to the rest of the body, such as being wounded.[24] Both types of process bring out the point that the mind-spirit complex (which Lucretius describes as a 'single nature') is both bodily in itself and closely integrated with the rest of the body.

The Epicurean account of the relation between psychological functions and the structure of the body is similar to the Stoic one, developed about the same time. Both theories assume a single locus of thoughts and emotions, located in the region of the heart. Both theories also see this locus as the organizing centre of a series of functions, including sensation, operating throughout the body as a

[21] Epic. *Ep. Hdt.* 66 (the comment seems to be a later addition to Epicurus' letter).

[22] Lucr. 3.136–44. This translation is based on that in LS 14, like subsequent translations from Lucretius cited here.

[23] Lucr. 3.145–52. [24] Lucr. 3.153–76.

whole.[25] A broadly similar division of roles can be found in the account offered slightly later by two medical writers, Herophilus and Erasistratus, working in Alexandria. Their accounts, based on anatomical investigation, and probably on human vivisection, allocate analogous functions to the brain and the central nervous system, respectively.[26] The Epicurean and Stoic theories were not based on direct study of anatomy, and were probably derived from earlier accounts, such as the heart-centred theory of Praxagoras, a late fourth-century medical writer.[27] Also, Plato's description of the relationship between psychological functions and bodily structure in the *Timaeus* may have been a source of influence, though Plato subdivides the functions and location of reasoning, emotions and desire in a way not found in the other accounts.[28] The Epicurean theory, like the Stoic one, assumes a close linkage between beliefs or reasoning and emotions or desires, a feature that is also important in Epicurean thinking about psychology in ethical contexts.[29]

V. INTERPRETATIVE AND PHILOSOPHICAL ISSUES

As noted earlier, some ancient critics of Epicureanism questioned whether their materialist and mechanical world-view enabled them to offer a credible psychological account of human beings as rational agents, capable of virtue and happiness.[30] However, there are strong grounds for arguing that this criticism is misguided, and that, in a number of ways, Epicureanism shows how a materialist theory of the psyche is compatible with giving a coherent account of rational

[25] For both theories the presence of emotions in the heart provides a reason for locating the mind or 'control-centre' there (Lucr. 3.140–2, cited above). A specific point of difference is that the Stoics allocate sensation to the mind, whereas this is the work of 'spirit' (*anima*) in Epicureanism.

[26] See von Staden 2000.

[27] See Annas 1992: 20–6; Aristotle also saw the heart as the main seat of psychological functions.

[28] See Pl. *Tim.* 69–72; see further on Plato's account and its later influence, Gill 2006b: ch. 5.

[29] See further Section VI below.

[30] For an extreme statement of this criticism (not solely directed against Epicureanism), see Gal. *Nat. Fac.* 1.12 (esp. Kühn II.28–9). For related criticisms, directed at the physical or body-based conception of the human good, see Cic. *Fin.* 2.107–10, and Plut. *Non posse* 1089D–1090C.

agency and ethical development. There is more scope for debate about how to analyse the assumptions about the relationship between psyche and body underlying this account, and this has formed an important issue of recent scholarly discussion.

In analysing Epicurean thinking on psychology and matter, it is useful to draw a comparison with Democritus. It seems clear that Democritus' atomic theory was the main influence on Epicurus' world-view. However, Epicurus adopts atomism in a form that he presents as being more subtle and credible than that adopted by Democritus. Democritus, in a famous statement, asserts: 'By convention sweet, by convention bitter, by convention hot, by convention colour, but in truth atoms and void'.[31] Although the precise meaning of this claim was debated in Antiquity and is disputed by modern scholars, Democritus would seem to deny that anything other than atoms and void count as real entities about which we can have knowledge. Epicurus, by contrast, while maintaining that body and void are the only things that exist in themselves, does not deny the reality or intelligibility of properties of phenomenal objects, such as colour. This is so even though he accepts that, in principle at least, all objects and properties are explicable in atomic terms.[32] This difference has a bearing on Epicurus' definition of the status of psychological functions and activities. These are, for Epicurus, properties of phenomenal objects (human beings and other animals) and as such they are real and intelligible.[33] It is consistent with this view that Epicurus sometimes explains animal behaviour in purely psychological terms and sometimes combines explanations given in psychological and in atomic terms. Although, on the view assumed here, psychological states are ultimately identical with atomic ones, this does not mean that psychological explanation has to be replaced in each case by atomic explanation. The relationship between the

[31] Democritus DK 68 B9 (SE *M.* 7.135).

[32] On Epicurean thinking on properties, see *Ep. Hdt.* 68-71. On the implications of this account for understanding Epicurean atomism and the contrast with Democritus, see Sedley 1999: 379–82; Warren 2002a: 7–9, 193–200; Gill 2006b: 24–5; also Morel, ch. 4 and O'Keefe, ch. 8, this volume.

[33] Defining the status of psychological states for Democritus is not easy from our available evidence, though it would be consistent for him to regard them as explicable only in atomic terms; see further Warren 2002a: 58–71, centred on discussion of DK 68 B 191.

thinking of Epicurus and Democritus on this subject is sometimes defined by reference to the ideas of reductionism or eliminativism. We can say, for instance, that both Epicurus and Democritus adopt a reductionist view of the mind or psyche in that both thinkers believe that psychological processes can be explained, ultimately, as physical – and specifically atomic – ones. But Democritus' position is also a form of eliminativism in that he regards properties of phenomenal objects as unreal and unknowable, and thus eliminates psychological states from the class of real, knowable entities in a way that Epicurus does not.[34]

It is consistent with this approach that we find, in Epicurean accounts, the combination of atomic and psychological explanations of animal activity, for instance in Lucretius' account of the origin of motion:

> Images of walking impinge on our mind and strike it, as I explained earlier. It is after this that voluntary action (*voluntas*) occurs. For no one ever embarks upon any action before the mind (*mens*) first previews what it wishes to do, and whatever it is that it previews there exists an image of that thing. So when the mind (*animus*) stirs itself to want to go forwards, it immediately strikes all the power of the spirit (*anima*) distributed throughout the limbs and frame; this is easily done, because the spirit is firmly interlinked with it. Then the spirit in turn strikes the body ...[35]

Presupposed in this passage is the Epicurean conception of thought, like perception, as a process of being affected by 'images' that are themselves, like the mind, structures of very small and fine atoms. The description of voluntary action and movement is thus, implicitly at least, an account of the operation of physical entities ('mind', 'spirit') that can be analysed in atomic terms.[36] However, there is no attempt to eliminate psychological language or to reduce this to *purely* physical or atomic terms. Also, the account gives emphasis to the idea that the mind is capable of voluntary action (*voluntas*), and

[34] For this account of the status of psychological states for Epicurus, see also O'Keefe 2002a: 158–60, and ch. 8, this volume, section 3b. For a different account, made in terms of emergent dualism, see discussion below. Epicurus is sometimes characterized as adopting a non-reductive view of the reality of properties (including psychological states) by contrast with the eliminative view of Democritus.

[35] Lucr. 4.881–90.

[36] See Lucr. 4.722–822, esp. 724–31, 777–815. On the atomic nature of the psyche, see Section III above.

that it exercises an active role in its thought processes ('previews') and in activating the 'spirit' to move the body. The implication is that atomic and psychological analyses of voluntary action are both valid and compatible.[37]

A similar general point emerges from certain fragmentary passages from Epicurus' *On Nature* 25 that have aroused much recent discussion. The main theme of these passages is that human beings are properly held responsible for their actions because of the way that they develop, by contrast with (at least wild) non-human animals. Like the account of voluntary action just noted, Epicurus' description of human development combines atomic and psychological analysis. But Epicurus rejects the idea that an atomic analysis implies the negation of psychological analysis and also rejects, most emphatically, the idea that it involves the denial of agency and responsibility. In doing so, he appears to be arguing against Democritus, or perhaps some post-Democritean thinkers, who supposed that the atomic theory required a deterministic conception of human action.[38] Two extracts illustrate the combination of atomic analysis and reference to human agency:

That which we develop – characteristics of this or that kind – is at first absolutely up to us; and the things which of necessity flow in through our passages [seeds directing us to various actions, thoughts and characters] from that which surrounds us are at one stage up to us and dependent on beliefs of our own making ...

And with these [bad people] we especially do battle, and rebuke them, hating them for a disposition which follows their disordered congenital nature as we do with the whole range of [non-human] animals. For the nature of their atoms has contributed nothing to some of their behaviour ... but it is their developments which themselves possess all or most of the responsibility for certain things.[39]

The passages from which these extracts are taken contain a number of textual and interpretative difficulties; but some points emerge

[37] See Everson 1999a: 551–2.

[38] See Sedley 1983: 29–36, Warren 2002a: 193–200. See also O'Keefe, ch. 8, this volume.

[39] Epic. *Nat.* 25 34.26–30 Arr. and 34.21–2 Arr. (extracts), translation as in Long and Sedley: LS 20 C(1) and B(2–3). For the most recent edition of this text, parts of which are found preserved in *PHerc.* 697, 1056, and 1191, see Laursen 1997, and for these sections see Laursen 1997: 32–3 and 19–20 respectively.

clearly. The description of human development is couched in part in atomic terms, for instance in the account of our 'congenital nature' and also, by implication at least, of the environmental influences or 'seeds' which 'flow in through our passages'. However, as in Lucretius' account of voluntary movement, atomic language is combined with psychological, and with a strong assertion of our agency or responsibility, in this case as regards the character that we develop. The second passage cited draws a contrast in this respect with animals, who are not able to develop in a way that runs counter to their inherited (specific) nature, a contrast that is also implied in Lucretius' comments on the physical basis of animal and human character traits cited earlier.[40]

Although the points just made are generally agreed by scholars, different accounts have been offered of Epicurus' ideas about the relationship between the psychological and atomic aspects of his analysis and about how to characterize his theory in modern terms. A notable feature of the passages in *On Nature* is the idea that 'we ourselves' or 'the developments' (*ta apogegennēmena*) play a major role as causes. Another is the contrast drawn between 'we' or 'developments', on the one hand, and 'atoms' or 'congenital nature' or 'original constitution', on the other.[41] These features have been interpreted in different ways. On one view (associated with the idea of 'emergent dualism'), in the course of development, mental capacities 'emerge', which are distinct from, and causally independent of, the atomic make-up of the person concerned.[42] On another, competing view, the contrasts drawn are not between mental and physical (atomic) but between different stages in the development of the person as a psychological, but also atomic, entity. The main relevant contrast is between the developing or developed character and the original or earlier nature or state. What Epicurus is stressing is the process by which we (as atomic entities and agents) shape our pre-existing characters by thought and conscious effort and not – as in the

[40] On this contrast see also Epic. *Nat.* 25 34.25.21–34 Arr. (LS 20j, only in LS vol. 2); recent text in Laursen 1997: 31–2. See also Lucr. 3.321–2: 'so slight are the traces of our human nature which reason cannot expel from us, that nothing stands in the way of our leading a life worthy of the gods', continuing the passages cited in text to n. 14 above. On the human-animal contrast, see also Annas 1993a: 65–70.

[41] See Annas 1993a: 57–9. [42] See Sedley 1983: 38–40; 1988: 321–2.

alternative view – by the exercise of purely mental causation on our physical make-up. The second view interprets Epicurus' theory as, in modern terms, that of 'ontological physicalism' or 'token identity physicalism', according to which each psychological event is identical with a physical (atomic) event.[43] The second view has predominated in recent discussions and is the approach I am assuming here.

I have pointed to certain ways in which Epicurean theory, although adopting a physicalist (and atomic) approach to psychology, does so in a form which allows scope for a conception of human beings as psychological (and rational) agents, capable of ethical responsibility. A related feature is that Epicurean thinking, in various ways and levels, conceives human beings, and to some extent other animals, as coherent psychophysical and psychological wholes and therefore in principle capable of unified agency. At a very basic level, the four types of psychic atom constitute a unified nexus or 'blend' (*krama*) that enables relatively complex and subtle processes such as sensation or thought. Also, the psyche (more precisely, the 'mind-spirit' complex) forms a coherent system that is integrated with bodily structure and functions.[44] A related feature is the idea that animal species such as human beings are natural kinds with their own psychological character, an idea seen by the Epicureans – perhaps surprisingly – as compatible with their rejection of natural teleology in general. Different species are reproduced from their own biological 'seeds'; and the survival of species over time reflects the fitness and coherence of their species-specific bodily make-up.[45] Also different species have distinct temperaments, reflecting the dominance of a certain type of psychic atom in their composition. The latter two points in particular explain Epicurus' use of the idea of a (relatively stable or structured) 'constitution' (*sustasis*) in connection with natural kinds. Adult human beings, in addition, are conceived as being relatively complex physical and psychological structures, in which advanced capacities such as that for reasoning and responsible action

[43] For these terms, see Everson 1999: 547–9, 558–9; and Annas 1993a: 59, n. 30, point 1. Other scholars holding this view include Hankinson 1998: 226–32; Bobzien 2000; and O'Keefe 2002a. See further Gill 2006a: 224–8, 2006b: 57–66. See also O'Keefe, ch. 8, this volume.

[44] See Section IV above.

[45] See Epic. *Ep. Hdt.* 38–9, Lucr. 1.159–73, 5.837–77, SE *PH* 3.17–18. See also Sedley 1998a: 193–8, 1999: 363–4, and Hankinson 1999: 500.

represent 'developments' from the original 'constitution'. One recent discussion presents the last point as helping to explain how the Epicurean version of atomism offers a credible account of human psychology and ethical agency. Epicurus does not assume that atomism requires that explanation must be made at the level of atomic constituents; certain entities 'cannot be understood other than as *systems* of atoms'. Hence, 'one cannot understand the behaviour of certain systems of atoms – i.e. humans – without describing it as the behaviour of a *system* – i.e. of the person – and so as having psychological causes'.[46] Thus, Epicurus' thinking about animals, especially humans, as systems or structures supports his view of them as agents capable of ethical agency and responsibility.[47]

VI. PSYCHOLOGY IN ETHICS

So far, this discussion has focused on Epicurean thinking on psychology as part of physics (the study of nature). But Epicurean ethics also deploys psychological ideas or language; how do these features relate to the Epicurean ideas already discussed here? This question raises the larger issue, how ethics and physics are related in Epicurean theory. Broadly speaking, although ethics and physics are independently formulated, they are seen as mutually supporting; and both branches of theory have an ultimately practical aim, to promote happiness, as understood in Epicureanism.[48] Also, both branches of theory presuppose similar ideas, including those of psychophysical and psychological unity or holism, as illustrated shortly.

One clear point of linkage between physics and ethics is that the recognition of human mortality is taken to be crucial for counteracting fear of death and thus enabling freedom from anxiety. For instance, in Book 3 of his poem, Lucretius argues that a proper understanding of our nature as temporary psychophysical (and ultimately atomic) units enables us to see that 'death is nothing to us' (3.830), and thus to free ourselves from fear of what death may hold.[49]

46 Everson 1999a: 549, 557, his italics. 47 See also Gill 2006a: 221–2; 2006b: 53–4.

48 See Epic. *Ep. Pyth.* 85–8. See also Sedley 1998b; and Gill 2006b: 27, 187–9.

49 Lucr. 3.94–416 offers thirty-three arguments for the inseparability of psyche and body, thus preparing for the conclusion stated in 830 and the ethical implications drawn in 831–1094. On Epicurean arguments against fear of death, see Warren 2004a and ch. 13, this volume.

Analogously, as just noted, in *On Nature* 25, Epicurus aims to show how an understanding of human development (framed in part in atomic terms) supports the claim that we are ethically responsible agents. More generally, a number of important and distinctive themes in Epicurean ethics reflect the idea of human beings as psychophysical units (fundamentally embodied psychological agents with a temporary life-span) that is central to Epicurean thinking about psychology as part of the study of nature. These ideas seem to be deliberately formulated in a way that runs counter to the contrast between psyche (or mind) and body that is so important in much Platonic and Aristotelian thought.[50]

For instance, the Epicurean definition of happiness or the goal of life as pleasure, characterizes this in terms that combine physical and psychological well-being, described negatively as absence of bodily pain and mental distress (*aponia* and *ataraxia*). The key function of the human mind is presented as that of reasoning out the best way to bring about a pleasurable or pain-free bodily and psychological state.[51] Other characteristic Epicurean categories and distinctions imply the same inclusive view of the human being as a psychophysical unit. One such distinction is between kinetic and katastematic pleasures (transient or episodic and stable or static pleasures). Although there is scope for debate about the precise way to interpret this distinction, it is clear that both types of pleasure include bodily and psychological dimensions; for instance, both absence of physical pain and mental distress are presented as katastematic pleasures.[52] A similar point can be made about the distinction between natural, necessary and empty desires. Although the clearest examples of natural and necessary desires are bodily ones, the basis of applying this distinction is the aim of achieving pleasure and avoiding pain across the board, in both bodily and psychological states.[53] An idea that seems to underlie much Epicurean thinking on pleasure is that simply *being alive* (that is,

[50] On this as a general point of contrast between Epicurean (and Stoic) thought and much Platonic and Aristotelian thought, see Gill 2006b: ch. 1.

[51] See Epic. *Ep. Men.* 127–32; Cic. *Fin.* 1.29–32, 37–9.

[52] See Cic. *Fin.* 2.9–10, DL 10.136–7.

[53] See Epic. *Ep. Men.* 127, *KD* 29. On these distinctions, and their interrelationship, see Annas 1993b: 190–8, and Woolf, ch. 9, this volume.

fulfilling one's nature and doing what is necessary to express this) is *inherently* pleasurable.[54] Our nature embraces both bodily and psychological aspects, and the key categories of Epicurean thinking on pleasure imply this picture of our nature.

Analogously, Epicurean ethical thinking implies a unified or holistic view of human psychological functions, and avoids the sharp contrast between reason and emotion or desire that figures prominently in much Platonic, and some Aristotelian, thinking about psychology. As in Stoic thought, it is assumed that emotions and desires are informed by beliefs and reasoning, rather than that they derive from a separate, non-rational, part of the psyche.[55] This assumption underlies the Epicurean distinction between 'natural' and 'empty' anger, that is, anger that is, or is not, based on an understanding of the true basis of pleasure and pain in human life.[56] This assumption also underlies the Epicurean critique of many human emotions (such as fear of death or greed and the craving for honour), which are regarded as based on misguided beliefs about what promotes human happiness.[57] The core Epicurean approach to the therapy of emotions, exemplified for instance in Book 3 of Lucretius' poem, presupposes that emotions such as fear can be fundamentally changed by changes in belief (such as recognising that 'death is nothing to us').[58] Earlier, it was noted that, in the Epicurean account of embodied psychology, reasoning and emotion are located in the same unitary centre (the mind), by contrast with the Platonic subdivision of psychological functions.[59] Epicurean thinking about emotions and desires in ethical contexts seems to reflect the same pattern, and to express a view about

[54] This idea may lie behind the (surprisingly) negative definition of pleasure in terms of *absence* of pain and distress (*aponia* and *ataraxia*); i.e. life *without* these drawbacks is inherently good. The connotations of the term 'katastematic' include expressing our human 'constitution' (*katastēma*) and doing so in a 'stable' or 'static' way. See further Gill 2006b: 109–113.

[55] See further Gill 2006b: 113–14.

[56] See Philod. *De ira* (*PHerc.* 182) XXXVII.52, XLII.22–34 Indelli. See also Annas 1992: 192–9; Procopé 1998: 174–82.

[57] See Cic. *Fin.* 1.59–61; Lucr. 3.978–1023.

[58] See text to n. 49 above; and on the Epicurean therapy of emotions, see Tsouna, ch. 14, this volume.

[59] See text to nn. 25, 28 above.

psychological unity or holism that parallels their thinking about the fundamental unity of the human being as a psychophysical entity.[60] In these respects, then, Epicurean thinking about human psychology in ethical contexts expresses similar or compatible ideas to those discussed earlier as part of the study of nature.

[60] See further on links between Epicurean thinking on ethics and their psychological and psychophysical holism, Gill 2006b: 100–26.

TIM O'KEEFE

8 Action and responsibility

I. INTRODUCTION

One of Epicurus' central concerns is to show how human agency exists within a world whose ultimate constituents are simply extended and indivisible bits of matter (atoms) whizzing around in empty space (the void). A common way of putting this concern is to say that Epicurus wishes to defend free will against the threat of determinism. After all, the Epicurean poet Lucretius asserts that *libera voluntas* – often translated as 'free will' – is incompatible with causal determinism, and Epicurus (famously or infamously) posits an indeterministic atomic motion, the 'swerve', in order to defend our freedom against this threat.[1]

However, framing the issue this way risks anachronistically over-simplifying and distorting the Epicurean position. First of all, Epicurus defends at least three different sorts of freedom:

(a) *Effective agency*, our ability to act as we wish to in order to get what we desire.
(b) *Self-formation of character*, our ability to modify our desires, hopefully in a way that allows us to attain happiness.
(c) *Moral responsibility*, our ability to be justifiably subject to praise and blame for what we do.

Secondly, Epicurus confronts a variety of threats to our freedoms, and none of them maps easily on to the threat that causal determinism is usually thought, in modern discussions, to pose to free will – the apparent incompatibility of causal determinism with the

[1] We have no references to the swerve in Epicurus' surviving writings, but given the sources that credit him with it, and the Epicureans' doctrinal conservatism, it almost certainly originated with him.

ability to do otherwise than one does, which is (supposedly) necessary for free will.[2]

In what follows, I will briefly sketch out how Epicurus thought the sorts of freedom listed above were under attack, and how he responded. Fair warning: this chapter doesn't advance a standard interpretation of Epicurus' position on freedom and the role of the swerve within it. No standard interpretation exists. The texts on this topic are suggestive and philosophically rich enough to fuel a huge range of views, but sketchy and obscure enough that no consensus has emerged.[3]

2. DETERMINISM, EFFECTIVE AGENCY AND BIVALENCE

2a. *Lucretius on free volition and the swerve*

Atoms naturally fall straight downwards, and they also move because of collisions and entanglements with other atoms. However, there is a third cause of atomic motion, a random swerve to the side by one spatial minimum, which saves us from the decrees of fate. Although widely derided in Antiquity, nowadays many hail the swerve as part of the first libertarian theory of free will.[4] Because of this, Lucretius' discussion of the swerve in *DRN* 2.251–93 has garnered a great deal of attention, as it is the most extended consideration we have of the swerve and freedom.[5]

Lucretius infers that imperceptible atomic swerves exist on the basis of what we can see, namely that animals act freely. His argument goes as follows:

(1) If atoms did not swerve, there would not be 'free volition' (*libera voluntas*).
(2) There is free volition.
(3) Therefore, atoms swerve.

Lucretius spends most of his argument (lines 261–83) pointing to the manifest truth of the second premise, and in so doing, he shows what

[2] See van Inwagen 1983: ch. 3 for an influential version of such an argument, and Kapitan 2002 for an overview of the recent debate.

[3] For a detailed consideration of the contested texts and the various interpretations they have spawned, see O'Keefe 2005; some of this chapter is adapted from that book.

[4] For example, see Huby 1967; Long and Sedley 1987: vol. 1, p. 107; Asmis 1990a: 275.

[5] Lucretius is also our main source (*DRN* 2.216–24) for the swerve's other role, as an origin of atomic collisions. See Morel, ch. 4, this volume, and ch. 5 of O'Keefe 2005.

sort of 'free volition' determinism threatens. Free volition is what allows creatures throughout the earth, both human and non-human, to do what they want to do and to advance wherever pleasure leads them. Lucretius establishes that free volition exists by showing that the body follows the mind's desire. He gives two examples. Both are meant to show that animals have an internal capacity to initiate or resist motion, and that this capacity distinguishes animal motion from the way in which inanimate objects are shoved around by external blows. Voluntary motion has an 'internal source' in a quite literal sense: it is produced by the animal's mind (*animus*), an organ in its chest.

The first example is of racehorses eager to burst from the gates (*DRN* 2.263–71). Lucretius claims that we see a slight delay between the external stimulus of the gates' opening and the resultant motion of the horses surging forward. This delay supposedly shows that motion initiated by the mind exists, as it takes some time for the mind's decision to move all of the matter of the horse in a co-ordinated manner. Motion caused by external blows, on the other hand, does not require time for internal processing: a horse struck from behind by another horse is immediately shoved forward.

The second example (*DRN* 2.272–83) appeals our own experience of situations such as being in a jostling crowd: we are not always helplessly shoved around by these outside forces but can sometimes fight against them to go where we wish. Imagine being carried down a river by its swift current unwillingly, sharp rocks looming downstream. Unlike an inanimate object, such as a log, we need not allow ourselves to be carried along but can fight against the current and swim for the shore in order to avoid danger.

The sort of freedom at stake here may be dubbed 'effective agency'. Two differences between it and 'free will' (as the phrase is often used) are worth underlining. First, effective agency is possessed by all animals that can do what they wish, including many that do not have the rational capacities needed to be rightly praised or blamed; many animals possess effective agency which do not have 'free will'.[6] Second, 'effective agency' need *not* involve the ability to do otherwise than one does. The

[6] We *hate* destructive wild animals like lions but cannot properly *blame* them. See Epic. *Nat.* 25 Arr. 34.25.21–34 (LS 20j; only in vol. 2). For the most recent edition of this text, parts of which are found preserved in *PHerc.* 697, 1056, and 1191, see Laursen 1997: 31.

horses Lucretius describes at the starting gates are not trying to decide *whether or not* to break from the gates, and a man caught in a current is not concerned with *whether or not* to swim for the shore. Instead, as Lucretius portrays it, volition is what allows them to move around in the world in order to obtain what they desire.[7] This ability to do as one wishes contrasts with the sort of 'two-way' power either to do or not to do something that is supposed by some to be necessary for free will.[8]

If we did not have this sort of volition, we would be utterly helpless. Epicurus probably has such helplessness in mind when he asserts that it would be better to believe in the meddling Olympian gods than to be a slave to the fate of the natural philosophers, since at least one can try to placate the Olympian gods, whereas the necessity of the natural philosophers would be inescapable. (*Ep. Men.* 133–4.)

If this is correct (it is controversial), then one influential and popular view of the role of the swerve in preserving our freedom is mistaken. Basically, on this view (a) determinism precludes us from having the sort of ability to do otherwise that is needed to have free will, (b) each free decision is constituted by atomic swerves in our minds, and (c) having decisions constituted by swerves in this way preserves our ability to do otherwise than we do because, for each action we perform, we could have done otherwise if those atomic swerves had not occurred as they did.[9] However, (i) this sort of 'two-sided' free will as a precondition of moral responsibility is not something the Epicureans wish to defend in the first place when they are talking about the swerve and our volitions, (ii) Lucretius does not work atomic swerves into his account of how volition arises and moves the body,[10] and (iii) even if Epicurus were concerned with a two-sided 'free will', a random atomic swerving in one's mind is an

[7] Bobzien 2000: 311 makes this point.

[8] See Bobzien 2000: 287–93 for more on this distinction.

[9] Bailey 1928: 838–42 and 1947: 318–23, 433–7; Purinton 1999, and Fowler's 2002 commentary on *DRN* 2.251–93 and app. 1 all advance (roughly) this view. See O'Keefe 2005: ch. 2 for a more nuanced discussion.

[10] Lucretius describes the atomic basis of *voluntas* and action in Book 4 of *DRN*. In his description, swerves play no direct role in the production of action. The action-theory in *DRN* 4 seems 'mechanistic', in the sense that, given the incoming stimulus and the state of the soul, action follows automatically. See Furley 1967: 210–26 and O'Keefe 2005: 37–42.

unpromising basis for the production of free and responsible actions, instead of random and blameless twitches.[11]

2b. *Epicurus on the Principle of Bivalence and the swerve*

Lucretius describes for us what sort of volition the Epicureans wish to protect against determinism. However, he does little to explain how causal determinism threatens its existence, or how introducing a random atomic swerve overcomes this threat.[12] For that, we need to turn to Cicero's *De Fato*, which describes a debate between the Epicureans, Stoics and Academic sceptics on issues of fate and freedom.

One of its central topics is the 'lazy argument', which is one member of a family of arguments, including the argument concerning tomorrow's Sea Battle in Aristotle's *De interpretatione* 9, that try to show that accepting the universal applicability of the Principle of Bivalence (PB) – the thesis that every proposition either is true or is false, including propositions about what will occur in the future – would have unacceptable consequences on our agency.[13] The type of determinism at issue here we might dub 'logical' determinism.[14] Here is a sketch of how this sort of argument goes.

You are sick, and you are trying to decide whether or not to call a doctor. However, if you accept PB, then either it is true (and has always been true) that you are going to recover from the disease, or true (and always has been true) that you will not recover (*Fat.* 29). But if either of two alternatives has been true from all eternity, that alternative is also necessary (*Fat.* 21), because the past is immutable.[15] And because there is no point in deliberating about what is necessary,[16] then it is pointless for me to worry now about whether or

[11] See Furley 1967: 163 and O'Keefe 2005: 44–6.

[12] See O'Keefe 2005: 30–2 and 35–7 for arguments that passages in Lucretius that are sometimes taken to show the role the swerve plays do not do so.

[13] For more on the sources and structure of these arguments, see Bobzien 1998: 76–81 and 180–93.

[14] This terminology comes from Long and Sedley 1987: vol. 1, p. 466.

[15] See *Fat.* 14. Diodorus and Chrysippus (and presumably Epicurus) consider the past necessary because it is unchangeable. See also *Fat.* 19–20, 21, 28, 29 and *DRN* 2.255: things that are true 'from eternity' or 'from infinity' are beyond our power to effect.

[16] *De int.* 9 18b31–6.

not to call the doctor, as if my present actions could change the outcome one way or the other (*Fat.* 28–9).

In connection with this argument, 'necessary' simply means what is inevitable or beyond our power to affect: mathematical truths, celestial motions and the past – Aristotle's examples of things we do not bother deliberating about – all cannot be changed by our efforts, and thus all are necessary. This immutability is also the reason the Stoic Chrysippus gives (against Cleanthes) for why the past is necessary (*Fat.* 14).

Contrast this argument with a typical argument for the incompatibility of free will and determinism: in this argument, the type of determinism is 'logical', not causal. Logical determinism is apparently incompatible with the contingency of the future (*not* with the ability to do otherwise), where this contingency is necessary for the effectiveness of deliberation and action (*not* for moral responsibility). Those important differences noted, it would be fair to dub Epicurus a 'lazy argument libertarian'. He asserts that it is obvious we engage in effective action and deliberation, that the future is therefore contingent, and accordingly he rejects 'logical' determinism (i.e. he rejects PB).[17]

Causal considerations are not present in the lazy argument as I described it. However, in order to escape the 'necessity of fate' that this argument would establish, Epicurus posited the swerve. Immediately after laying out the argument that the Principle of Bivalence would make everything in the future necessary (and in this sense fated), Cicero says, 'Epicurus thinks that the necessity of fate is avoided by the swerve of an atom' (*Fat.* 22).[18]

Both Epicurus and the Stoics think that logical and causal determinism are interentailing; let us call this the 'Interentailment Thesis'. Both the Stoics and Epicurus say that things which are true must have causes of their future being (*Fat.* 26; see also *Fat.* 19). The point is that, since the future is not yet – it has not obtained – there is not yet anything there in virtue of which a statement about the future can be true, unless there presently obtain conditions to bring about

[17] On most (although not all) interpretations of *De int.* 9, this is also Aristotle's position. For a brief discussion and pointers to further literature, see O'Keefe 2005: 135–7.

[18] Also see *Fat.* 18 and 48.

the state of affairs described by the statement.[19] (Likewise, for a statement about the future to presently be false, there must presently obtain conditions to preclude the state of affairs described by the statement.) So, if you are a 'lazy argument libertarian' like Epicurus and accept the Interentailment Thesis, you need some sort of physical mechanism – like the swerve – to underwrite the rejection of PB.[20]

Chrysippus' reply to the 'Lazy Argument' shows that this whole line of thought is misguided, since neither logical nor causal determinism are incompatible with effective agency. Just because it is fated that you will recover from a disease does not make your calling the doctor in order to recover from that disease pointless. Chrysippus says that certain events are 'co-fated': for instance, it is fated (and causally determined) *both* that I will recover from the disease *and* that I will call the doctor; it is through my fated action of calling the doctor that my fated recovery will occur (*Fat.* 30). As long as my calling the doctor is causally efficacious in bringing about its purpose, it is not pointless, and causally determined actions can be causally efficacious. Even if it is causally determined that you'll recover, counterfactuals like 'if you do not call the doctor, you'll die' can still be true.

3. ATOMISM AND SELF-FORMATION OF CHARACTER

3a. Reason and desire

Introducing the swerve, then, helps preserve our agency by securing the contingency of the future and thereby saving us from the 'fate of the natural philosophers'. But this is not the only threat to our freedom that Epicurus sees the need to counter. The greatest fruit of self-sufficiency is freedom (*SV* 77), freedom from being dependent on whims of chance to fulfil our desires. Such a dependency would

[19] The Interentailment Thesis is questionable, and it is rightly questioned by Carneades, the head of the sceptical Academy. See *Fat.* 26–33 and O'Keefe 2005: 140–9, 153–9.

[20] See O'Keefe 2005: ch. 6 for more details and argument. Warren 2006 also discusses the truth-conditions for statements concerning the past and future, and the ontological status of the past and future, for the Epicureans.

make us vulnerable and hence fearful (*Ep. Men.* 130–1). At the centre of the Epicurean ethical program is limiting one's desires in order to attain self-sufficiency.[21]

Epicurean psychology is hedonistic. Pleasure and pain motivate all of our action and lie at the root of every action (*Fin.* 1.42, 1.23).[22] Cases of evildoing are explained by saying that the malefactor has incorrect beliefs about what will bring him pleasure.[23] This *psychological* hedonism is the chief argument for their *ethical* hedonism. The good is the end to which all other things are means, and never itself a means to an end (*Fin.* 1.9). To discover what this end is, we ought to look at what creatures actually *do* pursue as the ultimate end of all of their actions, and this is to attain pleasure and avoid pain (*Fin.* 1.30).[24] Given that you desire pleasure, and you believe that doing *X* will bring you pleasure more effectively than any other available course of action, you'll do *X*.

This psychological hedonism does not threaten our freedom, however, because our beliefs are under our control. We live in a sick society that teaches us we need wealth and social status so that we can engage in continuous drinking bouts, enjoy the sexual favours of boys and women, and consume fish and the other dainties of an extravagant table (*Ep. Men.* 132). If our actions were controlled by such desires, this enslavement would lead to misery. But, Epicurus thinks, we can modify such desires, by using our reason. We can discover the limits of pleasure and distinguish between natural and necessary desires, merely natural desires, and vain and empty desires (*KD* 18–22, 29–30). We can ask, of every desire we have, 'what will happen if I get what I desire, and what will happen if I do not?' (*SV* 71). Using our reason, we can overcome hate, envy and contempt (DL 10.117). Reason allows us to do this by showing us that certain desires, temperaments and ways of life are not effective for getting us what we ultimately desire for its own sake, pleasure.

This reasons-responsiveness distinguishes us from other animals. Humans can control their own development, while non-human

[21] See Woolf, ch. 9, this volume.

[22] See also Cic. *Fin.* 1.30, *Fin.* 2.60ff., and Epic. *Ep. Men.* 128.

[23] *KD* 7, 10, *SV* 16, Cic. *Fin.* 1.32–3, 55.

[24] See O'Keefe 2001a: 273–6 for more on Epicurean psychological hedonism, and Cooper 1999a for an extended argument that Epicurus is only an ethical, and not a psychological, hedonist. Cf. Woolf 2004 for criticisms of Cooper's arguments.

animals cannot. Lucretius gives the clearest Epicurean statement of this doctrine. For example: lions are naturally irascible because their souls contain many fire atoms; stags are timid because they have more wind atoms (*DRN* 3.288ff.). People also have natural temperaments: some are naturally easily moved to anger, while others are too fearful (*DRN* 3.307–19). These differences cannot be erased entirely, but the traces of these natural temperaments that remain beyond the power of reason to expel are so trivial that they do nothing to impede our living a life worthy of the gods (*DRN* 3.320–2).[25] Other Epicurean authors also assert that it is our reasoning abilities that set us apart from animals. We can calculate the outcomes of different possible courses of action, whereas animals have only 'irrational memory'. Animals lack prudential concepts like 'healthy' and 'expedient', ethical concepts like 'fine' and 'base', and signs. They cannot take precautions before suffering something and cannot reflect on their lives as a whole and make them consistent.[26]

3b. *Atomism and the mind*

Epicurus wishes to preserve the efficacy of our reason. One part of this project is to account for the emergence and causal efficacy of things such as human reason within an atomistic world-view. Epicurus' efforts here are spurred by the troubles he thinks were encountered by his atomist predecessor, Democritus. Epicurus believes the following:[27]

(A) The basic constituents of the world are atoms and void. They are eternal and unchanging in their intrinsic properties. The stock of atomic properties, e.g. size, shape and resistance to blows, is very limited.

(B) Atoms cluster together to form aggregates, which are mutable and temporary. These compound bodies, which include all of the macroscopic bodies we see and our minds, are real.

(C) These aggregates have properties and powers that individual atoms do not, and in order to account for these properties and powers, we often need to look to the structural features of

[25] See Gill, ch. 7, and Tsouna, ch. 14, this volume.
[26] These authors are discussed in Annas 1993a: 66–9.
[27] See also Morel, ch. 4, this volume.

aggregates, which arise because of the spatial relations holding between the atoms that constitute the aggregate, the ways in which they have become entangled with one another, and so forth. These properties and powers are real, and include relational properties like being enslaved or being healthy.

Epicurus and Democritus share a commitment to (A). However, Epicurus thinks Democritus is overly restrictive in what he allows into his ontology, and hence encounters difficulties in his epistemology and his philosophy of mind. Let me first briefly describe their epistemological disagreement, as it will help illuminate their differences in philosophy of mind.

Famously, Democritus asserts that sensible qualities like sweetness, bitterness, and heat exist only 'by convention', whereas in reality there are atoms and the void (DK 68 B9). Because honey tastes sweet to some and bitter to others, Democritus infers that the honey is in itself neither. The Epicureans think that this eliminativism with regard to sensible qualities leads Democritus to deny that knowledge is possible.[28] To avoid this scepticism, which would make life impossible to lead, Epicurus staunchly defends the reality of sensible qualities. It is true, for instance, that there is a mixture of natures in wine such that a certain amount of it may affect one person one way, another person another way, and that wine is neither universally cooling nor universally heating.[29] But it does not follow from this that wine is 'no more cooling than heating', or that we are mistaken to say that the wine itself is cooling or heating, as long as we put in the proper qualifications: *for whom* the wine is cooling, and *under what circumstances*. In fact, this sort of relativity is just what we should expect if we understand the meaning of terms like 'being heating' or 'being nutritious', and to think otherwise is naive.[30] So, strongly affirming (C) allows the Epicureans to avoid scepticism. Even though sensible properties exist only at the macroscopic level, depend on the

[28] Plut. *Adv. Col.* 1108F. Whether Democritus thinks that knowledge is merely difficult or impossible to attain is disputed. See Hankinson 1995: 47–50 and 1998: 201–5 for an introduction to the texts and issues, Curd 2001 for an argument that Democritus is not a sceptic, and chs. 8 and 9 of Lee 2005.

[29] Plut. *Adv. Col.* 1109F–1110D.

[30] Polystratus *De cont. irr.* (*PHerc.* 336/1150), XXIII.26–XXVI.23 Indelli.

structural features of bodies for their existence, and are (in some sense) observer-relative, they are nonetheless real.[31]

Now on to the mind. Epicureans think (perhaps wrongly) that Democritus' eliminativism extends far beyond sensible qualities. Plutarch's *Against Colotes* gives the fullest statement of this Epicurean charge against Democritus.[32] In his version of Democritus' famous saying 'By convention, <this, that, and the other>, in reality atoms and void' (DK 68 B9), the Epicurean Colotes includes *compounds* among the things that are for Democritus merely 'by convention' and says that anybody who believes this couldn't conceive of himself as a human or as alive – presumably because humans are compound bodies (*Adv. Col.* 1110E). Plutarch agrees with this radical interpretation of Democritus' ontology, and he spells out the eliminative position as follows: atoms flying through the void collide and entangle with one another, and the resulting atomic aggregates may *appear* to be water, or fire or a human, but in reality nothing other than atoms and the void exists. Plutarch notes that a result of this is that colours and the mind (*psuchē*) do not exist.[33] So Epicurus also needs to find a way of defending the reality of the mind and of mental properties against the threat of Democritean eliminativism.

But the same sort of reply is available to the Epicureans in the case of compound bodies generally as it is in the case of sensible qualities: once we understand the meaning of predicates like *being heating* it would be naive to think that properties like being heating are unreal just because they're relative. Likewise, in the case of macroscopic bodies, Epicurus himself regularly refers to them as being merely aggregates of atoms, but he refuses to draw the conclusion that, as atomic aggregates, they are somehow unreal.[34] Epicurus admits that some things (atoms and void) are indestructible and unchanging, while

[31] See O'Keefe 1997 for further discussion.

[32] But see also Diogenes of Oinoanda 7.II.2–14 Smith.

[33] I think that this is an uncharitable reading of Democritus that is inconsistent with too many other things he says to be rightly ascribed to him: see O'Keefe 1997: 122–3 and Taylor 1999: 152. However, it is not a lunatic reading of Democritus, and some (e.g. Wardy 1988) defend it. Pasnau 2007 is agnostic but thinks this 'radical' reading has a lot going for it, and he gives a thoughtful discussion of what exactly the position amounts to.

[34] See Morel, ch. 4, in this volume and O'Keefe 2005: 68–9.

others (aggregates and their properties) are generated and mutable, but Colotes insists that Epicurus is wiser than Plato in applying the name 'beings' (*onta*) equally to all of them alike (*Adv. Col.* 1116C–D).

To put it in resolutely anachronistic terms, let us imagine a group of atoms arranged tablewise: Democritus (on the Epicurean interpretation) will say 'we thought that there was a genuine object there, a table, but this is mistaken; in reality there is just a bunch of atoms arranged tablewise, nothing else'.[35] The Epicureans, on the other hand, will say that a macroscopic object like a table can be *identified* with a bunch of atoms arranged tablewise, and as such, is perfectly real. Likewise with the mind.

Holding theses (B) and (C) need commit Epicurus to an 'emergent' view of the mind in only a weak sense. Somebody can hold that the mind is real and that it has powers and properties none of its constituent atoms do, while identifying the mind with a bodily organ that is nothing more than an atomic aggregate and mental events with bodily events that are explained from the 'bottom up' in terms of the motions of the atoms that compose the mind. In fact, I think that this *is* the Epicurean view, as the fullest and best-preserved Epicurean texts on the topic heavily point toward an Identity Theory of the mind.[36] However, this interpretation is contentious: it is clear that Epicurus wishes to preserve the reality of the mental (and of our reason, in particular) against the threat of Democritean eliminative materialism, but less widely accepted that he counters this threat by reaffirming the mind's reality within a reductionist theory. The controversies largely centre on how to understand the extant portions of Book 25 of *On Nature*, Epicurus' *magnum opus*. The passages we have contain a self-refutation argument against those who hold that everything occurs 'of necessity' (which I discuss below), and a description of human psychological development, including the relationship between psychological states and the atoms that constitute the mind.

Going into detail on these issues would far exceed the scope of this essay.[37] The text is in terrible shape (it was buried in the eruption of Mount Vesuvius in AD 79) and bristles with unexplained technical

[35] See van Inwagen 1990 for an extended argument that no (non-biological) composite material objects exist.

[36] See Gill, ch. 7, in this volume and O'Keefe 2005: 78–81.

[37] Readers wanting more detail can consult O'Keefe 2005: ch. 4. Atherton 2007 gives detailed criticisms of my reading of these texts and of the overall interpretation.

terminology. It is hard to overstate its obscurity. In it, Epicurus asserts that psychological 'products' (*apogegennēmena*) arise, and it is these products, and *not* the nature of the atoms, which are responsible for a person developing in the particular way he does. These products differ from the atoms in a 'differential' (*dialēptikon*) way, and they acquire the 'cause out of itself', which then reaches as far as the 'first natures' (*prōtōn phuseōn*).[38]

My best guess as to what any of this means, so that it is consistent with the other texts we have, is that we can *distinguish* between the psychological products and the atoms of the mind in thought (we can 'differentiate' between them; compare Epicurus' discussion in *Ep. Hdt.* 69 of how we do this with the permanent attributes of a body), even though the product is just an aspect of the atomic aggregate. However, once we do so, we see that the proper way to explain why people acquire the characters they do, e.g. why somebody is irascible, is by referring to the operations of these complicated psychological developments, not to the natures of the atoms that constitute the mind. For instance, an explanation of why some adult grew up to become a hot-head will be a complicated story referring to his beliefs, environment, ideals, etc., not just to the preponderance of fiery atoms in his mind. Our ability to shape our own character reaches as far as our 'first natures', i.e. to the congenital dispositions Lucretius discusses as amenable to reason. Others have read Epicurus as here asserting the causal *independence* of emergent psychological states from the atoms that constitute the mind, states which then exert 'downwards causation' and move the soul's atoms (the 'first natures'), or they think that Epicurus is here recognizing the incompatibility of atomic causal necessitation with explanations in terms of goals or reasons, while insisting that the latter are real.[39]

[38] See Laursen 1995 and 1997 for the latest edition of *On Nature* 25, parts of which are found preserved in PHerc. 697, 1056 and 1191. The passage discussed here is Laursen 1997: 19–23; an earlier version is Arr. 34.21–2 (LS 20B). See Gill, ch. 7, this volume, for further discussion of this text.

[39] Sedley 1983 and 1988 asserts that psychological states are 'radically emergent' and exert 'downwards causation'. For the incompatibility of causal necessitation and explanations in terms of goals or reasons, see Asmis 1990a and Wendlandt and Baltzly 2004. On Asmis' view (which is not based on *On Nature* 25), Epicurus is trying to accommodate goal-directed movement generally, with the swerve directly involved in every animal action. According to Wendlandt and Baltzly, Epicurus is (for broadly Davidsonian reasons) denying causal necessitation via the swerve in order to make room for normative explanations by reasons.

4. REASON AND RESPONSIBILITY

Finally, Epicurus is concerned to defend the appropriateness of our practices of praise, blame and punishment, in which we hold one another responsible for our actions. This concern is closest to our contemporary concerns regarding free will and determinism. Diogenes of Oinoanda (an Epicurean from the second century AD) says that all censure and admonition would be abolished if fate controlled what we did, but that Epicurus discovered the swerve and countered this threat. Epicurus, likewise, when arguing that some things 'depend on us', says praise and blame properly attach to such things, contrasting them with those due to chance or necessity, and in *On Nature* 25, he says that our practices of criticizing each other presuppose that the cause of actions is 'in ourselves'.[40]

These passages are suggestive, but they leave open what it is for our actions to 'depend on us', or for their causes to be 'in ourselves'. To help us understand what Epicurus means, we should examine his argument that it is self-refuting to deny that we are responsible for our actions.

A brief version of the argument is preserved as *Vatican Saying* 40: 'The man who says all events are necessitated has no ground for criticizing the man who says that not all events are necessitated. For according to him this is itself a necessitated event' (tr. Long and Sedley). As it stands, this seems plainly inadequate. If I deny that people are responsible for their actions, then I cannot consistently assert that the person who says that they are responsible is *blameworthy* for saying so. But for all that, my position may still be true and my opponent's false, and I can criticize his position as false and his arguments as inadequate.

On Nature 25 gives the argument in more detail. It follows Epicurus' discussion of how we can use our reason to develop our own character. Further evidence for this ability, says Epicurus, is that we rebuke, oppose and reform each other as if the responsibility for what we do lies also 'in ourselves', not just in our congenital dispositions and in our environment. To argue against this thesis and to maintain that everything we do happens of necessity is self-refuting,

[40] Diogenes of Oinoanda 54 Smith; Epicurus *Ep. Men.* 133; Epicurus *Nat.* 25 Arr. 34.26–30 (LS 20C); Laursen 1997: 32–41 has the latest text.

because the person who engages in debate assumes that he is responsible for reasoning correctly and his opponent is responsible for talking nonsense. (An alternative translation is that we rebuke, oppose and reform each other as if the *cause* for what we do lies in ourselves, and that the person who debates these matters assumes that he himself is the *cause* of his reasoning correctly and his opponent himself the *cause* of his talking nonsense.)

But this invites an obvious counter-argument. Perhaps I must presuppose certain things when I engage in debate, e.g. that I have *reasons* for my position, that my interlocutor has reason so that she can understand my arguments, and that by offering her those reasons, I may change her mind. The proposition 'human reason is ineffective' is not self-contradictory, but to *argue* for it does seem to be self-refuting. Nonetheless, even granted this, Epicurus' conclusion does not follow: just because our actions are necessitated does not imply that practices of praise, blame and debate are ineffective. We simply may be the sorts of creatures who necessarily act in such a way that rational considerations can play a role in determining what we do.

Epicurus responds that this counter-argument misses the point – the relevant senses of what 'depends on us' and of 'necessity' here involve the distinction between actions that are under our rational control and those that are not. According to Epicurus, our preconceptions of necessity and of our own responsibility arise by observing ourselves in action.[41] We see that sometimes we can do things we do not want to (e.g., submit to a root canal now to avoid greater pain later), and that we can dissuade others from doing something they are considering only because they are being threatened (e.g. convince someone not to betray his friend despite the prospect of the rack). It is from these observations that we arrive at the standards by which we delineate which actions are of necessity and which ones depend on us. We show our awareness of the distinction in our interactions: we try to dissuade others from actions that 'depend on us', which would be pointless for those that are of necessity.

According to Epicurus, to say that something is necessary for us but that we still have rational control over it is to misuse the term – to 'call necessitation empty'. To show that our actions really are all

[41] For more on *prolēpsis*, or 'preconception' see Asmis, ch. 5, and Atherton, ch. 11, this volume, and Asmis 1984: 19–80.

necessitated, one must 'prove that we have a preconception of a kind which has faulty delineations', i.e. prove that the empirical basis of our concept somehow fundamentally misrepresents the way things are. Since our observations of ourselves and others deliberating and arguing with one another are the basis of the concepts in question, an example of this would be proving that the reasons we thought drove our behaviour were really just after-the-fact rationalizations, and that both our 'reasons' and our behaviour had a common, sub-rational cause.[42] Unless somebody is perversely maintaining this sort of thesis, says Epicurus, or 'makes it clear what fact he is rebutting or introducing' in saying our actions happen of necessity, 'it is merely a word that is being changed'.[43]

The central point of Epicurus' theory, then, is that we are responsible agents because we are rational.[44] Any concerns about bivalence, determinism or the ontology of the mind are ancillary to preserving our ability, as rational agents, to act effectively, to improve our character by thinking about what we really need, to improve the characters of others through our practices of praise and blame and to attain tranquillity.

[42] See Wegner 2002 for an argument of this sort and Nahmias 2002 for a good summary and able criticisms.

[43] See O'Keefe 2005: 81–93 for a more detailed discussion; the preceding line of argument is still from *On Nature* 25 (see n. 37 for references).

[44] Annas 1993a: 70 gives this pithy summation.

RAPHAEL WOOLF

9 Pleasure and desire

Pleasure is the goal of life for an Epicurean. But it is pleasure of a particular kind that represents this goal, namely lack of pain in body (*aponia*) and lack of distress in soul (*ataraxia*).[1] It is clear that, for Epicurus, to be free from bodily pain and mental distress is, in and of itself, to be in a state of pleasure. He does not recognize a neutral state of neither pleasure nor pain; for a percipient subject, being without pain is already pleasant. Equally, however, Epicurus does not hold that the only pleasure to be had is freedom from pain. The pleasures of the profligate, which he tells us do not represent the Epicurean goal (*Ep. Men.* 131), certainly are pleasures as far as Epicurus is concerned, since he calls them that, though he adds that such pleasures do not generate a pleasant life – it is 'sober reasoning' that does so (*Ep. Men.* 132).[2]

An abridged version of this paper was read to the King's College London philosophy department staff seminar in February 2007; some of its themes were hatched in a presentation to a King's graduate seminar on the *Letter to Menoeceus* in Autumn 2006. I would like to thank the participants at both events for helpful discussion, and James Warren for valuable editorial input. Responsibility for the views expressed in this chapter is mine alone.

[1] *Ep. Men.* 131. In fact Epicurus does not hold simply that Epicureans do seek this end and others should, but that everyone as a matter of psychological fact seeks freedom from pain and distress as their goal of life. What he thinks non-Epicureans do in general is go about their pursuit of this goal in a misguided way. I have defended this view in Woolf 2004, and shall not return to the topic here. For a case against reading Epicurus as a psychological hedonist see Cooper 1999a: 485–94.

[2] Epicurus may have in mind here the Cyrenaics, his main hedonistic rivals, who advocate enjoying the pleasures of the moment. For discussion of Cyrenaic ethical theory, see Annas 1993b: 227–36, Long 1999. See also nn. 19 and 27 below.

These points will be elaborated and (where appropriate) qualified as we proceed.[3] But I wish to organize the discussion around an issue suggested by Epicurus' apparent coolness towards extravagance. It is perhaps tempting to see Epicurus as advocating a somewhat ascetic lifestyle here. In addition to his advocacy of sober reasoning and the rather scornful attitude towards the pleasures of the profligate, one might also mention remarks such as that bread and water provide the height of pleasure for one in need (*Ep. Men.* 131), as well as his advocacy of self-sufficiency as a great good (130).

Epicurus, to be sure, indicates that he is already aware that misunderstanding or malevolence may have caused opponents of his position to treat its positing of pleasure as the goal as tantamount to recommending luxury and lack of restraint (*Ep. Men.* 131).[4] It would, then, be a poignant historical irony if the figure of the Epicurean as lover of luxury should be so far removed from actual Epicurean doctrine, if this sets as a condition of the good life that one abstain from luxury and aim to satisfy only one's basic needs.[5]

Fortunately, it is a mistake to read Epicurus in quite this way. His attitude towards luxury turns out to be rather different from outright rejection, and a closer examination of this feature of his ethical stance may shed some broader light on his view of pleasure, its relation to desire, and its role in our lives.

I

Let me begin with perhaps a rather unlikely point of comparison. Consider this succinctly charming description of Wittgenstein's procedure in disposing of his inheritance:

[3] I shall focus mainly on Epicurus' own writings, both for reason of space and from a sense that the founder's words, where available, should have a certain primacy.

[4] An early source for this view may have been the Epicurean apostate Timocrates, who, we are picturesquely told, accused Epicurus of over-indulgence to the point of vomiting twice daily (DL 10.6). On Timocrates and his influence see Sedley 1976: 127–32, though Sedley's description of Epicurus' actual position as 'bordering on asceticism' (130) perhaps makes it unnecessarily hard to see how Timocrates' caricature might have taken hold.

[5] According to Erler and Schofield 1999: 643, 'Epicurus in fact extols a kind of asceticism, a reduction in the number and scope of our desires dictated by reason'. I shall argue that, notwithstanding his view on desire (discussed in section IV below), Epicurus by no means exhorts us to avoid luxury; in that sense he is no ascetic.

Born of a wealthy family, but convinced of the corrupting influence of money, he [Wittgenstein] gave away his inheritance to the rich, so as not to corrupt the innocent.[6]

One who has the attitude attributed here to Wittgenstein will regard luxury and material wealth in general as intrinsically harmful. To experience it is thereby to be corrupted; hence one should minimize the damage by bestowing it only on those who, already being in possession of it, are already corrupted. Epicurus' view is some distance from that of Wittgenstein.[7] Luxury, according to Epicurus, is in fact to be welcomed, just so long as its possession does not detract from the maintenance or attainment of a pain and trouble free state; and it need not do this, he holds, so long as one has the right attitude towards luxury: namely, that it is to be enjoyed if present, but not missed if absent.

Let me offer a somewhat mundane example. Imagine that one has a seat booked in economy class on a forthcoming flight. It turns out on arrival at the airport that there are spare seats in business class. (Let us for present purposes regard business class as a luxurious way to travel, and economy as at least allowing the satisfaction of basic needs.) The airline generously offers to upgrade a randomly selected group of passengers at no extra charge. A follower of Wittgenstein, shunning luxury as corrupting, will refuse the offer. The Epicurean, it seems to me, will accept. The Epicurean had no desire for or expectation of an upgrade, is perfectly content without one, and would remain so if unselected. Nonetheless, business class offers more opportunities for pleasure than economy, and the offer is therefore to be accepted. The good Epicurean will take these opportunities, but without any expectation or desire that they will come along again in the future, perfectly content, going forward, with economy class flights.

[6] Found at www.hotelfilosoof.nl (go to the 'Wittgenstein room'). I have not attempted to verify the view of Wittgenstein's psyche implied here. The Cambridge Wittgenstein archive (www.wittgen-cam.ac.uk) relates that after some earlier disbursements to Austrian artists of slender means Wittgenstein distributed his inheritance amongst his siblings. Notwithstanding his famously ascetic lifestyle, references to 'Wittgenstein' in this chapter should be read with scare quotes firmly in place.

[7] Were there contemporaries of Epicurus who advocated asceticism? The most plausible candidates are perhaps the Cynics, and it is interesting that Epicurus appears to have held that one should not adopt Cynic ways (DL 10.121). We are told that Crates the Cynic sold his property for a considerable sum and distributed the proceeds to his fellow-citizens (DL 6.87; compare Wittgenstein).

Consider now a third case, of someone who regards it as an ordeal to travel economy but who has booked an economy ticket in the erroneous belief that business class on this and other suitable flights was full (or perhaps it was simply too expensive). Our traveller arrives full of dread at the prospect of economy travel, is beset by anxious expectation at the possibility of an upgrade, and awash with relief at being one of those selected – but would have had despondency intensified if the offer had gone to others. Evidently this person has entirely the wrong attitude towards the situation from the point of view of maintaining equanimity in a properly Epicurean fashion; but what determines this is not the fact that the upgrade will be accepted if offered, since (I have suggested) the Epicurean will make the same choice. Luxury is not itself corrupting, but one's beliefs about its value may be, beliefs that Epicurus will term 'empty' (see section IV below). The Epicurean, one might think, strikes rather an attractive mean between the respective puritanism and fastidiousness, equally neurotic in their own way, of the other two characters in our scenario.

II

Let us turn to the texts both to flesh out the claim that one with a properly Epicurean attitude will opt for luxury in such circumstances, and to provide evidence in its favour. Perhaps the most important passage in this regard is the one that contains Epicurus' remarks on the value of self-sufficiency (*Ep. Men.* 130):[8]

We consider self-sufficiency a great good, not in order that in all circumstances we use little, but so that, if we do not have much, we be satisfied with little, having been genuinely persuaded that luxury (*poluteleia*) is most pleasantly enjoyed by those who need it least, and that what is natural is all easy to procure, and what is empty is hard to procure.

The passage suggests that, contra Wittgenstein, luxury is not necessarily to be avoided. To be exact, the avoidance of luxury is said not to be the aim of self-sufficiency; but it would be odd to emphasize this

[8] See here Irwin 1986: 103–4, who notes that the passage presents an outlook markedly different from asceticism; also Annas 1993b: 197. Irwin 1979: 194 maintains that *KD* 15 supports an ascetic viewpoint. But in contrasting nature's wealth with that of empty opinion the text targets not luxury itself but, in a familiar Epicurean way, the false belief that it can bring contentment.

point if Epicurus had some other reason, unstated here, for advocating such avoidance. His clear purport is that it is no part of the Epicurean life to shun luxury when it presents itself. Rather, the point is that one be content with the little that (Epicurus believes) is always ready to hand in the natural order of things, thus maintaining peace of mind, and bodily satisfaction, in all eventualities.

More strongly than this, equipped with the belief that little will always suffice, we should indeed choose plenty where available. For it could hardly be the case that Epicurus would declare luxury to be most enjoyable for the one who has no need of it unless he were advocating that, for the one who does have no need of it, it is to be opted for.[9] The logical structure of the earlier portion of the passage has a similar message: we advocate *x*, not in order that *y*, but so that if we don't have *z* (the opposite of *y*), we are content with *y*. Compare, for example: 'we advocate umbrellas, not in order that it may rain, but so that if we don't have dry weather we are content with rain.' Whoever made this perhaps unlikely declaration would be implying at any rate that dry weather is preferable to rain. Epicurus' wording likewise suggests that, in terms of our example, business class is preferable to economy, though the latter will suffice if the former is unavailable.

Nor, it seems to me, does Epicurus have the view that it is only the occasional enjoyment of luxury that is to be recommended,[10] too much being likely to corrupt in a way that may draw him rather closer than I have been urging to the outlook of Wittgenstein. What may encourage this reading is that he does say a little later that one should accustom oneself to a simple and non-luxurious way of life; and he offers various reasons in favour of doing this, one of which is that it puts us in a better position to deal with luxuries when we encounter them from time to time (*Ep. Men.* 131). So perhaps

[9] Epicurus is said to have written that, content with bread and water, a bit of cheese would enable him to 'live luxuriously' (*poluteleusasthai*, DL 10.11). While certainly emphasizing his own self-sufficiency, Epicurus does not seek to *restrict* the scope of 'luxury' to such modest items (as *Ep. Men.* 132 on the luxuries of the table makes clear), which would threaten to trivialize his remarks on the relation between luxury and need.

[10] So Brunschwig and Sedley 2003: 161. 'The life-style both preached and practised by the Epicureans was ... one of simple frugality, punctuated with just occasional feasts and other indulgences.'

Epicurus' point is that only a limited exposure to luxury is advisable, more than that being liable to cause a dependence that will make us crave it in its absence and be anxious about losing it even while we have it, thereby destroying the peace of mind that is at the core of Epicurus' ethical theory.

This is to read Epicurus the wrong way round. Absence of anxiety being a main part of the goal, we are not to strive for that which is difficult to obtain. If we do, then our beliefs are misguided, and we are in need of Epicurean therapy.[11] But we are not told to *confine* ourselves to the occasional bout of luxury, as if our task is to fend off all those other luxurious opportunities that are likely to befall us. Rather, luxury is not the sort of thing that tends to come our way at all; if it does, this will most likely be only occasional. Similarly, getting accustomed to a simple life is not a matter of *going out of our way* to ensure that, say, some suitably high proportion of our meals consists of plain fare. The latter is what nature provides whether or not we are prepared to compromise peace of mind by striving for what is not readily at hand.

Accustoming oneself to the simple life is not then primarily a matter of having to organize one's life in a certain way, though consequences for how one lives will undoubtedly follow. Accustoming oneself is *accepting* the simple life as adequate – getting used to it in the normal idiomatic sense of that phrase, with no implication that what one gets used to has to be, even if it generally will be, a permanent or near permanent condition. One who is thus accustomed to the simple life is then perfectly at liberty to enjoy spells of luxury, long or short, should these happen to come along. Epicurus evinces no particular sense that only a large quantity of simplicity with (at most) a small dose of luxury will keep one on the path of good living.[12] Rather, if one accepts simplicity as adequate to one's needs, luxury

[11] For more on the topic of therapy see Tsouna, ch. 14, this volume, with references.

[12] One of the reasons given by Epicurus for accustoming oneself to simplicity is that this conduces to health (*Ep. Men.* 131). Is he advising, on medical grounds, that luxury for the most part be avoided? Then why not say, more succinctly, that simplicity conduces to health? The emphasis on habituation makes a sharper point if it is recommending the benefit of being *psychologically* adjusted to the simple life, the idea of a healthy mental state having received prominence at the start of the *Letter* (cf. *to kata psuchēn hugiainon*, 122).

may be enjoyed with a wholeheartedness unavailable to one who would be discomfited by its removal.

To accustom oneself to a certain situation nonetheless would normally mean that one is at least in the situation to which one is accustoming oneself. If so, then there may be circumstances in which the subject does actually have to make a deliberate decision to practise simplicity, and avoid luxury, in order thereby to become accustomed to the former. This might apply to someone born to luxury, for example. But Epicurus is free to lay down a, so to speak, purely psychological procedure, such that one might, say, simply repeat to oneself until fully internalized that if luxury were to be lost, one would be quite content with simplicity.[13] If so, luxury need not militate against a properly Epicurean outlook even when it is all one has known and maybe will know.

This kind of procedure is clearly envisaged in a different but relevant case, namely one's attitude towards death, fear of which (Epicurus holds) is one of the main sources of human anxiety. Epicurus bids us accustom ourselves to *thinking* that death is nothing to us (*Ep. Men.* 124). Evidently we cannot get used to death in a sense that would require us to experience it (death in any case is incompatible with percipience, *ibid.*), but that is no reason to suppose that we cannot come to accept it as no evil. By the same token, it should be open to one who has no experience of the simple life to accept it as fully compatible with happiness. Just as we can truly enjoy life only if unafraid of death (*Ep. Men.* 125), so having no fear of simplicity equips us to get the most out of luxury should it be ours to enjoy.

III

It may seem at this point that luxury has a rather more respectable place in Epicurus' system than his undoubtedly scornful remarks about the pleasures of the profligate would indicate. One has to be a little careful here, however. As was noted earlier, the downgrading of such pleasures is made in the context of opponents' misinterpretation of the Epicurean goal. The goal is indeed freedom from disturbance,

[13] For a discussion of the cognitive mechanics of this kind of procedure see Bobzien 2006.

physical and mental, not feasting or drinking-bouts. It is as *falsely occupying* this role that such pleasures are to be scorned.

Moreover, in speaking of the pleasures of the profligate, Epicurus may be criticizing not so much a certain type of pleasurable activity (e.g. feasting or drinking), or the felt pleasure derived from such activity, as a certain type of person who may be found enjoying such activities. His point would be levelled against one who went for this kind of pleasure *heedlessly*, without factoring in considerations about, say, future bodily pain brought on by over-indulgence, anxiety caused by over-dependence, and so on.[14] As *KD* 10 implies, it is those who pursue these pleasures as if they brought freedom from pain and fear who deserve reproach; if that freedom were attained, Epicurus would not rebuke anyone for being 'filled with pleasures from all sides'.

That we have a critique of a thoughtless approach rather than a type of pleasure ('luxurious') as such is borne out by the contrast Epicurus draws with sober reasoning as that which, by seeking out the proper bases of choice and avoidance, generates the pleasant life (*Ep. Men.* 131). It is worth noting in this regard that Epicurus could in principle have made the contrast between *any* kind of pleasure, simple included, on the one hand, and reasoning on the other. Labelling the reasoning 'sober' lays stress on thoughtfulness, and we get a rhetorically more vivid contrast with drinking-bouts than we would with sips of plain water, but Epicurus does not say that it is sober *pleasures* as opposed to luxurious ones that generate the pleasant life. Reason and pleasure are the elements of the contrast, not pleasures of different kinds.

In the light of this, it seems right to take Epicurus' point to be advocacy of the thoughtful approach to pleasure, not the lauding of simple pleasures (which are unmentioned here) over luxurious ones. And this chimes well with his earlier description of the workings of a calculus of pleasure and pain in decision-making, such that one rejects pleasures that bring greater pains in their wake, and chooses pains that will result in greater pleasures (*Ep. Men.* 129). The decision

[14] Relevant here is Epicurus' claim that the virtuous and the pleasant life go hand-in-hand (*Ep. Men.* 132; *KD* 5). Injustice is to be avoided given the consequent fear of discovery (*KD* 34, 35), whilst striving for gain (ill-gotten or otherwise) will have limited appeal for one who regards happiness as independent of wealth (cf. *SV* 81).

procedure is described quite neutrally, without reference to simplicity or luxury, let alone to the former trumping the latter.[15]

Mention of the calculus does, however, strengthen the thought that an Epicurean would be expected to choose luxury over simplicity (say business class over economy) so long as equanimity were not thereby compromised. Doubtless part of the consideration would be whether this particular experience of luxury was indeed likely to cause, say, some degree of desire for it in its absence, which of course would be unhealthy on Epicurean terms. But there is no evidence that, as far as Epicurus is concerned, one who has accepted the simple life as nature's way – one who has accepted, thus, that luxury is not necessary for contentment – is liable to have that view changed by the mere fact of experiencing luxury. On the contrary he is clear, as we have seen, that to have accepted this is precisely to be in a position then to gain the maximum enjoyment of luxury. At this point, Epicurus has no wish to deny the obvious, that, subject to the details of the given case, sober reasoning might be expected to declare that luxury promises a greater quantum of pleasure than simplicity, and is thereby to be chosen.

This surely does not militate against Epicurus' dictum that bread and water bring the height of pleasure when brought to one in need. For it seems true to say that when one is suffering brute hunger and thirst (assuming this is what Epicurus has in mind in talking of need) the difference between simple and more elaborate fare is at least significantly attenuated in terms of pleasure produced, and is perhaps nullified or even reversed in some cases. So too with his immediately preceding remark that plain food gives the same pleasure as luxurious fare when the removal of pain caused by want is at issue (*Ep. Men.* 130). There are cases where luxury seems not to outflank simplicity in hedonic terms, and cases where it fairly obviously does. Epicurus seems no more than sensible in the way he acknowledges this.

His emphasis here on need is reflected in his earlier comments that we have need of pleasure when we are in pain through pleasure's absence, and that when we are not in pain we no longer need pleasure (*Ep. Men.* 128). The comments seem carefully restricted in their wording. Epicurus does not say that we cannot *get* pleasure when

[15] For detailed discussion of the calculus and its role in Epicurus' theory see Warren 2001a.

free from pain, just that we do not need it in such circumstances. That we do not need it does not in turn suggest that it is unreasonable for one to avail oneself of opportunities for pleasure nonetheless. The Epicurean offered the upgrade will indeed, let us assume, be without pain and distress either way. But the onus is surely on an opponent to argue that one can make sense of choice only in terms of need. Pending that, there seems nothing mysterious about choosing something on grounds other than that we are in need of it. Epicurus' theory both allows and encourages this possibility where pleasure is concerned.

IV

It might still be objected that luxuries are items that will be treated, under Epicurus' classification of desires, as objects of 'empty' or 'vain' desires. This is surely intended as a pejorative label, and so Epicurus cannot be as relaxed about the place of luxury in the good life as I have been arguing.

Let us briefly rehearse Epicurus' classification. Desires, he says, are either natural or empty. Natural desires are in turn subdivided into the necessary and the merely natural. Necessary desires are further subdivided into those necessary for happiness, for lack of trouble in the body, and for survival itself (*Ep. Men.* 127). Into which of these divisions will luxurious items fall? A scholiast on *KD* 29 (which contains a summary of the classification of desires) tells us that luxurious food counts as an object of natural but not necessary desire, honours such as garlands and statues being objects of desires that are neither necessary nor natural. Thus far we can say that Epicurus does not regard material luxury as 'empty' in a way that seemed at odds with a comfortable view of it.

Epicurus himself, though, goes on to temper the distinction somewhat. In *KD* 30 he discusses natural desires that do not (presumably for a person in the proper condition) lead to pain when unfulfilled; that these are non-necessary desires is made explicit in *KD* 26. When they are made the subject of intensity in their pursuit, this arises through 'empty opinion', precisely what was said to be the case with desires that are neither natural nor necessary in *KD* 29. The thought seems to be that since humans are so constituted as to necessarily suffer pain only when deprived of basic needs, a view that regarded anything more as greatly worth pursuing would be groundless.

But this should not lead us to suppose that luxury itself is under attack. Epicurus' point is that no one *needs* luxury, either for survival or for happiness. In that sense it is vain or empty to desire it in the way one might do if these states did require it – intense pursuit would not then presumably be groundless, though fortunately those items that are necessary turn out to be easy to procure in any case. Epicurus is comfortable with the idea of luxury as something that any reasonable person might choose if offered it. What he rejects, again, is both its puritanical disavowal and its strenuous pursuit. His classification of luxury as an object of empty desire reflects his attitude toward the latter conjunct; it does not entail the former.

Clearly it is important that Epicurus not be committed to the view that luxury, to the extent that it is to be chosen over simplicity, endows its possessor with a happier life. He tells us that freedom from bodily pain and mental distress is 'the goal of living blessedly' (*Ep. Men.* 128) – i.e. what living blessedly consists in; and luxury, on Epicurus' picture, has no necessary connection with the attainment of freedom from pain and distress. But one need not avow that just because luxury may reasonably be chosen over simplicity, it must therefore be regarded as making a corresponding contribution to the happiness of our lives. Indeed we might think that there would be something deeply misguided about a theory that made the happiness of a life turn on whether it was materially luxurious or not. It would be just as misguided to say that one can make sense of a choice only in terms of whether what is chosen is regarded as conducive to a happy life; choices do not have to be so grand! Epicurus can quite consistently treat luxury as choiceworthy without giving it a role in bringing about or sustaining a happy life, or (for that matter) regarding it as something that the chooser could only, in so choosing, be in need of.[16]

Still, we should be able to say that for Epicurus the life in which luxury is chosen over simplicity, with peace of mind maintained, is a more pleasant life than where it is not chosen, just insofar as luxury does, we are assuming, tend to offer more pleasure than simplicity.

[16] The statement at *Ep. Men.* 122 that 'we do everything towards the acquisition of this [viz. happiness]' concerns the situation in which happiness is absent (*apousēs*); it is consistent with the view that there may be other things worth choosing when happiness is attained. True, Epicurus has also just said that when happiness is present 'we have everything', but this may simply mean that those who are happy do not need, rather than could not reasonably choose, anything more.

Pleasure as freedom from pain and distress is attained independently of luxury; the latter cannot make our lives happier than they would otherwise be. But surely the obvious way to spell out why the latter is nonetheless choiceworthy is that it adds pleasure. We are, in being free from pain and distress, already in a state of pleasure, one which equates to happiness. But there seems nothing untoward, and something quite plausible, in allowing that pleasure (though not happiness) increases if I choose, say, business over economy.

V

However that may be, Epicurus on occasion seems to deny this possibility. In *KD* 18 (with support from *KD* 3), he states explicitly that bodily pleasure does not increase once the pain caused by want is removed.[17] Rather, he says, pleasure is merely embellished (or varied) in such circumstances.[18] What is motivating this statement? It seems to me that Epicurus is faced with the following problem. It is all very well to say that one's life is more pleasant but not happier if one takes the upgrade. But a hedonist ought to allow no measure of the quality of a life other than pleasure; indeed Epicurus' measure is quantity of pleasure, as his description of the calculus indicates. It is then rather harder to allow oneself the freedom to declare that pleasure behaves one way, happiness another: that pleasure can go on increasing without happiness increasing with it.

The heart of the problem for a hedonist is that pleasure does appear to behave differently from happiness, and Epicurus seems to recognize this.[19] At any rate, it is plausible to say that happiness might, so

[17] *KD* 18 in full: 'Pleasure in the flesh will not increase, but is only varied (*poikilletai*), once the pain of want is removed. The limit of pleasure in the mind is produced by reflection on the very things and those akin to them that used to provide the mind with its greatest fears.' The more involved point about the limit of mental pleasure is in harmony with the basic idea that beyond the removal of pain or distress there is no increase of pleasure.

[18] I prefer 'embellish' as a translation of Epicurus' verb *poikillein*, since it captures the Greek (whose root meaning is 'embroider') more precisely than does 'vary', while suggesting the idea of something one might reasonably opt for but do perfectly well without.

[19] The Cyrenaics went so far as to deny that their goal of pleasure was to be equated with happiness (DL 2.87–8). For discussion see Irwin 1991; O'Keefe 2002b, Tsouna 2002.

to speak, be a matter of getting a few big things in one's life right. One might disagree on what the big things were, but in Epicurus' version success would be the achievement of satisfaction of bodily need together with peace of mind. Once one has the core items in one's life right, one may want to say that doing well in other respects does not increase one's happiness in a significant way, or at all. To try to do justice to this conception, one might want to say that one's happiness may indeed be embellished by the addition of other good things, but not increased.

The pleasure of a life is, by contrast, arguably cumulative in a rather straightforward way (whether one considers the relevant amount to be 'net' of pain or not). If I have a lot of pleasure in my life, then a little more will increase the pleasantness of my life proportionately. If I have a little, then a lot will increase the pleasantness likewise, and so on. If this is right, then it seems arbitrary to treat pleasure as the sole measure of the quality of a life, while insisting that happiness and pleasure can diverge in the way they behave. Now at times (as *KD* 18 indicates) Epicurus seeks to square this circle by the rather drastic expedient of denying that pleasure actually does behave differently than happiness. Once we have achieved the pleasurable state that is freedom from bodily want and mental distress, the very pleasantness of our lives can no longer be increased. Thus pleasure does behave like happiness, and the relation promised by hedonism is maintained.

There is an alternative strategy that Epicurus seems to have worked with. This involves distinguishing more than one form of pleasure, and claiming that happiness is not to be equated with pleasure *tout court*, but with one of its forms. Thus we are told, with a citation of Epicurus' own words, that he distinguished 'katastematic' or 'static' pleasures from pleasures 'in motion' or 'kinetic' pleasures; and treated freedom from pain and distress as static, joy and delight as kinetic (DL 10.136).[20] One might thus talk of 'static'

[20] The correct way to label and characterize this distinction remains highly controversial (for discussion see e.g. Gosling and Taylor 1982: 365–96; Giannantoni 1984; Mitsis 1988: 45–51; Purinton 1993; Preuss 1994: 121–77; Stokes 1995; Striker 1996c; Cooper 1999a: 508–14; Nikolsky 2001). My own treatment attempts in a rather broad-brush way to understand what might be motivating the distinction; it makes no effort to get to grips with the linguistic niceties with which Epicurus (as reported) sets it out.

pleasure as consisting in a state of mental and bodily satisfaction. Once one is without pain in the body or distress in the mind, then static pleasure has reached its limit and cannot be increased. In this regard it can stand as a reasonable candidate for identification with happiness insofar as we treat happiness as a state and as one which may have determinate conditions for its achievement beyond which one would not be inclined to say it could be significantly, if at all, increased.

One might then contrast static pleasure with pleasure obtained in processes or activities (such as drinking, watching the sunset, or sitting in business class), free now to treat the latter as behaving differently from happiness. One maintains a hedonistic position by equating happiness with one form of pleasure, while remaining in harmony with the intuition that other things, luxurious or not, might increase the pleasantness of a life (and to that extent its goodness) without increasing its happiness.[21]

Though not marked by any explicit distinction of this kind in the *Letter to Menoeceus*, this seems to be the strategy that Epicurus chiefly employs in that work. He says that in stating pleasure to be the goal 'we mean not the pleasures of the profligate and those consisting in enjoying ... but lack of pain in body and of distress in soul' (*Ep. Men.* 131).[22] The wording quite naturally suggests that Epicurus has in mind two senses of the term 'pleasure' corresponding to two forms of pleasure. I take it that his generalization from the pleasures of the profligate to pleasures that consist in enjoying indicates that the contrast is not to be read primarily in terms of 'good' versus 'bad' pleasures, but as distinguishing static from kinetic, with the Greek rendered as 'enjoying' (*apolausis*) able to carry the sense of a process or activity.

[21] A life in which, for example, one's beverages consisted of more than just water might reasonably be described as a better life (other things equal) than one restricted to water; but it would be absurd to think that one then had to call the first life happier.

[22] Annas 1993b: 335 suggests, regarding the calculus, that it should bear little weight given that it is 'incompatible' with the goal being static pleasure, since the latter is 'something not amenable to quantitative measurement'. Yet Epicurus talks of the calculus and the goal in successive paragraphs of the *Letter* without exhibiting any sign of tension between them. It is open to him to say that if racked with anxiety I have a smaller amount of static pleasure than if mildly worried, and so on, with the limit being lack of worry altogether. There is nothing incoherent in treating maximization of static pleasure as the first priority in deploying the calculus.

What I have called the more drastic approach to the hedonist's problem, as found in *KD* 18, also has a presence in the *Letter*, albeit in the background. When Epicurus speaks without qualification of 'the limit of good things' being easily attained (*Ep. Men.* 133), he appears to be expressing the thought that good things – i.e. pleasures – do not increase beyond a certain point, so that pleasure *tout court* and happiness can reasonably be identified.

VI

One cannot be certain that Epicurus regarded these *as* alternative approaches to dealing with the problem of accounting, within a hedonistic framework, for the relation between pleasure and happiness.[23] But the claim that once one has attained freedom from pain and distress there is no extra pleasure to be had (only embellishment) seems a little strained. The strategy of marking off two different forms of pleasure, one to be identified with happiness, the other not, looks more promising. That said, one can see why Epicurus might not have wanted that to be the only string to his bow.

As noted above, what Epicurus meant by pleasure in stating that pleasure was the goal of life seems already at the time of the *Letter* to have been maligned and /or misunderstood – his opponents thought he meant feasting, drinking and the like, whereas he actually meant freedom from pain and distress. Presumably one major source of this opposition was a reluctance to consider freedom from pain and distress as (a form of) pleasure at all, rather than say (following in Plato's footsteps) as a neutral state that is neither pleasure nor pain. This was apparently the position of the Cyrenaics who, we are told, did not recognize static pleasure (DL 10.136); and Cicero no doubt reflects a tradition in selecting as his opening line of attack against Epicurus' ethics the denial that the Epicurean goal can properly be described as one of pleasure in the first place (*Fin.* 2.5–16). Explicitly marking off

[23] This nonetheless seems a more fruitful approach than denying that the static/kinetic distinction marks a genuine classification of pleasures at all, which requires discounting some significant evidence, in particular the testimony of Cicero. Denial is advocated by Nikolsky 2001, following the lead of Gosling and Taylor 1982: 365–96. The unevenness of our sources that is partly responsible for motivating the denial may instead be a sign that the classification was not a permanent fixture in Epicurean thinking.

static pleasure as a form of *pleasure* directly invites this kind of sceptical riposte. *KD* 18 does not place reliance on the distinction, though Epicurus could hardly have supposed it would be much less contentious to claim that pleasure could not be increased once pain is eliminated.

All of which raises the question: why would Epicurus insist that freedom from pain and distress *was* pleasure?[24] Why was he a hedonist at all? I have interpreted the content of *KD* 18 and the distinction between static and kinetic pleasure as alternative responses to a problem specific to hedonism. Was it not, then, open to a theory with a goal of life as stated to have presented itself differently? To this one might respond on Epicurus' behalf that to talk of being in neither pleasure nor pain, if this be the description of his goal that the opponent is urging on him, is, precisely in its connotation of neutrality, misleading. What is valuable about the state of freedom from pain and distress that the conscious Epicurean subject is in is that it is experienced as having a positive qualitative character. To apply the label 'pleasure' is simply to recognize that fact.

Epicurus is perhaps hampered by terminology here. We might speak in English of 'tranquillity' to describe this character,[25] and seek either to distinguish that from pleasure or to mark it off as a type thereof. But the Greek equivalent employed by Epicurus (*ataraxia*) is negative – literally 'lack of disturbance'; and the way that Epicurus describes his ideal state as a whole is negatively – 'neither pained in body nor distressed in soul' (*Ep. Men.* 131).[26]

The negative language all too easily suggests a state that, insofar as it consists of absence, could not feel like anything to be in. Whether through unavailability of terminology or his undoubted provocative streak, Epicurus' settling on a negative formulation could only have helped fuel assertions that his was not a genuinely hedonistic

[24] It has been well recognized that Epicurus' view of pleasure should be understood with reference to the formal conditions imposed by his eudaimonistic framework (see e.g. Hossenfelder 1986; Mitsis 1988: 11–58); the question remains why one might suppose such a state to be a pleasant one.

[25] See Striker 1996b.

[26] He does also speak in the *Letter* of the body's health (128), and elsewhere refers to its 'well-balanced condition' (*eustatheia*; cf. Plut. *Non posse* 1089D); but it might have seemed equally contentious to treat good health as necessarily pleasant.

doctrine;[27] or if it was, that it must really be advocating pleasures of quite a different sort, as those who associated it with the pleasures of the profligate maintained. But on the substantive point Epicurus remains (his critics notwithstanding) right. What he is describing is not a neutral state, but one with a felt character that is not unfairly captured in terms of pleasure – a relaxed freshness, let us say, that feels wonderful.[28] It is not Epicurus but one who would deny that being without pain or distress is (for a sentient subject) pleasant who, it seems to me, is in the grip of a theory.

It should also be noted that it is preferable, if not necessary, if we are to regard Epicurus as offering a theory that is not immediately incoherent, that the state of freedom from pain and distress be interpreted as having a felt character. When Epicurus explains why pleasure is to be regarded as the highest good (*Ep. Men.* 129), he appeals to 'feeling' (*pathos*) as the yardstick for decision about what to choose.[29] Judged thereby, pleasure and pain turn out to be the basis, respectively, of all choice and avoidance. In order for this claim to have relevance to, rather than simply undermine, the establishment of the thesis that freedom from pain and distress is the goal, Epicurus must, rightly or wrongly, be taking the pleasure that is freedom from pain as possessing a felt character. If not, application of the favoured criterion would fail to pick out the goal as choiceworthy.

Similarly, Epicurus calls pleasure the 'first and congenital' good (*Ep. Men.* 129), and this may allude to, or foreshadow, the so-called 'cradle argument', which, though not set out in any surviving material from Epicurus himself, receives formulation as part of basic Epicurean doctrine at Cic. *Fin.*1.30.[30] Fundamental here is an appeal

[27] Cyrenaics derided the Epicurean goal as the state of a corpse (Clem. *Strom.* 2.130), echoing Callicles' jibe about the life without need (and hence, as he sees it, without pleasure) at Pl. *Gorg.* 492e.

[28] There is some evidence that Epicurus regarded the state of being free from pain and distress as an intentional object – that in which the greatest pleasure (or more precisely joy) is taken. By itself this would give Epicurus a rather promiscuous (and correspondingly bland) hedonism, since, as ancient critics pointed out, one can rejoice in anything. There is of course nothing to prevent one rejoicing in that which has its own felt quality, so these two ways of regarding static pleasure are to that extent compatible. For elaboration and defence of the 'object' reading, see Purinton 1993.

[29] On *pathos* and pleasure see Konstan 2006a.

[30] For more detailed discussion of the argument see Brunschwig 1986; for a reconstruction of Epicurus' overall strategy in deriving his ethical doctrines see Sedley 1998b.

to the idea that all creatures from birth go after pleasure and avoid pain.[31] But in order for the argument to get off the ground, it is important that the potential convert to Epicurus' philosophy be prepared to accept the point about what the young seek as a reasonable one. Only then can one move on to consider the question of whether the point offers, as it would claim to, a self-evident lesson about what one *should* seek – namely pleasure, and ultimately the pleasure given by the absence of pain and distress. For the possibility of agreement on this key inference to arise, one needs assent to the initial picture. The supposition that what young creatures find attractive is the *feeling* of pleasure, albeit that which purportedly obtains when need has been satisfied, is far from implausible, as the notion that what is sought by them is an *absence* of feeling would not be. The conception of pleasure as a feeling should, on pain of irrelevance, then be carried forward to the official Epicurean account of what the highest pleasure is.

VII

With this in mind, let me now briefly discuss a rather different way of interpreting the Epicurean position which attempts to, as it were, 'bulk up' the goal by reading it in such a way that it will turn out to include the kinetic pleasures. If it does, then Epicurus' claim both that his position is hedonistic and that its goal marks the upper limit of pleasure looks smoother, pre-empting debate about whether mere lack of pain and distress is pleasant, let alone maximally pleasant.

What this reading needs to do is somehow tie kinetic pleasures to the idea of being free from trouble and pain; otherwise their inclusion in the goal looks arbitrary. Of course it is likely, even inevitable, that there will *be* a range of kinetic pleasures that the subject of static pleasure will enjoy in life; the question is what is the relation between the two such that one need not say that the former appear to be making an independent contribution as far as the goal is concerned.

One might say something along the following lines: what makes the kinetic pleasures pleasurable is just the fact that pain is absent when one experiences them.[32] In other words, static pleasure is the

31 Compare the reference at *Ep. Men.* 128 to the state of the 'creature' (*zōion*) that is free from pain and distress.

32 See here Striker 1996c: 207.

very thing that gives certain processes or activities their quality of being enjoyable. Taking a walk, for example, will be pleasant just insofar as, and only to the extent that, the walker is free from pain and distress. If so, then achievement of the official Epicurean goal will indeed bring with it the pleasures that an opponent would accept as such (albeit oddly characterized), and indeed the limit of pleasure, since there will be no kinetic pleasure to be had without it, and nothing independent of it to be added on.

Although this reading is ingenious and well-motivated, it does not seem to me to gain particularly strong support from the texts, though these are admittedly difficult. As a view about the nature of pleasure, it perhaps attributes something less plausible to Epicurus than what is being rejected. For it seems plainly false to say that the pleasure of e.g. walking consists wholly in the activity being performed without pain or distress.[33] No doubt the presence of such features might diminish the activity's pleasantness, but that hardly makes the latter dependent on their absence.

By contrast, one can see (or so I have suggested) that a state of freedom from pain and distress might be characterized as pleasant, thus obviating the need for a role for kinetic pleasure to create what looks like a hedonistic theory.[34] One can also, I think, see how it might be possible to regard the state of freedom from pain and distress as being one of a felt character that overshadows, in hedonic terms, the merely kinetic.[35]

[33] The claim is less plausible still if one takes (as I am inclined to, though the evidence makes certainty difficult) kinetic pleasure to include processes of relieving pain, such as eating when hungry.

[34] One might claim that what makes the state of freedom from pain and distress pleasurable is precisely the enjoyment when in it of a range and variety of kinetic pleasures. As Cooper 1999a: 509 puts it, 'only in this way [viz. by enjoying a variety of such pleasures] will a person be able constantly to enjoy the pleasure of the pain- and distress-free condition of mind and body'. This view, it seems to me, fails to do justice to the Epicurean emphasis on the pain and trouble free state as itself one of pleasure that is identifiable with happiness. Cooper's worry is that without the variety 'boredom (a distressing mental state) might set in' (*ibid.*). But an Epicurean would be entitled to ask what *makes* such a state distressing. If it implies some frustrated desire, this is already a misguided response.

[35] Doubt about this stronger claim may arise in part from the identification of magnitude with intensity. One can concede that the pleasure of, say, eating when famished is more intense than the pleasure of the breeze caressing one's face; it does not follow that the former pleasure is greater than the latter. By the same token, the pleasure of being without pain or distress may be greater, even if less intense, than other pleasant feelings.

VIII

There is more to say about the relation between kinetic and static pleasure than I can discuss here. In particular, delicate questions are raised by the weight that Epicurus at times seems to place on expectation and memory of pleasures as elements of the good life.[36] Are the expectations and memories themselves kinetic pleasures? Are the items that are expected or remembered? Did Epicurus hold that a life without such memories or expectations could not be a good one? He may have thought that the key thing was expectation that one's pain-free state would continue;[37] and it is not clear that this requires any commitment to kinetic pleasure as a component of good living.[38]

Again, one should not read Epicurus back to front. He is starting from a situation in which people will experience their share of kinetic pleasure in the ordinary course of life, but will have failed to attain freedom from pain and distress. In saying that the latter is the goal, he has no reason to concern himself with a wholly artificial scenario in which such freedom had been won but kinetic pleasures were mysteriously absent. If he is inclined to regard the good life as one in which the subject will continue to enjoy a range of kinetic pleasures, that is no more than one would expect in any real-life situation.[39]

Even if this is accepted, there still looks to be some tension. It is one thing to say that there is more pleasure to be got from a state of tranquillity than from anything else; quite another to say that there is

[36] For some relevant pieces of evidence see e.g. Plut. *Non posse* 1089D; DL 10.22; Cic. *Tusc.* 3.41, 5.96.

[37] This, together with actually being in that state, brings the highest joy (Plut. *Non posse* 1089D); see also *SV* 33, which asserts that with such a combination one might compete with Zeus for happiness, presumably implying that nothing further is required.

[38] Or, for that matter, as a means to it. One may need the activities of eating and drinking to keep the pain of want in abeyance, but one does not need that these activities be pleasant (even if they usually are) to do so. Where pain is unavoidable, Epicurus did hold that it can be combated through the joy of recollecting past pleasures, claiming to have availed himself of this technique on his deathbed (DL 10.22).

[39] One should also note that Epicurus seems often not so much to be insisting on the role of kinetic pleasure, as championing sensory pleasure against more intellectual varieties (not indeed to dismiss the latter but to bait those who downplay the former). This looks to be the thrust of Cic. *Tusc.* 3.41, and of the notorious paean to the pleasure of the stomach (Athenaeus *Deipn.* 12.546F).

no more pleasure to be got from anything else once tranquillity is attained. I have argued that Epicurus might in principle have no cause to assert this, given an appropriate division of labour between static and kinetic pleasure. But the unqualified denial in *KD* 18 that pleasure is increased beyond absence of pain shows that this cannot be the whole story.

It may then turn out that the notion of tranquillity is just what is needed. The pertinent feature of tranquillity is that it can serve to *unify* ideas of pleasure and happiness. Tranquillity is a pleasant state, but also a state of contentment, and it seems that we cannot succeed in picking it out under one of these descriptions without picking it out under the other. If one is prepared to equate happiness with contentment, this may suggest a convergence, and a corresponding covariance, between pleasure and happiness. It would then be odd to maintain that pleasure can be increased beyond a state of tranquillity but happiness merely embellished; either both can be increased or neither. Given the view that happiness is not such as to be increased by, say, whether one flies business rather than economy, Epicurus takes the more plausible option to be neither.

This is a gesture at grounding what I take to be Epicurus' core intuition once *KD* 18 is borne in mind: there is a state of well-being, within the reach of all of us to attain, beyond which it would be as much a misrepresentation to say that life's pleasantness could be increased, as its happiness. Whether a good Epicurean traveller can credibly defend the choice of business over economy as an embellishment, not an increase, of the pleasantness of one's life, I leave the reader to ponder.

ERIC BROWN

10 Politics and society

INTRODUCTION

Epicurean thoughts about politics contrast sharply with those of other prominent Greek and Roman philosophers. Plato, Aristotle and the Stoics agree that human beings are naturally political animals, by which they mean that to realize fully our natural capacities and be perfectly successful as human beings, we need to contribute to the *polis*. Accordingly, they believe that humans should start a family[1] and should, at least if circumstances are favourable, engage in politics.[2] These philosophers also agree that justice exists by nature and not by convention, by which they mean that standards of right and wrong for social life do not depend upon any particular agreements or customs.[3] The Epicureans differ. They discourage starting a family and engaging in politics, and they deny that justice exists by nature.

It would be a mistake, however, to infer that Epicureanism is apolitical. First, these sweeping contrasts need some qualification: the Epicureans do not absolutely reject ordinary politics and do not think that justice is *whatever* a society decides it is. Second, and more importantly, the Epicureans' pursuit of pleasure requires that they cultivate their own just community of friends, apart from the madding crowd. So although the Epicurean seeks to avoid traditional

For their comments on an earlier draft, I thank Jill Delston, Matt Evans and James Warren.

[1] Ancient doxographers widely assume that starting a family is a way of contributing to the *polis*. See Schofield 1991: 119–27.

[2] Plato, Aristotle and some of their followers qualify this by saying that some exceptional human beings should live as much like gods as possible, in a life of philosophical contemplation, instead of engaging in politics. See E. Brown forthcoming b.

[3] See E. Brown forthcoming a.

politics as much as he can, he is not apolitical. Rather, he adopts counter-cultural politics, rooted in his need for friendship and justice.

To explain the Epicurean's politics, I focus primarily on Epicurus, but especially in the final section, I also draw on two later Epicurean accounts of the origins of society, due to Hermarchus and Lucretius.[4]

ORDINARY POLITICS[5]

Epicurus understands the goal to be the absence of mental disturbance and physical pain (Epic. *Ep. Men.* 128 and 131). Thus, he proposes that success in life requires cultivating bulwarks against disturbance and pain and avoiding circumstances that are likely to give rise to disturbance and pain.[6] These two strategies can pull in two different directions. After all, the better one is equipped to shrug off what would pain most people, the less one needs avoidance, and the more one avoids pains, the less practice one has of the skills of absorbing troublesome circumstances without experiencing trouble. But when it comes to the business (*ta pragmata*) of the *polis*, Epicurus endorses the strategy of avoidance.[7] He insists that those who seek security from political power and honour are mistaken about how best to achieve freedom from fear (*KD* 7; cf. Lucr. *DRN* 5.1117–35), and he counsels against the political life (*SV* 58 and *KD* 14; cf. DL 10.119 and Plut. *Adv. Col.* 1126E–1127C).[8] He also counsels against contributing to the *polis* by starting a family: marriage and children are too much trouble.[9]

[4] The most significant fragment of Hermarchus' account is preserved by Porph. *Abst.* 1.7–12. For the title, scope and form of Hermarchus' work, see Obbink 1988; for fuller discussion of this particular fragment, see Vander Waerdt 1988. For Lucretius, see *DRN* 5.925–1457, with Furley 1978. We have only a whisper of Epicurus' own historical anthropology (*Ep. Hdt.* 75–6), but he evidently covered similar ground in *On Nature* books 12–13 (see the texts cited by Vander Waerdt 1988: 91 n. 20).

[5] Some of this section overlaps with E. Brown forthcoming b. For fuller discussion, see Roskam 2007.

[6] See Woolf, ch. 9, this volume.

[7] This appears to be his usual choice (see also Tsouna, ch. 14, this volume), perhaps in part because he believes that one can condition oneself without first-hand experience, as one can condition oneself to believe that 'death is nothing to us'. See also Woolf, ch. 9, this volume.

[8] See also Warren, ch. 13, this volume.

[9] See the textually problematic DL 10.119 with Chilton 1960 and Brennan 1996.

Epicurean avoidance of ordinary political activity is qualified in two important ways. First, the calculation that encourages withdrawal can go otherwise in special circumstances. If, say, one inherits children upon another's death, one should raise them carefully,[10] and presumably, if a pandemic of infertility or global enthusiasm for Epicureanism were to break out, one could recalculate one's opposition to producing children.[11] Also, if active Athenians were to resent the withdrawn Epicureans as 'free riders' who reap the benefits that Athens provides without contributing to the provision (cf. Plut. *Adv. Col.* 1127A), they might harass the Epicureans and make withdrawal more troublesome than engagement.[12] Or if the city is beset by war or an emergency that threatens the law and order the withdrawn Epicureans need for their sense of security (*KD* 14; cf. Plut. *Adv. Col.* 1124D), then they could calculate that engagement is the lesser of two evils. In fact, some Epicureans in the first century BC, such as Cassius, seem to have thought of Rome's civil wars as such a threat, and they engaged in politics.[13] Given these possible exceptions, Seneca aptly summarizes the view thus: 'Epicurus says that the sage will not engage in politics unless something intervenes' (*De otio* 3.2).

There is a second qualification to Epicurean withdrawal. The Epicureans need some property (e.g. *KD* 14), and to maintain their property, they need to be able to negotiate the local property laws. Epicurus, for example, wanted to leave the Garden to successors who, as metics (resident aliens), would not be legally able to own the land. But he understood the legal requirements and deftly satisfied them

[10] Such is suggested by Epicurus' will (DL 10.16–21), and provided for by DL 10.119 on the attractive emendation of Brennan 1996: 350–2.

[11] Epictetus *Diss.* 3.7.19 suggests that a society of Epicureans would simply die off. But if the Epicureans can explain why their own tranquillity requires painstaking actions on behalf of friends (including younger friends) – and I will argue in the next section that they can – then they could explain why their own tranquillity requires producing children as potential friends for their younger friends.

[12] This consideration might have motivated Democritus to endorse political engagement despite his acceptance of an ethical theory that is broadly similar to Epicurus'. See E. Brown forthcoming b, and for the connection between Democritean ethics and Epicurus, see Warren 2002a.

[13] See Momigliano 1941.

with his will.[14] This explains why the Epicureans say that the sage will go to court.[15]

Still, these are qualifications. The Epicurean prefers to live outside of traditional political entanglements, to 'live unnoticed' (551 Us.). The Epicurean does not, however, prefer to live alone. He prefers to live in a community of fellow prophets of painlessness.

FRIENDSHIP AND COMMUNITY[16]

The Epicurean community is defined by its members' friendship (in Greek: *philia*; in Latin: *amicitia*) with each other. This by itself is not unusual. It is a truism of Greek philosophy that fellow-citizens, at least in a good *polis*, are friends.[17] But Epicurus favours a community of friends outside of and quite unlike the traditional *polis*. Additionally, Epicurus' conception of friendship is much more demanding than the traditional ideal of 'civic friendship'. But from the start, critics charged the Epicureans in the community of friends with abandoning their principles, on the grounds that Epicurean hedonism cannot sustain genuinely demanding friendship.

According to the simplest version of the criticism, Epicurean hedonism requires that one pursue one's own pleasure and real friendship requires that one take pains on behalf of one's friends. But Epicurus can answer this charge. He first insists that although a friend is willing to help one, 'to sit with one when one is ill and to provide aid when one is in prison or in poverty' (Sen. *Ep*. 9.8 = fr. 175 Us.; cf. Plut. *Non posse* 1097C–D), the most important benefit that a friend provides is the confidence that he *will* help (*SV* 34; cf. DL 10.11). Knowing that future pains will be assuaged by friends is like knowing that sharp pains will be short, long pains dull (*KD* 28): it removes the disturbance caused by fear of future pain. Although this confidence depends

14 See Leiwo and Remes 1999 and Warren 2004a: 162–4.

15 See DL 10.120, where it is also reported that the Epicurean sage will leave behind words and show concern for property and the future. These reports all appear to fit Epicurean doctrine to Epicurus' will. Brennan 1996 plausibly makes a similar claim about DL 10.119.

16 My account in this section owes much to Evans 2004 and Shaw 2007: ch. 5, but I doubt that they agree with everything I say.

17 See, e.g., Arist. *EN* 8.1 1155a22–3, 8.9, and 8.11, especially 1161a30–2. Every Greek philosopher who discusses how a *polis* would ideally be constituted seeks to explain how the citizens of the *polis* could be friends.

upon the ordinary help that friendship also offers, its value is not reducible to that help. In fact, it is much more valuable than passing pleasures (cf. *SV* 34). A passing pleasure might exclude or absorb the experience of pain.[18] But confidence that future pains will be minimal and manageable excludes a principal source of mental disturbance and thus is crucial to providing mental tranquillity, and mental tranquillity is far more valuable than physical painlessness (Cic. *Fin.* 1.55–6; DL 10.137). That is why Cicero's Torquatus says that friendship, like the virtues, is always attached to pleasures (*Fin.* 1.68). Indeed, Epicurus believes that friendship is more useful for tranquillity than the virtues (*KD* 28; cf. *KD* 27 = *SV* 13 and *SV* 78), perhaps because friendship brings one the confidence that multiple virtuous people (one's friends) will help instead of just one (oneself).

Next, to show that one can be reliably confident that one's friends will help, Epicurus distinguishes between the ersatz 'utility friendship' that one cultivates merely for ordinary help and advantages and the genuine friendship that requires virtue or even is a virtue.[19] Epicurus here agrees with the majority opinion of Greek philosophers that genuine friendship is limited to the virtuous.[20] Although 'utility friendship' is unstable, a genuine friend, being wise, understands the importance of confidence to his tranquillity. He knows that any action that undermines the trust of friends undermines his own confidence and thus tranquillity, and is therefore not to be done. Conversely, he knows that actions that undergird the trust of friends support his confidence and thus tranquillity, and are to that extent to be done.

The unwise, by contrast, make mistakes about the causes of pleasure and pain (Cic. *Fin.* 1.55). A fool might misplace confidence in others – by misjudging their character – or he might mistakenly think that short-term pleasure is a more reliable path to his ultimate end

18 See *KD* 3 with Purinton 1993: 306.

19 *SV* 23, according to the ms. reading: 'Every friendship is by itself a virtue, but it takes its start from benefit.' (The interpretation of *SV* 23 is contested. See the discussion below.) Note also that genuine friends are those who are together filled up with pleasures (DL 10.120; cf. *SV* 39 and Cic. *Fin.* 2.84).

20 See also DL 10.118 with 117: 'Epicurus thinks ... that only the sage will experience gratitude towards his friends present and absent ...' (The text becomes corrupt at just this point.) For Aristotle, see, e.g., *EN* 8.3 1156b7–8 on 'perfect or complete (*teleia*) friendship', and for the Stoics, see, e.g., DL 7.124.

than actions on behalf of friends. Another fool might mistakenly suppose that he needs only to *appear* helpful to his friends in order to earn their trust and thus foster his own confidence. But if one merely *appeared* helpful, then one could never be free from the fear of being unmasked as a false friend (cf. *KD* 35, in the next section). The problem is not just that being unmasked would undermine one's friendships and thus one's confidence of others' help and thus one's tranquillity. The problem is that the *fear* of being unmasked already undermines one's tranquillity.

An Epicurean sage can plausibly maintain that even his *painstaking* actions on behalf of friends (e.g. *SV* 28 and Plut. *Adv. Col.* 1111B) are pleasant precisely because they sustain the trust of the friendship and thus his own confidence in the future and thus his own tranquillity. An example might help to display this thought's plausibility. Peeling potatoes can be a nuisance, especially if it brings on a painful hand cramp. But if one is peeling potatoes so as to make soup for friends, everything is different. Even the cramp, which otherwise could be reason to abandon the activity, cannot undermine the pleasure one takes in doing something for one's friends (and so sustaining one's friendships and thereby supporting one's confidence and tranquillity). The pleasure of mental tranquillity excludes or at least dwarfs the cramp in significance.

This might do for the simplest criticism. The critics will insist, however, that even if Epicureans can be friends most of the time, they will have to betray their hedonism to be friends in difficult circumstances. First, they will object that even if the pleasure of sustaining a friendship can exclude or at least dwarf minor pains, it cannot sufficiently counteract greater ones. So if an Epicurean finds himself in circumstances in which a friendship requires him to take significant pains, he will fail to do so. But on the day Epicurus recognized as his last, he wrote to Idomeneus or Hermarchus – our two sources disagree about this – and he said that he was enjoying a blessed day despite suffering 'urinary blockages and dysenteric discomforts which could not be more intense' (DL 10.22, tr. after Inwood and Gerson 1997: 76) because 'the mental joy that I get from remembering our past conversations compensates for all these things' (DL 10.22; cf. Cic. *Fin.* 2.96).[21]

[21] Cicero's rendering makes Epicurus say that his mental joy comes from recalling 'my theories and discoveries (*rationum inventorumque nostrorum*)'. (That is a royal

This suggests that one can think oneself to pleasure in the face of intense bodily pains. If this is plausible, then one can take pleasure in the most painstaking actions that benefit one's friends.[22]

The critics can press on with other imagined circumstances in which they do not expect the Epicurean to remain a reliable friend. What if one's friend becomes disabled or otherwise unable to provide one confidence that he will be helpful in the future? Ordinary intuitions suggest that if one is a genuine friend, one should continue to help. To satisfy this intuition, Epicurus must remind us that one needs a community of *many* friends (again, cf. *KD* 35, discussed below). In such a community, to maintain mutual trust with *A*, I also need to maintain mutual trust with *B*. For if *A* were to find out that I had abandoned *B*, I could not be confident that *A* would still trust me, and if I were to abandon *B*, I could not be confident that *A* would not find out. Thus, even if *B* were to suffer a debilitating

nostrorum, as Rackham 1931 and Woolf 2001 see.) Diogenes clearly records that it was 'our past conversations (*tōn gegonotōn hēmin dialogismōn*)'. I assume that the disagreement is due to Cicero's loose, somewhat uncharitable rendering. Cf. Plut. *Non posse* 1099D–E, and for the general point, see also *SV* 55 and Cic. *Fin.* 1.55.

[22] I am not sure whether one could enjoy – find pleasing – mental tranquillity even in the face of intense physical pain. I do think that Epicureans take this too far, however, when they say that the sage does not fail to achieve his end even on the rack (DL 10.118, Cic. *Tusc.* 2.17; cf. *Ep. Men.* 131, *SV* 47, Cic. *Fin.* 1.62–3 and *Tusc.* 5.27). That the sage will not lose his mental tranquillity is difficult to believe, but not impossible. That the sage will not lose his physical *painlessness* does not allow credence. It becomes tempting, then, to qualify the Epicureans' claim. Perhaps, distinguishing between a divine happiness that is genuinely pain-free and a mortal happiness that accommodates some physical pain, they mean that the sage can achieve – and is also guaranteed – only the latter sort of happiness and so not literal painlessness (see Long and Sedley 1987: vol. 1, p. 125). Unfortunately, this sits uneasily with Epicurus' insistence that 'a human being among immortal goods is not at all like a mortal animal' (Epic. *Ep. Men.* 135, and cf. *SV* 78, which names friendship as an immortal good; see also *SV* 33). Nor do I think it will do to assume that Epicurean painlessness requires only a net balance of more pleasure than pain. (That is to painlessness what fool's gold is to gold.) Nor do I think that the Epicureans actually believe that a person in the right state of mind can absorb painful experiences without feeling *any* pain. (Some people have had this thought, no doubt, but most of them – e.g. fire-walkers – appear to have trained their bodies to become inured to (at least some particular kinds) of physical pain.) Rather, the Epicureans seem to believe that a person in the right state of mind can absorb physical pains without thinking that they are anything but trivial. (Note especially Plut. *Non posse* 1088B–C and 1090A.) The sage experiences physical pains *as if* experiencing nothing at all, which is not exactly the same as experiencing nothing at all, although it might lend *some* (not to my mind enough, but *some*) credibility to the claim that the sage's painlessness is uninterrupted.

accident and become unable to reciprocate any helpful deeds, still the Epicurean friend of *B* has reason to continue helping *B*.[23]

But what if one is nearing the end of one's life and so cannot expect one's friends to be able to provide future help? Will confidence in the future continue to give one reasons to benefit one's friends? Epicurus needs to insist that the actions I perform for the sake of my friends please me as soon as I do them. As I am acting, I recognize that I am sustaining the mutual trust of the friendship, and so I am bolstering my confidence. Even if my soup-making is interrupted or my friends fail to make it over to enjoy the Vichyssoise, still I enjoyed the activity of making soup for my friends, because my action, undertaken to sustain mutual trust, already bolstered my confidence and tranquillity. After all, I can think, 'What friends we are that I undertake to make a surprise Vichyssoise, even knowing that they might not make it here to enjoy it!' Of course, if *everything* I do for the sake of my friends fails to help them, there would be cause for concern. But the pleasure brought by acting on behalf of friends does not require *on every occasion* the satisfaction of actually pleasing one's friends. There is still pleasure in doing what one can for the sake of one's friends, regardless of whether one experiences the benefits accruing to one's friends.

Epicurus' taxonomy of desires helps to clarify this line of thought.[24] According to his taxonomy, unnatural desires depend upon false opinion, and natural desires, which are free of false opinion, are necessary just in case their frustration brings pain and unnecessary otherwise (Epic. *Ep. Men.* 127, *KD* 29 with scholion, *KD* 30). Now, it might happen occasionally that one *must* do something for the sake of a friend in order to maintain the mutual trust of the friendship and so maintain one's confidence and tranquillity. In this case, the desire to do the action would be a necessary desire; pain would result from failure to satisfy such a desire. One might, for example, have a necessary desire to die for a friend, if (in special circumstances) not dying for one's friend would necessarily undermine one's trustworthiness and thus destroy one's confidence and tranquillity (*SV* 56–7; DL 10.121). (The critics cannot say that this would require the Epicurean to abandon his Epicureanism. He thinks,

[23] So, too, Evans 2004: 419–20. [24] See also Woolf, ch. 9, this volume.

'Death is nothing to us' (*KD* 2, *Ep. Men.* 124–7), and he concludes that he would be better off dead than alive with tranquillity lost.)[25]

But most actions one does for one's friends are not like this. They are motivated by *unnecessary* natural desires. Performing these actions brings pleasure, and failing to perform them does not bring pain. So starting these actions brings pleasure, and being prevented from completing them does not bring pain. Hence, I take pleasure in supporting the mutual trust between my friend and me not only when I act in ways that both of us recognize as beneficial and friendly but also when I act in ways that only I recognize to be such. Nor is this delusional pleasure. Part of the work of actually maintaining mutual trust is keeping oneself invested in the relationship.[26]

The critics have one last reproach. They maintain that a genuine friend must value his friend for her sake, not his own, and they claim that Epicurus' egoistic hedonism cannot sustain valuing others for their sake. Many scholars find Epicurus innocent of this charge, but I maintain that this one sticks.

Some scholars attribute to Epicurus a 'two-level' theory which distinguishes between one level of evaluating individual actions and another level of evaluating states or rules: actions are to be evaluated by reference to the preferred states or rules, and the states or rules are to be evaluated by reference to some ultimate criterion.[27] On this sort of theory, one should do actions even if they are not preferred by reference to the ultimate criterion, just so long as they are endorsed by reference to the preferred states or rules. So, on this interpretation, Epicurus could recommend an action even if it does not directly promote the agent's goal, just because it is an action of the type required by friendship, which does bring about the agent's goal.

But this is not the way Epicurus' evaluations go. He insists that one must refer *every* choice, *every* aversion, and *every* action to one's own

25 See Warren, ch. 13, this volume.

26 This reasoning can be extended to explain why the Epicurean should make a will, even though the execution of the will after his death cannot benefit him. The Epicureans believe that it is irrational to enjoy the anticipation of benefits one will not experience (just as it is irrational to fear harms one will not experience: *Ep. Men.* 125). But they can maintain that one's actions for the sake of friends bring pleasure to one as one does them, even if one does not or even cannot see those actions all the way to their completion. For a rich but less optimistic reckoning of Epicurean defences of will-making, see Warren 2004a: 162–99.

27 See O'Keefe 2001a. Cf. Schofield 2000: 442 and Warren 2004a: 188.

pleasure (*Ep. Men.* 128, *KD* 25).[28] So he must think that every action that is required for friendship sustains the greatest pleasure, precisely because it sustains the friendship that supports tranquillity, which is the greatest pleasure. And, in fact, Epicurus has no need and no desire to concede that actions on behalf of friendship might fail with reference to the ultimate criterion of pleasure. That is the way ersatz friends sometimes see things, but it is not the way the Epicurean friend who understands the source of his own security and tranquillity sees it.

Other scholars simply ascribe to Epicurus the view that friends and friendship are valuable for their own sake.[29] But Cicero testifies against this when he has Torquatus lay out three Epicurean approaches to friendship (*Fin* 1.65–70; cf. 2.82–5). After explaining the first approach, Torquatus notes Academic criticism to the effect that valuing friendship only for the sake of pleasure cripples it, and he explains that some 'more timid' – Cicero later calls them 'more recent' (*Fin.* 2.82) – Epicureans allowed that friends grow to value friends for their own sake (*Fin.* 1.69). Clearly, to provoke the Academic criticism and thereby set up the special concession of 'more timid', 'more recent' Epicureans, there must have been *less* timid, *earlier* Epicureans who declared that one's friendships and friends are valuable for the sake of one's pleasure alone. By far the most plausible reading assumes that Epicurus himself was among the early and bold Epicureans.[30]

Despite Cicero's testimony, many scholars nevertheless believe that Epicurus took the more timid line. They point first to *Vatican Saying* 23 (see note 19). But this sentence does not attribute to Epicurus the view that friendship is worth choosing for its own sake unless one makes two dubious moves. First, one must emend the sole manuscript so that it says not that every friendship is by itself a virtue but that every friendship is worth choosing for its own sake, despite

[28] So, too, Annas 1993b: 240–2, who says that Epicurus needs a two-level theory but cannot have it because of *KD* 25. O'Keefe 2001a: 299–301 attempts to fit *KD* 25 to a two-level theory; Evans 2004: 414–16 is rightly unpersuaded.

[29] There is no necessary connection between valuing friendship for its own sake and valuing friends for their own sake, but any hedonist who is prepared to compromise far enough to concede one of these claims might well concede the other. Most scholars attribute both to Epicurus. See Brescia 1955; Müller 1972: 112–29; Gemelli 1978; Rist 1980; Mitsis 1988: 98–128; and Annas 1993b: 236–44.

[30] Tsouna 2001: 161–4 argues that Philodemus is among the 'more timid', 'more recent' Epicureans.

the fact that the grounds for emending are not compelling.[31] Second, one must assume that Epicurus is the original author of the sentence, despite the facts that Epicurus is likely not the original author of several *Vatican Sayings* and that Cicero's testimony associates the view of the emended sentence not with Epicurus but with 'more timid', 'more recent' Epicureans.[32] With the text and the authorship in question, *Vatican Saying* 23 cannot serve as independent evidence that Epicurus takes friendship to be worth choosing for its own sake.

For evidence of a more timid Epicurus, some scholars look to Torquatus' account of the first Epicurean approach to friendship (*Fin* 1.65–8).[33] This is surely Epicurus' own approach: Torquatus precedes and ends his account of it with quotations of Epicurus, and Cicero notes that only this approach – in contrast with two others that follow it – contains words of Epicurus himself (*Fin.* 2.82).[34] But this approach does not hold that friends or friendship are worth choosing for their own sake. It says that we enjoy our friends' joy as much as we enjoy our own, and that the sage will be as disposed to act for his friend as he is for himself. But these claims are compatible with the insistence that the ultimate end of all our feelings and actions for our friends is our *own* pleasure. Indeed, the account insists on exactly this by the understatement that we should not seek our friends' pleasures *per se* as much as we seek our own. In sum, on Epicurus' account, we should seek our friends' pleasures as much as we seek our own, but we should seek only our own pleasures *for their own sake*. By this reasoning, we can and should seek friendship ever so much, but not for its own sake.[35]

So there is no evidence that Epicurus finds friendship or friends to be valuable for their own sake, no evidence that Epicurus contradicts his fundamental dictum that everything worth choosing is worth choosing for the sake of one's own pleasure (Epic. *Ep. Men.* 128–9, *KD* 25; cf. DL 10.34, Cic. *Fin.* 1.23).[36] He rejects the common belief

[31] E. Brown 2002: 76–8. [32] O'Keefe 2001a: 287–9 and E. Brown 2002: 78–9.

[33] See esp. Mitsis 1988: 100–2. [34] *Contra* O'Connor 1989: 184.

[35] For further detail about the inferences Torquatus attributes to this account, see O'Keefe 2001a: 289–97; E. Brown 2002: 70–1; and Evans 2004: 411–13.

[36] Of those scholars who attribute to Epicurus the belief that friendship and friends are valuable for their own sake, some (Mitsis 1988: 98–128 and Annas 1993b: 236–44) acknowledge the tension between this belief and his fundamental dictum. This is smart and forthright, but uncharitable. Others try to sidestep the problem by insisting that friendship is intrinsically *pleasant* or *pleasurable*. But this is insufficient.

that a friend must value his friend for her sake, and not for his own, and for this reason we might want to reject his conception of friendship. But Epicurus has a strong and consistent case that one should act for the sake of friends *because* by doing so, one fosters the trust that fosters the confidence that is necessary for one's own tranquillity. The more timid Epicureans, who in effect drop the 'because' clause, destroy Epicureanism's elegantly systematic insistence that one should act always for the sake of pleasure alone.[37]

Still, all the Epicureans, bold and timid alike, insist that one should cultivate friends. They urge that one should 'live unnoticed' with these friends, apart from the public sphere of a traditional political community, in their own, non-traditional community. The early Epicureans themselves tried to live this way, in Epicurus' Garden, just outside Athens' city-wall.[38] Of course, if the denizens of the Epicurean community forego procreation, their population – and with it, the tranquillity that their community of friends brings – will wane. So they will need to recruit new members from those who might become virtuous Epicureans,[39] and this will take some

It says only that friendship *brings* pleasure all by itself, which leaves intact the tension between the claims that everything is valuable for pleasure and that friendship is valuable for its own sake. The cleverest response notices that the tension – not a logical contradiction – would dissipate were Epicurus to hold that friendship is identical to (at least a part of) pleasure. Evans 2004: 418 n. 31 explains that Epicurus *could have* said that friendship is a mental state of confidence and trust, which is a part of painlessness. But Cicero's testimony makes it clear that Epicurus *did not* say this. I think he was right not to. If friendship is a psychological state, it is a state that embraces motivations to act in such-and-such ways; it is not the confidence and trust that *result* from such actions.

[37] The third Epicurean account is that friends contract to love each other no less than themselves (Cic. *Fin.* 1.70, 2.83). This is intelligible as a reinterpretation of the reasoning I attribute to Epicurus above. He makes trust or confidence the crucial bond, and some Epicureans evidently construed that trust or confidence as a contract. But as Cicero's response makes clear, this manoeuvre does not mollify the critics who insist that genuine friends must care for each other for the other's sake. Only the second Epicurean account mollifies the critics, and it does so by conceding the point at issue and wrecking the Epicurean theory.

[38] For an account of the historical Epicurean community, see Clay 1983b and ch. 1, this volume.

[39] For a speculative account of Epicurean recruitment, see Frischer 1982. Note that Epicureans will want to find new recruits even if they are themselves nearing the end of their lives, if my account above of why an Epicurean would want to benefit his friends is plausible. So Epicurus could have defended Diogenes of Oinoanda's decision, as an old man, to erect a gigantic wall that would proselytize for Epicureanism. For Diogenes' own reasons, see Warren 2004a: 181–6.

care, as not everyone is ready for genuine friendship (see *SV* 28 and 39). But the Epicureans seek a self-perpetuating community of friends.

But the Epicurean community is unlike most self-perpetuating political communities.[40] For one thing, it lacks many traditional political institutions. For another, it does not restrict membership to people from one *polis*, or even to Greeks, and so there is a potential for cosmopolitanism in the Epicurean community of friends.[41] Differing as it does from a traditional political community, does the Epicurean community of friends serve as a political ideal?

JUSTICE AND IDEAL POLITICS

Curiously, it is not even clear at first that Epicurus' theory of justice allows him to say that a community of sages would be just. On the one hand, Epicurus is clear that no one can live pleasantly without living justly (Epic. *Ep. Men.* 132, *KD* 5). This would suggest that the ideal community of friends is full of justice (cf. Diog. Oin. 56.I.6–12 Smith). On the other hand, Epicurus is clear that there is no justice without a convention that rules out inflicting and suffering harm (*KD* 32–3) and that sages have no need for such laws to govern themselves alone since they would never recognize any reason to harm each other (*KD* 21, 530 Us.; cf. Hermarchus *ap.* Porph. *Abst.* 1.8.4). This suggests that the harmonious community of friends is devoid of

[40] It does, however, resemble the ideal communities envisioned in the *Republic* written by the founding Stoic, Zeno of Citium. Zeno assumed that an ideal political community would be peopled exclusively by Stoic sages, and so would have no need of law-courts and ordinary political institutions. The evidence is collected and discussed by Baldry 1959. My suggestion here is developed in E. Brown forthcoming c: ch. 6. See also Schofield 1991.

[41] Diogenes of Oinoanda embraced this potential: '... so-called foreigners really are not, for in relation to each section of the earth, each has its own fatherland, but in relation to the whole circumference of this world, the entire earth is the single fatherland of all and the world is one home' (30.II.14–III.11 Smith). Diogenes and other later Epicureans explain this cosmopolitanism by suggesting that humans enjoy a natural 'love of humanity (*philanthropia*)' (Diog. Oin. 3.V.4–8 Smith and Philod. *De pietate* 1103–8 Obbink) or that every human being is naturally suited to become virtuous (Lucr. *DRN* 3.319–22). (See also Hermarchus *ap.* Porph. *Abst.* 1.7.1, with Vander Waerdt 1988 against Long and Sedley 1987: vol. 2, p. 137.) But the evidence suggests that Epicurus himself was less than fully cosmopolitan, on the grounds that sages must come from certain peoples (DL 10.117 and 226 Us.; cf. *KD* 32 and Philod. *De dis* 3 (*PHerc.* 157/152) XIV Diels).

justice. Justice, on this view, would be a virtue born of conflict, useful for restraining the unwise and protecting the wise (530 Us.) but out of place in an ideally harmonious community.

In response to this problem, it is tempting to think that Epicureans recognize two kinds of justice, one a virtue of persons (that would be present in the ideal community) and the other of society (that would not).[42] One might even suppose that personal justice is natural (dependent upon facts about our psychology) whereas societal justice is conventional (dependent upon what we agree upon). But these are the wrong distinctions to draw. The surviving fragments give no whisper of a distinction between personal and societal justice or of a contrast between natural and conventional justice. Moreover, Epicurus has no need of either distinction to be consistent.[43]

What is natural is the concept of justice. Human beings form the natural concept (*prolēpsis*) of the just as that which benefits (*sumpherein*) reciprocal community (*hē pros allēlous koinōnia*) (*KD* 37–8). Thus, when 'just' is used not in vain but to refer to actually just things, it refers to things that are beneficial to a reciprocal community (*KD* 37, cf. *Ep. Hdt.* 37–8). That is why Epicurus' *Principal Doctrines* concerning justice (*KD* 31–8) start with the declaration that 'nature's justice is a token (*sumbolon*) of benefit toward not harming each other and not being harmed' (*KD* 31).[44] This is to say, there are facts of nature that favour certain other-regarding actions and disfavour others. Actions are not just or unjust merely because someone says they are (Hermarchus *ap.* Porph. *Abst.* 1.12.2).

Although being beneficial to reciprocal community is necessary for something to be just, it is not yet sufficient, according to Epicurus. He says that justice is not anything in itself, but is dependent upon a convention (*sunthēkē*) made to avoid harming each other and being harmed (*KD* 37–8). He draws out the consequence that for those who cannot make such a convention – nonhuman animals and primitive humans (cf. Lucr. *DRN* 5.925–1010) – nothing is just or unjust (*KD* 37; Hermarchus *ap.* Porph. *Abst.* 1.12.5–6).

[42] See Mitsis 1988: 59–97, esp. 91–2, and Annas 1993b: 293–302.

[43] With the argument that follows, see also Armstrong 1997 and O'Keefe 2001b.

[44] *Sumbolon* is commonly translated as if it were interchangeable with *sunthēkē* (convention). That seems to me to be forced, and to miss the importance of starting out with the natural concept of the just. See also Schofield 2000: 440 n. 11.

There are, then, two necessary and jointly sufficient conditions defining just and unjust actions (*KD* 37–8). An action is unjust if and only if it is proscribed by a convention made to avoid harming each other and being harmed *and* this convention actually benefits reciprocal community. An action is obligatory for a just person if and only if it is prescribed by a convention made to avoid harming each other and being harmed *and* this convention actually benefits reciprocal community. People are just and unjust derivatively from these specifications. As a first approximation, the just person is the one disposed to do what is just and the unjust person the one not so disposed.

This is only a first approximation because Epicureans distinguish three ways in which one might be disposed to do what is just, and only one of these ways belongs to the truly just person. One might do conventionally approved and actually beneficial actions because one simply sees that they are beneficial to the reciprocal community and thus to one's own tranquillity. To act upon simply seeing where advantage lies is to be free from countervailing temptations. This fully just disposition requires the wisdom of recognizing the limits of pleasure and pain (cf. Cic. *Fin.* 1.52–3). Another person might need to be reminded occasionally of where her advantage lies (Hermarchus *ap.* Porph. *Abst.* 1.10.2), or she might need to calculate carefully to determine this (Hermarchus *ap.* Porph. *Abst.* 1.8.2). Such a person is not fully virtuous, but is making progress toward virtue. A third sort of person, however, is so unwise that he will do what justice requires only out of fear of punishment that awaits those who fail to abide by the convention (Hermarchus *ap.* Porph. *Abst.* 1.7.3–4, 1.8.2–4).[45]

But if the wise and just person readily does what is beneficial for the community without need of reminders or penalties, then why does Epicurus think that a convention is necessary for justice? It is not because the demands of social life call for each of us to *compromise* his own pursuit of what is best for him. Glaucon, in Plato's *Republic*, tells a story of this sort, where weak individuals who would be best off harming others and not being harmed if they could pull this off reach a compromise agreement to avoid harming each other (Pl. *Rep.* 358e–359b). But Epicurus believes that no one can harm others without thereby harming himself. Anyone who resists the agreement

[45] For more on the distinction between the sage's motive to do what is just and the fool's motive (i.e. fear), see Vander Waerdt 1987.

and seeks to harm others will fail to achieve his good of tranquillity and painlessness because he cannot be secure in the belief that his treachery will go undiscovered and unpunished (*KD* 35, *SV* 7; Lucr. *DRN* 5.1151–60; Cic. *Fin.* 1.50–1; Plut. *Non posse* 1090C–D). Moreover, human beings need the co-operation of other human beings in order to avoid being harmed. Primitive humans who did not have the benefits of society faced constant threats of death from the natural world (Lucr. *DRN* 5.982–8 and 1007–8). Tranquillity requires security from wild animals and confidence of readily available food, and both of these require co-operation with other human beings.[46]

This need for co-ordinated behaviour to avoid harm and achieve benefits for mutual community is precisely the reason why a convention is required. It is not enough for all of us to see that some co-ordinated behaviour is needed. None of us reaps the benefits of security unless we see that the *same* pattern of co-ordinated behaviour is required. And we will not grasp this unless we actually communicate and come to an agreement about what behaviour is right and what wrong.[47] This holds even if we are all sages. The community of sages needs justice even though sages need neither laws nor the fear of punishment to encourage them to do as justice requires.[48]

Epicurus is not a pure conventionalist about justice. Nor is he like most limited conventionalists who restrict the content of justice by placing limitations on the procedures used to generate the

[46] Notice that the convention is formed to avoid harming each other and to avoid *being harmed*, and not just being harmed *by each other*. Both Lucretius and Hermarchus emphasize the threats wild animals pose and the need for peaceful community to ward them off. See Hermarchus *ap.* Porph. *Abst.* 1.10.2–3. These points are well emphasized by O'Keefe 2001b. Notice, too, that the contrast between Epicurean conventions and Glaucon's contract makes it clear that the Epicurean convention is not a response to a prisoner's dilemma, *contra* Denyer 1983.

[47] See Lucr. *DRN* 5.1019–23: humans who do not yet have language nonetheless communicate to produce an alliance (*amicitiem*). The word *amicitia* – often 'friendship' – calls to mind Torquatus' third Epicurean account of friendship as a convention (see n. 37 above). This association is sometimes resisted on the grounds that this particular *amicitia* consists merely in preventing each from harming the other. But that is false. The alliance also serves to protect the women and children, and the threats to the women and children are not all from other humans. This shows how the alliance serves to *benefit* the mutual community, and it brings the alliance closer to the Epicurean account of friendship.

[48] So, too, O'Keefe 2001b.

convention. Rather, Epicurus recognizes limitations on the *substance* of the convention, however it is formed: no agreement about right and wrong that fails to benefit reciprocal community defines what is just. So justice must have some reality independent of what any community has agreed. Still, justice is the same for all human beings only insofar as all have the same *concept* of justice; what is in fact just for these people here is not what is in fact just for those there (*KD* 36). This is not, as it was for Aristotle, a matter of recognizing that some things – for example, which side of the road one should drive on – need to be fixed as right or wrong though nature is indifferent as to which way they are fixed (Arist. *EN* 5.7). It is, instead, a matter of recognizing that *everything* that is right or wrong depends upon the community's particular circumstances, from the local environment to the way the community has been shaped by its history,[49] and upon the way in which the community agrees to respond to those circumstances.[50] Some actions might be conventionally and beneficially prohibited everywhere, but this would be a coincidence and subject to change (*KD* 37–8). It is built into the nature of the just that what is just is relative to particular facts that are subject to great variation.[51]

This point suggests why there is not a more concrete Epicurean 'political philosophy'. If the right and wrong of communal life varies from place to place and time to time, it is not easy to pronounce generally on the right regimes and procedures. But there remains the community of wise friends. This community, as is now clear, is full of justice because its members virtuously obey the norms of right and wrong that are fixed by a beneficial convention. Even without traditional institutions of politics, this would seem to be a political community.

49 *KD* 36. For the importance of a community's history, see Hermarchus *ap*. Porph. *Abst*. 1.10.4–11.5 with Morel 2000.

50 Nothing that any Epicurean says implies that there is one unique set of conventions that would be beneficial for a given particular community. For all that they say, there might even be significantly divergent sets of conventions that would just as readily benefit that community.

51 There are other ways of construing Epicurus' recipe of naturalism and conventionalism. Contrast, for example, the conventionalist reading of Müller 1972, Goldschmidt 1977, and Vander Waerdt 1987 with the naturalist interpretation of Alberti 1995.

Surely this is the Epicurean's political ideal? In one sense, yes, Epicureans must think that every community of human beings would be better than it is if every member of it were an Epicurean sage. But in another sense, caution is required. There are, in fact, very many ways of realizing a community of Epicurean friends. The purest community of friends would depend upon the security that only a world of exclusively sages could produce, and such a world is but a millennial promise (but see Diog. Oin. 56 Smith). Until such a world comes into being, a community of friends must do what is appropriate for its circumstances to realize security and tranquillity. In most circumstances, the community of friends *requires* the presence of a favourably disposed, traditional political community nearby, to guarantee security against potentially powerful enemies. So, Epicureans, who seek an ideal political community apart from the traditional *polis*, cannot be entirely apart from traditional politics.[52]

[52] So, too, Long 1986.

CATHERINE ATHERTON

11 Epicurean philosophy of language

INTRODUCTION

Is there such a thing as 'Epicurean philosophy of language'? There was, of course, no division or discipline so labelled within the Epicurean system. But that is a merely superficial objection: almost since there have been philosophers at all, they have been reflecting on many of the phenomena and problems now staked out as their territory by today's philosophers of language, although what earlier philosophers thought was worth investigating about language will not necessarily chime with modern priorities. Thus when we ask of any classical text the sorts of questions pursued by today's philosophers of language – such as how we manage to talk about the world, and to say true and false things about it; how language is related to thought; what a theory of meaning should look like – what we do not find may be at least as significant as what we do, just as what their contemporaries may have thought valuable or vulnerable in Epicurean theorizing need not coincide with our judgements.

The deep problem may be that Epicurean contributions derived importance from their role in some other enterprise than that of pursuing an interest in language *per se*. Epicureans, like Stoics, could be powerful arguers, resourceful, subtle, dogged (cf. Cic. *Fin.* 1.63) – but the school's insistence on keeping one's eyes on the prize was more powerful still. That prize was – typically for Hellenistic philosophers – ethical. It consisted in attaining and retaining stable

I would like to thank James Warren and David Blank for comments on earlier versions of this paper. Many of the topics touched on here will be discussed at greater length in a forthcoming book and several articles.

happiness; and the philosopher's goal was defined as the provision of instructions to that end (Epic. *Ep. Men.* 122; cf. Porphyry *Ad Marc.* 31). The Epicureans seem to have taken the trimming of philosophical fat very seriously indeed: thus the only reason to try to explain celestial phenomena, which philosophy alone can do, is that they otherwise may worry and frighten us (Epic. *KD* 11, 12, cf. *Ep. Hdt.* 81–4, *Ep. Pyth.* 85). Philosophy is to be integrated into ordinary life (*SV* 41), neither tacked on to it as an intellectual pastime, nor valued, as *hoi polloi* value a standard education, as a competitive activity to help one cut a *bella figura* in company (45).

There is far more to be said for this deeper, more specific objection. The surviving texts, which yield information not merely about the linguistic theorizing itself, but about its context, aims and limitations, do not point to an over-arching theoretical framework for the topics touched on by Epicureans that is narrower than the whole compass of their philosophy. Further, where those topics find modern correlates, such as the relation of thought to language or of truth and language (and on some problems the modern philosopher of language would explore the Epicureans seem to be silent, and *vice versa*), there are more assumptions to be found than forays into explicit theorizing, while one crucial theory (of linguistic communication) may have been extrapolated from Epicurean texts by an ancient interpreter. The Epicurean theory of the origins of language owes its status to its contribution to ethical instruction.

SOUNDS, THINGS AND ANTICIPATIONS

The majority of scholars agree that Epicureans should be described, in modern terms, as intensionalists; a minority holds out for an extensionalist interpretation. On this latter view,[1] a direct signifying relation holds between language and things in the world (individuals or tokens of types; perhaps other things too, such as properties and relations); on the former,[2] a role would also be played by (something like) meanings, that is, mental items of a sort, most likely

[1] Cf. *e.g.* De Lacy 1939: 85; De Lacy 1978: 184; Asmis 1984: 26–7; Annas 1992: 167; Glidden 1983, 1985.

[2] So Long 1971: 120–1; Sedley 1973: 14–16; Goldschmidt 1978: 163–4; Long and Sedley 1987: vol. 1, p. 89. Everson 1994 ascribes a form of intensionalism to the school (106–7), while recognizing the extensionalist implications of other evidence (87).

'preconceptions' or 'anticipations' (*prolēpseis*). Such a theory ought to furnish an account not only of the signifying relation, but also of what anticipations contribute. More importantly, however, the evidence points to interest above all in the phenomenon of communication *via* language, rather than in the direct relation between language and the world.

Thus two non-Epicurean authors – Plutarch *Adv. Col.* 1119F–1120A and Sextus Empiricus *M* 8.13 – who strongly support the extensionalists show signs of having adapted their source-material to a non-Epicurean conceptual framework, a Stoic-style tripartite scheme of things in the world, linguistic signifiers, and *lekta* or the incorporeal significations of sentences (and some sentence-parts) and the contents of thoughts expressible thereby,[3] with Epicureans, the story goes, rejecting the latter entirely. Now a principled rejection of this scheme would have been a reasonable move on the part of the Epicureans, who were thorough-going materialists themselves,[4] and it would have been reasonable to credit them with it later on: but the original Epicurean theory certainly cannot have been constructed as response to a (mature) Stoic rival, which was only developed by third-generation Stoics such as Chrysippus. Furthermore, Sextus' report, which is concerned with a specific question: *What sorts of thing do the doctrinaire philosophers say are the bearers of truth-values?*, tacitly flags its claim that the Epicurean answer was 'vocalizations' (*phōnai*) as an inference from the school's exclusion of the possibility that they are instead *lekta* of a kind, *viz.* propositions (cf. Asmis 1984: 144 n. 7; Hossenfelder 1996: 233), as if Sextus had been unable to discover what the school itself had to say on the matter.

Again, while there is evidence that Epicureans did accept the existence of a signifying relation between language and the world,[5] our principal sources do not make it central. It is not appealed to in a

[3] Cf. DL 7.41–2, 55, 62–3, 66–8; Ammonius *in De Int.* 2.26ff.

[4] Sedley has argued (1983, 1988) that Epicurean metaphysics countenances emergent mental properties, a contentious thesis which is anyway irrelevant to whether the school would have allowed incorporeal *lekta* into the fold (see Gill, ch. 7 and O'Keefe, ch. 8, this volume). The Stoic theory is hobbled by dependence on objects the incorporeality of which renders them causally inert (Clement *Strom.* 8.9.26.3–4, Stobaeus 1.13.1).

[5] For Epicurean talk of expressions 'signifying' things: see e.g. Philod. *Rhet.* 2a, XLIX.5 Longo Auricchio; Dem. Lac. *Po.* 2 XLIV.7–8, XLV.5–8 Romeo; *Ap.* XL.4–5, 11–12 Puglia. But see main text, below.

key text for us, *Ep. Hdt.* 37–8, where a methodological rule states that vocal sounds' 'subordinates' (*hypotetagmena*) are the things we must 'have grasped (*eilēphenai*)' for doubts and puzzles to be settled and for opinions to be verified; the absence of semantic vocabulary is in any case striking, even though what 'subordinates' are is not explained. The preferred interpretation[6] has been to identify them with the 'first thought-objects' mentioned in the justification for the rule which follows: 'for the first thought-object (*to prōton ennoēma*) corresponding to each (vocal) sound must be kept in view (*blepesthai*) and must stand in no further need of proof'. It is then further argued, or assumed, that a '(first) thought-object' is (more or less) the same thing as an anticipation, although for some reason Epicurus has avoided that term here,[7] anticipations, roughly speaking, being psychological constructs from repeated sensory and emotional experiences, allowing identification of objects as belonging to a kind (and perhaps recognition of individuals too). It is significant, again, that our investigation must extend to an item which evidently belongs to psychology and epistemology.

Interpretation has tended to go further still, toward a thesis that anticipations are subordinate to sounds in the very specific sense that they are their meanings, culminating in the (re-)construction of an Epicurean counterpart to the tripartite semantic scheme referred to earlier, with anticipations in place of *lekta*.[8] But there is certainly no direct evidence in its favour, and elsewhere anticipations play a crucial part in quite a different context: what looks to be an explanation, not of the relation between language and the world *per se*, but of linguistic communication, at DL 10.33: 'As soon as "man" is spoken (*rhēthēnai*), the pattern (*tupos*) thereof is also thought of (*noeitai*) immediately, in connection with an anticipation, the senses leading the way'. This third kind of item, the *tupos* or pattern which

[6] So Long 1971: 124; Long and Sedley 1987: vol. 1, p. 101; Hossenfelder 1996: 228; Striker 1996a: 38.

[7] Cf. Bailey 1926: 176; Asmis 1984: 22 with n. 9, 1999: 263, 277; Long and Sedley 1987: vol. 1, p. 89, cf. vol. 2, p. 92; Everson 1994: 104; more references in Glidden 1983: 196 n. 6.

[8] Cf. e.g. Bignone 1920: 73; Long 1971: 121; Arrighetti 1973: 36; Sedley 1973: 14, 20-1; Long and Sedley 1987: vol. 1, pp. 89, 101; Schenkeveld 1999: 196. Alternatively, subordinates could be things in the world, in which case Epicurus' rule will make sense because it is only by prior experiential grasp of a word's extension that cognitive access can be had to the corresponding thought-object.

belongs to a bit of language because it is brought to mind by it, could be the 'first thought-object' of the *Letter*; if so, a 'pattern' or 'shape' (*morphē*) would be (in Diogenes' words) '(primarily) subordinate' to a sound as what is (first) summoned to mind by it – it waits on it, so to say, like a general's troops or a manager's underlings[9] (although why it is 'first' is not yet clear). Access to patterns *via* language and thought would be made possible by the mind's having been put into a state of 'anticipating' them by sensory exposure (to what has 'often appeared from the outside', *viz*. a pattern), and they will then function as recognitional resources.

Thus the role of patterns or (first) thought-objects and/or anticipations will be epistemic, not semantic, for they will explain how we grasp how words are used, and how we mean things using words, but not, strictly speaking, what words signify (cf. Barnes 1996, 1999: 196; Everson 1994); and in a sense they will be rough equivalents of intensions, fixing the extensions of names, although not psychological in nature. Yet while what determines whether an object fits an anticipation is whether it belongs to the kind associated therewith, what determines whether this or that vocal sound in a community's language is associated with a given anticipation is, in contrast, merely whether it happens to be associated in that community with the things perception of which is the basis for formation of the anticipation that constitutes receptiveness toward the relevant pattern. Under optimal conditions, word-use and -understanding will be shared by individuals because the anticipation associated therewith will have a similar causal history in all users in a community. Such uniformity will strike us as implausible at best (cf. Long 1971: 120), and we shall see later that Epicureans did appeal to something other than contemporary standard usage to explain sound/thing pairings.

The vocalization/thing relation, therefore, need not always have been thought of by Epicureans as one of signifying – which in turn may account for the apparent paucity of evidence that it is.[10] We cannot be certain, however, that DL 10.33 is authentically Epicurean: it may report an extrapolation from Epicurean sources which applied,

[9] Non-philosophical usage of the verb is usually either military or more generally organizational: e.g. Polybius 3.36.7 (an interesting exception at 18.15.4); Plut. *Nic.* 23; Ael. *Tact.* 15.1, 26.7.

[10] See n. 5 for examples.

but nowhere articulated, the underlying theory – if so, an important omission. Note, too, that utterances' intentional properties (to use the modern jargon) will, it seems, be wholly dependent on the so-far unexplained intentional properties of users or their mental states. Something analogous seems to hold in the case of truth-values, as we shall see.

Whatever relation is in question may not be one between 'words' and 'things', as is often assumed, for example, at *Ep. Hdt.* 37, where Epicurus speaks of '(vocal) sounds' (*phthongoi*).[11] While *phthongos* was not common in philosophical discourse (cf. Asmis 1984: 24),[12] it was in literary language – to mean 'talk' or 'speech' – and was also applied, for example, to the sound made by a bird or animal or by the wind. It and its cognates were to become fixtures in Epicurean sources, as at DL 10.31 and Diogenes of Oinoanda 12.II.12–III.3, 47.II.2 Smith (cf. 106.1). In *Nat.* 28, Epicurus uses it and *vocalization* amongst other terms (*lexis, onoma*) for bits of language, apparently without distinction of meaning.[13]

Against this background, Epicurus' choice of term in so prominent a text suggests a conspicuous refusal to specify even whether the 'sounds' in question are specifically human; and by using it just after 'vocalizations' instead (36 [*bis*], cf. 52), he is demonstrating a well-known, and apparently influential, aversion to the sorts of rigid, technical linguistic concepts and categories being hammered out by contemporary experts in dialectic, especially Stoics (e.g. DL 7.39, 46-8) and the then emergent discipline of grammar.[14] For Epicurus, dialectic is useless because 'it is sufficient for natural philosophers to proceed in accordance with things' sounds' (10.31), while Cicero's Epicurean spokesman Torquatus assigns to natural philosophy the capacity to know 'the force (*uis*) of words, the nature of speech (*orationis*), and the rational principle' governing logical consequence and contradiction; Epicurean canonic (epistemology and methodology)

[11] An exception is Everson, 1994: 79 n. 16, who recognizes the term's vagueness, translating it *utterance*.

[12] Important background texts for this term include Plato *Phileb.* 18c1 and (especially) *Crat.* 429e–430a; cf. also Plut. *Quaest. Plat.* 1010A.

[13] Sometimes *lexis* (sing.) seems to function as the equivalent of *language* generally; e.g. 13.IX.3.

[14] Cf. Sen. *Ep.* 89.11; SE *M* 1.49, 272 (with Blank 1998: xlvii–l, 286, 307), 7.14–15 (but cf. 22); DL 10.30; Polystratus *De cont. irr.* XIII.25–9, XIV.2–7, XV.22–7 Indelli.

ensures that 'we will never be defeated by anyone's talk, and so abandon our belief' (*Fin.* 1.63, cf. 2.6, 18).

TRUTH

Sextus' report (*M* 8.13) of theories about truth-value-bearers lists a third possibility: 'the mind's change of state' (*hē tēs dianoias kinēsis*).[15] Although labelled scornfully by Sextus 'apparently a schoolman's invention', this could have been the Epicurean candidate for the job (cf. *Ep. Hdt.* 50–1). As a broad generalization, there would be nothing odd, in the logic of the Hellenistic and later periods, about assigning truth-values to beliefs – which, however, were typically so described insofar as they stood in the right sort of relation to primary truth-value bearers (whether propositions[16] or declarative sentences,[17] internally structured in subject-predicate fashion) giving the beliefs' contents; and believers were standardly thought of as assenting to such a truth-value bearer.[18] In contrast, the linguistic items regarded as true or false by Epicurus himself do not seem to have been specifically sentences or their significations, but in general vocal sounds (cf. *Nat.* 28 13.II.7–12 Sedley), vocalizations (6.I.8–13) and linguistic expressions (13.VII.4–5, where the use of the term 'subordinated' of concepts (*ennoiai*) is striking; cf. Philod. *Rhet.* (?) *PHerc.* 250 fr. V.6–7 (II 190 Sudhaus); Diogenianus *ap.* Euseb. *Praep. Ev.* 4.3.6). That is, the application of a vocalization (etc.) to a thing seems to be a matter of, or tantamount to, expressing an opinion about it, something DL 10.33 also suggests. The implicit identification (*Ep. Men.* 124) of the false suppositions ordinary people have about the divine with their 'assertions' (*apophaseis*) about it suggests indifference to any distinction between claiming that something has a certain property, and subscribing to a concept according to which it possesses that property. Thus the tentative conclusion reached earlier about the Epicurean explanation of how words signify (to the extent that there was such a thing, as opposed to an Epicurean theory of linguistic communication) must be emended; for it now seems that

15 Long and Sedley 1987: vol. 1, p. 195, Everson 1994: 84 translate 'the process that constitutes thought', but this is a far less likely interpretation of the Greek.

16 E.g. DL 7.58, 63-4; Porphyry *ap.* Amm. *in De Int.* 44.19ff.

17 E.g. Amm. *in De Int.* 7.29ff.; Galen *Inst. log.* 2.1.5-4.1K.

18 I leave aside here whether Epicureans accepted the 'assent' model of belief.

that theory extended beyond anticipations to other types of concepts or beliefs – including false ones not well-grounded in experience[19] – which can nonetheless play the part of 'subordinates'.

That use of names was conceived of in this way can be made consistent with evidence suggesting that beliefs (and mental states generally) were thought of by Epicureans as prior to and independent of language, on the assumption that naming constitutes expression of a pre-existing belief, as in the strongly imagistic conception of thought attested by Aëtius (4.8–10) and especially Lucretius (4.779–817; cf. Annas 1992: 165). On the other hand, *Nat.* 28 12.VI.2–VII.9 Sedley lists believing 'imagistically' (*phantastikōs*) alongside believing 'through reason/discourse, that is, theoretically (*dia logou dē theōrētikōs*)' and 'inclusively' (*perilēptikōs*), neither of which can depend intrinsically on the use of images (cf. respectively *Ep. Hdt.* 59 with 47, 62–3; 56, 57, 60, 66, 67–8, 70–1). Philodemus' *On signs* (fr. 1.1–6 De Lacy and De Lacy) may suggest that even inferential thought was conceived of as proceeding, in effect, by detection of similarities between appearances (cf. J. Allen 2001: 230–1; cf. DL 10.32).

Even a partial application of such a model would have to explain how the mind correctly (for the most part) maps the iconic structure of visual (or other perceptual) representations of objects on to whatever structure(s) linguistic complexes are assumed to enjoy, and *vice versa*, so as to be capable of moving between structures of these very different types. As it is, the Epicurean explanation remains obscure of how 'the mind's imagistic focus' (*phantastikē epibolē tēs dianoias*) on the property of e.g. flying (cf. *Ep. Hdt* 69 for such acts of attention to properties) is related to formulation or understanding of (an utterance of) the sentence *Theaetetus flies*, or of the form of the verb *fly* which occurs in it. Nor is it clear how the fact of predication, or the acts of *e.g.* communicating a belief, doubt or inquiry (*Ep. Hdt.* 37), could be conveyed by or translated into perceptual images. The complexity of the problem is increased by what Asmis (1984: 25) has well described as the school's 'refusal to peg ontological distinctions to grammatical distinctions'. While the Stoic *lekton* theory brings with it its own fair share of difficulties, it does provide solutions of a sort to all these problems, by systematically linking thoughts with

[19] These may be the 'doxastic concepts' which require confirmation: *KD* 24, with Asmis 1984: 62–3.

structured contents and both with sentences, and by distinguishing between the content of a thought and the acts of asserting, doubting, commanding (etc.) it. Also likely to be troublesome is the possibility that certain (kinds of) thoughts are available only to subjects with access to a natural language (a possible example at Lucr. 5.1022–3), even if not all beliefs require the believer to have access to a natural language (cf. Long 1971: 119; Everson 1994: 106 n. 81) – a controversial theoretical claim already in need of defence. We are left to speculate that thoughts intrinsically enjoy quasi-linguistic structuring, in something like the way postulated by today's 'language of thought' hypothesis.

This final problem also brings to our attention the fact that any extensionalist theory is notoriously open to objection on the grounds of failing to take into account intensional contexts and intentionality, major challenges to the dominant model in today's semantics: that of the specification of (contextually sensitive) sentence-meaning by way of truth-conditions. We have no reason to believe that Epicureans – or anyone until very recently – wanted to reduce meaning to truth in this way (but see Everson 1994: 86–91). If Epicureans took an extensionalist approach to signification, it was most likely because of suspicions about the ontological credentials and the explanatory usefulness of *lekta* and their ilk.

Belief in non-existents was, in contrast, recognized as a problem, but again for different reasons from those cited by today's philosophers. Nor was it framed directly as a problem about language (*e.g.* about what the names *Fury* [SE *M* 8.63–4] or *ghost* refer to, if anything), although the school's acceptance of the dependence of language on thought, and its assimilation of acts of naming, beliefs, and concepts, should licence some inferences at least. Belief in such things as Furies or ghosts had to be reconciled with central ontological, epistemological and ethical doctrines: the only autonomous existents are bodies and void, the only other existents being their properties; all appearances have external physical causes which those appearances faithfully represent; and 'there are no such things' as the scary monsters of myth and legend, as ghosts, or as the torments of the traditional underworld (the gods are another matter). Doctrinal harmony was achieved by shifting responsibility for error to the human faculty of belief and its failure to be appropriately cautious about identifying the ultimate causes of appearances (*Ep. Hdt.* 50–1; Lucr. 4.383–6; Diog. Oin. 9.v.3–13 Smith).

Of particular interest for us are the 'empty (vocal) sounds' which are to be avoided by proper use of 'first thought-objects' in *Ep. Hdt.* 37, there being a strong temptation to suppose that these are precisely sounds which have sense but fail to refer (cf. Everson 1994: 104–7). But even if beliefs about non-existents – including our acceptance of dream-images as veridical – can be given real causes external to the soul, *viz.* atomic *simulacra* (Lucr. 4.465; Diog. Oin. 69.II.1–3 Smith), it is the *contents* of beliefs or dreams which affect feelings and behaviour; analogously, what the theory identifies as the two-dimensional referents of *Fury* or *ghost* cannot be what subjects wrongly believe is being talked about. That Epicureans (and their opponents) had, however, somehow failed to see this difficulty is perhaps suggested by Diogenes' explanation of dreams (10.I.4–8 Smith). In any case, an interpretation which distinguishes between reference and sense obviously does not employ Epicurean concepts, and so cannot be directly exegetical.

As an alternative, we may tentatively apply to beliefs about non-existents the model set up earlier of the role played by anticipations and/or first thought-objects in linguistic communication. Everyone who possesses the concept of, say, a Fury will spontaneously associate the same kind of physical objects – atomic films, in such cases – both with that concept (i.e. the mind's standing readiness to accept and identify such images) and also with the name *Fury*. But possession of the concept of a Fury would amount to no more than a belief that *this* is what a Fury looks like, with no built-in commitment to the image's representing a three-dimensional continuant. This does not mean that anticipations are existentially quantified – as in Everson's reconstruction (1994: 105) – while mere concepts are not, for the distinction in play is one between two modes of physicality. The 'emptiness' of, say, Orestes' Fury-related utterances will accordingly lie in the fact that the real things with which the name *Fury* is associated, in Orestes' usage as in ours, simply cannot possess the properties, such as being alive or conscious, which he keeps trying to predicate of them, explicitly or implicitly. Any attempt to apply such names to these otherwise ontologically respectable bearers will result in sounds which are 'empty' precisely because their components contradict one other – the speaker might as well have said nothing at all – and in general Epicurus is warning us off talk about impossible combinations of properties, as those are prescribed by things' first thought-objects or anticipations. This will not be limited to ectoplasmic *simulacra*. It will extend to non-existent theoretical items (*e.g.* the 'element' fire, Lucr. 1.645–54, 665–83), to real things some have misunderstood (*Ep. Hdt.* 68, on 'empty talk' about the soul) and to the purely intentional objects which appear to be introduced by the Epicurean methods for determining the truth-value of beliefs (SE *M* 7.203ff., DL 10.34, with *Ep. Hdt.* 38, *KD* 24). Analogous problems are raised by what is known of Epicurean explanations of talk about things which no longer exist (Lucr. 1.464ff.) or do not yet exist.

THE ORIGINS OF LANGUAGE

The handful of primary and secondary texts we have for the Epicurean theory of glossogenesis conforms, to a considerable degree, to the picture constructed so far of Epicurean thinking about language.

First, it assumes the priority, both logical and psychological, of thought over (public, natural) language(s). This emerges from the very structure of that account, as summarized by Epicurus himself (*Ep. Hdt.* 75–6): in the remote past, vocalizations, mediated by the vocalizers' psychological states – their sensory appearances and feelings – were produced by primitive humans in response to the things which those vocalizations ultimately came to name.[20] Vocalizers' psychology and physiology (what Epicurus calls 'the natures of men') were in turn systematically shaped in part by the vocalizers' physical environment. Thus the fact that names are names *of* things – are associated with them, or signify them, or whatever – was determined by the prior facts that people had thoughts and feelings about those things, and that they came to use their natural, instinctive vocalizations to 'mark' them, as Lucretius says (*notare*, 5.1043, 1058, 1090). The systematic, community-wide correlations between externals on the one hand, and feelings, thoughts and vocalizations on the other, which made these 'marks' so useful, are the results of the fact that the former cause all the latter, directly or indirectly.

The scene for this development has been set in the passage just before Lucretius' account of the origins of language, which describes

[20] This interpretation borrows freely from Sedley 1973: 18 and Brunschwig 1994b, especially 26–31 (probably the most thorough and penetrating analysis); cf. also Giussani 1892–6: vol. 1, p. 277; Atherton 2005.

how early humans were beginning to expand their social associations beyond kinship groups, and must, therefore, have been in need of more precise and accurate means of communication than gestures and mumbling (5.1020–7). This passage points to a uniform approach to the doctrinal positioning of glossogenesis, for Epicurus' own original account of the origins of language probably,[21] and Diogenes' certainly (12.II.11–V.14 Smith),[22] were contributions to a naturalistic explanation of the emergence of civilization. Lucretius' aim too is to reassure us that humans have managed their own elevation from savagery by bootstrapping themselves into civilization, without divine teleological help or guidance. The linguistic theory is strikingly original, in part because it makes variation amongst languages something natural, in part for laying a naturalistic foundation for a superstructure of rational refinement. For after names are in place,[23] a second, bipartite,[24] stage takes over, at which rationality (*logismos*) intervenes both to improve and to add to existing stocks of names, thereby accommodating the other main type of ancient glossogenetic theory, that appealing to the deliberate 'imposition' (*thesis*) of words. Traditionally the province of some mythical or divine figure, in Epicurus' version this is assigned to normal communities and a few gifted individuals.

Lucretius attributes language's origins to two co-operating factors, nature and usefulness (5.1028–9): but it is clear that our ability to use the sounds which nature 'forced' our ancestors to make is itself something natural, in that it represents the exploitation of unlearned,

[21] The *Ep. Hdt.* account is probably a summary of Epicurus' original explanation in *Nat.* 12, which certainly discussed the rise of religion (cf. Philod. *De pietate* 225–31 Obbink), a topic dealt with by Lucretius at 5.1161–94.

[22] That Diogenes' account of glossogenesis belongs to natural philosophy is proved by the absence from the relevant fragments of the maxims which run along the bottom of the inscription's ethical portion: cf. Smith 1993: 82, 99.

[23] It is quite clear that the first stage produces names, not some approximation to them: not only does Epicurus imply as much (note 'names too did not come into being at the start by imposition'), but he describes the second stage as improving people's 'indicatings' (*dēlōseis*) (cf. Diog. Oin. 12.IV.1–2) – impossible if such things were not already in place.

[24] A bipartite second stage is to be preferred to two separate stages since Epicurus does not add another temporal adverb to mark off this part of his account, and since there is no reason in principle to suppose that theoretical names were introduced only after communal improvements had concluded, especially as such improvements are probably on-going.

involuntary vocalizations in the service of the innate human ability to use signs for objects in communication with others. That ability Lucretius brilliantly detects in the as yet languageless child's untaught, spontaneous use of gestures to achieve shared focus on objects around it (1030–2); it is still disputed whether Lucretius' loading of our faculties as naturally goal-directed in this way reflects Stoicizing influences.[25] But an implicit allusion, at best, to the existence of other languages may lurk in 5.1036, and the statement of the theory's core, compressed as it is into a single phrase – 'in relation to different feelings (*pro vario sensu*)' (5.1058) – would be obscure had Epicurus' own version not survived. In the immediate context, just before the catalogue of animal vocalizations varying by species and situation (1056–86), this summary may even be misleading, since the sample *sensus* at work in animals are explicitly limited to their emotional states (1061), saying nothing of perceptions; and the catalogue not much to the point without the key thesis that sign-use is as natural for us as is vocalization. Lucretius' argumentation also makes salient two serious difficulties for the Epicurean theory.[26]

The first is its reliance on a causal linkage, running from external object *via* internal state to vocalization, which removes control over vocalization from vocalizers. Epicurus' general principle governing the emergence of civilization (*Ep. Hdt.* 75) has nature 'taught and subject to necessity (*didakhthēnai te kai anagkasthēnai*) by things themselves', and Lucretius says that nature 'coerced (*subegit*)' our ancestors to vocalize. Yet the sort of 'necessity' or 'coercion' which yields a particular vocalization as the invariable, or at least typical, effect of a particular external feature, can at best provide a system of shared associations in community members. Unless utterances can be freed from this causal chain, they will inevitably lack communicative (as opposed to informational) content.

[25] The theory in question is that of 'appropriation' (*oikeiōsis*): DL 7.85; Plut. *Stoic. Repug.* 1038B (both from Chrysippus). For the debate, cf. e.g. Sorabji 1993: 163-4; Schrijvers 1999: 102 (*pro*); Robin 1962: 3: 142–3, Pigeaud 1984: 139–40; Boyancé 1963: 243 (*contra*). Lucretius might find it hard to quarrel with the teleologist Galen's description of a two-year-old's ability to learn to say words without special instruction in how to shape its tongue as a 'work of nature (*ergon tēs phuseōs*)' (*Comm. in Hipp. epid.* VI 17B K, 234.7–14, 237.1–2).

[26] I discuss both at greater length in Atherton 2005.

The automatic, uncontrolled character of the originary human cries is emphasized in Proclus' report that, according to Epicurus, the earliest language users 'did not impose names knowledgeably (*epistēmonōs*), but as being moved naturally, like coughers, sneezers, bellowers, howlers and groaners' (*in Crat.* 17.13–16). The 'naturalness' of names would thus be traceable to the 'naturalness' *of naming*, which is as natural to us as are seeing and hearing – something the natural sign-using behaviour highlighted by Lucretius would support. Epicurus could have presented his theory as a deliberate counter to Plato's knowledgeable or expert name-giver,[27] and an assimilation of naming to perceptual activity would, in one way, be especially appropriate, given that it is the causal 'purity' of the latter's products which grounds their criterial status.

Diogenes' version, at least as we have it, lacks even this stab at a positive explanation, focusing instead on negative campaigning, now partly lost, against the rival name-giver theory. This may originally have contained, besides appeals to the absurdity of the name-giver's being able to unite his community (12.IV.6–V.4, cf. *DRN* 5.1050–1) and (probably) of his even being understood by them (12.V.4–14, cf. 5.1052–5), the important, but dangerous, argument that he could not have had the anticipation [*notities*] of the usefulness of names, since this could not arise had 'others too not used vocalizations amongst themselves' (5.1046–7). But if a putative name-giver could not construct this anticipation without appropriate experience of names in use, whence did the real name-givers – primitive humans as a whole, or sub-groups of them – get their anticipation thereof, so that each 'could know and see in his mind what he wanted to do' (1049)? We must suppose that *all* humans were somehow able to imagine (cf. 5.1102–4; cf. 1361ff., 1379–83) the use of vocalizations as signs for communication, by combining – not necessarily reflectively – their own innate sign-using capacity with observed and remembered vocalization-thing correlations. On that basis, there will be no need for the intolerable nonsense of a divine name-giver, such as Diogenes' Hermes (12.III.4–8). It is striking that both he and Diogenes focus their efforts on making the theory's naturalistic foundation plausible

[27] Demetrius Lacon's text sadly becomes lacunose just as he is about to tell us what 'by nature' (*phusei*) means in the context of the first soundings-out of names (*Ap.* LXVII.7–10); one tempting possibility is 'untaught' (*adidaktōs*).

(cf. *DRN* 5.1056, 1089–90), at any rate by contrast with its rival (Diog. Oin. 12.III.7–8, IV 3–8 Smith).

Two other shortcomings deserve brief mention. First, Lucretius stresses the articulacy of primitive human cries (5.1088), without, however, explaining just what it contributes, or how it came about that we alone enjoy this property. Second, Epicurus and Lucretius present themselves as explaining the origins of 'names', 'words', 'vocalizations' or 'expressions', without further differentiation, so that it is Diogenes alone (12.II.12–III.3 Smith) who refers to the 'first soundings-out of nouns and verbs' (or of 'words and phrases')[28] by 'earth-born men' (cf. Lucretius 5.1411), thereby recognizing, implicitly or explicitly, the phenomenon of syntax, something modern linguists and philosophers argue is at once essential and unique to human languages. We are quite in the dark as to whether causal chains led from objects or their properties through appearances to vocalizations to the vocal emission of, say, particles, prepositions, or conjunctions, let alone of complete sentences (cf. Everson 1994: 93).

The pre-eminence of nouns and verbs could be explained if the school thought that the objective ontological distinctions between agents and patients, on the one hand, and actions and passivities on the other, were automatically embedded, through perception, in our conceptual apparatus, and hence in our naming-systems. (Epicureans would not have been alone in so privileging nominals and verbs: cf. e.g. Plut. *Quaest. Plat.* 1010A). If so, our broader cognitive endowment will have played yet another key role in Epicurean explanations of the origins of language. The existence of a capacity for learning from experience, for example, is implicit in Diogenes' claim that what produced the expertises were 'needs and external impacts, together with time' (13.II.8–11 Smith), as well as in the accounts of early man given by Diodorus Siculus (1.8, 90) and Horace (*Sat.* 1.3.96ff.), which show some signs of Epicurean influence.[29]

[28] For the first interpretation, see e.g. Spoerri 1959: 137, Brunschwig 1994b: 34; for the second, e.g. Bollack 1977: 795, followed by Smith 1993: 373.

[29] Diodorus allows for local differentation in the development of languages (1.8.4); Horace, for the influence of *utilitas* generally (*Sat.* 1.3.98), and for gradual shaping of sounds and significations alike (101).

LINGUISTIC NORMS

Lucretius' appeal to the infant's pointing activity shows that achievement of joint attention-focusing is central to the Epicurean model of linguistic communication. Even when the communicator lacks some of the relevant verbal and cognitive resources, the intentionality of thought is assumed to be passed on to linguistic structures, and assumed too is an untaught acceptance of other humans as loci of thought who can share focus on externals. Use of the system of linguistic communication sketched earlier does not require understanding of its underlying psychological mechanism. But intelligent reflection on both system and mechanism turns out to be an indispensable component of Epicurean philosophy in general and of its methodology in particular.

The failures of communication which such reflection will reveal turn out to be laid overwhelmingly at the door of inappropriate associations between concepts and vocalizations. Attention to the deleterious effects of ambiguity on philosophical discourse, especially as regards the school's own writings (e.g. *Nat.* 2, 24.49.9ff. Arr., where Epicurus accuses certain persons of forming a false belief 'on account of the homonymy of *fineness*'), can be interpreted as one example of the practice, mentioned in the second part of Epicurus' glossogenetic account, of eliminating ambiguities; and philosophers will naturally rank amongst that stage's rationally-motivated, theoretically-based name-givers. Very few known Epicurean texts appeal to ambiguity kinds other than homonymy; those which we do have are, unsurprisingly, far less tied to Epicurean categories and concepts (e.g. Demetrius Lacon *Ap.* XXXI.1–6, *Po.* 2 XLIV with DL 7.62; cf. Romeo *ad loc.*, 1988: 225). And while ambiguity was a target for Epicurean canonic, as Seneca claims (*Ep.* 89.11) and as Epicurean practice plainly confirms, the relevant evidence suggests a worrying deficiency in the relevant theoretical resources, especially in contrast with the important contributions made to the definition and classification of ambiguity by Aristotle in rhetoric (*Rhet.* 1407a31–2), literary criticism (*Poet.* 1461a25ff.) and logic (*Soph. El.* 165a3-13, 166a6–16, 33-8, b1–8), and by the Stoics in dialectic, with implications for numerous fields of study (DL 7.62; cf. Atherton 1993).

Epicurus did write a work *On ambiguity* (*Peri amphibolias*) (*Nat.* 28 13.v.2 Sedley), but, beyond the possible implications of the context in which it is mentioned, we know nothing about what topics it may have discussed; one speculative possibility is the question whether transfers of names from the observable to the theoretical realm (cf. *Nat.* 28 13.V.8–12 Sedley; cf. *Ep. Hdt.* 67, 70) result in cases of ambiguity (e.g. *to kenon* 'the void', originally the ordinary phrase '(the) empty'). Almost nothing is known about which criteria were laid down for ambiguity, and especially about what role was played in judgements about ambiguities by intuitions about usage or about the relation between ambiguity and the phenomenon of 'commonness' or 'sharing' (*koinotēs*) of names. Not only is this latter not explicitly identified with ambiguity or homonymy, there are often good reasons for supposing that these are precisely *not* in play, as in a well-known passage from Philodemus' *On anger* in which the topic of dispute is the right way to understand the key term *anger* (*thumos*) in the school's thesis 'that the wise man will become angry' (*De ira* XLIII.41–XLVI.16 Indelli). Here a claim that the word's significations (or associated anticipations) have nothing in common would be highly implausible. (Aristotle might have argued instead, for example, that anger is something 'said in many ways'; cf. Atherton 1993: 107 for similar Stoic terminology.)

Of course, Epicureans could still have argued for just that conclusion; or they could have brought other distinctions to bear. Concepts and categories commonplace in the literary-critical and philosophical mainstream were certainly put to work when needed, as in Philodemus' distinction between strict and extended or catachrestic uses of the words *expertise, expertly* (*Rhet.* 2a.1674 XIX.2–5, XXX.19ff., XLI.27ff. Longo Auricchio, with Blank 1995: 182–3). To date, however, the principle(s) on which the general distinctions between catachrestic or figurative and ambiguous usages were constructed are unknown (contrast e.g. Simpl. *In Cat.* 8.22ff., 10.27ff., 32.25–6, 81.7–14).

CONCLUSIONS

The linguistic naturalism which is the fruit of the Epicurean account of glossogenesis will tend to work in favour of linguistic conservatism. Existing usages will not always serve, but can typically boast the stamp of natural legitimacy, for they have, for the most part, been passed on unchanged within communities, as each new generation learns afresh from its elders what our most distant ancestors learned from nature: linguistic ontogeny, on the whole, recapitulates phylogeny, so that, as a rule, Epicurus' 'first' thought-objects (*Ep. Hdt.* 37) will be 'first' both historically and psychologically. Hence we ignore at our peril the guidance afforded by the learned system of anticipations associated in memory with vocal sounds, a system which is constructed from experiences and in turn guides us to identification of the things in the world with which those terms are associated in our community's usage. Other sorts of belief, in contrast, including those coded as applications of names, require testing, and some of them will be shown up to be, not false, but 'empty', by naming impossible combinations of (real) objects and properties. It hardly needs be said that against this epistemologically optimistic background, robust explanations will be needed of both the origins and the prevalence of 'false presuppositions' (such as those about the gods: *Ep. Men.* 122–3).

Our sources have pointed to an almost exclusive focus within the Epicurean school on the cognitive value of language and on its correct use in practice. Even though answers to some of the philosopher of language's traditional questions have been brought to light – as, for instance, with the relation between thought and language – we have found little by way of explicit theorizing about them, and the emphasis seems always to be on the analysis and assessment of a linguistic practice geared to successful communication, above all of philosophical doctrine. Language knowledge itself has turned out to be simply a special kind of memory, of a system of sound-concept/*tupos*-thing correlations. That model seems to have been at least facilitated by the school's general lack of interest in explaining the phenomenon of syntax. Such indifference is perhaps the clearest measure of the gulf between Epicurean theorizing about language and its counterparts, ancient and modern alike. The real lesson of this investigation must be that the school followed its own agenda so closely that, even where problems can be seen to be shared between it and philosophy of language today, that overlap does not extend either to the motivation for solving those problems, or, in large part, to the sorts of theoretical resources brought to bear on them and the methodological rigour with which they were attacked.

The school's isolation may indeed seem to have had grave consequences, if (as the evidence may suggest) the Epicureans were unable to complete their own limited range of theoretical linguistic projects – such as the explanation of glossogenesis – or to engage successfully in the practices of communicating and defending their own teachings, and of identifying and eliminating the language-related prejudices and errors which dog ordinary people and other philosophers alike. Those projects and practices, dictated by the school's overriding ethical interests, comport a narrowly utilitarian evaluation of the concepts and categories put to work therein. Hence any apparent failures at the level of explanation (such as the implausibility of certain aspects of Epicurean anti-teleology and naturalism, *e.g.* that intentionality is something 'natural', that humans articulate vocal sounds 'naturally', that our cognitive apparatus is broadly reliable ...) would, by the Epicureans' own lights, be outweighed not merely by the broader theoretical success of the school's doctrines and by its undermining of its rivals (e.g. the inspired or privileged name-giver), but also by the practical achievement of its members in, quite simply, improving their own lives and those of the people with whom they engage. A final judgement has yet to be passed on the appropriateness, and the success, of this strategy.

DAVID BLANK

12 *Philosophia* and *technē*: Epicureans on the arts

A widely publicized trait of ancient Epicureanism was its opposition to *paideia*, the set of disciplines or subjects of instruction which instilled culture and bestowed prestige on the Greek elite and included the so-called 'liberal' arts, usually: grammar or literature, rhetoric, dialectic, geometry, arithmetic, astronomy, music. Epicurus was said to have turned to philosophy when he could not learn from his grammar teacher about 'Chaos', at the beginning of Hesiod's theogony (DL 10.2). Later, he wrote to his pupil Pythocles to 'Hoist the sails of your skiff and avoid all of *paideia*' (DL 10.6=163 Us.; cf. Plutarch, *Non posse* 1094D), and to another pupil he said: 'I call you blessed, Apelles, because you have set out for philosophy undefiled by any *paideia*' (Athenaeus *Deipn.* 13.588A=117 Us.).

Epicurus' attitude to the arts is conditioned by the privileged position he accords philosophy: you should do philosophy all your life because it is never untimely to care for the health of your soul (*Ep. Men.* 122). Other disciplines do not meet this high standard of necessity and are criticized for it. Sextus Empiricus notes that two groups attacked the arts: the Epicureans did so because the arts 'contributed nothing to the perfection of wisdom' (or else in order to cover up Epicurus' ignorance in such things), while the Pyrrhonians avoided a dogmatic attack of this sort (and did not suffer from the ignorance of an Epicurus), but found the same sort of controversy and puzzles in the arts as they did in philosophy too (*M* 1.1 and 1.5). Sextus says (*M* 1.7) his polemics against the arts will select the most effective arguments from both camps, and for this reason his *Against the Professors of the Liberal Studies* (*M* 1–6) is a principal source for Epicurean attitudes to the arts (*technai*; sing. *technē*). Sextus' own sources for this material appear to be from the second–first centuries

BC, perhaps including Philodemus and his master Zeno of Sidon. Philodemus' own writings are our other most important source for Epicurean attitudes to the *technai*. A number of them are devoted to the arts, especially rhetoric, poetics and music. In addition, we have Philodemean treatises on other *technai*, e.g. household management, frank criticism in philosophical training, conversation. At least some of the latter *technai* were discussed in works included in Philodemus' ensembles of treatises on virtues and vices and on affections, and they appear to have had a similar purpose, to serve as both theoretical and practical guides for both accomplished Epicureans and their pupils in the daily life of an Epicurean school or 'garden' of 'friends'.

The Epicurean notion of *technē*, we are told, is a method producing something useful for life.[1] Philodemus gives a definition of the common conception of *technē*, by which he proposes to judge whether the three types of rhetoric qualify as *technai*: 'expertise is conceived and spoken of among the Greeks as a state or disposition arising from observation of certain common and elementary things extending through many particular cases, which grasps something and which accomplishes something of such a sort that none of those who have not learnt it can do in a similar way, whether fixedly and firmly or conjecturally'.[2] Philodemus here concentrates on other aspects of what makes a *technē*, ignoring for the moment whether its product is always advantageous or not, about which he has particularly strong feelings when it comes to rhetoric.

Sextus usually begins his attacks on the arts by distinguishing theoretically and practically orientated forms of them; he then attacks only the former: e.g. 'higher grammar', which deals with the nature of linguistic elements, etc., not 'lower grammar' or 'grammatistic', the simple art of reading and writing, which is very useful for life (*M* 1.44–56); astrology which casts horoscopes, not the kind which observes the stars and is useful for navigation (*M* 5.1–2); music as the science of melodies, tones, rhythms, etc., and 'musical' experts like Aristoxenus, not music as experience of playing musical instruments (*M* 6.1–4).[3] In Sextus' book against the musicians, there

[1] Sch. D. Thr. 108.27=227b Us.; cf. Diog. Oin. 12.II 4–11 Smith, where 'needs gave rise to all the *technai*'; Lucretius 5.1069.

[2] *Rhet.* 2a, *PHerc.* 1674 XXXVIII.2–18 Longo Auricchio (revised text in Blank 2003); cf. XXX.12.ff.

[3] See Blank 1998: 113–18.

follows a further distinction (6.4–6), between two kinds of attack on the *technē* of music, parallel to the one in *M* 1.1–7: some people dogmatically try to show that music is not a discipline necessary for happiness, but is actually harmful, by refuting the arguments brought by musicians in its favour; others aporetically destroy all of music by shaking the musicians' fundamental hypotheses. Sextus' first group of opponents of music are Epicureans, the second Pyrrhonians.

Like Sextus, in his treatise *On Household Management* (*De oec.*)[4] Philodemus notes (XVII.14–27) that of certain skills there are two kinds. Of baking there is a non-technical sort which is adequate to fulfil one's own need for sustenance, and a technical sort. In the same way, there are two kinds of household management. It is bad to be committed to doing all one can according to the rules of art to increase one's property, rather than managing one's estate easily using reason itself and the ordinary experience which is sufficient for estate management but not for excessive money-making (XVI.25–39).

So the sage should perhaps not be called an expert (*technitēs*) and producer of great wealth quickly acquired. For there is in fact a kind of experience and ability concerning money-making too, of which a good man will have no share, nor will he watch out for the best opportunities to use an ability of this kind, since all these things are characteristic of a money-loving man. Nonetheless, economy is just like a number of other areas in which, although there are good craftsmen, each one of us could achieve pretty well what is sufficient for our needs, as we see in the making of bread and the preparation of food. For anyone is capable of doing such things for himself to the extent necessary, even though there is also such a thing as an expert discipline (*empeiria entechnos*) regarding them. Now something similar appears to be the case with the acquisition and preservation of money as well. For, even if we are not experts at amassing and keeping it, like some people are, and we do not take care for it in a concentrated and persistent way, still many people seem to be not bad at it, at least as far as getting the things they need and so not failing vainly and [completely]; and among these one must count the good man (*spoudaios*). (*De oec.* XVII.2–40)

The philosopher will have a non-technical knowledge of household management or economy, which he needs to provide for his needs and the support of his friends; the technical kind of economy is an art of

[4] *PHerc.* 1424, ed. Jensen. For a general account of this treatise, see Tsouna 2007a, ch. 8.

money-making, and a true philosopher would hardly place such importance on acquiring wealth, which would be unseemly and would distract him from the cultivation of friendship and philosophy, the things which bring him the greatest pleasure. Philodemus' text is full of deprecating references to the labour involved in a serious, technical approach to money-making and to the worries that come with it, and how these are not necessary for living well, managing properly, or even being wealthy (e.g. XVIII.7ff., XIV.23–XV.3): one must look at the moral end (*telos*), not at whether one has more or less money (XIX.4ff.), and the wise man will find that excessive enrichment 'is not profitable when measured against its pain' (XIX.23–32).

When Philodemus thinks of a *technē* as useful for life, then, he means useful for living the life of an Epicurean philosopher. There are many arts which, while useful in certain contexts, are not useful for one who would live the life of a philosopher. And household management is a good example: for people who have chosen to set great store by money, it is certainly important to know how to make and conserve it. But the sort of focus on such activities demanded of one who pursues them seriously is actually destructive of the Epicurean life. On the other hand, if the Epicurean life demands a certain modicum of worldly goods and leisure and is even made better by having the means to treat friends well (e.g. XXIV.19–XXV.4, XXVI.1–14), household management demands some attention even from the Epicurean sage. The key point is to have the priorities of the sage and approach household management with an eye to those priorities. The Epicurean prescription means that there is a form of household management which it befits a sage to learn and practise, but that this is a non-technical form of the art.

Society as a whole inculcated the importance of money-making in citizens, as it did with the liberal arts, especially grammar and rhetoric. Members of the elite worried about being caught out by a poetic citation unknown to them, being unable to cap a companion's improvised verses after a feast, not to mention being unable to defend themselves in court and acquire prestige in political life by their oratory. Professors of literature and rhetoric often enjoyed a high regard and advertised for their subjects by emphasizing their importance. Although his words are usually cited in proof of Epicurean boorishness, Epicurus (see above) congratulated Apelles, not so much for being uneducated as for coming to philosophy without having been corrupted by the liberal arts. This 'corruption' would have involved being persuaded by the various claims of professors regarding the importance of the arts they teach: grammar is competent to understand literature, literature contains many starting points for the acquisition of virtue, so grammar is useful and necessary for happiness (*M* 1.270–1), and it is the starting point for learning all the other arts and teaches about reality, as the 'Siren song' of the professors claims (*M* 1.41–2); the modes and rhythms of music can manipulate our emotions and mould our characters with the same results as philosophy, not by ordering us about vehemently, but with charming persuasion, so musical expertise is valuable (*M* 6.7).

In reply, Epicurus said that 'writing is not toilsome for those who do not aim at the constantly changing criterion' of good writing (Dionysius of Halicarnassus, *On Composition* 24=230 Us.). Metrodorus attacked the offer of social status by literary education when he said one ought not to be bashful if one does not know 'on whose side Hector was, the first verses of Homer's poetry, or the middle verses either'.[5]

Such considerations are evidence of two related questions which are, to some extent, distinguishable: is it appropriate for the Epicurean to pursue one or another of the *technai* as a way of life; is there anything which can be gained for the conduct of the philosophical life by the Epicurean from the body of expert knowledge of any *technē*? The answer to both questions is, generally speaking, 'no', but the emphases fall differently with regard to different kinds of expertise.

Rhetoric was a viable and prestigious profession in the Hellenistic and Roman world, its practitioners divided, roughly, into politicians, who spoke in assemblies and law-courts to persuade public opinion, and 'sophists', who spoke at festivals and other public gatherings to create a festive mood, curry favour, and enhance their own reputation for eloquence. Following Metrodorus' arguments against the Cynics in his *On Wealth* (*Oec.* XXII.17–18), Philodemus surveys the acceptability for the Epicurean philosopher of the usual sources of income. The philosopher will not choose the military or political life of action, the art of horsemanship, using slaves to work mines, or cultivating

[5] Plut. *Non posse* 1094D = Metrodorus *De poem.* I, fr. 24 Körte. Plutarch also complains that the Epicureans deprive themselves of all the pleasures of liberal studies (1092Dff.).

the land with his own hands (XXII.17–XXIII.9). He might, on the other hand, let others cultivate his farmland (XXIII.9–18), or accept rent from tenants and profit from the expertise of his slaves, so long as the slaves' activities are not unseemly (XXIII.18–22). These are the second and third best ways for the philosopher to get income, as they minimize contact with unpleasant people and allow him a pleasant life, leisured retirement with friends, and a most respectable source of income. The best way (XXIII.22–36) is to share his philosophical discourses with those who are able to understand them, and from such men to receive gifts of thanks and veneration, as did Epicurus. These discourses should only be 'truthful, free of competition, and, briefly, serene, since earning one's living by sophistic or competitive speeches is no better than doing so by demagogic or sycophantic ones' (XXIII.30–6). Here, the life of the sophist is juxtaposed with those of political and judicial oratory, lives of action whose benefits cannot outweigh their toils, leaving the philosopher to make truthful, non-competitive, serene philosophical discourses.

The life of a professional musician was not so eligible for a member of the Hellenistic or Roman elite, but playing and singing to the lyre were parts of traditional education and were, at least on the Greek side, considered part of the aristocrat's life. Philodemus, however, produces a lengthy demolition of the claims of the Stoic Diogenes of Babylon, following Damon of Oa and Plato's *Republic*, that music and its modes and rhythms were important in moulding the character of the young and in modifying behaviour by, for example, soothing the angry (e.g. *De mus.* 4, col. 146.30–147.11 Delattre = *PHerc.* 1497.32–3; cf. Sextus, *M* 6.19ff.). He further argues that music distracts us from what is needful and brings happiness (*De mus.* 4, col. 62.38-42 Delattre = *PHerc.* 1578 fr. 20), and

> it is typical of small-minded people with nothing worthwhile to which they can dedicate themselves, let alone which would make them happy, to toil over learning (to play music) in order to amuse themselves now and again, people who do not see the abundance of public performances or the possibility of partaking in them all the time around the city, if they want to do so, and who do not consider that our nature refuses (to listen to music) for too long and quickly tires of it. (*De mus.* 4, col. 151.8–25 Delattre = *PHerc.* 1497.37)

He contemptuously says he will forbear to mention 'that the pleasure which comes from music is not necessary, while learning and practising music in order to amuse oneself is toilsome (*epiponon*) and excludes one from the things which are most important for our well-being, and the continual inactivity (*apraxia*) of one who childishly sings or plays the lyre assiduously (*energōs*)' (*De mus.* 4, col. 151.29–39 Delattre = *PHerc.* 1497.37).

In a list of things the Epicurean sage will or will not do (DL 10.117–21b), in addition to statements that he will not engage in politics or be a tyrant (119), that he will leave treatises behind but not speak at festivals, we read 'and only the sage would converse correctly about music and poetry; and he would not compose poems assiduously'.[6] Thus, the sage's attitude to writing poetry is apparently similar to his attitude to performing music: it is too much trouble and distracts from philosophy to learn and to practise it, but it is fine to listen to it with enjoyment, so long as the ears will tolerate. Plutarch also cites (*Non posse* 1095C–D) from Epicurus' work *Puzzles* (*Diaporiai*) remarks apparently directed against Plato's discussion of the 'lovers of sights and sounds' in *Republic* 5.475d–476b: 'the sage is a lover of sights (*philotheōros*) and takes as much pleasure as anyone else in concerts and Dionysiac spectacles'.[7] Plutarch takes these remarks to be contradicted when Epicurus advises even cultured kings to tolerate even battle tales and vulgar clowning at their symposia, rather than discourses about musical and poetic questions. But the enjoyment of spectacles can be a harmless and relatively passive pleasure, if kept within limits, while the discussion of 'questions', the arcane problems with which cultured guests tried to show off to one another, required hard study in addition to the desire to shine in front of others. That kind of behaviour might actually suggest that the cultured show-off is a flatterer of the king, someone who cultivates his patronage by dint of his scholarship; it is, perhaps, another way of making music or poetry one's profession, one which Epicurus warns kings against and presumably also considered unsuitable for the philosopher.

[6] The two parts of this sentence are fr. 569 and 568 respectively; on their text and interpretation, see Asmis 1995: 21–2 and 32–3 with Sider 1995: 35–6 and Clay 1995: 5; I read *energōs*, as in the passage of *De mus.* above (with Sider), rather than *energeiai* (Usener).

[7] On this passage, see Asmis 1995: 19–20. Similarly, in Diogenes' passage about the sage we are told 'and he will be more delighted than other men by festivals (*theōriai*)' (DL 10.120a). This use of *theōriai*, which can refer to processions or missions to religious festivals, may be related to the use of *philotheōros* cited by Plutarch.

Evidently, if the sage would be the only one who could converse correctly about music and poetry it is not because he is able to hold learned conversations about 'musical problems and the philological questions of critics' (*Non posse* 1095C). The philosopher's expertise is in philosophy, and if he is to discuss music and poetry, there must be a properly philosophical way of doing so.

We can see what this may have involved from Sextus' *Against the Grammarians*. The three parts of grammar – the expertise devoted to the study of what is in poets and prose-writers – (i) correct writing and speaking; (ii) the study of the people, places and things, as well as the plots of poetry and prose-writing; (iii) the judgment of literary works, especially regarding their moral suitability – are critiqued by Sextus from both the Pyrrhonist and Epicurean points of view. The Epicurean critique,[8] probably based on Zeno of Sidon's demolition of a grammatical treatise by Asclepiades of Myrlea, is especially well represented in the final, critical part of grammar, which judged poetry.

Sextus begins (*M* 1.270–6) by repeating a number of arguments given by grammarians on behalf of the usefulness of poetry and therefore of grammar as the expertise devoted to expounding it. These include a critique of philosophers, especially Epicurus and Pyrrho, who have picked up the nudges (*aphormai*) toward wisdom and happiness given in the poets' *gnōmai* or sentential statements and even stolen them. These arguments are then answered point for point: the poetic passages which are truly useful for life, especially their *gnōmai*, are clear and in no need of exegesis, while their unclear parts, e.g., foreign stories and allegories (*ta ainigmatōdōs ekpheromena*), are useless; a *gnōmē* is merely an assertion, but our intelligence demands proof, which is the province not of grammar, but of philosophy; if grammar is useful because poets make many useful statements, it will be useless when they make statements opposite to those, which would be injurious to life and make poetry dangerous; and if the good statements are to be distinguished from the bad, that is the job of philosophy, not grammar; it is only crowd-pleasers, not real philosophers, who use poets as witnesses, and the detractors of grammar, Pyrrho and Epicurus, did not mean the same things as the poetic

[8] Blank 1998: xliv–l: 'These are the things said by the others on this head, especially the Epicureans' (*M* 1.299).

passages which are said to be like what they wrote; the poets in any event also say the opposite of these things; the poetic precepts said to have been borrowed by philosophers are also found in the sayings of ordinary people; the poets often say things much worse than what most people believe; since poetry is such a mixed bag and grammar cannot show which bits we should believe, grammar is useless; the fact that poetic citations have been useful to states by resolving controversies does not show that grammar is more useful to the state than, e.g. dancing, and it certainly does not make grammar useful for us to learn, any more than their usefulness to states makes it desirable for us to learn cobbling and blacksmithing (*M* 1.277–95). At the conclusion of this litany, two points are emphasized (296–8). First, poets are of little or even no use for life, since they aim at entertainment (*psychagōgia*) and employ falsehood to that end, while philosophers and other prose-writers aim to instruct us in useful things. Second, poetry strengthens and exacerbates human passions. This last point is also made in Philodemus' critique of Diogenes of Babylon's thesis that certain forms of music could be used to soothe violent emotions and promote excellence in desire (*erōtikē aretē*, *De mus.* 4, col. 43.37–44 Delattre = *PHerc.* 1572, fr. 4). Philodemus argues that these passions and their opposites could be brought about, not by music *per se*, with its rhythms and modes which operate only on the irrational sense of hearing, but by the thoughts in the poetry which is set to music and exhort people to excess (*De mus.* 4, col. 120.2ff. Delattre = *PHerc.* 1497.6, col. 128.4–129.15 Delattre = *PHerc.* 1497.14–15). He adds that Diogenes incorrectly attributed Erato's contribution to 'erotic excellence' to music, rather than to poetry, or even better to philosophy (15.15ff.).

Thus, poetry says many things which are morally good or bad and can incite the listener to good or bad actions, emotions and character. It is best to inculcate the good in such matters via prose-writing, which does not mix the true with the false, strive for obscurity, or distract the soul from good precepts by means of poetic and musical devices. But insofar as poetry is to be a source of precepts, philosophy – not grammar – is required to tell the good from the bad. We can see such a process in Philodemus' *On the good king according to Homer*.[9] This book is

[9] On this work, see Murray 1965 and 1984, Asmis 1991. The latest full edition is Dorandi 1982, and a new edition is in preparation by J. Fish.

dedicated to Lucius Calpurnius Piso Caesoninus, Caesar's father-in-law and a prominent Roman politician, but it is addressed to a wider public as well. In it Philodemus points out the beneficial precepts about monarchs in Homer's text. He does this by taking a particular topic, such as that the good king does not love war and conflict, and citing various statements which support the thesis. Thus, 'friendless, lawless, homeless is he who loves terrible strife' (*Iliad* 9.63–4) is adduced along with other items, like Zeus' statement that Ares was the most hateful of the gods to him, as was Achilles among mortal kings, and the introduction of Nestor as eager to resolve discord in disputes with Agamemnon (*PHerc.* 1507 XXVII–XXIX Dorandi). Philodemus also demonstrates that Telemachus' journey is a commentary on the education of the good prince.[10] He points out that Homer prized wise counsel over force of arms, so that he called Nestor 'protector of the Achaeans' (*Iliad* 8.80 etc.) and gives him other praises as well, and he also praises Odysseus, saying that the Phaeacians' ship 'carries a man of godlike counsels' (*Od.* 13.89) and other such things (XXXII.10–XXXIII.20 Dorandi). At the end of the work Philodemus tells Piso that he has tried to show the 'starting points toward correction' in Homer's text (43.16–19 Fish). Perhaps this refers, among other things, to the places where Philodemus has shown that the impression made by some Homeric passages which seem to be immoral may be corrected. So, Philodemus implies that when Ares and Aphrodite are caught *in flagrante* and bound by Hephaestus, the apparently licentious scene dissuades one from adultery, even while using unsuitable characters to do the job (XX.2–8 Dorandi revised by Fish as col. 30.2–8). Plutarch, in *How the Young Man Should Read Poetry*, often notes starting points which can tell the reader that apparently immoral passages actually show the poet's probity.[11]

In *On the good king according to Homer* Philodemus has not only written a book about Homer, but also shown himself familiar with technical Homeric criticism, lending credibility to his account of how to read Homer, and perhaps to show how the work of philologists can only lead up to the really important interpretative and didactic work of the philosopher. The Epicurean must also learn about the technical precepts of the arts for a different reason, so that he can

[10] See Fish 1999.

[11] See Asmis 1991: 23; Obbink 1995: 191 n. 8; and Fish (forthcoming).

show their uselessness and argue that his companions ought not to spend their time, energy and money on learning them, nor should they think they will be missing anything, if they follow this advice.

Philodemus' *On poems* (*De poem.*) presents a critique of the poetic theories of other philosophers, such as Aristotle in Book 4, and specialists in poetry such as Crates of Mallos and a number of theorists treated by Crates and called by Philodemus 'critics' (*kritikoi*) in Books 2, 3 and 5. These 'critics', including Crates, who actually used that name for his own school, espoused a number of competing 'euphonist' theories of poetry, and Philodemus allows us to follow a very fertile Hellenistic debate known otherwise only from later representatives of such a theory, particularly Dionysius of Halicarnassus. They held a poem should be judged solely on the way it sounded rather than on what it said, content being outside of poetic expertise. Crates says that certain 'philosophers' charged the 'critics' with making pleasure the criterion of good verse because good verses please the irrational ear. Crates and the 'critics' replied that their accusers are actually doing just that, especially the proponents of evident things and of perception (*De poem.* 1, 128.22–5 Janko).[12] In *De poem.* 5 Crates again criticizes 'philosophers' – Philodemus takes him to be alluding unjustly to Epicureans – who allegedly claimed that there is no 'natural excellence' (*phusikon agathon*) in verse, so that all judging must be based on rules (*themata*),[13] but the rules can only be arbitrary and differ from one person to another (*De poem.* 5, *PHerc.* 1425 XXV.2–30 Mangoni, with Janko 2000: 122–3). While he agrees with what Crates said about 'the philosophers', that there is no natural criterion of good verse, Philodemus thinks that these 'philosophers' overlooked the 'conceptions' (*ennoiai*, here used in the same sense as *prolēpseis*)[14] 'of good and bad verse and poetry', and they 'were wrong' because these conceptions actually do enable a universal judgement (*koinē krisis*) which Philodemus treats as natural:

12 On all this material, see the introduction of Janko 2000 and that volume's marvellous reconstruction of the text of *De poem.* 1.

13 See Atherton, ch. 11, this volume, on the *phusei vs. thesei* ('by nature vs. by imposition') debate over the imposition of names on things. On *themata* cf. Blank 1998: 182–3 and Rispoli 2006.

14 See Asmis, ch. 5, this volume.

Since *qua* verse a verse provides no natural benefit either in diction or content, on this account there are laid down fixed aims for excellence, in diction to imitate that which teaches in addition useful things, and in content to partake of what is between that of wise people and vulgar ones. These criteria exist whether one thinks so or not, and one must judge with reference to them. For I leave aside the fact that, even if there is an imitation in such a form (and verse is that which imitates as best it can), in such a form most of all will it provide a judgment common to all, but it could not provide one for those who have classified a poem in accord with each rule.[15]

Philodemus' criterion has three important characteristics: it is rational and by referring to the way in which diction teaches and also to what is taught it rules out the thesis of the 'critics' that only the sound should be judged; being a 'common conception', it is a non-technical criterion, available to any layman who can use his reason, and it actually disallows the judgement of verse with reference to arbitrary rules; it is not complex and does not require much knowledge of particular standards of excellence. Treatises on poetry, Philodemus says, ought not to give detailed treatments of desirable and undesirable characteristics, but concentrate on giving general principles which allow the expression of the preconceptions (*tas prolēpseis ektupousthai*) of the good poem (5, XXX.25–33 Mangoni), and what one says about poetry must be anchored in 'the common conception' and what we 'preconceive' as the excellence of verse (5, XXXIII.32–6 Mangoni). Given his insistence that the only standard which can be applied universally is the common conception, Philodemus can hardly think one can have a valid 'expert' or technical knowledge of how to write or judge poetry. The non-technical way in which the rational person judges such matters is quite adequate for his purposes.[16]

Was there also a proper way for the philosopher to write poetry? Philodemus himself was a writer of polished and witty epigrams, some of which allude to the Epicurean life and philosophy,[17] and we must presume that he felt he could do this without 'toil' and that he could at least tell himself that his relationship with Piso was not that

[15] *De poem.* 5, XXV.30–XXVI.20, text and trs. Janko 2000: 131 and n. 1; for the interpretation see also Asmis 1992.

[16] On these claims in their application to poetics, rhetoric and music, see Blank 1995: 181–6.

[17] On these, see Sider 1997.

of flatterer to potentate. Lucretius' philosophical poem presents a different set of problems, all of which are difficult and have been much discussed by scholars. Epicurus had made clarity (*saphēneia*) the sole quality of good speaking and writing (e.g. DL 10.13), and for that reason the philosopher writes in a relatively plain prose style. But Philodemus does allow for the use of some devices, particularly metaphor, to make clear what is in itself unfamiliar,[18] and he thinks that good poems need not always strive for clarity, since it is not always possible for them to say clearly what they want to say (*De poem.* 5, XXXI.11–32 Mangoni). Perhaps, then, when the philosopher wants to say things which do lend themselves to clarity, he may use poetry and some of its devices to add charm and clarity both – or, at least, Lucretius may have thought this was the case: 'not without good reason do I set such clear verse about an obscure matter, tingeing all with muses' charm' (1.933–5) – especially when addressing one who is not yet a philosopher.[19]

We have seen that Philodemus does not allow that it is good for the philosopher to earn his living in any of the three traditional branches or 'parts' (*merē*) of rhetoric: political, forensic, panegyric. The young men of the Greek and Roman elite were expected to play a political role, but this was evidently not going to be desirable for an Epicurean philosopher.[20] Philodemus attacks political and forensic rhetoric on a number of fronts. In his second book *On Rhetoric*,[21] Philodemus cites one of the Epicureans who taught in Rhodes and Cos that

> Epicurus and Metrodorus did not allow that either the political or the forensic or the panegyric branch of rhetoric involves expertise, but said that the political and forensic branches require rehearsal, practice and a sort of empirical research, while the panegyric branch, they said, consists in rehearsal, practice and habituation at a certain kind of speaking, without practical research. Moreover, he expresses his view that according to the Great Men

[18] Metaphor etc., is discussed in *Rhet.* 4, *PHerc.* 1673 IIIff. [Sudhaus I 164ff]. Philodemus must feel that this does not always contravene Epicurus' injunction to use words in their primary senses (*Ep. Hdt.* 37).

[19] See, e.g., Clay 1995: 6–7, along with the contributions of Asmis, Sider, Wigodsky and Armstrong in Obbink 1995.

[20] On the Epicurean opposition to politics, see Scholz 1997: 251–314, Brown, ch. 10 this volume.

[21] For the structure of this work, perhaps in ten books, see Dorandi 1990a and Longo Auricchio 1997.

it is totally impossible for there to exist an expertise of persuading mobs; and that it is their doctrine also that the aforementioned rehearsal, practice and experience do not produce persuasion either always or for the most part, and that it sometimes turns out that non-rhetorical discourses are more persuasive than rhetorical ones.[22]

These Epicureans go so far as to think that 'even if, hypothetically, someone does have an ability which always persuades the many, this is the cause not of goods but of great evils' (2a 1674 LVI.3–9). Philodemus agrees with them about political and forensic rhetoric, the kinds that seek to persuade crowds. These require research (*historia*) and practice (*meletē*; also *tribē*),[23] but there is no expert knowledge of them, by which he means a set of rules which enable one who has learnt them to persuade crowds reliably about particular matters, in a way which one who has not learnt them cannot do.[24] He clearly thinks that Epicurus and his immediate followers rejected political rhetoric in part because such an art could not have observed (*paratetērēkenai*) what can persuade crowds and the good politician could not have calculated empirically (*epilelogismenos*) what is such as to evoke anger, pity, choice, or avoidance, and make consistent use of it.[25] Thus, there is no expertise of speaking to assemblies and courtrooms, nor can there be.

Philodemus uses one passage of Metrodorus in three of his books *On Rhetoric*:

But in fact, while many points in the founders' texts make this clear, what is in Metrodorus will suffice to show clearly that this experience too of speaking in assembly and arguing cases arises from a certain practice and from research into the affairs of cities: 'Is it the case, then, that one speaks of rhetorical capacity in regard to the discerning of what one who is going to be and will continue to be happy should or should not do, and one says that this is the capacity which comes about from natural philosophy (*physiologia*), or does one [say this about] political experience (*empeiria*), according to which one

[22] *Rhet.* 2a, *PHerc.* 1674 LIV.10–LV.15, LVI.3–9 Longo Auricchio, revised text and translation in Blank 2003: 71–2.

[23] He often echoes the *Gorgias* and its terms to characterize rhetoric; e.g. 463b4, 500d8, 501a7 with Blank 1998: xxiiff.

[24] See the definition of *technē* in *Rhet.* 2a. *PHerc.* 1674 XXXVIII.2–18 translated above, p. 217; also, XLII.8–XLIII.11 Longo Auricchio.

[25] *Rhet.* 2a, *PHerc.* 1674 XXXV.10–20 Longo Auricchio, revised text in Blank 2003: 74 n. 21; see also 2a 1674 XXVIII.13–17, 26–9.

could, from practice and research (*historia*) of the affairs of the city, see fairly well what benefits the mob'? And, a bit further on, 'For what is it that theory provides, for instance the theoretical knowledge of choices and avoidances, or that about political consequences, which comes from historical research?'[26]

Metrodorus is arguing, in his work *Against those who say that Good Politicians are made by Natural Philosophy*, against Nausiphanes of Teos, the 'Democritean' who taught Epicurus, though the latter denied that he learnt anything from him.[27] Metrodorus says that Nausiphanes claimed that natural philosophy is the source of ethical advice, counsel about what to choose or avoid in order to lead a blissful life, and understanding of what actually does benefit or harm crowds or the city. But Metrodorus thinks that ethical advice can be based only on philosophy, while political advice comes from something else, *viz.* political practice and study of what has happened in the city's past. As Philodemus then points out, knowledge of the atomic structure of the audience's souls cannot provide a basis for a reliable expertise of persuasion,[28] nor can knowledge of the natural end, given that each person in the crowd judges on the basis of the (usually false) opinions he already has, not necessarily with reference to the natural goal.[29] While there can be no expertise of consistently persuading crowds, there can be one of giving ethical individual advice in the context of relationships in the Epicurean Garden, and that expertise is what Philodemus refers to as 'frank criticism' (*parrhēsia*).[30]

On the other hand, Philodemus disagrees with the view of the Epicureans of Rhodes and Cos that panegyric rhetoric consists only in practice and habit and a commonly agreed style of speech and differs from political and forensic rhetoric only in having no need of research into political affairs. Instead, he argues throughout a long stretch of *Rhetoric* 2 that 'sophistic' actually is a *technē* and was recognized as such by the Epicurean founding fathers.[31] This

26 *Rhet.* 2b, *PHerc.* 1672 XXI.36–XXII.25 Longo Auricchio, slightly revised and translated in Blank 2003: 78–9; the other passages are *Rhet.* 8, *PHerc.* 1015 ii.1–15 (text in Blank 2003: 79 n. 41) and *Rhetoric* 3, *PHerc.* 1506 XL.20–3 and XLI.5–9 Hammerstaedt.

27 See Clay, ch. 1, this volume.

28 *Rhet.* 8, *PHerc.* 1015.xv.9–21 + 832.8.1–15 (text in Blank 2003: 80–1).

29 *Rhet.* 8, *PHerc.* 1015.xvi.2–20; VIII, *PHerc.* 1015.xvii.9–20 (texts in Blank 2003: 82).

30 See Tsouna, ch. 14, this volume.

31 This is adumbrated at *Rhet.* 2a, *PHerc.* 1674 XXXVII.10–16 Longo Auricchio (revised text in Blank 2003: 73), then argued at length; see also Longo Auricchio 1985.

'sophistic' is 'an expertise of composing discourses and making displays' (*Rhet.* 2a, *PHerc.* 1674 XXIV.1–5 Longo Auricchio); it is the body of expert knowledge of rhetoric, which constitutes at least some of what is taught in the rhetorical schools run by 'sophists'. As we have seen, however, the Epicureans did not think that a philosopher should spend his time giving display speeches at festivals, so it is not the case that Philodemus is commending the 'panegyric' branch of rhetoric. Indeed, he denies that rhetoric has as its 'parts' the panegyric, political and forensic, just as it is not the case that one part of dog (the 'dogfish' or shark is the sea animal and another part is the land animal (*Rhet.* 2a, *PHerc.* 1674 LVIII.4–16 Longo Auricchio). I suspect that he calls the methodical, expert aspect of rhetoric 'sophistic' to differentiate it from 'panegyric' and to limit it to what is taught in the sophists' schools, as opposed to what is actually practised at festivals. Philodemus also repeats Epicurus' arguments against attending the sophists' schools, which cannot make one a good politician (e.g., 1674 XVII.2–13, 1674 XX.13–XXI.11) and are therefore a waste of money for all those who go there with that intention. After all, the kinds of rhetorical tricks used by sophists in their displays and festival speeches, their parisoses, antitheses, end-rhymes, etc., would not be tolerated in a courtroom or assembly, and would be counterproductive (1674 X.3–XI.34, with *Rhet.* 3, *PHerc.* 1426 III.15–V.10 Hammerstaedt).

To judge from the cases of poetics and music, we should expect this 'sophistic' to have only a small basis of true rules, and that is what we see: 'sophistic rhetoric is an expertise concerning displays such as they make and the disposition of discourses such as they write and improvise. However, we say that it has method, but not much of it, just as poetics does not either' (*Rhet.* 2b, *PHerc.* 1672 XXII.29–39 Longo Auricchio). In *On Rhetoric* 4[32] Philodemus treated the parts and precepts of rhetoric taught by others, beginning with a discussion of general claims about rhetoric as the only teacher of conversation, the mother of all sciences, counsellor of war and peace, guarantor of a good income, especially in comparison with philosophy, which

[32] The book is preserved in pieces of two copies, the largest parts being *PHerc.* 1007/1673 and *PHerc.* 1423, edited in Sudhaus 1892, I 162–225 and I 147–61. My discussion is indebted to the work of R. Gaines, who is producing a new edition with commentary.

leaves one open to attack from sycophants, slaves and tyrants, and does not prepare for a public life. Philodemus denies all this and argues against the life of the rhetorician, especially one involved in political and judicial speaking, comparing it negatively to the philosophical life.[33] Next, he gives a lengthy technical treatment of rhetorical style, followed by delivery, arrangement and invention. The last topic is the kinds of speech, where the focus is on epideictic or panegyric, forensic and deliberative speaking having been quickly dismissed as not arising from the expertise taught by the sophists (*PHerc.* 1007/1673 XXXIa.4–XXXIIa.6 [I 212–13 Sudhaus]). The discussion of panegyric centres on the fact that one cannot truly praise things or people for qualities they do not have or even cannot have, nor can one praise without knowing whether to praise for the benefit of the one praised, of someone else, or of us ourselves. Further, knowledge regarding the things sophists praise and censure is not confined to sophists, but poets and even philosophers can also do these things, so that this is an ability belonging to everyone. If the sophists want to say instead only that they know the sort of praises and censures which are commonly used and taught, then Philodemus will not object, since 'it is the same as saying that the works of rhetoricians are of rhetoricians' (1007/1673 XLa.1–24 [I 220–1 Sudhaus]).

As with poetry, we see that this sophistic *technē*, insofar as it can do anything valid, must rely on understanding which is available to rational persons in common, rather than on rules which its practitioners make up. We may even think that it is philosophers who are best suited to praise and censure appropriately, and Philodemus did indeed write a treatise *On Praise* (1007/1673 XXXVIIIa.15–XXXIXa.1 [I 219 Sudhaus]).[34] Philodemus says (1007/1673 VII.6–14 [I 151 Sudhaus]) that, since there is 'one naturally beautiful kind of discourse', one should ignore the kind of discourse composed according to arbitrary rule (*thema*). But since sophistic rhetoric is said by Philodemus to have a modicum of method, may we not think that the philosopher may use that small amount of method and compose in the naturally beautiful mode to enhance the effectiveness of the

[33] This comparison is also the subject of another book of Philodemus' treatise, preserved in a number of pieces, the chief of which is *PHerc.* 1669, edited in Sudhaus 1892, I 225–70.

[34] See Gaines 2003 and 2004: 217–18.

'philosophical discourses' he gives to his companions, both oral and written, and for which he will receive their merited thanks and admiration? The proper expertise of the philosopher is philosophy, and that is also the basis for the proper approach to music, poetry and rhetoric, as also to everything in life.

JAMES WARREN

13 Removing fear

The Epicureans set the absence of mental disturbance, *ataraxia*, as the goal of human life and claimed that it is identical with the greatest mental pleasure. They can be expected, therefore, to offer an account of the psychology of mental disturbance and the proper methods for managing and eradicating it. Their basic conception of value, that pleasure is the only good and pain the only bad, is supplemented by the assurance that we should feel no anxiety about our chances of living a good life since pleasure is easy to obtain and pain is easy to avoid. In addition, they identified two major sources of common mental disturbance: fear of the gods and the fear of death, and they dedicated considerable effort and philosophical ingenuity to the removal of these. Before we come to consider their arguments in detail, it is important to look at the general Epicurean account of the sources and nature of mental disturbance since this provides the general framework for their understanding of how mental disturbance should be tackled. Epicurus explains both the importance of this project and also the prime causes of disturbance at *Ep. Hdt.* 81:

We must recognise in addition to all these that the most powerful disturbance in human souls arises from the belief that the heavenly bodies are blessed and immortal and also at the same time have intentions and actions and powers inconsistent with this. It also comes from constantly anticipating or suspecting that some everlasting evil is to come, either because of myths or else in fear of the very absence of perception in death (as if that concerns us). Disturbance is also suffered not because of opinions but because of some irrational state of mind which causes those who set no bounds to what is feared to undergo just as much or even more intense disturbance than they would if they believed these things. Peace of mind (*ataraxia*) is both having been released from all these cares and also possessing the constant recollection of general and most important truths.

Above all, Epicurus diagnoses mental disturbance, anxiety, and fear as the result of ignorance and false opinion (which the Epicureans often term *kenodoxia*).[1] In so saying, he does not deny that fear, like other emotions, also has important affective or non-cognitive aspects, including disturbing feelings of mental pain. But a cognitive fault of either ignorance or misapprehension lies at the root of all these other aspects. These two sources are sometimes conflated: someone may be said to be 'ignorant' of natural philosophy if they believe falsely, for example, that there is only one cosmos. But they can also be distinguished as Epicurus does here: fear caused by ignorance is fear generated by an inability to explain some phenomenon in any way or to provide any kind of guidance about what may occur in the future. We can imagine someone being terrified by an earthquake because she simply has no conception of what is happening and why. Contrast this with someone who is fearful because she believes, falsely, that the earth is shaking because the gods are angry. This person has an explanation of the phenomenon to hand, but the explanation is incorrect and not only causes immediate mental disturbance but also will – so the Epicureans inform us – lead to further concerns and unnecessary behaviour.

This dual explanation of mental disturbance is important for the Epicureans because it allows them to respond to a particular criticism of their view. Some critics argued that if the Epicureans were simply interested in removing fear then they ought to hold that non-rational animals are in fact ideally placed for living a good life. A dog, for example, cannot form the sort of beliefs needed to have an incorrect view of death or the gods. Should we, therefore, strive as far as possible to remove our beliefs entirely?[2] Such a suggestion is absurd because humans are rational creatures and the Epicureans are interested in offering a conception of the human good. And it is precisely

[1] For more discussion of the Epicurean analysis of fear and its role in the formation of incorrect desires see Konstan 2006a, 2007: 64–103; Tsouna 2006: 81–7 and 2007a: 32–50. Generally on ancient accounts of fear see Konstan 2006b. For a discussion of the nature of modern fear see Bourke 2005.

[2] See, for such criticisms and for the Epicurean response, Philod. *De dis* I (*PHerc.* 26) XII–XV Diels and Warren 2002a: 136–42.

by use of our reasoning abilities that we can come to form the correct views of the gods and death and therefore attain and enjoy *ataraxia*.[3] But these reasoning abilities must be used in the right way: Epicurus notes that it is possible to be very well informed about the heavens by having a comprehensive knowledge of celestial motions, the rising and setting of the stars and planets and so on, but nevertheless fail properly to understand what the heavenly bodies are and the proper explanation for their motions (*Ep. Hdt.* 79). Such beliefs, in the absence of understanding, are ultimately no better than simple ignorance or error. What is needed is the comprehension of an explanatory account of such potentially worrying topics and, the Epicureans assure us, not only will possession of the truth remove uncertainty but it will also demonstrate that there is in fact nothing at all to fear when it comes to the gods or our own mortality. That proper understanding can then be itself a source of pleasure since it will generate and support a disturbance-free life.[4] The twin tasks of removing false conceptions and instilling true beliefs can be seen at work in the Epicurean attack on both the fear of the gods and also the fear of death, precisely the two specific concerns noted here.[5]

It is worth noting at the outset that we have good evidence for the Epicureans' paying close attention to the way in which these two kinds of fear are connected. The remains of the first book of Philodemus' work *On the gods* explicitly raise the question which of the two sources of fear is the most damaging.[6] From column XVI.18 to the end of the surviving rolls, Philodemus pursues this question and, in the process, makes a number of observations about the interconnection between the two kinds of fear. He notes, for example, that certain conceptions of the gods – in particular, the idea that they are concerned with human behaviour and sit in judgement over us in the afterlife – tend to exacerbate the fear of death. Similarly, the fear of death itself sometimes takes the form of a concern about what might

[3] The Epicurean ideal of *ataraxia* is one of continuing undisturbed mental activity, not the mere absence of mental disturbance (since this would also be true of death). Similarly, *aponia* is not merely the absence of physical pain (since a stone feels no pain) but continuing undisturbed physical activity. On reason as a source of pleasure see also Woolf, ch. 9, this volume, and Warren 2007a: 138–41.

[4] See Lucr. *DRN* 1.146–54, 6.35–42.

[5] For more on the psychology of moral development see Bobzien 2006: esp. 220–8.

[6] The most recent edition is Diels 1916.

happen to us in some kind of afterlife and might therefore reinforce certain conceptions of the gods. Col. XXIV.20ff. then turns to consider the kinds of belief which lie behind these fears:

> In general, concerning these anxieties there is a distinction between two sets of beliefs. For the fear of the blessed gods for the most part arises on the basis of unconsidered beliefs, whereas the fear of death for the most part arises out of latent and unarticulated beliefs. The former are easier to cure than the latter, because fully ridding oneself of a latent, hidden, source of anxiety is difficult and it is not possible to throw off such weighty foolishness. Indeed, even wise words are unable to take away these people's wound; in general, humans for no good reason make out that infinity itself is something evil. (*De dis* 1.XXIV.20–34 Diels)

Philodemus here stresses how the fear of the gods can at least be addressed directly because people tend to be conscious of what they believe about the subject. They need only to think properly about what they happen to believe to notice the inconsistencies and then change their view. In the case of death, on the other hand, fear is usually driven by a set of unarticulated and unnoticed beliefs common to most humans which first have to be identified and then brought properly to the notice of the person concerned. Only then can a therapeutic process begin.[7] Both fears, as Philodemus stresses here, are widespread and tenacious. As Epicurean texts like to point out, the misconceptions they are fighting against are common and easily transmitted.[8] Like doctors attempting to stem a virulent contagion, the task is difficult and demanding of both the Epicurean doctor and his patient. Fortunately, however, the Epicureans are well armed with a number of arguments to address these concerns. But it is worth remembering that they require attention and perseverance; as Epicurus advises, it is necessary to 'accustom yourself to the thought that death is nothing to us' (*Ep. Men.* 124), presumably by thinking over and internalizing the Epicurean point of view, integrating it with one's other relevant beliefs. For example, Lucretius offers a picture of someone who professes the belief that death is nothing to him, but whose actions betray that he has not entirely come to terms with the full import of this conclusion (*DRN* 3.870–93). In fact, as

7 Compare Diog. Oin. fr. 35 Smith on evident and non-evident fears of death.

8 See, for plague imagery, in particular Diog. Oin. 3.IV.4–V.8 with Warren 2000b.

Voula Tsouna's chapter in this volume demonstrates, the Epicureans offered a sophisticated psychological analysis of the best means of ethical improvement and education.[9] My chapter, however, focuses on the argumentative structure of their account and the reasoning behind the various conclusions they thought could be integrated into the ideal standpoint on the gods and death.

THE GODS

It might be surprising that the Epicureans believe that there are gods at all, since their cosmology offers an account of the universe and its functioning which has no need for creating or governing divinities.[10] Further, their ethical system as a whole is based primarily on a conception of human nature which again makes no reference to any divine source of value.[11] But they are impressed by the thought that everyone – at least everyone worth paying any attention to – thinks that there are gods. And Epicurean epistemology places great store by any belief which is the subject of such universal consent even if universal consent by itself is no guarantee of truth.[12] The *Letter to Menoeceus* 123 offers a concise summary of the Epicurean view.

> First, think that god is an imperishable and blessed living thing – as the shared conception of god has been set down – and in addition think nothing which is either inconsistent with god's imperishability or alien to his blessedness. Believe about god everything which serves to uphold the combination of blessedness and imperishability. For there are gods; for the recognition of them is clear. But they are not as the many think they are, for they are not consistent in how they conceive the gods. The person who denies the gods of the many is not impious, but impious is he who attributes to the gods what the many believe.[13]

As Philodemus notes, and Epicurus makes clear both here and, as we have already seen, in *Ep. Hdt.* 81, anxieties about the gods are generated by an inconsistency between various evident beliefs. The universal consensus on which the Epicureans rest their belief that

[9] See also Tsouna 2006, 2007a. [10] See Morel, ch. 4, and Taub, ch. 6, this volume.
[11] See Woolf, ch. 9 and Brown, ch. 10, this volume.
[12] Cf. Cic. *ND* 1.43–5. See Asmis, ch. 5, this volume, and Obbink 1989: 190–4 and 2002.
[13] Cf. Philod. *De pietate* 1138–46 Obbink ; Aët. 1.7.7 (361 Us.).

there are gods also, we are told, holds that all gods are imperishable and that they live a perfectly happy existence. These two – imperishability and blessedness – are the essential characteristics of divinity against which are evaluated all other claims about the gods. They can be used both to rule out certain characteristics as being inconsistent with this essential pairing and also used to generate other positive characteristics which necessarily follow from them. (Epicurus himself is generally reluctant to offer a more specific description of the gods, but other Epicureans were less reticent. For example, Philodemus argues that the gods must speak Greek since they must be rational if they lead a perfect existence, and Greek is the language of all rational animals.)[14]

In combating anxiety about the gods, the most important task is the removal of false beliefs, since for the most part anxieties about the gods are caused not by not knowing enough about their lives so much as by having incorrect beliefs about them.[15] In particular, the most pernicious and dangerous belief about the gods is that they are in the least concerned about our world and its inhabitants. Epicurean texts consistently remind us that the gods are entirely indifferent to us and to the world, and necessarily so. For example, the ordered motion of the heavenly bodies was often cited as evidence for the intelligent governance of the cosmos. Epicurus insists that no such inference should be made and, moreover, that to do so generates a conclusion inconsistent with the essential characteristics of the gods (see Lucr. *DRN* 5.82–90).

This same form of argument is used regularly to rule out any thought that the gods take an interest in our world. Were they to have any interest in there being a world like ours, or in its being constructed in a certain way, or in its inhabitants behaving in certain ways, then this implies that should these interests not be promoted, then the gods would somehow be in a worse state than they might otherwise enjoy. But the gods cannot enjoy anything other than the

[14] See Philod. *De dis* 3 (*PHerc.* 157/152) xiv Diels. This book seems generally to be concerned with clarifying various details about the gods' lives. Similarly, Demetrius Lacon argues that the gods are anthropomorphic since reason is not found in anything other than human form: *De forma dei* (*PHerc.* 1055, Col. xv–xvi). For more on Epicurean anthropomorphic theology cf. Cic. *ND* 1.46–51 and 71–102 and Santoro 2000a: 50–60, and 2000b.

[15] Philod. *De pietate* 2226–40: the fear that the gods will punish unjust deeds is sometimes as harmful as the imagined punishment would be.

best state possible. They cannot be troubled, anxious, or fearful so their happiness cannot be contingent on anything else (*Ep. Hdt.* 76–8). How misguided – not to say arrogant – is it to think that the perfect gods are somehow upset if we fail to honour them properly or pleased if we perform the correct rituals at the right times?[16] And why should we believe that the gods had any interest in creating a cosmos or governing it once it had come-to-be?[17] Certainly they would not have done so merely for us humans' benefit. Any such commitment would suggest that before the cosmos was formed they were less happy than they might have been, and this would be inconsistent with their essential nature.

Other Epicurean arguments undermine the notion of interventionist gods by emphasizing various faults and evils in the world which humans have to endure.[18] How are they to be explained? Lactantius gives the following concise Epicurean argument against the Stoics and their view of a benevolent and omnipotent god:

> Either god (i) wishes to prevent evils and cannot, or (ii) he can and does not want to, or (iii) he neither wants to nor can, or (iv) he both wants to and can. If (i), he is weak, which is impossible for god. If (ii), he is malevolent, which is equally alien to god. If (iii), he is malevolent and weak, so not a god. If (iv) – the only real possibility for a god – then where do evils come from? And why does he not prevent them? (Lactantius *On the anger of god* 13.19 (374 Us.))

For the Epicureans, the only possible conclusion from such arguments is that in the face of human suffering and natural evils the Stoic view of divinity is hopelessly misguided. But unlike some modern proponents of the 'Argument from Evil', the Epicureans do not conclude that there are no gods at all. Rather, since there are gods, they must be neither interested in nor necessary for the affairs of our cosmos.

The significance of such arguments is not merely that we might eventually generate a correct account of the gods. Rather, removing these inconsistencies leads directly to positive benefits in our lives. Thinking that the gods themselves might be subject to any kind of anxiety or concern is not only inconsistent with the universal true belief that they enjoy a perfect existence, but it is also detrimental to

[16] Cf. Cic. *ND* 1.21–2. [17] Cf. Lucr. *DRN* 5.156–94.
[18] E.g. Lucr. *DRN* 5.195–324. See also Lactantius *Inst.* 3.17.8 (370 Us.).

our own chances of living a good life. Ascribing anxieties to the gods can lead only to anxiety in ourselves as we try desperately to placate them. Indeed, false conceptions about the gods can lead people to commit terrible atrocities. For example, if only Agamemnon had known that the gods have no control over the prevailing winds between Aulis and Troy and, in any case, were not interested in even extreme acts of sacrifice, then the horrific killing of his daughter Iphigenia and the attendant pain and anguish could have been averted. This famous example from Lucretius' poem (*DRN* 1.80–101) is part of a stretch of argument in which he responds to the accusation that the Epicureans are 'atheists' since they hold that the gods play no role in governing the cosmos and human affairs.[19] The line of argument he takes is the same as Epicurus offered in *Ep. Men.* 123 (above) and is echoed in Philodemus' treatise *On piety*. True piety involves having the right view of the gods and worshipping them for the right reason: not because they care about us, but because doing so is a route to our own happiness. Having rid ourselves of inconsistent beliefs about the gods, it becomes possible to think about the gods in a way which will have a positive effect on our own well-being. The Epicureans notoriously were encouraged to take part in traditional religious rituals, a practice which many ancient critics took to show a degree of doubt or bad faith in their own conceptions of the gods. But in response, the Epicureans insist that by taking part in such rituals it is possible to reinforce a true and beneficial view of divinity which is not only free from the anxiety-inducing aspects of the common conception, but also provides a clear image and paradigm of a good life to which every Epicurean can aspire.[20] Indeed, the Epicureans were happy to join other schools and philosophical movements in asserting that someone living the good life becomes 'god-like'. For the Epicureans, of course, this does not mean that such a person attains any kind of immortality, if we take that to mean an everlasting existence; accepting and welcoming our mortality is part of the process of removing the fears of death and living a good life (*Ep. Men.* 124). But a mortal human can achieve a god-like existence in the sense that he can live a perfectly and

[19] For the accusation see e.g. Cotta in Cic. *ND* 1.121–4 and cf. Obbink 1989; 1996: 1–23.
[20] See Lucr. *DRN* 6.68–79, Philod. *De pietate* 730–1390 Obbink.

completely happy life which is unconcerned by the inevitability of his death.[21]

This might make us wonder why it is necessary to think of the gods as imperishable. In the arguments surveyed so far the demonstrative work is primarily being done by the conception of the gods as enjoying a perfect, concern-free, existence. The imperishability of the gods, their other essential characteristic, is more puzzling. No doubt, it is part of the common and shared conception (*prolēpsis*) of the gods and therefore should be acknowledged. But it notoriously presents a difficulty by making the gods an apparent exception to the general Epicurean thesis that all conglomerations of atoms are merely temporary: the atoms will eventually disperse to form new conglomerations (see Cotta in Cic. *ND* 1.68 and cf. SE *M* 9.58). If the gods are indeed real living things, dwelling in the spaces between one cosmos and the next, then how can they be exempt from erosion and eventual decay? This uncomfortable combination of Epicurean physics and their theist beliefs has led some commentators to wonder whether the gods do not take the form of real, objectively existing, living things at all but are more likely 'thought constructs' generated by humans from the receipt of certain streams of atomic *eidōla*. The positive evidence for this latter view is not as clear as it might be, however, and ancient and modern critics alike are perhaps right to find the Epicureans' commitment to theism somewhat difficult to reconcile with their general cosmology.[22]

DEATH

Death, so Epicurus tells us, is for most people the 'most frightening of evils' (*Ep. Men.* 125). The Epicureans, however, are confident that this view is seriously mistaken and that we can all be persuaded of the

[21] See Warren 2000a, Erler 2002.

[22] The sources are notoriously difficult to interpret. See esp. *KD* 1 (and the scholion to it in DL); Cic. *ND* 1.49, 105–10; Philod. *De pietate* 34–201, 320–75 Obbink. The 'realist' view of anthropomorphic divine beings living outside the cosmos is defended most recently by Babut 2005 but see also Mansfeld 1993. The 'idealist' view of the gods as thought constructs can be traced in modern scholarship in English back to Scott 1883, but see also Long and Sedley, 1987: vol. 1, pp. 144–9. Obbink 1989 and 2002 offers support for the 'idealist' view based on sections of Philodemus' *De pietate* and at 2002: 214 n. 104 gives further bibliographical references. Purinton 2001 offers some further ammunition for this interpretation.

truth of the famous claim that 'death is nothing to us', provided we think properly through the Epicureans' arguments and, in addition, work hard to integrate this new and truthful belief into our general outlook on the world.[23]

The core of the Epicurean argument can be stated very succinctly:[24]

> Death is nothing to us; for what is dispersed does not perceive, and what does not perceive is nothing to us. (*KD* 2)

> Therefore death, the most terrifying of evils, is nothing to us, since for the time when we are, death is not present; and for the time when death is present, we are not. Therefore it is nothing either to the living or the dead since it is not present for the former, and the latter are no longer. (*Ep. Men.* 125)

> Therefore death is nothing to us, nor does it matter to us at all, since the nature of the soul is understood to be mortal. (Lucr. *DRN* 3.830–1)

Other Epicurean arguments, including the famous 'Symmetry argument' which asserts that we should think of post mortem time in just the same way that we think of the time before our birth (see Lucr. *DRN* 3.832–42 and 972–7), argue for the same conclusion.[25] The argument depends heavily on the Epicurean conviction that the soul is mortal. Like any other composite body, it eventually dissolves into its constituent atoms. The soul is so fragile and composed of such small and mobile atoms, that it dissolves immediately at the point of a living thing's death.[26]

On this basis, the Epicureans make two related claims about the state of affairs after an individual's death.

(1) After the dissolution of the soul there is no *perception* of pleasure and pain

(2) After the dissolution of the soul there is no *subject* of harm; the individual ceases to exist.

[23] The Epicurean arguments appear to be rather well known in antiquity and to have generated some sophisticated discussion. See, for example, the opening of Cic. *Tusc.* 1, discussed in Warren, forthcoming.

[24] I concentrate here on the argumentative core of the Epicurean position. For further discussion of some of its nuances see Warren 2004a and, for Philodemus' approach in *On death*, Tsouna 2007a: 84–5 and 239–311.

[25] For a defence of this view of the Symmetry argument and references to other discussions see Warren 2004a: 57–108.

[26] On Epicurean psychology see also Gill, ch. 7, this volume. For more on the Epicurean account of dying see Warren 2002b and Taylor 2007.

For the Epicureans, either of this pair of considerations would be sufficient to show that death is nothing to us. If pleasure and pain are the only sources of value, death can be neither a positive (pleasant) nor a negative (painful) state. Also, if after death there is no persisting subject, then there is no sense in which Metrodorus, for example, can be said to exist after the point of his death. So there is no sense in asking what state of well- or ill-being we should then assign to Metrodorus. For death to be an evil for Metrodorus then he must persist as a subject affected by that bad. If death is the end of personal existence then he is after death unavailable to be a subject of that bad. So death is not bad for Metrodorus, and so is not to be feared.

The two claims are, of course, related: the presence of a functioning soul is a necessary condition for perception of pleasure and pain. But it is useful to keep them distinct. (1) will have force only on the acceptance of a hedonist thesis relevantly like the Epicureans'; (2) will have force for many more accounts of what the value of a human life consists in. Before we pass on to various criticisms of the Epicurean view, there are evidently, we should note, two basic ways in which people may have mistaken beliefs which cause them to fear death. They may believe that after death they will be able to perceive pleasure and pain. More likely, they may believe they will in fact persist in some relevant sense after death and can therefore be subject to harm. It is hardly surprising, therefore, that the Epicureans expend considerable effort in showing that such views are incorrect. They also note, however, that the project of removing such false beliefs may be complicated by the difficulty many people feel in isolating and articulating precisely what they do believe on such issues. As Philodemus pointed out (above p. 237), beliefs relevant to the fear of death are often 'latent' and have to be uncovered before they can be cured.[27]

It would be possible to reject the Epicurean view on the basis of some positive account of post mortem survival, but most modern philosophical approaches to the question tend to agree that death is the end of one's personal identity. From this starting point, there are two principal strands of criticism designed to retain the possibility of death being a harm. The first argues that death is a harm which can affect someone even in the absence of post mortem survival. The

[27] Compare Lucr. *DRN* 3.870–93.

most effective versions of this criticism evade the Epicureans' argument by finding a sense of harm which is consistent with their account of the nature of death and also finds an appropriate subject for such a harm. In addition, they offer answers to Epicurus' question of *when* death can be a harm.

The most popular type of anti-Epicurean view offers a 'comparative deprivation account' of the harm of death.[28] People are harmed by death, on this account, insofar as, because they die as and when they do, they do not experience the goods of life *which they would have experienced had they died at a time later than they did.* In essence, this compares the life actually led with an alternative, longer, life which is assumed to contain more goods (perhaps more pleasures). The alternative life is therefore better and, in comparison, the shorter life is worse. So by preventing this alternative better life, death has harmed the individual in question. The account answers (1) by asserting that there are harms which need not be perceived by the subject of the harm.[29] But why should we accept this? Anyone convinced by Epicurean hedonism would remain unmoved. (Alternatively, if we do find such harms plausible, this will weaken or prevent a commitment to Epicurean hedonism.) The account answers (2) by locating the time of the harm: it is suffered either before death, or else it is somehow eternally true that the person is harmed, or perhaps timelessly true; the preferred answer will depend on a thought about *when* the counterfactual claim is true.[30] The Epicureans themselves pointed out that, viewed as a kind of deprivation or loss, the supposed evil of death seems to be of a very peculiar kind. As ancient sources point out, it is difficult to think of the deceased being deprived of the goods of life if this means that he is 'missing out' on them – whether or not he is aware of the loss. For there is no subject persisting after death and it seems odd to conceive

[28] There is a large and rapidly growing secondary literature on this issue. But, for a general introduction, see, for example, Nagel 1979, Feldman 1992. For defences of Epicurus see, for example, Rosenbaum 1986 and 1989. For more discussion and references to some recent literature see Warren 2004a: 17–55.

[29] Nagel 1979: 5 gives the famous example of a case of undiscovered betrayal: 'the natural view is that the discovery of betrayal make us unhappy because it is bad to be betrayed – not that betrayal is bad because its discovery makes us unhappy'.

[30] For a discussion of the different options see Warren 2004a: 46–50.

of a 'loss' in which there is no subject at all after the disappearance of the supposed goods.[31]

There are other potential weaknesses with this anti-Epicurean stance. First, it assumes that it is indeed possible that someone might die later than they in fact do. In a determined universe, therefore, this counterfactual account would not hold. But also, in order to avoid the uncomfortable thought that it might also be true that people are harmed by being born later than they might, this counterfactual account will try to resist the symmetrical claim that such people do not experience the goods of life *which they would have experienced had they been born at a time earlier than they did*. The explanation for this asymmetry is generally couched in terms of a description of personal identity consistent with the idea that the timing of birth is somehow necessary and the timing of death merely contingent.[32] In that way, death – rather than non-existence *per se* – is seen as somehow robbing us of goods we would otherwise have enjoyed.[33]

There are other questions it must face. First, since we are all going to die at some time, we can ask: Is therefore *every* death an evil? Is someone who lives to be over a hundred years old and who enjoys a full and active life until the very end nevertheless to be pitied because they did not live to be two hundred years old? Instead perhaps death's badness is limited to the duration one can realistically be expected to live *unless one dies earlier*. Still, in that case is the death of a ninety-year-old not so bad for the ninety-year-old as the death of a sixteen-year-old is for that sixteen-year-old? And is the death of an infant still worse? Alternatively, we might stipulate that deaths are bad only for people for whom the relevant counterfactual is true. If it is the case that by continuing to live I would have experienced no more goods (say that the only prospect was that I continue to experience long periods of excruciating pain) then death is not a loss. Is it therefore a good thing in such cases? Presumably so, since this counterfactual would be true: 'by dying at that point X missed out on various evils which he *would have experienced had he died later*'.

[31] See Lucr. *DRN* 3.894–911; Cic. *Tusc.* 1.87–8.

[32] See, for some options: Nagel 1979, 8 and n. 3; Kaufman 1996; Warren 2004a: 78–81.

[33] For an ancient attempt to maintain a similar asymmetry between post mortem and pre-natal non-existence see Cic. *Tusc.* 1.9–14.

The second principal criticism of the Epicurean view claims that they misplace the source of people's fear. They assume that in fearing death we primarily fear the state of being dead, the everlasting nothingness which will succeed the end of life. But it is quite possible that this is not the prime source of anxiety. It is possible to be entirely indifferent about that state – perhaps even rightly so – but still fear death in the sense of it being an end to life. It is not at all incoherent not to fear 'being dead' but, while alive, nevertheless to be anxious that one's life and its various projects, hopes and desires, will inevitably come to an end. And, perhaps more important, it is possible to fear not that life will come to an end but more specifically that it might come to an end *too soon*. Since a mortal life will end, there is a sure threat that its value will be diminished: a longer life would contain more good than a shorter life and so it is always bad to die earlier rather than later. Further, it can be argued that it is rational for someone to be concerned – even anxious – about this possibility even during life. This threat of premature death might affect the plans, desires and projects one takes up with overall adverse effects.

The simple concern that we will eventually die is perhaps most easily disposed of. For various reasons it is plausible to think that the alternative, an everlasting life, would not itself be desirable.[34] In that case, a longer life might be preferable to a shorter one, but an infinitely long life would not be preferable to a finitely long life. Epicurus explicitly insists that a correct estimation of a good life will remove the desire for an everlasting life since it will show that a good life can be achieved within a finite time. This stance is, paradoxically, part of what it means for someone to achieve a 'god-like' life (*Ep. Men.* 124). Nothing of value would be added to a good Epicurean life were it to last forever. Now, this still allows that a life could be cut short prematurely and this could be a reasonable source of anxiety. We may not want a life never to end, but still not want it to end just yet. Against this concern, the Epicureans insist that a good life is within the grasp of even the young (and they offer certain prodigious examples of youthful ataraxic Epicureans) and, once attained, the limit of mental and physical pleasures is not made any more valuable by lasting. A good Epicurean life need not have

[34] See Warren 2000a. On the desirability or otherwise of immortality see also Williams 1973, Fischer 1999, Moore 2006.

a particular duration: once the good life has been achieved, there is no sense in which it can be cut short prematurely since it is already complete.[35] (Philodemus says that a wise Epicurean will live his life 'already, as it were, prepared for burial', *De morte* 4, *PHerc.* 1005, XXXVIII.14–19 Kuiper). Clearly, this is a radical and revisionist account of what constitutes a 'complete life' and we might be left wondering not only about its plausibility and the chances of it offering an attractive goal for us to pursue, but also about various consequences which might follow. There is therefore a serious concern about not whether the Epicureans' arguments are consistent or plausible, but whether the Epicurean life they describe is one we would want to live. For example, it is not clear, given that we are supposed not to be concerned about the duration of life once in this ideal state, what reason there might be for an Epicurean sage to keep on living. Unlike the Stoics, the Epicureans seem to have generally frowned on suicide, but their good life appears to offer no sufficient reasons for its prolongation. In short, we might wonder if the price for a life without fear of death in any sense is much too high: it is a life we cannot imagine wanting to attain or to continue living.[36]

[35] See Rosenbaum 1990 and Warren 2004a: 109–59.

[36] Cf. Warren 2004a, 161–212. For the Epicurean attitude to suicide see also Englert 1994, Cooper 1999b. Tsouna 2007a: 256–7, 262–4 and 269–77 (cf. Tsouna 2007c) argues that in *De morte* Philodemus accepts that a good life does indeed require some duration for completeness.

VOULA TSOUNA

14 Epicurean therapeutic strategies

Like other Hellenistic philosophers, the Epicureans assume that the principal goal of philosophy is to secure one's happiness,[1] and that that result can be achieved only by removing the principal causes of human suffering, namely the vices (*kakiai*) and certain emotions or passions (*pathē*).[2] Considered in the light of a normative conception of nature and psychic health,[3] these are diseases of the soul that philosophy must cure and thus restore the soul to its healthy natural state, much as medicine treats the ailments of the body aiming to restore its unimpeded functioning. Therapy consists in purging from the soul the elements of moral disease, in putting into the soul the right elements, and often in both. However, from the practical perspective, the important aspect of the therapy is purgatory: the removal of features that cause disturbance and unhappiness rather than the replenishment of whatever knowledge we lack. Epicurus is the first member of the school to compare philosophy to medicine and the philosopher to the medical doctor (221 Us.). Lucretius (first century BC), Philodemus (first century BC), Diogenes of Oinoanda (second century AD) and other Epicureans are also wedded to the so-called medical analogy. They too perceive the philosopher as a kind of doctor who cures disturbance and anxiety and helps us achieve the supreme good, pleasure *(hēdonē)* or the absence of pain *(aponia)*. The medical model suggests that philosophical therapy is an ongoing activity integrated into the context of ethical *praxis*. The important

[1] Cf. Sextus' formulation of the Epicurean definition of philosophy as 'an activity that secures the happy life by means of arguments and reasonings' (*M* 11.169).

[2] For the sake of brevity, I shall use 'emotions' interchangeably with 'passions', i.e. in the negative sense of harmful emotions, unless I indicate otherwise.

[3] Cf. Nussbaum 1994: 29–32.

thing is to live the philosophical life, not merely to be engaged in theoretical discourses.[4]

The Epicureans' commitment to the medical model varies according to their particular interests, purposes, and methods. They do not explicitly isolate a specifically 'therapeutic' aspect of philosophy or a genre of 'therapeutic' argument. Moreover, their reliance on the medical model does not appear to exclude the parallel use of other complementary or even competing models.[5] Even so they all agree that the supreme good cannot be attained unless we are healed from our troubles and fears, and each of them proposes several strategies to that effect.

I

The identification and classification of Epicurean strategies is not a straightforward matter. For the goal of therapy can be pursued in many different ways. Moreover, questions can be raised concerning the exact nature and range of therapeutic techniques. Notably, it is unclear whether all Epicurean arguments should be considered 'medical'. A related issue is whether the properly therapeutic aspects of Epicureanism concern only the correction of moral error or, alternatively, extend to theoretical instruction enabling us to avoid error in the first place. Indeed, while corrective and didactic functions often appear to overlap (as in e.g. Lucr. *DRN* 3), they also can be dissociated. Epicurean strategies sometimes depend on Epicurean doctrine, but other times are not attached to it: they derive from other schools, notably the Stoics and the Peripatetics, or are consistent with their teachings.[6] For the Epicureans realize, as their rivals do, that psychic diseases require a plurality of methods because they can be complex and hard to cure. Indeed, the methods that they use exhibit remarkable variations in the psychic powers that they address. In particular, they may rely more or less on the faculty usually called reason and

[4] See P. Hadot 1995: 49–70.

[5] A different interpretation is defended by Nussbaum 1994 regarding Hellenistic philosophers in general. Cf. also David Sedley's review of Nussbaum 1994 (Sedley 1994), and also Diskin Clay's review of that work (Clay 1996: 501).

[6] For example, Philodemus takes the description of the enraged man from Stoic sources and he cites the methods of Aristo of Ceos in order to combat arrogance.

they may or may not involve other faculties as well. This last point requires further clarification and a brief look at the Epicurean view of the nature of the passions.[7]

Passions such as erotic love, anger, and the fear of death are related to particular dispositions (*diatheseis*) to believe certain things and to feel and behave in certain ways, under certain circumstances, for certain reasons. They are evil *precisely because* they are causally connected with wicked dispositions. But strictly speaking they are not identical with them. An irascible person is not always angry (cf. Philodemus *De ir.* XXVII.19–23) and someone who tends to fear dying at sea does not always make his fear manifest (cf. Philodemus *De mort.* XXXIII.9ff.). The Epicureans strongly suggest that the emotions consist of cognitive and non-cognitive elements. This applies to all kinds of emotions healthy or destructive, passionate as well as mild.[8] All emotions comprise desires, and desires are classified into natural and empty depending on the kinds of beliefs on which they are based (*KD* 29); therefore, emotions too are probably classified in a similar manner. Later Epicureans suggest that the passions (including anger and the fear of death) belong to the category of unnatural or empty emotions, precisely because they are related to empty beliefs or presumptions about their objects. These beliefs are both false and harmful and give rise to reactions with the same characteristics. They mainly concern the issues whether there is evil at hand and whether one reacts to it in an appropriate manner.[9] They have descriptive as well as evaluative components, and it seems that the Epicureans address them both. The main means of doing so are arguments. As for the extra-cognitive features of the passions, we find that they are distinct if not independent from beliefs.[10] They include feelings and imaginings and account for the particular experiential quality that

[7] See Annas 1989 and, more recently, Cooper 1999a; Erler and Schofield 1999; Everson 1999a; Nussbaum 1994; and Sorabji 2000.

[8] Epicurus suggests that the arousal of emotions involves both beliefs and a focusing of the *pathos* at something definite (*Nat.* 25 34.18–20 Arr. = Laursen 1995: 108–9 and 1997: 14–17); see Annas 1992: 191–2.

[9] For discussion of the emotions as value judgements in Chrysippus see, recently, Sorabji 2000: 29–47.

[10] It is not clear how the different aspects of individual emotions, notably beliefs and feelings, are related to each other. On this point, see Tsouna 2007a: 42–4.

each emotion has, i.e. for the way in which it is felt.[11] The Epicureans seem to think that arguments are insufficient to treat these aspects of the emotions, but need to be complemented by other techniques of persuasion. However, it is important to emphasize that, unlike (for instance) the dietary recommendations of Posidonius and Galen, all Epicurean techniques are cognitive in a broad sense, while many of them are strictly intellectualist and, indeed, judgemental. In this respect at least, the Epicureans come closer to Chrysippus than to Posidonius, Panaetius or Galen. Lastly, we should bear in mind that, for the Epicureans as for every other Hellenistic philosopher, therapeutic exercises are intended to engage one's whole being and, therefore, they involve many factors: intellectual as well as moral, self-reflective as well as instinctual, dispositional and also behavioural, drawing on reason and sensibility, memory, imagination and sensitivity.

Therapy may be practised in different contexts and the therapist may address his patients in different ways and by different means. We can draw a broad distinction between therapy exercised in life between the members of an Epicurean group and the therapy available to mankind with the aid of Epicurean writings. The paradigm of the former kind is the interaction between the teacher and the student within an Epicurean school. Philodemus' *On frank speech* (*De lib. dic.*) gives us important information about the nature and goals of this interaction as well as its principal method: *parrhēsia*, frank speech.

Parrhēsia is a generic method of moral correction, of which other devices (though not all) are species or individual applications. It consists primarily in the candid criticism that an Epicurean teacher addresses to a student who has been at fault. Ideally, the process begins on the student's own initiative: he goes to the teacher because he feels an 'itching' at what he has done and is confident that he will receive help. He realizes, however dimly, that the unpleasantness of the treatment will be vastly outweighed by its benefits (*De lib.dic.* fr. 49.2–5). And if he has good character, he trusts that the teacher will assist him out of disinterested motives. The treatment is complex

[11] The clearest statement to this effect is found in Philodemus' *On anger*. Natural anger (*orgē*), which is an acceptable kind of anger, differs from empty or inacceptable anger (*thumos*) in its experiential quality (cf. *poiotēti*: *De ir.* XLV.34–7): it does not feel like empty anger (XLIII.41–XLIV.35).

and could be long. It is determined by the diagnosis of the error, touches on both reason and feeling, and is more or less severe depending on the case. The Epicurean teacher tailors his frank speech to the pupil's personality and character, the kind of error that he has committed, and its magnitude. So, frank speech can be mild (*metrion*) or harsh (*sklēron*) and bitter (*pikron*); more intense towards pupils with a strong character, but less intense towards more tender persons. Compare a doctor who chooses his medicines in accordance with the patient's physical constitution, the kind of malady affecting him, and its severity. If the doctor's preferred method of treatment fails, he tries another method in the same patient or in a different one. Something similar holds for the teacher: if mild criticism fails to correct the error, he applies harsher criticism and may increase further its intensity in order to achieve his goal (*De lib. dic.* frs. 64.3–13, 66.1–16).

In principle, *parrhēsia* is exercised by all to all, although the standard relation is that between the teacher and the student. The good teacher is prompted by affection and benevolence, while the student is expected to submit to the admonition with respect and trust. Ideally, both know that, even if the correction is painful, the student will benefit from it. *Parrhēsia* may or may not be exercised in front of one's fellow-students. In any case, it never amounts to an attack on one's personality, but concentrates only on specifics. Once an error is corrected, it is also forgiven and forgotten. Past sinners, like everybody else, take their turn in criticizing their fellow-students or, if they are not in a position to correct them, in reporting them to the teachers. The teachers too are open to criticism and are willing to admit their mistakes and failures (sometimes to students but usually to their colleagues). They address their students with no passion (fr. 48.2)[12] and no self-complacence, and have no motive other than the students' own good. Their attitude to *parrhēsia* is entirely consistent with their avowed beliefs about the method. They persuade 'through deeds and not just through speaking' (fr. 16.5–7).

Epicurean therapy and the Epicurean way of life are cultivated also through the study of Epicurean writings, some of which concern, among other things, the *parrhēsia* of Epicurean sages. It is a job of the instructors to handle such texts in appropriate ways and, more

[12] The context indicates that the conjecture *a[pathōs]* is correct.

generally, to collect and preserve the school's tradition in a variety of forms: compilation of notes, distribution of works, textual criticism, composition of epitomes, and training in how to read and understand books. Therapy through texts is available not only to those who receive an Epicurean education in the relevant institutions, but also, importantly, to every careful reader of these texts. In fact, the major figures of the school appear acutely aware of the healing power of their writings. Epicurus says that one purpose of philosophical writings is to enable us to help ourselves (*Ep. Hdt.* 35). Lucretius frequently points to the importance of reading and rereading his poem as well as to the progress that his readers will make in that way. Philodemus too appears to realize that some form of therapy should be available for broader audiences at all times: in his ethical works, he lays out therapeutic strategies that his readers will be able to apply to themselves. His treatises are books as well as drugs, registers of therapeutic wisdom as well as exemplifications of treatment carrying a therapeutic value of its own.[13]

II

A large part of Epicurus' conception of therapy is cognitive in the narrow sense that it consists in arguments. It also relies on a concrete methodology, which is conducted according to rules of enquiry and which Epicurus follows in all his endeavours.[14] His arguments principally aim at removing ignorance or false beliefs lying at the source of much of our anxiety and disturbance, notably the fear of the gods and the fear of death. This holds for his arguments in ethics, as well as in physics, astronomy, meteorology and other domains of philosophy (cf. *Ep. Hdt.* 81).

However, Epicurus does not overlook the extra-cognitive aspects of therapy. For alongside the importance of reading, studying and understanding the cardinal tenets of the system, he constantly stresses the role of repetition and memorization. In these ways the teachings take firm hold of our soul, enable us to help ourselves in particular situations, and ensure that we shall never get disturbed whether awake or asleep (cf. *Ep. Hdt.* 35–6, *Ep. Pyth.* 84, *Ep. Men.*

[13] Cf. Diogenes of Oinoanda fr. 3.V.14–VI.2 Smith. [14] See, for instance, Asmis 1984.

135). So far as we know, these practices remain central also to the therapeutics of Epicurus' followers.

Epicurus suggests that what we experience and commit to memory tends to get associated with a number of thoughts, some of which are true and others false. If we assess them in the light of the Epicurean criteria of truth (especially in the light of our preconceptions, *prolēpseis*, which are themselves memory-derived concepts), we end up having true beliefs or knowledge. Extended to ethics, this account of memory suggests that committing firmly to memory the cardinal principles of the Epicurean doctrine is not merely a matter of remembering them, but rather of determining the contents and the direction of our way of thinking.[15] In fact, this appears to be one main purpose of Epicurean compendia (*epitomai*) whose basic structure resembles that of memory handbooks. The better we remember the cornerstones of Epicurean thought, the easier we associate them with particular situations at hand and, moving from one thing to another, from one true belief to another, we end up making the right choice. Epicurus' insistence on repetition and practice indicates that the relevant trains of thought become increasingly faster to the point of building quasi-automatic moral reflexes. Later Epicureans still debate issues concerning the mechanism and impact of memorization: Philodemus tries to explain precisely how the memorization of the principles of Epicureanism brings about one's peace of mind, refuting a rival Epicurean position on the same topic (*De elect.* XI.7–20). While repetition and memorization are distinct from arguments, Epicurus and his followers give no indication that these strategies can *replace* arguments and achieve *alone* the patient's healing.

III

One reason why Lucretius' *De rerum natura* has drawn much attention is that it has appeared to many to reconcile successfully two elements that by their very nature go against each other: poetry and teaching, artistic inspiration and didactic intent.[16] As we saw, the three basic elements of the medical model are the doctor/teacher, the

[15] Cf. Frede 1990: 240.

[16] A recent discussion of this topic is found in Volk 2002: 1–24 and 67–118. My own treatment in this section owes much to hers.

patient/student, and the medicines/teachings that achieve the cure. In close parallel, *De rerum natura* exhibits all three fundamental features of didactic poetry: the speaker/teacher, the listener/student, and the subject matter taught. The speaker leaves no doubt that he takes seriously both his poetic craft and his philosophical mission. His model is Empedocles, eminently a didactic poet whose subject matter is, at least in part, philosophical.[17] However, the famous simile of the honeyed cup (1.936–50, 4.11–25) indicates that poetry plays a subordinate role with regard to the transmission of Epicurean doctrine. As the physician smears with honey the rim of a cup in order to beguile the child to drink the wormwood and regain health, so the speaker uses poetry, 'the sweet honey of the Muses' (1.947, 4.22), to beguile his addressee to take in the harsh truths of Epicurean philosophy and achieve well-being. And although the honey might appear at first glance necessary (for without the honey the child might refuse the wormwood and, likewise, without the sweetness of the verses the addressee might turn away from Epicureanism), nonetheless the speaker suggests that even such sweeteners do not guarantee success (1.948–9) and that, in any case, the important thing is the medicine but not the honey, the philosophical content more than the poetic form.

The recipient of the speaker's teachings is Memmius, a poetic persona as unspecified as the speaker and a rather untalented novice in philosophy. He too serves specific therapeutic goals. On the surface, many of the poetic and rhetorical techniques of the poem appear calculated, precisely, to overcome Memmius' shortcomings and help him assimilate Epicurean philosophy, especially Epicurean physics and their implications for our emotional life. Moreover, his philosophical inadequacy appears deliberate: we do not want to be like him and, therefore, we shall exert ourselves far more than Memmius in order to understand and accept the poem's teachings.[18] Other formal features of the poem as well have not just didactic, but specifically therapeutic, dimensions. The poet conveys the impression that he is creating the poem as he goes along and, correspondingly, Memmius and we, the readers, are learning and becoming liberated from the fear of the gods and the fear of death as we follow

[17] On the relation between Lucretius and Empedocles, see Sedley 1998a.
[18] Cf. Mitsis 1993: 123ff., and Volk 2002: 81ff.

that ongoing process.[19] The repeated use of the first person plural indicates that our active participation is required for the poem to attain its goals. The poet presents the teaching-and-learning process as a journey along a certain path: of the poet, who describes himself as a charioteer nearing the finishing line (6.92–5); of Memmius, who initially may have entertained doubts about the nature of the path that he is urged to enter (1.80–2); of the readers who will begin their own journeys towards the truth; of Epicurus, who 'marched far beyond the flaming walls of the world and traversed the immeasurable universe in thought and mind' (1.72–4) and returned carrying the knowledge of the natural world as his prize (1.74–7); and perhaps also the journey of Odysseus, to whom the readers of *De rerum natura* can liken themselves.[20] There is considerable urgency in undertaking the journey. For the fear of the gods, the fear of death, the fear of disease, the troubles of erotic love and other similar conditions inflict on us the supreme evil, pain, so that we cannot be happy unless we purge our mind (1.43–54). Epicurus is the only person in the history of mankind to show us the road to healing and salvation.[21]

Turning to individual therapeutic techniques, we find that, in accordance with Epicurus' practice, Lucretius uses an impressive arsenal of arguments, some of which he is the first Epicurean author known to use. One such example is the famous Symmetry Argument (3.832–42, 972–5), intended to combat anxieties related to death: just as the infinity of time preceding our birth has been nothing to us, so the stretch of time after our death will also be nothing to us (3.972–5); our attitudes should reflect that fact.[22] Other examples are found in the first two books of the poem, which defend the principal claims of Epicurean physics. Regardless of their differences in provenance and scope, these arguments too have a clear therapeutic intent: by removing false beliefs concerning the universe and the ways in which the

[19] Volk 2002: 12ff., calls this feature 'poetic simultaneity' and provides an informative discussion of it.

[20] Volk 2002: 20–6, points out that the travel metaphor is typical of poems which exhibit poetic self-consciousness and poetic simultaneity.

[21] Cf. Nussbaum 1994: 269–71.

[22] Depending on how the argument is interpreted, it seems intended primarily to address the fear of being dead or, alternatively, the fear of mortality. There is an extensive philosophical literature on the Symmetry Argument, whose most important pieces are summarized and discussed in Warren 2004a.

gods might be involved in its workings, they eliminate a major source of mental trouble and lead us towards a correct and beneficial conception of these matters.

Moreover, like Epicurus, Lucretius invites his audience to study and reflect on the principles and arguments presented, in order not to be overborne by fear (1.102–6) and to be able to see 'into the heart of hidden things' (1.145). He too emphasizes the importance of memorization (2.581–5) and presents the Epicurean doctrine by touching upon its chief points (cf. 3.261). He too takes care to repeat often the most important points of his analysis; the claims that the soul is mortal and that death is nothing to us are cases at hand. Lucretius clearly believes that such techniques help us not just learn, but internalize the teachings of the poem. Many passages indicate why there is need to do so, e.g., the passage describing the man who professes to believe that with death comes lack of sensation but worries about the disposal of his remains (3.870–93). Rather than invoking any notion of the unconscious, we should read these verses as revealing the patient's inconsistency and self-deception.[23] Epicurus would have concurred that, in such cases, additional instruction is required to achieve the sufferer's cure.

Lucretius also uses rhetorical and literary resources. Sometimes he anticipates conclusions for which he has not yet argued, other times he suspends a conclusion which he has already amply defended, yet other times he disrupts the logical flow of his exposition with digressions. These elements are not failures in logic, but effective therapeutic techniques.[24] Other such techniques include the immense wealth of images and metaphors, the use of imagery to create conceptual associations (as opposed to making explicit claims), changes of tone and nuances, and the personification of Nature in the famous diatribe at the end of the third book of the poem.[25]

[23] Cf. Gladman and Mitsis 1997.

[24] Asmis 1983 gives some earlier bibliography on this charge and offers a plausible refutation of it. She suggests that Lucretius' poetry serves throughout the rhetorical aim of persuasion: poetic and rhetorical elements are joined together to create a kind of 'philosophical rhetoric'. While I am sympathetic to this view, I am reluctant to accept Asmis' stronger claim that Lucretius has structured his entire philosophical presentation along rhetorical guidelines

[25] On the speech of Nature (3.931–71) see, recently, Reinhardt 2002.

One last feature of *De rerum natura* has puzzled readers: the frequent depiction of scenes of horrific suffering, in particular of the plague that afflicted Athens towards the beginning of the Peloponnesian war. Competing interpretations suggest that such scenes bear testimony to Lucretius' disturbed psyche; they illustrate how Lucretius' poetic imagination often runs ahead of his didactic goals; or they express displaced forms of anxiety about death primarily by depicting images of violating the boundaries of the body.[26] In fact, the uncontrollable and chaotic circumstances in which horrible pain and death occur have a therapeutic purpose.[27] They constitute the final test as to whether the readers have truly internalized the teachings of the poem and can look upon even these deaths without anxiety and fear. If they can, Lucretius' poetic art has perfomed its miracle. If they cannot, the readers should return to the poem and reflect on it again.

IV

Various other therapeutic techniques can be found in Epicurean works. They urge us to cultivate an impartial perspective, i.e., a perspective which is objective and natural as opposed to one that is subjective and human. It is valuable because it enables us to detach ourselves from the things that people ordinarily prize, including life itself.[28] Reinforcement of various kinds is also used. Philodemus emphasizes that it fortifies the students against error (*De elect.* XI.7–20) and discusses it (e.g., in the forms of repetition and memorization) in connection with frank speech (*De lib. dic.* fr. 63.4–13, fr. 16.1–5, cf. fr. 14.5–10, Col. IIb.2–10). Another Epicurean technique is redescribing familiar things in an unfamiliar light.[29] One of the most famous examples is Lucretius' suggestion that, in order to escape the snares of erotic love, one should try to avoid self-delusion and see the objects of one's desire for precisely what they are (*DRN* 4.1141–54): relabel 'the sweet disorder' as 'dirty and rank', the 'modest' as 'dump', the 'slender' as 'too skinny to live', and 'the woman who is all kiss' as 'one with thick lips'

[26] Cf. Segal 1990. [27] Cf., for instance, Erler 1997.

[28] Cf. Philod. *De mort.* XXXIX.15–25, *De inv.* fr. 18 1–9.

[29] This technique may include, but is not restricted to, what Sorabji 2000 (222–3) discusses under the heading of 'relabelling'. His account and mine overlap in part, but they focus on different types of cases.

(cf. 4.1159–70).[30] Relabelling is often driven by theory, as in the above examples, but in many cases it is simply chosen for psychological effect. Soldiers falling gloriously in battle 'are killed like farm animals in the ranks' (*De mort.* XXVIII.37–XXIX.2), and the heroes of Plataea became 'bird food and dog food' (XXXIII.21–2).

Another group of exercises has to do with time and may also involve conceptions of the self.[31] The passions displace one's happiness away from the present to some uncertain future and force us to think wrongly, in general, about all temporal modes. One reason is that the desires involved in, e.g., anger and lust, are of a special kind. They do not concern the present and cannot be satisfied in the present; in truth, they cannot be satisfied at all. However, we should not infer that, without any qualifications, for the Epicureans 'only the present is our happiness'.[32] For on the one hand, the Epicureans contend that pleasure is complete at every moment, death cannot affect present happiness, and the sage's contemplation of nature reveals to him timeless truths.[33] On the other hand, they also believe that the pleasures of the past and those anticipated in the future are relevant to present happiness (cf. DL 10.22, 137, Cicero *Fin.* 1.60), and that we should think rightly about the past and the future rather than think of them not at all.

Like Epicurus and Lucretius, Philodemus stresses the universal and atemporal nature of the sage's perspective in connection with the supreme good and with death.[34] But he is also the first Epicurean explicitly to dissociate a *carpe diem* attitude from one's true enjoyment of present pleasures (*De elect.* XVII.3–20). The good Epicurean should deliberately focus his attention on *past* pleasures in order to round off his mental survey of his life and die content (*De mort.* XXXIX.15–25). Philodemus' conception of the hedonic calculus shows the role of anticipation and foresight in the rational pursuit

[30] Cf. on the 'good money-maker', Philod. *De oec.* XX.1–32. On this topic, see Betensky 1980; R.D. Brown 1987; Clay 1983a; W. Fitzgerald 1984; Nussbaum 1994: 140–91; Schrijvers 1970; and Sorabji 2000: 222.

[31] Cf. Sorabji 2000: 228–52; Nussbaum 1994: 192–238; P. Hadot 1995: 217–37. Individual strategies concerning our attitudes to temporal modes and to personal identity are also discussed by contemporary philosophers. Parfit 1984 has greatly influenced modern interpretations of the Symmetry Argument.

[32] Cf. P. Hadot 1995: 217–37.

[33] Cf. Robin 1962: 150–2.

[34] Philodemus uses these techniques extensively: *De mort.* XII.11, XIX.1–6, XII.28–30, XXXVII.1–5, XXXIX.15–25.

of pleasure and avoidance of pain.[35] Moreover, he maintains that anticipation and hope add to our happiness so long as they are of the right kind and are directed towards the right objects. We should nurture good hopes for the future: hopes that we shall remain healthy or recover from disease (*De elect.* XXIII.7–13), share our goods with others and get benefits in return (XXII.17–21), retain our friendships and make more (XIV.5), and conduct philosophical conversations in tranquillity and leisure (*De oec.* XXIII.1–20). All the same, we must not disregard present and past pleasures on account of a future that may never be ours. For in that case we would be deprived of every enjoyment (*De elect.* XIX.12–14) and would cut ourselves off 'from every means to a better life, exactly like men sentenced to death' (*De elect.* XVIII.9–11).

Philodemus highlights the therapeutic value of concepts of the self by using them in new contexts. We find them in his treatment of individual vices and passions, principally in connection with issues of rationality, self-control and self-knowledge. *On frank speech* points out that people too keen on pleasure or too afraid of pain shrink at *parrhēsia* (*De lib.dic.* fr. 30.1–11), and those affected by vices do the same because they are irrational and do not know themselves. On the other hand, seeking correction implies a certain level of awareness of oneself. *On arrogance* describes arrogant people as having no knowledge of themselves (*De superb.* fr. 1) for, if they did, they would register negative reactions towards themselves, would grieve about their own condition, and would seek to improve themselves (cf. *De superb.* II.1–33, V.5-6, XVIII.37-8). Those susceptible to flattery may falsely believe that they merit the flatterer's praise, or they may be dimly aware of the fact that they do not (*De adul.*, *PHerc.* 1457 fr. 14.5–10). In either case, their therapy requires that they get to know their own selves. *On anger* holds a mirror in front of the enraged man

[35] Epicurus seems to have sharply differentiated the anticipation of future pains in the context of the hedonic calculus from the Cyrenaic exercise of anticipating suffering and misfortune. While the former is part of a rational enterprise, the latter makes us suffer about evils that have not yet happened (Cicero *Tusc.* 3.32). This remark suggests that the kind of anticipation involved in the hedonic calculus is not accompanied by intense joy or fear but, at most, by mild feelings of similar kinds. In truth, the Epicureans seem to think that it is appropriate to distance oneself from intentional states projected into the future, since they can always be cancelled by the reality of death. Cf. Warren 2001a.

and invites him to look at himself. If he does not like the picture, he will endeavour 'to become himself' again: get cured of the passion and retrieve his rationality and self-control.

Shifting attention is also a strategy related to temporal modes and many Epicureans use it, including Epicurus at his deathbed. A distressed person may feel happier by focusing on a pleasant memory, a much anticipated future event, or something that distracts him at present. Such shifts are often prompted or accompanied by belief. Take the case of anger. Often we actively try to distract ourselves, precisely because we have become convinced that nothing terribly bad has happened to us after all. In other exercises, the emphasis is on the shift of attention, not of belief. Melody, which is irrational, cannot directly affect emotions and judgements, which are rational: 'it only distracts people into switching their attention, just like sex and drunkenness' (*De mus.* IV, 129.1–7 Delattre).

Lastly, there is a therapeutic device which cannot be readily classified under some general heading and has not received much attention in the literature. We may call it moral portraiture. In outline, it consists in drawing vivid if elliptical portraits which bring out characteristic features of certain types of persons, good or bad, serene or disturbed. It is used by many schools but plays a particularly prominent role in Epicurean authors. It is determined by their conception of the philosophical life and, in the later history of the school, by institutional celebrations of Epicurus and his associates as moral paradigms.

These portraits are often organized in an antithetical manner which facilitates their principal purpose, namely to 'put-before-the-eyes', to compel us to imagine just what it is like to be superstitious, arrogant, irascible, etc., and also what it is like to be the opposite. The success of the technique depends on the literary qualities of the representation. In particular, we must be induced to assume that a single person can believe and do everything that the portrait represents[36] – that there is a single coherent character who has the dispositional, behavioural, moral, and theoretical features depicted. If the technique works, we feel aversion not only towards isolated elements, such as arrogance or rage, but towards the entire personality of someone arrogant or irascible. We simply do not want to be that

[36] See Nehamas 1998: 3.

sort of person but just the opposite. For the most part, such portraits serve the Epicurean philosophical agenda nicely. They work apotreptically as much as protreptically, and contribute to the removal of disease and the restoration of moral health. They are also self-referential to a degree. For Epicurean authors must have endorsed for themselves the moral ideal that they represent so well.

V

To conclude, let us consider some objections against the Epicurean therapeutic model. Like the physician of the body, the doctor of the soul occupies a position which may appear asymmetrical with regard to his patients. Although he takes into account his patients' perception of their own condition, he critically assesses it according to a kind of expertise that his patients do not often fully possess; it is essential that they trust and even obey him if the therapy is to work. But, in contrast to medicine, the practice of philosophy requires intellectual initiative on the part of the student and reciprocity between the parties. Similarly, perhaps learning how to engage in dialogue is not an Epicurean objective, since the school puts so much emphasis on authority and trust. Additional charges are that some Epicurean practices numb one's intellect and critical spirit, discourage the fair consideration of competing alternatives, and ascribe to arguments merely instrumental value.[37]

There may be some truth to these criticisms. However, they are mitigated considerably by the following considerations. First, the treatise *On frank speech* establishes that frank speech, as practised in life between the members of an Epicurean school, is not at all a passive process akin to brainwashing but, on the contrary, it requires the student's active participation in his own healing.[38] Recall that the therapeutic process usually begins on the student's own initiative (*De lib.dic.* fr. 49.2–5). Believing that one has bronchitis could be unrelated to the presence of the disease or to the antibiotics prescribed for its cure. On the other hand, realizing that one's rage at

[37] Cf. Nussbaum 1994: 13ff., 14–16, 45–7, 69ff., 130–2, 137–9.

[38] In fact, Philodemus makes clear that the teacher bears little or no responsibility for failing to cure morally corrupt people, much as the doctor cannot be blamed for failing to heal an incurable disease (*De lib. dic.* fr. 69.1–8).

one's neighbour is inappropriate is essential to its subsequent removal. Patients can contribute to their own treatment by maintaining positive thoughts and attitudes. In particular, they must struggle to keep down their own defences and preserve their trust in the teacher's good will. They must learn to bear the discomfort caused by frank criticism and feel grateful for it. In general, they need to make constant mental and psychological efforts in order to benefit from the teacher's candour, develop their self-awareness, and get rid of their faults. On a practical level, they may help the therapist in his job by reporting the errors of their fellow-students. Or they may undertake the role of the therapist by applying *parrhēsia* to their peers. Occasionally, *parrhēsia* involves the switching of roles between teachers and students, and it also obtains between peers (students, teachers, or even sages). Second, although parrhesiastic exchanges do not have the structure of dialogue, nonetheless, in some respects, they come surprisingly close to the paradigm of engaging in dialogue, namely Plato's Socrates.[39] Each such exchange represents either a communal or a personal exercise, or both. It is a mental and psychological itinerary that presupposes, crucially, self-examination and self-criticism.

Third, it would seem that Epicurean students are not deprived of critical spirit and that they become cognizant of the views of their rivals. Consider the extant remains of Epicurus' *On Nature*, and even more so the complex dialectical structures of Philodemus' *On poems* I, *Rhetoric* I *and* II, *On music*, and also *On signs*, *On anger*, and the writing tentatively identified as *[On choices and avoidances]*. Epicurean dialectical arguments in these works vary in rigour and clarity and can be unfair or fallacious. However, they can also impose high intellectual demands on their readers. For instance, these last must be able to distinguish the positions of different rival factions – sometimes a formidably difficult task; follow the development of an argument to its conclusion; understand the reasons why a certain position should be rejected; be able to separate the stronger from the weaker reasons to that effect; and so on. Popular writings too, such as epitomes, require a certain degree of sophistication. I doubt that a student could really digest Epicurus' *Letter to Herodotus* if he were not able to grasp the highly condensed formulations of doctrines and

[39] Cf. P. Hadot 1995: 89–93.

arguments found in that work. In short, Epicurean students may well be partial, but this does not entail that they reject alternative views merely on authority or that they endorse their own without reflection.

Fourth, although the Epicureans set stringent ethical constraints upon therapeutic arguments, it does not follow that they would have been happy to substitute for reasoning a drug that would make one forget all empty beliefs and retain only true ones, assuming that such a drug existed.[40] Epicurus does say that if we had never been bothered by fears concerning things in the heavens and death, as well as by our ignorance of the limits of emotion and desire, we would not stand in need of the science of nature (*physiologia*: *KD* 11), but these claims are counterfactual. In truth, we *are* very disturbed by these fears. And we can be cured only by making use of our reason (*logismos*) throughout our life (*KD* 16). Precisely because we are rational beings, we find it impossible to enjoy unadulterated pleasures without knowing the nature of the universe (*KD* 12) and, like Epicurus, we reach serenity in our lives 'most of all by engaging constantly in the science of nature' (*Ep. Hdt.* 37). As Philodemus remarks, we successfully accomplish our moral choices only when we measure them by the ends laid down by nature (*De elect.* XI.17–20), namely when we perform correctly the hedonic calculus. And since our ability to do so is the very stamp of human rationality, no drug can ever take its place.

[40] Nussbaum 1994: 128.

CATHERINE WILSON

15 Epicureanism in early modern philosophy

INTRODUCTION

The recovery of Epicurus' natural and moral philosophy in the Renaissance and its dissemination in the early modern period had a significant effect on the evolution of philosophy. The theses of the plurality of worlds, their self-formation, the non-existence of any god or gods concerned with the affairs of men and women, and the centrality and validity of the hedonic motive in human life, came under extended scrutiny in the seventeenth and eighteenth centuries. Although it was once customary to regard Epicureanism as a fringe movement represented in the seventeenth century almost uniquely by the enigmatic Pierre Gassendi, it is now increasingly recognized that Epicurus' letters and sayings, and his follower Lucretius' Latin poem, *On the nature of things*, contributed to the formation of a rival image of nature – the corpuscularian, mechanical philosophy – that replaced the scholastic synthesis of Aristotelianism and Christian doctrine, and that found special favour in the new scientific academies of Europe. Robert Boyle, the chief English spokesman for the new philosophy observed that

> The atomical philosophy invented or brought into request by Democritus, Leucippus, Epicurus, & their contemporaries, tho since the inundation of Barbarians and Barbarisme expelled out of the Roman world all but the casually escaping Peripatetic philosophy, it have either been wholly ignored in the European schools or mentioned there but as an exploded system of absurdities yet in our less partial & more inquisitive times it is so luckily revived & so skillfully celebrated in diverse parts of Europe by the learned pens of Gassendus, Magnenus, Descartes, & his disciples our deservedly famous countryman Sir Kenelme Digby & many other writers especially those that handle magnetical and electrical operations that it is now grown

too considerable to be any longer laughed at, & considerable enough to deserve a serious inquiry.[1]

Like many of his contemporaries, however, Boyle harboured grave reservations. The passage quoted appeared in an essay written in 1652-4, 'Of the Atomicall Philosophy', which Boyle later instructed was 'without fayle to be burnt' after his death. Epicureanism was almost synonymous, for early modern philosophers, with atheism, and so with the denial of divine creation, providence, the immortality of the soul, heaven and hell, and moral right and wrong. While Epicurus had admitted the existence of the gods, insisting that piety was to be cultivated, the view usually ascribed to him was that, as Cicero put it, religion was 'invented by wise men in the interest of the state, to the end that those whom reason was powerless to control might be led in the path of duty by religion'.[2]

ATOMISM AND MECHANISM

The chief sources for Epicurean doctrine in the Latin West were Cicero's thorough and generally balanced discussions in *On the Nature of the Gods*, the *Tusculan Disputations*, and *On Ends*, Plutarch's *Morals*, and the polemics of Lactantius in *The Wrath of God* and the *Divine Institutions*, together with hostile mentions in other patristic writings. Diogenes Laërtius' account of Epicurus in Book 1 of his *Lives of the Philosophers* was brought to Italy in the early fifteenth century, and his valuable chapter included reproductions of Epicurus' letters to Herodotus, Pythocles and Menoeceus, references to his lost work, *On Nature*, and forty short maxims dealing with cosmological, anthropological and ethical topics. Lucretius' poem was recovered as well in the early fifteenth century and had appeared in a number of European editions before 1600.[3]

The invention of the printing press furthered the dissemination of careless and libertine writings as well as a massive devotional and theological literature for Christians, and unbelievers seemed to the godly to be multiplying without limit. Several well-known atheistic circles existed in England in the late 1500s, amongst them Sir Walter Raleigh's band of free-thinkers, and a group collected by Henry

[1] Boyle 2000: 13: 227. [2] Cicero *ND* 1.118.
[3] On the reception of Lucretius in the modern era, see Johnson and Wilson 2007.

Percy.[4] Giordano Bruno, who had visited England in 1583-5, aroused audiences with his lectures against Aristotle, and,while he disavowed material atomism, he admired Epicurus and Lucretius. He taught the multiplicity of worlds and was executed for heresy in 1600.[5] Epicurean poetry instructed readers that life was brief and followed by an endless sleep, that men and beasts were no different and experienced the same pleasures and desires, and that one ought to enjoy life to the fullest as long as possible.[6] Marin Mersenne remarked despairingly in the 1620s that there were over 50,000 atheists in Paris alone;[7] and Epicureanism, or 'Epicurism', was regarded in Italy, France and England, as a corrupting force, dragging men into a condition of degradation and promoting malice and social unrest. In *Natures Embassie, or, The Wilde-mans Measures* of 1621, Richard Braithwaite portrayed his contemporaries as 'drawne and allured by the vaine baits and deceits of worldly suggestions ... Every one ... a hogge wallowing in the mire of their vaine conceits ....[8] The cause, he said, was Epicurism, the 'private and peculiar Sect', which 'thought that the *chiefe good* consisted in a voluptuous and sensuall life, expecting no future doome after the tearme and end of this life'. Their philosophy, 'like a noisome and spreading Canker, eats into the bodie and soule of the professor, making them both prostitute to pleasure and a very sink of sinne'.[9]

Simultaneously, practical chemists were voicing their dissatisfaction with the scholastic interpretation of chemical entities and processes. Their laboratory experience was less congenial to the notion that the world consisted of a multitude of different substances composed of matter and form ('hylomorphism'), each with its own essence, than to the notion that perceptual and chemical qualities depended on the motion and arrangement of invisible particles. As Daniel Sennert wonderingly pointed out in 1618, the doctrine of

[4] Kargon 1966: 7. See also Hill 1972: 173–4; 1977: 317–19.

[5] See Yates 1966: 221. [6] Charles-Daubert 1998: 74–5.

[7] Parisian Epicureans of the early seventeenth century included Gabriel Naudé, Elio Diodatai and François de la Mothe le Vayer, and, on the periphery, the storywriter Cyrano de Bergerac, and the playwright Molière. See Lennon's 'dramatis personae' in Lennon 1993: 63–102.

[8] Braithwaite 1621: 129. It was common in Antiquity to compare Epicureans to pigs, sometimes with a positive spin: see Horace *Epodes* 1.4.16. On their repudiation of the accusation, see Warren 2002a: 129–31.

[9] Braithwaite 1621: 129.

atoms was not new in his own time, and was indeed older than Aristotle. '[E]very where amongst Philosophers and Physicians both Ancient and Modern', he mused, 'mention is made of these little Bodies or Atomes, that I wonder the Doctrine of Atomes should be traduced as Novelty.' 'All the Learnedest Philosophers', he says, 'have acknowledged that there are such Atomes, not to speak of *Empedocles, Democritus, Epicurus,* whose Doctrine is suspected, perhaps because it is not understood.'[10]

Francis Bacon's 'Democritean' (this euphemism carried less moral and religious baggage than 'Epicurean') *Cogitationes de rerum natura* (1605) and his *De principis atque originibus* (1612), although they were not published until 1653, defended the study of matter and cited the effects of mechanical processes on qualities. The Epicureans held individual atoms to be colourless, but regarded perception as accomplished by means of films or *eidōla* that were emitted from the surface of a body. The dependence of perceived colours on illumination, the position of the observer, and mechanical processes, such as the whipping up of sea water by the wind, was detailed at length by Lucretius in Book 2 of *On the nature of things*. While most modern philosophers rejected the theory of coloured films, the position that sensory qualities are relative, observer-dependent entities was available to seventeenth-century philosophers, and eagerly adopted by them. Boyle and Locke distinguished neatly between the 'primary' qualities of bodies – magnitude, figure and motion; and the 'secondary properties' – colour, taste, texture – that they held were caused by the action of subvisible bodies on the sensory organs of observers. The powers of bodies to purge, poison and to effect other changes on neighbouring bodies, they referred also to the motion and interaction of the particles composing them.

Writing from Florence in 1623, Galileo Galilei introduced a particle-theory of heat, light and colour in *The Assayer* and presented a theory of infinitely minute atoms in the *Two New Sciences* (1638).[11] René Descartes, probably inspired by the Dutch physicist Isaak Beeckman, married a mechanical system of corporeal nature,

[10] Sennert 1660: 446.

[11] According to Paolo Redondi, his troubles with the Church owed more to his Democritean leanings than to his relatively inoffensive Copernicanism. Redondi 1987: 333–5; see however Finocchiaro 1989: 202–4.

incorporating a Galilean analysis of qualities, to a Platonic theory of the soul in his *Meditations* (1640) and his *Principles of Philosophy* (1644). Descartes took some care to distance himself from Parisian libertinism and materialism. He referred in a letter to one of his critics to 'that inane philosophy conflated of atoms and the void, usually ascribed to Democritus and Epicurus, and others like it, which have nothing to do with me'[12] and he denied the possibility of atoms – indivisible least particles – on the grounds that they conflicted with God's power to do anything whatsoever.[13] In his *Meditations*, he entertained – though only to reject it – the Epicurean possibility that all his ideas were caused by material things and that 'God' named nothing more than the idea of a fictitious incorporeal entity. His overall aim was to reintroduce the main concepts and claims of classical atomism, minus the commitment to uncuttables and the void, into textbook natural philosophy. In his *Meditations* he argued that corporeal substance has 'all the properties which I clearly and distinctly understand, that is, all those which, viewed in general terms, are comprised within the subject matter of pure mathematics'.[14]

Meanwhile, in France, Epicureanism was decisively recast by the anti-Aristotelian humanist scholar, Pierre Gassendi, who maintained friendly relations with members of Parisian libertine circles, whilst managing to remain above suspicion. Likely encouraged by his conversations with Beeckman, whom he met at Dordrecht in 1629,[15] his *De vita et moribus Epicuri libri octo* in 1647 was an apology for Epicurus, devoted to an account of the life and reputation of his author. Having rejected Aristotelian ontology and the conception of scientific knowledge as demonstrative knowledge of essences and natures, Gassendi accepted the Epicurean premise that experience is the basis of knowledge, and he insisted that the aim of research in physics was to establish probability rather than certainty. Further, he endorsed the ontology that Aristotle had conspicuously rejected, and he tackled the traditional objections against atoms, insisting that 'there is nothing to prevent us from defending the opinion which decides that the matter of the world and all the things contained in it is made up of atoms, provided that we repudiate whatever falsehood

[12] Descartes 2000: 84. [13] Descartes 1985: vol. I, p. 231.
[14] Descartes 1985: vol. II, p. 55. [15] See Jones 1989: 169.

is mixed in with it'.[16] He edited and translated Diogenes Laërtius' Book 10, and, in his *Syntagma philosophi Epicuri* and his posthumously published *Syntagma philosophicum*, he married atomism to theology, explaining that God created the atoms and set them in motion, and that the phenomena of the world were generally to be explained as a result of the interaction, collision and entanglement of these tiny bodies. Gassendi's declared commitments to a providential world order and to an immortal, incorporeal soul have struck some interpreters as insincere, but the persistence of controversy testifies to the great care he took in his presentations, and to the likelihood that Gassendi's stance amounted, in Bloch's phrase, to an agnostic *refus de choisir*.[17]

English philosophers influenced by Gassendi's Epicureanism included Kenelm Digby, whose *Two Treatises* had appeared in 1644, Margaret Cavendish, and Thomas Hobbes. Cavendish announced in her preface to *The World's Olio* of 1655 that it was better to be an atheist than superstitious; atheism fostered humanity and civility, whereas superstition only bred cruelty. Cavendish's friend, Walter Charleton, the main vector for Epicurean philosophy in England, edited and published J.B. van Helmont's *A Ternary of Paradoxes*, which discussed corpuscular effluvia, in 1650. He followed it with the *Darknes of Atheism* in 1652, with its cautious reference to the 'pure and rich Metall' hidden amongst detestable Epicurean doctrines, and with his *magnum opus* – in fact an elaborate paraphrase of Gassendi – the *Physiologia Epicuro-Gassendo-Charletoniana*, in 1654. Within a few years, *Epicurus' Morals* (1656) and a dialogue on Lucretian mortalism (1657), had given an airing to Epicurean moral philosophy and antitheology. Though a plenist who took some states of matter to be irreducibly fluid, Hobbes went further than any of the other moderns in his *Leviathan* (1651), in which he asserted that all that existed was body, that all effects were produced by bodies in motions, and in which he reinvented the Epicurean account of justice as a non-aggression pact forged amongst hostile parties. Thomas Stanley devoted over one hundred pages to Epicurus in the third volume of his *History of Philosophy* which appeared in 1660.

[16] Gassendi 1972: 398.
[17] Bloch 1971: 108–9; see also Johnson 2003; and Osler 2003.

Boyle began to publish corpuscularian treatises beginning in the late 1650s. In the *Sceptical Chemist* of 1661, and in *The Origin of Forms and Qualities* of 1666, he voiced his commitment to what he called the 'Corpuscularian or Mechanical' philosophy in language such as the following:

I plead ... for such a Philosophy, as reaches but to things purely Corporeal, and distinguishing between/ the first *original of things*; and the subsequent *course of Nature*, teaches ... not onely that God gave Motion to Matter, but that in the beginning He so guided the various Motions of the parts of it, as to contrive them into the World. (furnish'd with the *Seminal* Principles and Structures or Models of Living Creatures,) and establish'd those *Rules of Motion*, and that order amongst things Corporeal, which we are wont to call the *Laws of Nature* ....; the Phaenomena of the World thus constituted, are Physically produc'd by the Mechanical affections of the parts of Matter, and ... operate upon one another according to Mechanical Laws.[18]

Later, however, in numerous tracts and essays, Boyle emphasized the insufficiency of this mechanical philosophy to explain many observed phenomena and its subordination to theology. Though Isaac Newton in turn professed disdain for hypotheses concerning unobservable processes that did not admit of experimental or mathematical demonstration, he followed Gassendi, Descartes and Boyle in giving a stamp of approval to corpuscularianism in Book 3 of his *Principia mathematica philosophiae naturalis* (1687), and in the last Query of the first Latin edition of his *Opticks* (1706).[19] The *Principia* were prefaced by an influential Latin 'Ode', written by the suspected atheist Edmund Halley, that drew on Lucretius' poem implying flattering parallels between Newton and Epicurus as liberators of humanity.[20]

Bold philosophers, like Descartes and, at least for a time, Cavendish, were willing to set aside the Christian doctrine of hexameral creation in favour of a self-forming universe of multiple planetary systems.[21] Where Aristotle had maintained that there was only one world, with the earth at its centre, Epicurus acknowledged an infinity of *cosmoi*,

18 Boyle 2000: vol. VIII, p. 104. 19 Newton 1952: 400.

20 See Albury 1978. Bentley, Albury notes, was one of the Examiners who had rejected Halley's application for Savilian Chair of Astronomy on the grounds of his unorthodoxy; he, too, was close to Newton.

21 Cavendish 1664b: 6, 43.

and seventeenth century 'new philosophers' adjoined the Copernican doctrines of heliocentrism and the plurality of worlds to their corpuscularianism. To be sure, Descartes presented his speculations on cosmogenesis as referring to another, alternative world in the *Treatise of Light*, as only possible in the *Discourse*, and as hypothetical and false in the *Principles*, deferring to the account in Genesis. 'There is no doubt that the world was created right from the start with all the perfection which it now has.'[22] But he ventured the position that 'The laws of nature are sufficient to cause the parts of this chaos to disentangle themselves and arrange themselves in such good order that they will have the form of a quite perfect world ...'.[23] In the *Treatise of Man*, he maintained that animals were purely corporeal machines; with the exception of the human mind, a spiritual substance, there were no souls, spirits, species, forms, virtues or powers present in matter. In his *Principles of Philosophy* he insisted that matter left to itself would assume all the forms of which it was capable. The baby, he insisted, is generated mechanically in the womb from a mixture of material fluids, just like any other object.[24] These points were also the focus of his *Discourse on Method* of 1637.

THINKING MATTER AND THE MORTALITY OF THE SOUL

Although the Epicurean hypothesis of subtle soul atoms found no adherents other than Gassendi amongst the major philosophers of the seventeenth century, the notion that suitably organized corporeal substance might be able to think was very much alive and was on the minds of many of the Objectors to Descartes' *Meditations*.[25] Henry Oldenburg noted in his third letter to Spinoza that '[T]he controversy about what Thought is, whether it is a corporeal motion or some spiritual act, entirely different from the corporeal, is still unresolved'.[26] Gassendi had amplified his objections to Cartesian dualism into a lengthy *Disquisitio Metaphysica*, and Spinoza in his *Ethics* (1677) pursued the notion that extended and thinking

22 Descartes 1985: vol. I, p. 256. 23 Descartes 1985: vol. I, p. 91.
24 Descartes 1985: vol. III, pp. 134–5. 25 Descartes 1985: vol. 2, p. 284.
26 Oldenburg, in Spinoza 1985: vol. I, pp. 168–9.

substance – the corporeal world and God – might be the very same unique substance.

Despite his earlier waverings, by 1683 Locke's reflections on personal identity had, according to Michael Ayers, already veered away from his early mind–body dualism, and assumed 'a starting point more favourable to the materialists'.[27] His *Essay on Human Understanding* of 1689, though organized around the corpuscularian philosophy and the causal theory of perception and ideation associated with it, did not mention thinking matter. But in the second edition, Locke noted that it was entirely possible that God, rather than joining to our bodies a thinking, immaterial substance, had 'given to some Systems of Matter fitly disposed, a power to perceive and think', in virtue of which suitably organized systems might exhibit, not only vegetable life, but also animal perception, and human reason. What certainty can anyone have, Locke asked,

> that some perceptions, such as *v.g.* pleasure and pain, should not be in some bodies themselves, after a certain manner modified and moved, as well as that they should be in an immaterial Substance ... Body as far as we can conceive being able only to strike and affect body; and Motion, according to the utmost reach of our *Ideas*, being able to produce nothing but Motion ....[28]

Like many of his English counterparts, Locke had adopted Gassendi's views on our ignorance of essences, and on the vagueness and philosophical uselessness of the concept of substance, whether material or immaterial. With his double negation – our inability to know that God has not given the power of thought to matter – Locke carefully avoided affirming ontological doctrines about what really exists. Denying that his aim was to 'anyway lessen the belief of the Soul's Immateriality', he emphasized that 'it becomes the Modesty of Philosophy, not to pronounce Magisterially, where we want that Evidence that can produce Knowledge'.[29] He invoked the Epicurean principle that we have access only to appearances, now theorized by reference to a theory of 'ideas', which are either simple, or else complex combinations that originate directly in the motions and impressions of the bodies surrounding us.[30] Though the language of ideas is typically given a strictly Cartesian reading, Lockean ideas are more

[27] Ayers 1991: vol. II, p. 255. [28] Locke 1975: 540–1.
[29] Locke 1975: 541–2. [30] Locke 1975: 104–18.

appropriately read as Epicurean appearances, localized inside the mind. Like Gassendi and Hobbes, Locke began his exposition of Man, not with Epicurean material first principles – this would have been a needlessly provocative move, but with sensory appearances and the imagination, moving on to their putative material causes. As Ayers aptly remarks, Locke wanted to 'demonstrate that scepticism about that which thinks in us is compatible with a belief in immortality'.[31] He tried to show how religion and morality could tolerate the possibility of materialism, and he shifted the focus from ontological questions about the nature of the soul to questions about the effects of a belief in its immortality on moral motivation.

For Epicurus, the central aim of philosophy was to free humans from 'the fears of the mind'.[32] Some fears are aroused by celestial and atmospheric phenomena such as storms, earthquakes, hail and eclipses that are taken as manifestations of divine wrath. Other fears are aroused by reflection on human mortality. The fear of death is dissipated by the realization that every composite entity is perishable, that a full and enjoyable life can be lived in the time allotted to mortals, and that the condition of being dead cannot logically be experienced and so is not an evil.[33] As early modern philosophers became increasingly convinced of the dependence of experience on physiological processes in the sensory organs, nerves and brain, the Epicurean postulate that the death of the body is the end of human existence came to seem increasingly compelling. Descartes' assertion of an immortal, incorporeal soul in the *Meditations* perplexed many readers of his other texts and aroused considerable cynicism.[34] Yet mortalism threatened the basis of the Christian religion and the authority of the Church, with its promise of eternal life for obedient believers. The intensity with which the issue of the mortality of the soul was pursued indicates intense engagement with the Epicurean position, but Epicurus' doctrine found little favour. Whatever their private doubts might have been, it was not worthwhile for philosophers to risk prosecution under blasphemy laws and condemnation of their other doctrines merely to advance such an unwelcome and

[31] Ayers 1991: vol. II, p. 205. [32] See Warren, ch. 13, this volume.
[33] See Warren 2004a and ch. 13, this volume.
[34] On the rehabilitation of Descartes as a good Catholic philosopher after his placement on the Index of Prohibited Books, see Lennon 1993: 239.

possibly pernicious doctrine. Even Spinoza, who had been excommunicated from the Jewish community for denying the soul's immortality,[35] seemed in his *Ethics* to favour a less aggressive Averroist doctrine of the absorption of the individual into the mind of the whole at death.

Leibniz, an opponent of Epicureanism who saw the necessity of constructing an entire rival system of immaterial atomism or 'monadology', appealed to the latest microscopical discoveries as evidence that 'birth' is only growth and development, and he argued that 'death' is only collapse and condensation, so that all living creatures are naturally eternal. The incorporealist bias of the philosophers has helped to define the discipline down to the present day. Kant, for example, famously argued that human beings are not entitled to assert the truth of materialism, lacking as they do epistemological access to the supersensible realm in which the answers to questions about God, the immortality of the soul and its free will are hidden. These entities, along with the existence of a future state, he insisted, were necessary postulates of practical reason, preconditions of moral behaviour and moral judgement.

ETHICAL HEDONISM

Epicurus had asserted forthrightly, 'I know not how to conceive the good, apart from the pleasures of taste, sexual pleasures, the pleasures of sound, and the pleasures of beautiful form.'[36] At the same time, he expressed scorn for 'drinking bouts and continuous partying and enjoying boys and women, or consuming fish and the other dainties of an extravagant table'. He recommended prudence and foresight and insisted that living honourably and justly was living pleasantly.[37] He assigned, however, no value to suffering – nullifying the import of Christian martyrology – and he considered that living virtuously was advantageous, precluding molestation by others, guilt, mental troubles, and the sequelae of overindulgence.

The vindication of pleasure was as significant a feature of early modern moral philosophy as its acceptance of corpuscularianism. Epicureanism furnished an alternative to Stoic and Christian rigourism,

[35] See Nadler 2001. [36] Epicurus, *On the telos*, cited at DL 10.6.
[37] Epicurus *Ep. Men.* 131–2. See for details Woolf, ch. 9, this volume.

and it brought the issue of basic human welfare, understood as the satisfaction of non-intellectual needs, to the fore. Lorenzo Valla's remarkable dialogue *De Voluptate* (1431), later retitled *De Vero Bono*, described by Lynn Joy as containing 'one of the most ambitious projects for reform in the history of ethics',[38] set a Stoic, a Christian, and an Epicurean in debate to the advantage of the last-named. In Thomas More's *Utopia* (1516), sensory pleasure was effortlessly integrated with the pursuit of knowledge and with social equality in a context of minimal religion. The Utopian philosophers agree that 'all our Actions, and even all our Virtues terminate in Pleasure, as in our chief End and greatest Happiness; ...'[39] Carefully observing the Epicurean maxim that pleasures that draw pains after them should be avoided, the Utopians devote themselves to enjoyments of the mind and also of the body. The latter arise, according to More, when we 'feed the internal Heat of Life by eating and drinking', or when we are relieved of surcharge or pain in 'satisfying the Appetite which Nature has wisely given to lead us to the Propagation of the Species'.[40] More's Utopians are not mortalists; they despise as 'men of base and sordid minds' and bar from public office and high honours those who 'so far degenerate from the Dignity of human Nature, as to think that our Souls died with our Bodies, or that the World was governed by Chance, without a wise overruling Providence ...'[41] Such persons are allowed nevertheless to dispute in private with priests 'for the Cure of their mad Opinions', for it is a maxim amongst the Utopians that belief cannot be compelled.

Gassendi had planned, but apparently did not complete a seventh book for his *Exercises Against the Aristotelians* of 1624, which was to show 'in what way the greatest good depends on pleasure and how the reward of human deeds and virtues is based upon this principle.' The lengthy compilation of his writings published by François Bernier in 1699 under the title *Three Discourses of Happiness, Virtue and Liberty* began confidently and warmly: 'Mankind having a natural Inclination to be happy, the main bent and design of all his Actions and Endeavours tend chiefly that way. It is therefore an undeniable Truth, that Happiness, or a Life free from Pain and Misery, are such

[38] Joy 1992: 573; see also D.C. Allen 1944. [39] T. More 1751: 96.
[40] T. More 1751: 101–2. [41] T. More 1751: 144–5.

things as influence and direct all our Actions and Purposes to the obtaining of them.'[42]

The Cartesian Antoine Le Grand, along with Walter Charleton, and later Charles de Marguetel de Saint Denis, sieur de Saint-Évremond, promoted openly Epicurean systems of morals. They insisted that Epicurus had been unjustly maligned by his enemies, and the earlier image of the Epicurean pig swilling in a filthy trough was replaced by a new image of the Epicurean as a man of taste, refinement and delicate feeling. Charleton proposed to create in his reader 'a very great dearnesse towards [Epicurus] not a patron of Impiety, Gluttony, Drunkenness, Luxury, and all kinds of Intemperance'. Felicity, he decided was 'that good, to which all other Goods ought to be referred, and cannot itself be referred to any other thing'.[43] Saint-Évremond, a paragon of worldliness and tenderness, admired by even the chaste and virtuous Mary Astell, said that 'Honours, Reputation, Riches, Amours, & well-manag'd Pleasures, are a mighty Relief, against the Rigours of Nature and the Miseries of Life'.[44] We live, he urged, 'in the midst of an infinite number of Goods and Evils, with senses capable of being affected with one, and tormented with the other; without very much Philosophy, a little Reason will make us relish good things as deliciously as possible, and instruct us to bear the bad with all the patience we can'.[45] David Hume, in his *Enquiry Concerning the Principles of Morals* (1751), emphasized the sensuous aspects of life and the pleasures afforded by wealth and the enjoyment of society. The virtues, he had maintained in his earlier *Treatise of Human Nature*, were such because they were either agreeable or useful, to society or to their possessors. They lacked any form of supernatural warrant.

JUSTICE AS CONVENTION

Epicurus had insisted that natural justice was 'a symbol or expression of expediency, to prevent one man from harming or being harmed by another'.[46] Justice was not a Platonic Form but a designation for some set of local customs, dependent on the needs and wishes of the community instituting it. The Epicurean view that only the atoms

[42] Gassendi 1699: 1. [43] Charleton 1670: 7. [44] Saint-Évremond 1714: vol. II, pp. 43–4.
[45] Quoted in Mayo 1934: 89. [46] Epicurus *KD* 31.

were eternal, and that all social structures, as well as living creatures, had emerged in time, and in some cases altered over time, forced and enabled the atomists to give constructive accounts of the origins of civil life – to take men as having sprung from the earth like mushrooms – and also to suppose that existing social arrangements were highly contingent. Pictorial representations of the life of early man and the origins of civilization, a counter-narrative to the Old Testament, based on the Lucretian account derived from Epicurus, as well as on corresponding accounts in Horace and Ovid, were fashioned by Cranach the Elder, and by Piero di Cosimo (1462–1522).[47]

Epicureanism's egalitarian premises and its treatment of the origins of the social contract were revived by Grotius, Hobbes, and Pufendorf, and left their mark on both Hobbes's *Leviathan* and Rousseau's *Discourse on the Origins of Inequality* (1755). Bernd Ludwig cites in this connection the Preface by Thomas Creech to his translation of *De rerum natura*. 'Hence also the admirers of Mr. Hobbes may easily discern that his Politics are but Lucretius enlarged; His State of Nature is sung by our Poet: the rise of Laws; the beginning of Societies; the Criterions of Just and Unjust exactly the same, and Natural Consequents of the Epicurean origin of Man; no new adventure.'[48] Locke, by contrast, appeared decisively to reject human agreement as the basis of the moral law in his early draft of a moral treatise, the *Questions concerning the Law of Nature*, composed in 1664.[49] The opening chapters of his *Essay*, expressed his horror at the local customs – cannibalism, infanticide, bestiality – that some communities deemed to meet their needs and express their wishes; he demanded rather an absolute standard for morality, that he thought human beings could come to ascertain through intellectual effort. Nevertheless, he acknowledged the role of convention and agreement in morals and politics: '[W]hatever is pretended', he says, 'these Names, *Vertue* and *Vice*, in the particular instances of their application, through the several Nations and Societies of Men in the World, are constantly attributed only to such actions, as in each Country and Society are in reputation or discredit.'[50] He referred to the 'secret and tacit consent' established in 'Societies, Tribes, and

[47] The cycle is treated in detail in Miller 2005; see also Prosperi 2007.

[48] Ludwig 2005. A more tentative view was taken by Haas 1896.

[49] Locke 1990: 179–80. [50] Locke 1975: 353.

Clubs of Men in the World: whereby several actions come to find Credit or Disgrace amongst them according to the 'Judgment, Maxims, or Fashions of that place'.[51] These admissions, rather than the moral realist convictions he expressed elsewhere, impressed Locke's critics, who were sceptical at the same time of his rationalism. They were however entirely consonant with the observations of eighteenth century anthropologists regarding the plurality of moral and political systems that could confer stability and harmony on a society.

The rejection of the theory of the divine right of kings, and the development of the Utilitarian view that the function of the state is to make men happy, or at least to remove as many as possible of the ubiquitous obstacles to their making themselves as happy as possible, is unthinkable in the absence of renewed attention to Epicurean moral and political theory. Gassendi and Charleton were responsible for the reintroduction into philosophy of the view that ethics was the study of the common good rather than the study of personal virtue, and this reintroduction had far-reaching consequences, especially in British moral philosophy. Hume, scorning the 'monkish virtues', insisted in his *Enquiry* that utility pleases, and he tried there and elsewhere to account for moral approval and disapproval of actions by reference to the contribution the observance of certain norms made to social harmony. J.S. Mill, himself a model of moral probity, expressed his approval of the Epicurean maxim: *Carpe diem*[52] and noted of his predecessor, Jeremy Bentham, 'The generalities of his philosophy itself have little or no novelty: to ascribe any to the doctrine that general utility is the foundation of morality, would imply great ignorance of the history of philosophy, of general literature, and of Bentham's own writings. ... In all ages of philosophy, one of its schools has been utilitarian – not only from the time of Epicurus, but long before.'[53] The opening paragraphs of Mill's own *Utilitarianism* (1863) were devoted to a characteristically gentle and lucid exposition of the misconceptions that still surrounded Epicureanism in his own time.[54] Another student of Democritus and Epicurus, Karl Marx, generalized their attacks on the superstitions of religion and amplified the Lucretian account of class division and social conflict.

[51] Locke 1975: 353. [52] Mill 1963–91: vol. x, p. 420.
[53] Mill 1950: 54. [54] Mill 1963–91: vol. x, pp. 209–10.

CRITICS OF EPICUREANISM

Already by 1660, Margaret Cavendish had decided that atomism was philosophically unacceptable. 'It is not probable that Chance should produce all things in such Order and Method,' she reflected, 'such Curious Compositions, such Subtil Contrivances, such Distinctions of Several Kinds, Sorts, Times, Seasons, such Exact Rules, Fixt Decrees, Perfect Figures, Constant Succession and the Like, unless every Single Atome were Animated.'[55] In her *Observations on Experimental Philosophy* of 1666, she alleged that atomism shows a want of depth in the theorist.

[T]he corpuscularian or atomical writers, which do reduce the parts of nature to one certain and proportioned atom, beyond which they imagine nature cannot go, because their brain or particular finite reason cannot reach further, are much deceived in their arguments, and commit a fallacy in concluding the finiteness and limitation of nature from the narrowness of their rational conceptions.[56]

Similar objections were voiced by later critics, including Edward Stillingfleet, Boyle, Cambridge Platonists, and Leibniz. Stillingfleet, who took up arms against 'the Atomical or Epicurean Hypothesis' as 'that which makes the most noise in the world'[57] in his *Origines Sacrae* of 1662, devoted over a hundred pages to its refutation and served up phrases – 'blind and fortuitous concourse' 'merely causal concourse of Atoms' – that reverberated in the polemical literature. Stillingfleet's arguments rested on the sheer implausibility of supposing that atoms could join together to form an orderly world with thinking beings in it. These arguments had little originality – physico-theology is the staple of Cicero and Lactantius – but he presented them with considerable rhetorical force.

[W]hen I see a *thousand* blind men run the *point* of a *sword* in at a key hole without *once* missing; when I find them all *frisking* together in a *spacious* field, and exactly meeting all at last in the very *middle* of it; when I once find, as *Tully* speaks, the *Annals* of *Ennius* fairly written in a *heap* of *sand*, and as *Keplers wife* told him, a *room full* of *herbs* moving up and down, fall into the

[55] Cavendish 1655: c2r. [56] Cavendish 2003: 199.
[57] Stillingfleet 1662: vol. III, p. 282.

exact *order* of *sallets*, I may then think the *Atomical Hypothesis probable*, and not before.[58]

Stillingfleet allowed nevertheless that a theistic particle theory might 'give us a tolerable account of many Appearances as to Bodies'.[59] Henry More in turn insisted that 'the curious frame of Mans Body, and Apparitions' were the most telling arguments against the atheist.[60] More's co-religionist, Ralph Cudworth, though well aware of the 'Feigning Power' of the human soul to represent imaginary objects, devoted almost a third of his nearly nine-hundred-page *True Intellectual System* of 1678 to the refutation of the 'Atheistic Corporealism' of Hobbes and Descartes. Having eliminated forms from his ontology and reduced qualities to dispositions, Boyle, meanwhile, struggled with the question of the human soul, admitting the radical inadequacy of the Cartesian arguments for its immortality. He hoped to find experimental evidence for the Resurrection and also for witchcraft and demonic activity, and he endowed the Boyle Lectures to continue his struggle against atheism, materialism and mortalism, as well as to combat Judaism, Islam and other alleged heresies.

Concerned to remove all hints of impiety from the Newtonian dynamical cosmology he admired, Richard Bentley, the first Boyle Lecturer, preached a set of six sermons in 1692. His *Confutation of Atheism from the Faculties of the Soul, alias Matter and Motion cannot think* rested on his alleged demonstration that matter could not generate sense and perception, and that the structure of the animal body could not have arisen by mechanical means. He raised the old doubts about the ability of senseless and randomly moving atoms to arrange a cosmos, to produce well-formed animals and men, and to coalesce into thinking beings. Nevertheless, he defended Boyle's corpuscularian philosophy as friendly to the doctrine of immortality, and he described gravity as the cement which held the universe together and as the 'fiat and finger of God'. Bentley contended directly against the Epicurean thesis that religion is a human invention for the domination and control of credulous populations, but much of his argument in favour of the Christian religion and its account of things turned on the consoling powers of religion, the uses

[58] Stillingfleet 1662: vol. III, p. 378. [59] Stillingfleet 1662: vol. III, p. 239.
[60] H. More 1653: 151.

of faith, rather than its epistemological validation. Suppose men are told, said Bentley,

> ... that all about them is dark senseless Matter, driven on by the blind impulses of Fatality and Fortune; that Men first sprung up, like Mushrooms, out of the mud and slime of Earth; and that all their Thoughts, and the whole of what they call Soul, are only various Action and Repercussion of small particles of Matter, kept a-while a moving by some Mechanisms and Clock-work, which finally must cease and perish by death.[61]

The sweetest Enjoyments of Life, Bentley said, 'will become flat and insipid, will be damp'd and extinguish'd, be bitter'd and poison'd by the malignant and venomous quality of this Opinion'. It is a 'firmer foundation for Contentment and Tranquillity', he went on, 'to believe that All things were at first created, and since are continually order'd and dispos'd for the best, and that principally for the Benefit and Pleasure of Man ...'[62]

Leibniz, who accepted Copernicanism and mechanism, considered the Epicurean hypothesis of worlds and living beings formed by chance to be possibly true, but massively unlikely. He argued that the mere existence of something rather than nothing, and the variety of entities and effects in nature and the simplicity of its underlying laws were evidence of intelligent design. It is as 'little credible as to suppose that a library forms itself one day by a fortuitous concourse of atoms. For it is always more likely that something is done by ordinary ways than to suppose that we have fallen into this happy world by chance'.[63]

EPICUREANISM AND EXPERIMENTAL SCIENCE

Epicureanism in its original form, it might be observed, was not especially favourable to the open-ended investigation of nature.[64] Epicurus claimed that, while a general acceptance of atomism produced the appropriate attitudes and moral emotions, 'special inquiry' was useless, there was nothing in 'the knowledge of risings and settings and solstices and eclipses and all kindred subjects that

[61] Bentley 1693: 11–12. [62] Bentley 1693: 24. [63] Leibniz 1989–: vol. VIII, p. 1810.
[64] Epicurus *Ep. Pyth.* 78–9. See Taub, ch. 6, this volume.

contributes to our happiness'. Further, '[i]f we had never been molested by alarms at celestial and atmospheric phenomena, nor by the misgiving that death somehow affects us, nor by neglect of the proper limits of pains and desires, we should have had no need to study natural science'. Both ignorance of the causes of celestial phenomena and excessive anxiety about arriving at the proper account of them in perfect detail destroyed tranquillity, he thought.[65] The boundaries to knowledge were set by the invisibility of the atoms, and by the subordination of science to moral and psychological needs. Later philosophers as well grappled with the epistemological problems posed by atomic invisibility and the perils of inference to the best explanation. One might wonder why the theory of atoms was taken up so eagerly by experimental philosophers in the absence of weighty evidence for its truth.

In appealing to an old tradition, the new Epicureans signalled their respect for the ancients and their distance from the radical fringe of prophets and utopian reformers. While especially keen to read the book of nature, they could show that they did not reject all the books of men, that they valued the contributions of the past and saw their own work in light of it, questioning only the exaggerated status of Aristotle vis-à-vis other great philosophers of Antiquity. Scepticism was at the same time a weapon – against the Cartesian pretention to have explained everything, and vain superstition alike. The experimentalists could further capitalize on the old complaint that Aristotelian philosophy was pagan through and through, by suggesting that Epicureanism was in fact easier to marry to Christianity than Aristotelianism. God was given a new role as master and commander of the mindless atoms. Like Gassendi, Boyle considered God's action necessary to 'dispose that *Chaos*, or confus'd heap of numberless Atoms into the World, to establish the universal and conspiring Harmonie of things; and especially to connect those Atoms into those various seminal Contextures, upon which most of the more abstruse Operations and elaborate Productions of Nature appear to depend'.[66] By repudiating Aristotle and the old philosophy of forms and virtues as heathen and idolatrous, the experimentalists established (barely and controversially) their Christian credentials and settled in their own minds the permissibility of their activities. Epicurean

[65] Epicurus *Ep. Pyth.* 85–6. [66] Boyle 2000: vol. III, p. 259.

insouciance regarding the correctness of particular explanations was eroded in stages, as experimental science came to adopt an explicit commitment to uncovering the truth about the operations of subvisible particles.

Tying the experimental philosophy to a classical system gave it a sense and a dignity that distinguished the methodical investigation of the scientific academies from the casual curiosity of the Renaissance virtuoso. This enlargement was especially important for the aristocratic Boyle, who, without denying that his aim was utility, had to distinguish his own activity from that of the greedy alchemist, working for profit amongst stinks and smells. The triviality into which the Royal Society's activity often descended in its early years, the target of so many satires, was countered by the elevated philosophical rhetoric of Boyle's defence of his 'Anaxagorean' – or modified Epicurean – theory of corporeal nature.

The moderns did not share the relatively passive attitude of their ancient forebears. The atoms of ancients were destined to remain forever invisible and were no more under the control of man than Aristotelian hylomorphs were. This entailed that human beings had to resign themselves to relying on sense-perception – the standard of truth – and try to enjoy life for as long as they were able. Bacon, Descartes and Boyle were aware, by contrast, of the increasing power and the greater potential power of human beings to effect technological changes in the world, and the possibility that, with improved optical instruments, it might one day be possible to see into the interior workings of things. They often tried to justify their largely curiosity-driven endeavours in humanitarian terms; the production of new drugs to cure the ills of humanity – understood as mechanical problems arising in the body, rather than as the wages of sin – was a recurrent theme.[67]

CONCLUSIONS

The transmission of the Epicurean legacy began with the general acceptance of material corpuscles as units of interest to natural science, the doctrine of primary and secondary qualities, nominal and real essences, and with the favouring of mechanical over animistic

[67] Boyle 2000: vol. II, p. 86.

explanations. But it sank deeper roots as well. The philosophically and morally attractive features of Epicureanism were its seamless integration of human beings into the rest of animated nature, the postulate of human equality that it implied, and the notion that pain and pleasure, both psychological and physical, mattered, regardless of who was experiencing them and what that person's status or merits might be. The Epicurean presentation of law and justice as needing legitimation in terms of the benefits to men of submitting to authority was a rejection of *de facto* hierarchies. These characteristically modern doctrines, accordingly, have ancient roots. Though often veiled, and sometimes ambivalent, the reception of Epicurean doctrines, from the early modern period down through the mid nineteenth century, amongst a wide sample of philosophers, was extensive and largely positive.

BIBLIOGRAPHY

Adam, Antoine (ed.) (1964) *Les libertins au* XVIIe *siècle*, Paris.

Alberti, A. (1995) 'The Epicurean theory of law and justice', in *Justice and Generosity*, ed. A. Laks and M. Schofield, Cambridge: 161–90.

Albury, W.R. (1978) 'Halley's ode on the *Principia* of Newton and the Epicurean revival in England', *Journal of the History of Ideas* 39: 24–43.

Algra, K.A., J. Barnes, J. Mansfeld and M. Schofield (eds.) (1999) *The Cambridge History of Hellenistic Philosophy*, Cambridge.

Algra, K.A., M.H. Koenen and P.H. Schrijvers (eds.) (1997) *Lucretius and his Intellectual Background*, Amsterdam.

Allen, D.C. (1944) 'The rehabilitation of Epicurus and his theory of pleasure in the early Renaissance', *Studies in Philology* 41: 1–15.

Allen, J. (2001) *Inference from Signs: Ancient Debates about the Nature of Evidence*, Oxford.

Althoff, J. (1999) 'Zur Epikurrezeption bei Laktanz', in *Zur Rezeption der hellenistischen Philosophie in der Spätantike*, ed. T. Fuhrer and M. Erler, Stuttgart: 33–53.

Angeli, A. (1981) 'I frammenti di Idomeo di Lampsaco', *Cronache Ercolanesi* 11: 41–101.

(1988a) *Agli amici di scuola (PHerc. 1005): Edizione, traduzione, e commento*, La Scuola di Epicuro 7, Naples.

(1988b) 'La scuola epicurea di Lampsaco nel *PHerc.* 176 (fr. 5 coll. I, IV, VIII–XXIII)', *Cronache Ercolanesi* 18: 27–51.

Angeli, A. and M. Colaizzo (1979) 'I frammenti di Zenone sidonio', *Cronache Ercolanesi* 9: 47–133.

Annas, J. (1989) 'Epicurean emotions', *Greek, Roman and Byzantine Studies* 30: 145–64.

(1992) *Hellenistic Philosophy of Mind*, Berkeley.

(1993a) 'Epicurus on agency', in J. Brunschwig and M. Nussbaum (eds.), pp. 53–71.

(1993b) *The Morality of Happiness*, Oxford.

Armstrong, D. (1995) 'The impossibility of metathesis: Philodemus and Lucretius on form and content in poetry', in Obbink (ed.), pp. 210–32.
(2004) 'All things to all men: Philodemus' model of therapy and the audience of *De morte*', in Fitzgerald, Obbink and Holland (eds.), pp. 15–54.
Armstrong, J.H. (1997) 'Epicurean justice', *Phronesis* 42: 324–34.
Arrighetti, G. (1973) *Epicuro. Opere: introduzione, testo critico, traduzione e note*, 2nd edn, Turin.
Asmis, E. (1983) 'Rhetoric and reason in Lucretius', *American Journal of Philology* 104: 36–66.
(1984) *Epicurus' Scientific Method*, Ithaca.
(1990a) 'Free action and the swerve', *Oxford Studies in Ancient Philosophy* 8: 275–90.
(1990b) 'Philodemus' Epicureanism', *Aufstieg und Niedergang der römischen Welt* II 36, 42369–406.
(1991) 'Philodemus' poetic theory and *On the Good King According to Homer*', *Classical Antiquity* 10: 1–45.
(1992) 'An Epicurean survey of poetic theories (Philodemus *De poem.* 5, cols. 26–36)', *Classical Quarterly* 42: 395–415.
(1995) 'Epicurean poetics', in Obbink (ed.), pp. 15–34.
(1999) 'Epicurean epistemology', in Algra, Barnes, Mansfeld and Schofield (eds.), pp. 260–94.
Atherton, C. (1993) *The Stoics on Ambiguity*, Cambridge.
(2005) 'Lucretius on what language is not', in *Language and Learning. Proceedings of the 9th Symposium Hellenisticum*, ed. B. Inwood and D. Frede, Cambridge: 101–38.
(2007) 'Reductionism, rationality and responsibility: a discussion of Tim O'Keefe, *Epicurus on Freedom*', *Archiv für Geschichte der Philosophie* 89: 192–230.
Auvray-Assayas, C. and D. Delattre (eds.) (2001) *Cicéron et Philodème*, Paris.
Ayers, Michael (1991) *Locke*, 2 vols., London.
Babut, D. (2005) 'Sur les dieux d'Épicure', *Elenchos* 26: 79–110.
Bacon, Francis (1860–4) *Works*, ed. J. Spedding, R. Ellis, D. Heath and W. Rawley, 15 vols., Boston.
Bailey, C. (1926) *Epicurus: The Extant Remains*, Oxford.
(1928) *The Greek Atomists and Epicurus*, Oxford.
(1947) *Titi Lvcreti Cari. De Rervm Natvra: Libri Sex*, Oxford.
Baldry, H.C. (1959) 'Zeno's ideal state', *Journal of Hellenic Studies* 79: 3–19.
Baltes, M. (2000) 'Zur Nachwirkung des Satzes "to makarion kai aphtharton oute auto pragmata ekhei", in Erler (ed.), pp. 93–108. Reprinted in *ΕΠΙΝΟΗΜΑΤΑ. Kleine Schriften zur Antiken Philosophie und Homerischen Dichtung*. Hg. von Marie-Luise Lakmann, ed. M. Baltes, Leipzig (2005): 27–47.

Barnes, J. (1989) 'The size of the sun in antiquity', *Acta Classica Universitatis Scientiarum Debreceniensis* 25: 29–41.

(1996) 'Epicurus: meaning and thinking', in *Epicureismo greco e romano*, ed. G. Giannantoni and M. Gigante, Naples: 197–220.

(1999) 'Linguistics 2: meaning', in Algra, Barnes, Mansfeld and Schofield (eds.), pp. 193–213.

Benferhat, Y. (2005) *Cives Epicurei. Les Épicuriens et l'idée de monarchie à Rome et en Italie de Sylla à Octave*, Brussels.

Bentley, Richard (1693) *The Folly and Unreasonableness of Atheism*, London.

Betegh, G. (2006) 'Epicurus' argument for atomism', *Oxford Studies in Ancient Philosophy* 30: 266–84.

Betensky, A. (1980) 'Lucretius and love', *Classical World* 73: 291–9.

Bett, R. (forthcoming) *The Cambridge Companion to Ancient Scepticism*, Cambridge.

Bienert, W.A. (1978) *Dionysius von Alexandrien. Zur Frage des Origenismus im dritten Jahrhundert*, Berlin, New York.

(1981) 'Dionysius von Alexandrien', *Theologische Realenzyklopädie* 8: 767–71.

(1985) 'Dionysius der Große und Origenes', *Studia patristica* 16, ed. E.A. Livingston, Berlin: 219–23.

Bignone, E. (ed.) (1920) *Epicuro. Opere, frammenti, testimonianze*, Bari.

Blank, D.L. (1995) 'Philodemus on the technicity of rhetoric', in Obbink (ed.), pp. 178–88.

(1998) *Sextus Empiricus, Against the Grammarians (Adversus mathematicos I), translation with introduction and commentary*, Oxford.

(2003) 'Atomist rhetoric in Philodemus', *Cronache Ercolanesi* 33: 69–88.

(2007) 'The life of Antiochus of Ascalon in Philodemus' history of the Academy and a tale of two letters', *Zeitschrift für Papyrologie und Epigraphik* 162: 87–93.

Bloch, Olivier (1971) *La philosophie de Gassendi*, The Hague.

Bobzien, S. (1998) *Determinism and Freedom in Stoic Philosophy*, Oxford.

(2000) 'Did Epicurus discover the free will problem?', *Oxford Studies in Ancient Philosophy* 19: 287–337.

(2006) 'Moral responsibility and development in Epicurus' philosophy', in Reis (ed.), pp. 206–29.

Bollack, J. (1977) Review of Chilton 1971, *Gnomon* 49: 790–5.

Booth, A.P. (1994) 'The voice of the serpent. Philo's Epicureanism', in *Hellenization Revisited*, ed. W.E. Helleman, Lanham: 159–72.

Boulogne, J. (2003) *Plutarque dans le miroir d'Épicure. Analyse d'une critique systématique de l'Épicurisme*, Villeneuve-d'Ascq.

Bourke, J. (2005) *Fear: A Cultural History*, London.

Boyancé, P. (1963) *Lucrèce et l'épicurisme*, Paris.

Boyle, Robert (2000) *Works*, ed. Michael Hunter and Edward B. Davis, 14 vols., London.

Braithwaite, Richard (1621) *Natures Embassie, or, The Wilde–mans Measures Danced Naked by Twelve Satyres*, London.

Brennan, T. (1996) 'Epicurus on sex, marriage, and children', *Classical Philology* 91: 346–52.

Brescia, C. (1955) 'La φιλία in Epicuro', *Giornale italiana di filologia* 8: 314–32.

Brown, E. (2002) 'Epicurus on the value of friendship (*Sententia Vaticana* 23)', *Classical Philology* 97: 68–80.

(forthcoming a) 'The emergence of natural law and the cosmopolis', in *The Cambridge Companion to Greek Political Theory*, ed. S. Salkever, Cambridge.

(forthcoming b) 'False idles: the politics of the "quiet life" in Greek and Roman antiquity', in *A Companion to Ancient Political Thought*, ed. R. Balot, Oxford.

(forthcoming c) *Stoic Cosmopolitanism*, Cambridge.

Brown, R.D. (1987) *Lucretius on Love and Sex*, Leiden.

Brunschwig, J. (1986) 'The cradle argument in Epicureanism and Stoicism', in Schofield and Striker (eds.), pp. 113–44.

(1994a) 'Epicurus' argument on the immutability of the all', in J. Brunschwig, *Papers in Hellenistic Philosophy*, Cambridge: 1–20; originally published as 'L'argument d'Épicure sur l'immutabilité du tout', in *Permanence de la philosophie: mélanges offerts à Joseph Moreau* (Neuchâtel, 1977): 127–50.

(1994b) 'Epicurus and the problem of private language', in his *Papers in Hellenistic Philosophy*, Cambridge: 21–38; originally published as 'Épicure et le problème du "langage privé"', *Revue des sciences humaines* 43 (1977): 157–77.

Brunschwig, J. and M. Nussbaum (eds.) (1993) *Passions and Perceptions: Studies in Hellenistic Philosophy of Mind, Proceedings of the 5th Symposium Hellenisticum*, Cambridge.

Brunschwig, J. and D. Sedley (2003) 'Hellenistic philosophy', in *The Cambridge Companion to Greek and Roman Philosophy*, ed. D. Sedley, Cambridge: 151–83.

Capasso, M. (2003) 'Filodemo e Lucrezio', in *Le jardin romain: Épicurisme et poésie à Rome. Mélanges offerts à M. Bollack*, ed. A. Monet, Lille: 77–107.

Castner, C.J. (1988) *A Prosopography of Roman Epicureans*, Frankfurt.

Cavendish, Margaret (1655) *Philosophical and Physical Opinions*, London.

(1664a) *Philosophical Letters*, London.

(1664b) *Poems and Fancies*, London.

(2003) *Observations on Experimental Philosophy*, ed. Eileen O'Neill, Cambridge.

Charles-Daubert, Françoise (1998) *Les libertins érudits en France au* XVIIe *siècle*, Paris.

Charleton, Walter (1650) *A Ternary of Paradoxes*, London.

(1652) *The Darknes of Atheism*, London.

(1657) *The Immortality of the Soul*, London.

(1670) *Epicurus' Morals, Collected Partly Out of His Own Greek Text, In Diogenes Laertius, And Partly Out of The Rhapsodies of Marcus Antoninus, Plutarch, Cicero, & Seneca; And Faithfully Englished*, London.

(n.d.) Bodleian MS. Smith 13.

Chilton, C.W. (1960) 'Did Epicurus approve of marriage? A study of Diogenes Laertius x.119', *Phronesis* 5: 71–4.

Clarke, M.L. (1973) 'The Garden of Epicurus', *Phoenix* 27: 286–7.

Clay, D. (1973) 'Sailing to Lampsacus. Diogenes of Oenoanda, New Fragment 7', *Greek, Roman and Byzantine Studies* 14: 49–59. Reprinted in Clay (1998), pp. 189–99.

(1980) 'An Epicurean interpretation of dreams', *American Journal of Philology* 101: 342–65. Reprinted in Clay (1998), pp. 211–31.

(1983a) *Lucretius and Epicurus*, Ithaca and London.

(1983b) 'Individual and community in the first generation of the Epicurean school', in *ΣΥΖΗΤΗΣΙΣ. Studi sull'epicureismo greco e romano offerti a M. Gigante*, Naples: vol. I, pp. 255–79. Reprinted in Clay (1998), pp. 55–74.

(1984) 'The means to Epicurus' salvation. The "Crux" at Diogenes of Oenoanda, NF 7 II 12', in *Studi in Onore Adelmo Barigazzi, Sileno* 10 (1984) 169–75. Reprinted in Clay (1998), pp. 200–6.

(1986) 'The cults of Epicurus', *Cronache Ercolanesi* 16: 11–28. Reprinted in Clay (1998), pp. 75–102.

(1989) 'A lost Epicurean community', *Greek, Roman and Byzantine Studies* 30: 313–35. Reprinted in Clay (1998), pp. 232–56.

(1990) 'The philosophical inscription of Diogenes of Oenoanda. New discoveries 1969–1983', *Aufstieg und Niedergang der römischen Welt* II 36, 4: 2446–559, 3231–2.

(1992) 'Lucian of Samosata. Four philosophical lives (Nigrinus, Demonax, Perigrinus, Alexander Pseudomantis)', *Aufstieg und Niedergang der römischen Welt* II 36, 5: 3406–50.

(1995) 'Framing the margins of Philodemus and poetry', in Obbink (ed.), pp. 3–14.

(1996) 'Deep therapy', Review of Nussbaum 1994, in *Philosophy and Literature* 20: 501–5.

(1998) *Paradosis and Survival: Three Chapters in the History of Epicurean Philosophy*. Ann Arbor.

(2000) 'Diogenes and his gods', in Erler (ed.), pp. 76–92.

(2007) 'L'Épicurisme: école et tradition,' in *Lire Épicure et les Épicuriens*, ed. A. Gigandet and P.-M. Morel, Paris: 5–27.

The Compact Edition of the Oxford English Dictionary (1971), Oxford.

Conroy, D. (1976) 'Epicurean cosmology and Hellenistic astronomical arguments', unpublished Ph.D. thesis, Princeton University.

Cooper, J. (1999a) 'Pleasure and desire in Epicurus', in his *Reason and Emotion: Essays on Ancient Moral Psychology and Ethical Theory*, Princeton: 485–514.

(1999b) 'Greek philosophers on euthanasia and suicide', in his *Reason and Emotion: Essays on Ancient Moral Psychology and Ethical Theory*, Princeton: 515–41.

Crönert, W., (1907) 'Die Epikureer in Syrien', *Jahreshefte des Österreichischen Archäologischen Instituts* 10: 145–52.

Cudworth, Ralph (1678) *The True Intellectual System of the Universe*, London.

Curd, P. (2001) 'Why Democritus was not a skeptic', in *Essays in Ancient Greek Philosophy*, vol. VI: *Before Plato*, ed. A. Preus, Albany: 149–69.

Daiber, H. (1992) 'The *Meteorology* of Theophrastus in Syriac and Arabic translation', in *Theophrastus: His Psychological, Doxographical, and Scientific Writings*, ed. W.W. Fortenbaugh and D. Gutas, New Brunswick, NJ: 166–293.

De Lacy, P.H. (1939) 'The Epicurean analysis of language', *American Journal of Philology* 60: 85–92.

De Lacy, P.H. and E.A. De Lacy (eds.) (1978) *Philodemus: On Methods of Inference*, La Scuola di Epicuro 1, 2nd edn, Naples.

Delattre, D. (2003) 'Présence ou absence d'une copie du *De rerum natura* à Herculaneum?', in *Le jardin romain: Épicurisme et poésie à Rome. Mélanges offerts à M. Bollack*, ed. A. Monet, Lille: 109–16.

(2007) *Philodème de Gadare, Sur la Musique* IV. *Introduction, texte, traduction, notes et indices*, 2 vols., Paris.

Denyer, N. (1983) 'The origins of justice', in *ΣΥΖΗΤΗΣΙΣ: Studi sull'Epicureismo greco e romano offerti a Marcello Gigante*, vol. I, Naples: 133–52.

Des Places, E. (1973) *Numénius. Fragments*, Paris.

Descartes, René (1985) *Philosophical Writings*, tr. and ed. J. Cottingham, R. Stoothoff and D. Murdoch, 3 vols., Cambridge.

(2000) *Philosophical Essays and Correspondence*, ed. R. Ariew, Indianapolis.

Diano, C. (1974) *Epicuri ethica et epistulae*, Florence.

Diels, H. (1879) *Doxographi graeci*, Berlin.

(1916) *Philodemos über die Götter. Erstes Buch*, Berlin.

(1917) *Philodemos über die Götter. Drittes Buch*, Berlin.

Dihle, A. (1971) 'Sine ira et studio', *Rheinisches Museum* 114: 27–43.

Dontas, G.W. (1971) *Eikonistika, Archaiologikon Deltion A* (Studies) 26: 16–33.

Dorandi, T. (1982) *Filodemo. Il Buon Re secondo Omero*, La Scuola di Epicuro 3, Naples.

(1990a) 'Per una ricomposizione dello scritto di Filodemo sulla Retorica', *Zeitschrift für Papyrologie und Epigraphik* 82: 59–87.

(1990b) 'Gli arconti nei papyri ercolanesi', *Zeitschrift für Papyrologie und Epigraphik* 84: 121–33.

(1991a) *Ricerche sulla Cronologia dei Filosofi ellenistici*, Stuttgart.

(1991b) *Filodemo. Storia dei Filosofi Platone e l'Academia*, La Scuola di Epicuro 12, Naples.

(1999) 'Organization and structure of philosophical schools', in Algra, Barnes, Mansfield and Schofield (eds.), pp. 55–62.

(2000) 'Plotina, Adriano e gli Epicurei di Atene', in Erler (ed.), pp. 137–48.

Eckstein, P. (2004) *Gemeinde, Brief und Heilsbotschaft. Ein phänomenologischer Vergleich zwischen Paulus und Epikur*, Freiburg.

Edelstein, E.J. and L. Edelstein (1945) *Asclepius. A Collection and Interpretation of the Testimonies* II, Baltimore.

Englert, W.G. (1987) *Epicurus on the Swerve and Voluntary Action*. Atlanta.

(1994) 'Stoics and Epicureans on the nature of suicide', *Proceedings of the Boston Area Colloquium in Ancient Philosophy* 10: 67–98.

Erler, M. (1992) 'Orthodoxie und Anpassung. Philodem, ein Panaitios des Kepos?', *Museum Helveticum* 49: 171–200.

(1993) 'Philologia medicans. Wie die Epikureer die Schriften ihres Meisters lasen', in *Vermittlung und Tradierung von Wissen in der griechischen Kultur*, ed. W. Kullmann and J. Althoff, Tübingen: 281–303.

(1994) 'Epikur – Die Schule Epikurs – Lukrez', in *Grundriss der Geschichte der Philosophie* IV, ed. H. Flashar, Philosophie der Antike: Die hellenistiche Philosophie I, Basel: 29–490.

(1997) 'Physics and therapy', in Algra, Koenen and Schrijvers (eds.), pp. 79–92.

(1999) 'Hellenistische Philosophie als "praeparatio Platonica" in der Spätantike *(am Beispiel von Boethius' "Consolatio philosophiae")*', in *Zur Rezeption der hellenistischen Philosophie in der Spätantike*, ed. T. Fuhrer and M. Erler, Stuttgart: 105–22.

(ed.) (2000) *Epikureismus in der späten Republik und der Kaiserzeit. Akten der 2. Tagung der Karl-und-Gertrud-Abel-Stiftung vom 30. September–3.Oktober 1998 in Würzburg*, Stuttgart.

(2001a) 'Epicurei, Epicurus', in *Augustinus-Lexikon* II, ed. C. Mayer, Basel: 858–61.

(2001b) 'Selbstfindung im Gebet. Integration eines Elementes epikureischer Theologie in den Platonismus der Spätantike', in *Platonisches Philosophieren*, ed. T.A. Szlezák, Hildesheim: 155–71.

(2002) 'Epicurus as *deus mortalis: homoiosis theoi* and Epicurean self-cultivation', in *Traditions of Theology: Studies in Hellenistic Theology, its Background and Aftermath*, ed. D. Frede and A. Laks, Leiden: 159–81.

(2003) 'Exempla amoris. Der epikureische Epilogismos als philosophischer Hintergrund der Diatribe gegen die Liebe in Lukrez *De Rerum Natura*', in *Le jardin romain : Épicurisme et poésie à Rome. Mélanges offerts à Mayotte Bollack*, ed. A. Monet, Villeneuve-d'Ascq: 147–62.

(2004) '"Et quatenus de commutatione terrenorum bonorum cum divinis agimus ...". Epikureische Diesseitigkeit und christliche Auferstehung bei Augustinus und Lorenzo Valla', in *Abwägende Vernunft*, ed. F.-J. Bormann, Berlin: 78–90.

Erler, M. and M. Schofield (1999) 'Epicurean ethics', in Algra, Barnes, Mansfeld and Schofield (eds.), pp. 642–74.

Ernout, A. and L. Robin (eds) (1962) *Lucrèce. De rerum natura. Commentaire exégétique et critique*, 2nd edn, 3 vols., Paris.

Evans, M. (2004) 'Can Epicureans be friends?', *Ancient Philosophy* 24: 407–24.

Everson, S. (1990) 'Epicurus on the truth of the senses', in *Epistemology*, ed. S. Everson, Companions to Ancient Thought 1, Cambridge: 161–83.

(1994) 'Epicurus on mind and language', in *Language*, ed. S. Everson, Companions to Ancient Thought 3, Cambridge: 74–108.

(1999a) 'Epicurean psychology', in Algra, Barnes, Mansfeld and Schofield (eds.), pp. 542–59.

Everson, S. (ed.) (1999b) *Psychology*, Companions to Ancient Thought 2, Cambridge.

Farrell, J. (2007) 'The architecture of the *De rerum natura*', in Gillespie and Hardie (eds.), pp. 76–91.

Farrington, B. (1939) *Science and Politics in the Ancient World*, London.

(1967) *The Faith of Epicurus*, London.

Feldman, F. (1992) *Confrontations with the Reaper. A Philosophical Study of the Nature and Value of Death*, Oxford.

Feltroe, C.L. (1904) *DIONYSIOU LEIPSANA. The letters and other Remains of Dionysius of Alexandria*. Cambridge, 1904 (*Dionysius von Alexandrien, das erhaltene Werk*, eingel., übers. und mit Anmerkungen vers. v. W.A. Bienert, Stuttgart 1972).

Ferguson, J. and J.P. Hershbell (1990) 'Epicureanism under the Roman Empire', *Aufstieg und Niedergang der römischen Welt* II 36, 4: 2257–327.

Ferrary, J.-L (1988) *Philhellénisme et impérialisme. Aspects idéologiques de la conquête romaine du monde hellénistique, de la seconde Guerre de Macédoine à la Guerre contre Mithridate*, Paris.

(2007) 'Les philosophes grecs à Rome (155–86 av. J.-C.)', in *Pyrrhonists, Patricians, Platonizers: Hellenistic Philosophy in the Period 155–86* BC, ed. A.M. Ioppolo and D.N. Sedley, Naples: 17–46.

Finocchiaro, M.A. (1989) *The Galileo Affair: A Documentary History*, Berkeley and Los Angeles.

Fischer, J. (1999) 'Why immortality is not so bad', *International Journal of Philosophical Studies* 2: 257–70.

Fish, J. (1999) 'Philodemus on the education of the good prince: *PHerc.* 1507, Col. 23', in *Satura: Collectanea philologica Italo Gallo ab amicis discipulisque dicata*: 71–7.

(2002) 'Philodemus' *On the good king according to Homer*: columns 21–31', *Cronache Ercolanesi* 32: 187–232.

(forthcoming) 'Philodemus' *On the good king according to Homer*: Political protreptic or Homeric scholarship?', in *Proceedings of the 25th International Congress of Papyrologists*, Michigan 2007.

Fish, J. and K. Sanders (forthcoming) *Epicurus and the Epicurean Tradition*.

Fitzgerald, J.T., D. Obbink and G.S. Holland (eds.) (2004) *Philodemus and the New Testament World*, Leiden.

Fitzgerald, W. (1984) 'Lucretius' cure for love in the *De rerum natura*', *Classical World* 78: 73–86.

Föllinger, S. (1999) 'Aggression und Adaptation. Zur Rolle philosophischer Theorien in Arnobius' apologetischer Argumentation', in *Zur Rezeption der hellenistischen Philosophie in der Spätantike*, ed. T. Fuhrer and M. Erler, Stuttgart: 13–31.

Fowler, D. (2000) 'The didactic plot', in *Matrices of Genre. Authors, Canons, and Society*, ed. M. Depew and D. Obbink, Cambridge, Mass.: 205–19.

(2002) *Lucretius on Atomic Motion: A Commentary on* De rerum natura 2.1–332, Oxford.

Fowler, D. and P. Fowler (1997) 'Introduction' to *Lucretius: On the Nature of the Universe*, Oxford.

Frede, M. (1990) 'An empiricist view of knowlege: memorism', in *Epistemology*, ed. S. Everson, Companions to Ancient Thought 1, Cambridge: 225–50.

(1999) 'Epilogue', in Algra, Barnes, Mansfeld and Schofield (eds.), Cambridge, pp. 771–97.

Frischer, B. (1982) *The Sculpted Word: Epicureanism and Philosophical Recruitment in Ancient Greece*, Berkeley.

Fuhrer, T. (2000) 'Zwischen Skeptizismus und Platonismus. Augustins Auseinandersetzung mit der epikureischen Lehre in *Conf.* 6', in Erler (ed.), pp. 231–42.

Furley, D. (1966) 'Lucretius and the Stoics', *Bulletin of the Institute of Classical Studies* 17: 55–64. Reprinted in Furley (1989), pp. 183–205.

(1967) *Two Studies in the Greek Atomists*, Princeton.
(1971) 'Knowledge of atoms and void in Epicureanism', in *Essays in Ancient Greek Philosophy*, ed. J.P. Anton and G.L. Kustas, Albany: 607–19. Reprinted in Furley (1998), pp. 161–71.
(1978) 'Lucretius the Epicurean on the history of man', in *Lucrèce*, ed. O. Gigon, Geneva: 1–37. Reprinted in Furley (1989), pp. 206–22.
(1981) 'The Greek theory of the infinite universe', *Journal of the History of Ideas* 42: 571–85. Reprinted in Furley (1989), pp. 1–13.
(1987) *The Greek Cosmologists*, Cambridge.
(1989) *Cosmic Problems: Essays on Greek and Roman Philosophy of Nature*, Cambridge.
(1996) 'The earth in Epicurean and contemporary astronomy', in *Epicureismo greco e romano: Atti del Congresso Internazionale, Napoli, 19–26 Maggio 1993*, ed. G. Giannantoni and M. Gigante, Naples: vol. I, pp. 119–25.
(1999) 'Cosmology', in Algra, Barnes, Mansfeld and Schofield (eds.), pp. 412–51.
Gaines, R. (2003) 'Philodemus and the Epicurean outlook on epideictic speaking', *Cronache Ercolanesi* 33: 189–98.
(2004) 'Cicero, Philodemus, and the development of late Hellenistic rhetorical theory', in Fitzgerald, Obbink and Holland (eds.), pp. 197–218.
Gale, M.R. (2000) *Virgil on the Nature of Things*, Cambridge.
Galilei, Galileo (1953) *Opere*, Milan.
Gallo, I. (1980) *Frammenti biografici da papyri* II*: La biografia dei filosofi*, Rome.
Gargiulo, T. (1981) 'PHerc. 222: Filodemo sull'adulazione', *Cronache Ercolanesi* 11: 103–27.
Gassendi, Pierre (1647) *De vita et moribus Epicuri libri octo*, Lyon.
(1668) *Institutio logica: et Philosophiae Epicuri syntagma authore P. Cl. Petro Gassendo*, 2nd edn, London.
(1699) *Three Discourses of Happiness, Virtue and Liberty*, tr. F. Bernier, London.
(1962) *Disquisitio Metaphysica*, tr. and ed. Bernard Rochot, Paris.
(1972) *The Selected Works of Pierre Gassendi*, tr. and ed. Craig Brush, New York and London.
Gemelli, B. (1978) 'L'amicizia in Epicuro', *Sandalion* 1: 59–72.
Gercke, A. (1885) 'Chrysippea', *Jahrbuch für klassische Philologie Supplement Band.* 14: 691–748.
Giannantoni, G. (1984) 'Il piacere cinetico nell'etica epicurea', *Elenchos* 5: 25–44.
Gigandet, A. (2001) *Lucrèce. Atomes, mouvement. Physique et éthique.* Paris.

Gigante, M. (1975) 'Philosophia medicans in Filodemo', *Cronache Ercolanesi* 5: 53–61.

(1983a) 'L'inizio del quarto libro "Della Morte" di Filodemo', in his *Ricerche Filodemee*, 2nd edn, Naples: 115–61.

(1983b) 'La chiusa del quarto libro "Della Morte" di Filodemo', in his *Ricerche Filodemee*, 2nd edn, Naples: 163–234.

(1992) 'Das zehnte Buch des Diogenes Laertios. Epikur und der Epikureismus', *Aufstieg und Niedergang der römischen Welt* II 36, 6: 4302–7.

(1995) *Philodemus in Italy: The Books from Herculaneum*, Ann Arbor.

(1999) *Kepos e Peripatos. Contributo alla Storia dell'Aristotelismo Antico*, Naples.

(2000) 'Seneca, ein Nachfolger Philodems?', in Erler (ed.), pp. 32–41.

Gill, C. (2006a) 'Psychophysical holism in Stoicism and Epicureanism', in *Common to Body and Soul: Philosophical Approaches to explaining Living Behaviour in Greco-Roman Antiquity*, ed. R.A.H. King, Berlin: 209–31.

(2006b) *The Structured Self in Hellenistic and Roman Thought*, Oxford.

Gillespie, S. and Hardie, P. (eds) (2007) *The Cambridge Companion to Lucretius*, Cambridge.

Giussani, T. (1892–6) *Lucreti Cari De rerum natura libri sex, revisione del testo, commento e studi introduttivi*: vol. I, *Studi lucreziani*; vols II–IV, with E. Stampini; 3rd edn, V. D'Agostino, *Commento e note*, Turin.

Glad, C.E. (1995) *Adaptability in Epicurean and Early Christian Psychagogy: Paul and Philodemus*, Leiden.

Gladman, K.R. and P. Mitsis (1997) 'Lucretius and the unconscious', in Algra, Koenen and Schrijvers (eds.), pp. 215–24.

Glidden, D. (1983) 'Epicurean semantics', in *ΣΥΖΗΤΗΣΙΣ. Studi sull' Epicureismo greco e latino offerti a Marcello Gigante*, 2 vols., Naples: vol. I, pp. 185–226.

(1985) 'Epicurean *prolêpsis*', *Oxford Studies in Ancient Philosophy* 3: 175–217.

Glucker, J. (1978) *Antiochus and the Late Academy*, Hypomnemata 56, Göttingen.

Goldschmidt, V. (1977) *La doctrine d'Épicure et le droit*, Paris.

(1978) 'Remarques sur l'origine épicurienne de la "prénotion"', in *Les Stoïciens et leur logique*, ed. J. Brunschwig, Paris: 155–69.

Gordon, P. (1996) *Epicurus in Lycia. The Second-Century World of Diogenes of Oenoanda*, Ann Arbor.

Gosling, J.C.B. and C.C.W. Taylor (1982) *The Greeks on Pleasure*, Oxford.

Goulet, R. (2000) 'Épicure de Samos', in *Dictionnaire des philosophes antiques* 3, ed. R. Goulet, Paris: 154–81.

Griffin, M. (1989) 'Philosophy, politics and politicians', in Griffin and Barnes (eds.), pp. 1–37.

Griffin, M. and J. Barnes (eds.) (1989) *Philosophia Togata*, Oxford.

Guthrie, W.K.C. (1940) Review of Farrington 1939, *Classical Review* 54: 34–5.

Haake, M. (2007) *Die Philosoph in der Stadt*, Munich.

Haas, Albert (1896) *Über den Einfluss der epikureischen Staats – und Rechtsphilosophie auf die Philosophie des 16. und 17. Jahrhunderts*, Berlin.

Hadot, I. (1969) *Seneca und die griechisch-römische Tradition der Seelenleitung*, Berlin.

Hadot, P. (1987) 'Théologie, exégèse, révélation, écriture, dans la philosophie grecque', in *Les règles de l'interprétation*, ed. M. Tardieu, Paris: 13–34.

(1995) *Philosophy as a Way of Life*, tr. M. Chase, Oxford.

Hammerstaedt, J. (1992) 'Der Schlußteil von Philodems drittem Buch über Rhetorik', *Cronache Ercolanesi* 22: 9–117.

Hankinson, R.J. (1995) *The Sceptics*, London and New York.

(1998) *Cause and Explanation in Ancient Greek Thought*, Oxford.

(1999) 'Explanation and causation', in Algra, Barnes, Mansfeld and Schofield (eds.), pp. 479–512.

Hershbell, J.P. (1992) 'Plutarch and Epicureanism', *Aufstieg und Niedergang der römischen Welt* II 36, 5: 3355–83.

Hill, C. (1972) *The World Turned Upside Down*, London.

(1977) *Milton and the English Revolution*, London.

Hobbes, Thomas (1996) *Leviathan*, ed. Richard Tuck, Cambridge.

Hossenfelder, M. (1986) 'Epicurus – hedonist malgré lui', in Schofield and Striker (eds.), pp. 245–63.

(1996) 'Epikureer', in *Sprachtheorien der abendländischen Antike*, ed. P. Schmitter, Tübingen: 217–37.

Huby, P. (1967) 'The first discovery of the freewill problem', *Philosophy* 42: 353–62.

Huffman, C. (2005) *Archytas of Tarentum: Pythagorean, Philosopher and Mathematician King*, Cambridge.

Hume, David (1998) *An Enquiry concerning the Principles of Morals*, ed. Tom Beauchamp, Oxford.

Indelli, G. (1978) *Polistrato. Sul disprezzo irrationale delle opinioni popolari.* Edizione, traduzione e commento, La Scuola di Epicuro 2, Naples.

(1988) *Filodemo. L'ira.* Edizione, traduzione e commento, La Scuola di Epicuro 5, Naples.

Indelli, G. and V. Tsouna-McKirahan (1995) *[Philodemus]. [On Choices and Avoidances]*, La Scuola di Epicuro 15, Naples.

Ingenkamp, H.G. (1971) *Plutarchs Schriften über die Heilung der Seele*, Göttingen.

Inwood, B. (ed.) (2003) *The Cambridge Companion to the Stoics*, Cambridge
Inwood, B. and L. Gerson (1997) *Hellenistic Philosophy: Introductory Readings*, 2nd edn. Indianapolis.
Irwin, T.H. (1979) *Plato, Gorgias*, Oxford.
(1986) 'Socrates the Epicurean?', *Illinois Classical Studies* 11: 85–112.
(1991) 'Aristippus against happiness', *The Monist* 74: 55–82.
Isnardi Parente, M. (1990) 'Diogeniano, gli epicurei e la τύχη', *Aufstieg und Niedergang der römischen Welt* II 36, 4: 2424–45.
Janko, R. (2000) *Philodemus On poems Book 1*, edition, translation and commentary, Philodemus: The Aesthetic Works 1/1, Oxford.
Jensen, C. (1907) *Philodemi περὶ οἰκονομίας qui dicitur libellus*, Leipzig.
(1911) *Philodemi περὶ κακιῶν liber decimus*, Leipzig.
Johnson, M.R. (2003) 'Was Gassendi an Epicurean?', *History of Philosophy Quarterly* 20: 339–59.
Johnson, M.R. and C. Wilson (2007) 'Lucretius and the history of science,' in Gillespie and Hardie (eds.), pp. 131–48.
Jones, C.P. (1986) *Culture and Society in Lucian*, Cambridge, Mass.
Jones, H. (1989) *The Epicurean Tradition*, London.
(1992) 'Epicureanism in Renaissance moral and natural philosophy', *Journal of the History of Ideas* 53: 573–83.
Judeich, W. (1931) *Topographie von Athen*, 2nd edn, Munich.
Jürss, F. (1991) *Die epikureische Erkenntnistheorie*, Berlin.
Kahn, C. (1985) 'Democritus and the origins of moral psychology', *American Journal of Philology* 106: 1–31.
Kapitan, T. (2002) 'A master argument for incompatibilism?', in R. Kane *The Oxford Handbook of Free Will*, Oxford: 127–57.
Kargon, R.H. (1966) *Atomism in England from Hariot to Newton*, Oxford.
Kaufman, F. (1996) 'Death and deprivation; Or, why Lucretius' symmetry argument fails', *American Journal of Philosophy* 74: 305–12.
Kleve, K. (1989) 'Lucretius in Herculaneum', *Cronache Ercolanesi* 19: 5–27.
Konstan, D. (1972) 'Epicurus on "up" & "down" (*Letter to Herodotus* § 60)', *Phronesis* 17: 269–78.
(2006a) 'Epicurean "passions" and the good life', in Reis (ed.), pp. 194–205.
(2006b) *The Emotions of the Ancient Greeks: Studies in Aristotle and Classical Literature*, Toronto.
(2007) *Lucrezio e la Psicologia Epicurea*, Milan.
(forthcoming) 'Epicurus on the gods', in Fish and Sanders.
Konstan, D., D. Clay, C.E. Glad, J.C. Thom and J. Ware (1998) *Philodemus: On Frank Criticism. Introduction, Translation and Notes*, Atlanta.
Körte, A. (1890) 'Metrodori Epicurei fragmenta', *Jahrbücher für klassische Philologie*, Supplement Band. 17: 531–97.
Kühn, C. (1822–33) *Galeni opera omnia*, Leipzig.

Kuiper, T. (1925) *Philodemos over den Dood*, Amsterdam.

Laks, A. (1991) 'Epicure et la doctrine aristotélicienne du continu', in *La physique d'Aristote et les conditions d'une science de la nature*, ed. F. de Gandt and P. Souffrin, Paris: 181–94.

Lalonde, G.V. (2006) '*IG* I[3] 1005 B and the boundary of Melite and Kollytos', *Hesperia* 75: 83–119.

Lana, I. (1991) 'Le lettere a Lucilio nella letteratura epistolare', in *Sénèque et la prose latine. Neuf exposés suivis de discussions*, ed. P. Grimal, Geneva: 253–89.

Laursen, S. (1995) 'The early parts of Epicurus *On nature* 25th book', *Cronache Ercolanesi* 25: 5–109.

(1997) 'The later parts of Epicurus *On nature* 25th book', *Cronache Ercolanesi* 27: 5–82.

Lee, M. (2005) *Epistemology after Protagoras: Responses to Relativism in Plato, Aristotle, and Democritus*, Oxford.

Leibniz, Gottfried Wilhelm (1989–) *Vorausedition*, Akademie der Wissenschaften Münster.

Leiwo, M. and P. Remes (1999) 'Partnership of citizens and metics: The will of Epicurus', *Classical Quarterly* 49: 161–6.

Lennon, T.M. (1993) *The Battle of the Gods and Giants: The Legacies of Descartes and Gassendi, 1655–1715*, Princeton.

Lévy, C. (2000) 'Philon d'Alexandrie et l'épicurisme', in Erler (ed.), pp. 122–36.

Locke, John (1975) *An Essay Concerning Human Understanding*, ed. P. H. Nidditch, Oxford.

(1990) *Questions Concerning the Law of Nature*, ed. Robert Horwitz and Jenny Strauss Clay, tr. Diskin Clay, Ithaca.

Long, A.A. (1971) 'Aisthesis, prolepsis and linguistic theory in Epicurus', *Bulletin of the Institute of Classical Studies* 18: 114–33.

(1986) 'Pleasure and social utility. The virtues of being Epicurean', in *Aspects de la Philosophie hellénistique*, ed. H. Flashar and O. Gigon, Geneva: 283–324.

(1999) 'Aristippus and Cyrenaic hedonism', in Algra, Barnes, Mansfeld and Schofield (eds.), pp. 632–9.

Long A.A. and D.N. Sedley (1987) *The Hellenistic Philosophers*, 2 vols., Cambridge.

Longo Auricchio, F. (1977) 'ΦΙΛΟΔΗΜΟΥ ΠΕΡΙ ΡΗΤΟΡΙΚΗΣ libros primum et secundum', in *Ricerche sui papiri ercolanesi*, ed. F. Sbordone, vol. 3. Naples.

(1978) 'La scuola di Epicuro', *Cronache Ercolanesi* 8: 21–37.

(1985) 'Testimonianze dalla "Retorica" di Filodemo sulla concezione dell'oratoria nei primi maestri Epicurei', *Cronache Ercolanesi* 15: 31–61.

(1988) Ermarco: *Frammenti*, La Scuola di Epicuro 6, Naples.

(1997) 'New elements for the reconstruction of Philodemus' *Rhetorica*', in *Akten des 21. internationalen Papyrologenkongresses*: 2.631–5, Stuttgart and Leipzig.

Ludwig, Bernd (2005) 'Cicero oder Epikur: Ueber einen "Paradigmenwechsel" in Hobbes' politischer Philosophie', in *Der Einfluss des Hellenismus auf die Philosophie der fruehen Neuzeit*, ed. Gabor Boros, Wiesbaden: 159–80.

Makin, S. (1993) *Indifference Arguments*, Oxford.

Mangoni, C. (1993) *Filodemo. Il quinto Libro della poetica* (*PHerc.* 1425 e 1538), La Scuola di Epicuro 14, Naples.

Mansfeld, J. (1992) 'A Theophrastean excursus on god and nature and its aftermath in Hellenistic thought', *Phronesis* 37: 314–35.

(1993) 'Aspects of Epicurean theology', *Mnemosyne* 46: 172–210.

(1994) 'Epicurus Peripateticus', in *Realtà e Ragione, Studi di Filosofia antica*, ed. A. Alberti, Florence: 29–47.

(1999) 'Sources', in Algra, Barnes, Mansfeld and Schofield (eds.), pp. 3–30.

Markschies C. (2000) 'Epikureismus bei Origenes und in der origenistischen Tradition', in Erler (ed.), pp. 190–217.

Masi, F. (2006) *Epicuro e la Filosofia della Mente. Il* XXV *Libro dell'Opera* Sulla Natura, Sankt Augustin.

Mayo, T. (1934) *Epicurus in England 1650–1725*, Dallas.

Melville, R. (1997) (tr.) *On the Nature of the Universe, by Lucretius, a new verse translation*, Oxford.

Militello, C. (1997) *Filodemo: Memorie Epicuree (*PHerc. *1418 e 310)*, La Scuola di Epicuro 16, Naples.

Mill, J.S. (1950) *On Bentham and Coleridge*, ed. F.R. Leavis, Westport, Conn.

(1963–91) *Collected Works*, 33 vols., Toronto.

Miller, M. (2005) 'Epicureanism in Renaissance thought and art: Piero di Cosimo's paintings on the life of early man', Lecture, American Philological Association, Boston.

Mitsis, P. (1988) *Epicurus' Ethical Theory: the Pleasures of Invulnerability*, Ithaca and London.

(1993) 'Committing philosophy on the reader: didactic coercion and autonomy in *De Rerum Natura*', in *Mega nepioi: il destinatario nell' epos didascalico*, ed. J.S. Clay *et al.*, Materiali e discussione 31: 111–28.

Momigliano, A. (1935) 'Su alcuni dati della vita di Epicuro', *Rivista di filologia e di istruzione classica* NS 13: 302–16.

(1941) Review of Farrington 1939. *Journal of Roman Studies* 31: 149–57.

Moore, A.W. (2006) 'Williams, Nietzsche, and the meaninglessness of immortality', *Mind* 115: 311–30.

More, Henry (1653) *An Antidote Against Atheism*, London.

More, Thomas (1751) *Utopia Containing an Impartial History of the Manners, Customs, Polity, Government, &c. of that Island*, tr. Thomas Burnet, London.

Morel, P.-M. (1996) *Démocrite et la recherche des causes*, Paris.

(1998) 'Démocrite. Connaissance et apories', *Revue Philosophique de la France et de l'étranger*: 145–63.

(2000) 'Épicure, l'histoire et le droit', *Revue des études antiques* 102: 393–411.

(2003) 'Corps et cosmologie dans la physique d'Epicure. *Lettre à Hérodote*, § 45', *Revue de métaphysique et de morale*: 33–49.

(2007) 'Method and evidence: on Epicurean preconception', *Proceedings of the Boston Area Colloquium in Ancient Philosophy* 23: 25–48.

Müller, R. (1972) *Die Epikureische Gesellschaftstheorie*, Berlin.

Murray, O. (1965) 'Philodemus on the good king according to Homer', *Journal of Roman Studies* 55: 161–82.

(1984) 'Rileggendo *Il buon re secondo Omero*', *Cronache Ercolanesi* 14: 157–60.

Nadler, S. (2001) *Spinoza's Heresy: Immortality and the Jewish Mind*, Oxford.

Nagel, T. (1979) 'Death', in his *Mortal Questions*, Cambridge: 1–10.

Nahmias, E. (2002) 'When consciousness matters: A critical review of Daniel Wegner's *The Illusion of Conscious Will*', *Philosophical Psychology* 15: 527–44.

Nehamas, A. (1998) *The Art of Living*, Berkeley.

Newton, Isaac (1952) *Opticks*, 4th edn, ed. I.B. Cohen, New York.

Nikolsky, B. (2001) 'Epicurus on pleasure', *Phronesis* 46: 440–65.

Nussbaum M. (1986) 'Therapeutic arguments: Epicurus and Aristotle', in Schofield and Striker (eds.), pp. 31–74.

(1994) *The Therapy of Desire*, Princeton.

Obbink, D. (1988) 'Hermarchus, against Empedocles', *Classical Quarterly* 38: 428–35.

(1989) 'The atheism of Epicurus', *Greek, Roman and Byzantine Studies* 30: 187–223.

(1992) '"What all men believe–must be true": common conceptions and *consensio omnium* in Aristotle and Hellenistic philosophy', *Oxford Studies in Ancient Philosophy* 10: 193–231.

(1995) (ed.) *Philodemus and Poetry. Poetic Theory and Practice in Lucretius, Philodemus, and Horace*, Oxford.

(1996) *Philodemus. On Piety I*, Oxford.

(2002) '"All gods are true" in Epicurus', in *Traditions of Theology. Studies in Hellenistic Theology, Its Background and Aftermath*, ed. D. Frede and B. Inwood, Leiden: 183–221.

(2007) 'Lucretius and the Herculaneum library', in Gillespie and Hardie (eds.), pp. 33–40.

O'Connor, D.K. (1989) 'The invulnerable pleasures of Epicurean friendship', *Greek, Roman and Byzantine Studies* 30: 165–86.

O'Keefe, T. (1997) 'The ontological status of sensible qualities for Democritus and Epicurus', *Ancient Philosophy* 17: 119–34.

(2001a) 'Is Epicurean friendship altruistic?', *Apeiron* 34: 269–305.

(2001b) 'Would a community of wise Epicureans be just?', *Ancient Philosophy* 21: 133–46.

(2002a) 'The reductionist and compatibilist argument of Epicurus' *On nature*, Book 25', *Phronesis* 47: 153–86.

(2002b) 'The Cyrenaics on pleasure, happiness, and future-concern', *Phronesis* 47: 395–416.

(2005) *Epicurus on Freedom*, Cambridge.

Oliver, J.H. (1938) 'An inscription concerning the Epicurean school at Athens', *Transactions of the American Philological Association* 69: 494–9.

Olivieri, A. (1914) *Philodemi Περὶ παρρησίας libellus*, Leipzig.

O'Meara, D.J. (1999) 'Epicurus neoplatonicus', in *Zur Rezeption der hellenistischen Philosophie in der Spätantike*, ed. T. Fuhrer and M. Erler, Stuttgart: 83–91.

(2000) 'Epikur bei Simplikios', in *Epikureismus in der späten Republik und der Kaiserzeit*, ed. M. Erler, Stuttgart: 243–51.

Osler, M. (2003) 'Early modern uses of Hellenistic philosophy: Gassendi's Epicurean project', *in Hellenistic and Early Modern Philosophy*, ed. Jon Miller and Brad Inwood, Cambridge: 30–44.

Parfit, D. (1984) *Reasons and Persons*, Oxford.

Pasnau, R. (2007) 'Democritus and secondary qualities', *Archiv für Geschichte der Philosophie* 89: 99–121.

Pigeaud, J.-M. (1984) 'Épicure et Lucrèce et l'origine du langage', *Revue des études latines* 62: 122–44.

Preuss, P. (1994) *Epicurean Ethics: Katastematic Hedonism*, Lewiston.

Procopé, J. (1998) 'Epicureans on anger', in *The Emotions in Hellenistic Philosophy*, ed. J. Sihvola and T. Engberg-Pedersen, Dordrecht: 171–96.

Prosperi, V. (2007) 'Lucretius in the Italian renaissance', in Gillespie and Hardie (eds.), pp. 214–16.

Puglia, E. (ed.) (1988) *Demetrio Lacone. Aporie testuali ed esegetiche in Epicuro (PHerc. 1012). Edizione, traduzione e commento*, Naples.

Purinton, J. (1993) 'Epicurus on the *telos*', *Phronesis* 38: 281–320.

(1999) 'Epicurus on "free volition" and the Atomic Swerve', *Phronesis* 44: 253–99.

(2001) 'Epicurus on the nature of the gods', *Oxford Studies in Ancient Philosophy* 21: 181–231.

Rackham, H. (tr.) (1931) Cicero, *De finibus bonorum et malorum*, Cambridge, Mass.

Raubitschek, A.E. (1949) *Dedications from the Athenian Acropolis*, Cambridge, Mass.

Redondi, P. (1987) *Galileo: Heretic*, Princeton.

Reinhardt, T. (2002) 'The speech of Nature in Lucretius' *De rerum natura* 3.931–71', *Classical Quarterly* 52: 291–304.

Reis, B. (ed.) (2006) *The Virtuous Life in Greek Ethics*, Cambridge.

Richter, G.M.A. (1984) *The Portraits of the Greeks*, abridged and revised by R.R.R. Smith, Ithaca, New York.

Rispoli, G.M. (2006) '*Thema* tra retorica e filosofia', in *Papers on Rhetoric*, ed L.C. Montefusco, Rome: 203–25.

Rist, J.M. (1972) *Epicurus. An Introduction*, Cambridge.

(1980) 'Epicurus on friendship', *Classical Philology* 75: 121–9.

Robert, L. (1980) *A travers l'Asie mineure. Poètes et prosateurs, monnaies grecques, voyageurs et géographie*, Paris.

Robin, L. (1962). See Ernout and Robin 1962.

Romeo, C. (ed.) (1988) *Demetrio Lacone. La poesia (PHerc. 188 e 1014). Edizione, traduzione e commento*, La Scuola di Epicuro 9, Naples.

Rosen, F. (2002) 'Utility and justice: Epicurus and the Epicurean tradition', *Polis* 19: 93–107.

Rosenbaum, S. (1986) 'How to be dead and not care: a defense of Epicurus', *American Philosophical Quarterly* 23: 217–25.

(1989) 'Epicurus and annihilation', *Philosophical Quarterly* 39: 81–90.

(1990) 'Epicurus on pleasure and the complete life', *Monist* 73: 21–41.

Roskam, G. (2005) 'The displeasing secrets of the Epicurean life. Plutarch's polemic against Epicurus' political philosophy', in *Plutarco e l'età ellenistica. Atti del Convegno Internazionale di Studi. Firenze, 23–24 settembre 2004*, ed. A. Casanova, Florence: 351–68.

(2007) Live Unnoticed: *On the Vicissitudes of an Epicurean Doctrine*, Leiden.

Saint-Évremond, Charles de Marguetel de Saint Denis, sieur de (1712) *Epicurus' Morals, to which is added, an essay in Epicurus' Morals written by Monsieur Saint-Évremond*, tr. John Digby, London.

(1714) *Works*, ed. Pierre des Maizeaux, 3 vols., London.

Santoro, M. (2000a) *[Demetrio Lacone] [La forma del dio] (PHerc.* 1055) Naples.

(2000b) 'Il pensiero teologico epicureo: Demetrio Lacone e Filodemo', *Cronache Ercolanesi* 30: 63–70.

Schenkeveld, D. (1999) 'Language', in Algra, Barnes, Mansfield and Schofield (eds.), pp. 197–225.

Schiebe, M.W. (2003). 'Sind die Epikureischen Götter "Thought–Constructs"?', *Mnemosyne* 56: 703–27.

Schiesaro, A. (1990) *Simulacrum et imago: gli Argomenti analogici nel* De rerum natura. Biblioteca di 'Materiali e discussioni per l'analisi dei testi classici' 8, Pisa.

Schmid, W. (1955) 'Eine falsche Epikurdeutung Senecas und seine Praxis der erbauenden Lesung (Epic. Gnom. Vat. 60)', *Acme* 8: 119–29.

(1962) 'Epikur', in *Reallexikon für Antike und Christentum* v, ed. T. Klauser, Stuttgart: 681–819. Repr. in W. Schmid: *Ausgewählte philologische Schriften*, ed. H. Erbse, J. Kueppers, Berlin 1984:151–266.

Schofield, M. (1991) *The Stoic Idea of the City*, Cambridge.

(1996) 'Epilogismos: an appraisal', in *Rationality in Greek Thought*, ed. M. Frede and G. Striker, Oxford: 221–37.

(2000) 'Epicurean and Stoic political thought', in *The Cambridge History of Greek and Roman Political Thought*, ed. C. Rowe and M. Schofield, Cambridge: 435–56.

Schofield, M. and G. Striker (eds.) (1986) *The Norms of Nature: Studies in Hellenistic Ethics*, Cambridge.

Scholz, P. (1997) *Der Philosoph und die Politik. Die Ausbildung der philosophischen Lebensform und die Entwicklung des Verhältnisses von Philosophie und Politik um 4. und 3. Jh. v. Chr.*, Frankfurter althistorische Beiträge 2, Stuttgart.

Schrijvers, P.H. (1970) Horror ac divina voluptas: *Études sur la poétique et la poésie de Lucrèce*, Amsterdam.

(1999) *Lucrèce et les sciences de la vie*, Leiden.

(2007) 'Seeing the invisible: A study of Lucretius' use of analogy in *De rerum natura*', in *Lucretius*, ed. M. Gale, Oxford Readings in Classical Studies, Oxford: 255–88.

Scott, W. (1883) 'The physical constitution of the Epicurean gods', *Journal of Philology* 2: 212–47.

Sedley, D. (1973) 'Epicurus *On nature*, book XXVIII', *Cronache Ercolanesi* 3: 5–83.

(1976) 'Epicurus and his professional rivals', in *Études sur l'Épicurisme antique*, Cahiers de philologie 1, ed. J. Bollack and A. Laks, Lille: 119–59.

(1982) 'Two conceptions of vacuum', *Phronesis* 27: 175–93.

(1983) 'Epicurus' refutation of determinism', in *ΣΥΖΗΤΗΣΙΣ. Studi sull'Epicureismo greco e romano offerti a M. Gigante*, vol. 1, Naples: 11–51.

(1988) 'Epicurean anti–reductionism', in *Matter and Metaphysics*, ed. J. Barnes and M. Mignucci, Naples: 295–327.

(1989) 'Philosophical allegiance in the Greco–Roman world', in Griffin and J. Barnes (eds.), pp. 97–119.

(1994) Review of Nussbaum 1994, *TLS* (24 June 1994).

(1996) 'The inferential foundations of Epicurean ethics', in *Epicureismo greco e romano*, ed. G. Giannantoni and M. Gigante. Naples: 313–39. Repr. with minor changes as Sedley (1998b).

(1998a) *Lucretius and the Transformation of Greek Wisdom*, Cambridge.

(1998b) 'The inferential foundations of Epicurean ethics', in *Ethics*, ed. S. Everson, Companions to Ancient Thought 4, Cambridge: 129–50.

(1999) 'Hellenistic physics and metaphysics', in Algra, Barnes, Mansfeld and Schofield (eds.), pp. 355–411.

(2003) 'Philodemus and the decentralisation of philosophy', *Cronache Ercolanesi* 33: 31–41.

(2004) 'Lucretius', *Stanford Encyclopedia of Philosophy*, http://plato.stanford.edu/entries/lucretius.

(2007) *Creationism and its Critics in Antiquity*, Berkeley.

(forthcoming) 'Epicurus' theological innatism' in Fish and Sanders (eds.).

Segal, C.P. (1990) *Lucretius on Death and Anxiety*, Princeton.

Sennert, Daniel (1660) *Epitome philosophiae naturalis*, Wittenberg, 1618, tr. as *Thirteen Books of Natural Philosophy*, London.

Shaw, J.C. (2007) *'Plato and Epicurus on pleasure, perception, and value'*, Ph.D. dissertation, Washington University in St Louis.

Sider, D. (1995) 'Epicurean poetics: response and dialogue', in Obbink (ed.), pp. 42–57.

(1997) *The Epigrams of Philodemos*, New York and Oxford.

(2005) *The Library of the Villa dei Papiri at Herculaneum*, Los Angeles.

Simpson, D. (1985) 'Epicureanism in the *Confessions* of St. Augustine', *Augustinian Studies* 16: 39–48.

Smith, M.F. (1993) *Diogenes of Oinoanda. The Epicurean Inscription*. La Scuola di Epicuro, Suppl. 1, Naples.

(1996) 'An Epicurean priest from Apamea in Syria', *Zeitschrift für Papyrologie und Epigraphik* 112: 120–30.

(2000) 'Digging up Diogenes. New Epicurean texts from Oinoanda in Lycia', in Erler (ed.), pp. 64–75.

(2003a) *Supplement to Diogenes of Oinoanda, the Epicurean Inscription*, La Scuola di Epicuro, Suppl. 3, Naples.

(2003b) 'Herculaneum and Oinoanda, Philodemus and Diogenes. Comparison of two Epicurean discoveries and two Epicurean teachers', *Cronache Ercolanesi* 33: 267–78.

Snyder, H.G. (2000) *Teachers and Texts in the Ancient World*, London and New York.

Solmsen, F. (1953) 'Epicurus on the growth and decline of the cosmos', *American Journal of Philology* 74: 34–51.

Sorabji, R. (1993) *Animal Minds and Human Morals: The Origins of the Western Debate*, London.

(2000) *Emotion and Peace of Mind*, Oxford.

Spinoza, Baruch (1985) *Collected Works*, vol. I, ed. and tr. Edwin Curley, Princeton.

Spoerri, W. (1959) *Späthellenistische Berichte über Welt, Kultur, und Götter: Untersuchungen zu Diodor von Sizilien*, Schweizerische Beiträge zur Altertumswissenschaft 9, Basel.

Staden, H. von (2000) 'Body, soul, and the nerves: Epicurus, Herophilus, Erasistratus, the Stoics, and Galen', in *Psyche and Soma: Physicians and Metaphysicians on the Mind–Body Problem from Antiquity to Enlightenment*, ed. J.P. Wright and P. Potter, Oxford: 79–116

Stillingfleet, Edward (1662) *Origines Sacrae: A Rational account of the grounds of Christian Faith, as to the truth and divine authority of the Scriptures and the matters therein contained*, 3 vols., London.

Stokes, M. (1995) 'Cicero on Epicurean pleasures', in *Cicero the Philosopher*, ed. J. Powell, Oxford: 145–70.

Striker, G. (1977) 'Epicurus on the truth of sense impressions', *Archiv für Geschichte der Philosophie* 59: 125–42. Reprinted in her *Essays in Hellenistic Epistemology and Ethics*, Cambridge: 77–91.

(1996a) 'κριτήριον τῆς ἀληθείας' in her *Essays on Hellenistic Epistemology and ethics*, Cambridge: 22–76. English translation of the original German version published in *Nachrichten der Akademie der Wissenschaften zu Göttingen*, I Phil.-hist. Klasse 2 (1974), Göttingen: 48–110

(1996b) '*Ataraxia*: happiness as tranquillity', in her *Essays in Hellenistic Epistemology and Ethics*, Cambridge: 183–95.

(1996c) 'Epicurean hedonism', in her *Essays in Hellenistic Epistemology and Ethics*, Cambridge: 196–208.

Sudhaus, S. (ed.) (1892–6) *Philodemi volumina rhetorica*, Leizpig. Repr. Amsterdam 1964 (vol. I 1892, vol. II 1896).

Taub, L. (2003) *Ancient Meteorology*, London.

Taylor, C.C.W. (1980) '"All perceptions are true"', in *Doubt and Dogmatism: Studies in Hellenistic Epistemology*, ed. M. Schofield, M. Burnyeat and J. Barnes, Oxford: 105–24.

(1999) *The Atomists: Leucippus and Democritus. Fragments: A Text and Translation with a Commentary*, Toronto.

(2007) 'Democritus and Lucretius on death and dying', in *Democritus: Science, the Arts and the Care of the Soul*, ed. A. Brancacci and P.-M. Morel, Leiden: 77–86.

Tepedino Guerra A. (1985) 'Il *PHerc.* 1678: Filodemo sull'invidia?', *Cronache Ercolanesi* 15: 113–25.

(1994) 'L'opera filodemea *su Epicuro* (*PHerc.* 1232, 1289β)', *Cronache Ercolanesi* 24: 5–54.

Timpe, D. (2000) 'Der Epikureismus in der römischen Gesellschaft der Kaiserzeit', in Erler (ed.), pp. 42–63.

Tsouna, V. (2001) 'Cicéron et Philodème: quelques considérations sur l'éthique', in *Cicéron et Philodème: la polémique en philosophie*, ed. C. Auvray-Assayas and D. Delattre, Paris: 159–172.

(2002) 'Is there an exception to Greek eudaimonism?', in *Le Style de la pensée*, ed. M. Canto-Sperber and P. Pellegrin, Paris: 464–89.

(2006) 'Rationality and the fear of death in Epicurean philosophy', *Rhizai* 3: 79–117.

(2007a) *The Ethics of Philodemus*, Oxford.

(2007b) 'Philodemus and the Epicurean tradition', in *Pyrrhonists, Patricians, Platonizers. Hellenistic Philosophy in the Period 155–86* BC, ed. A.M. Ioppolo and D.N. Sedley, Rome: 339–97.

(2007c) Review of Warren 2004, *Rhizai* 4: 195–202

Usener, H. (1887) *Epicurea*, Leipzig. Repr. Stuttgart 1966.

Valla, Lorenzo (1977) *On Pleasure,* tr. A. Kent Hieatt and Mariella Lorch, New York.

Van Inwagen, P. (1983) *An Essay on Free Will*, Oxford.

(1990) *Material Beings*, Ithaca.

Vander Waerdt, P.A. (1987) 'The justice of the Epicurean wise man', *Classical Quarterly* 37: 402–22.

(1988) 'Hermarchus and the Epicurean genealogy of morals', *Transactions of the American Philological Association* 118: 87–106.

Vlastos, G. (1965) 'Minimal parts in Epicurean atomism', *Isis* 56: 121–47.

Vogliano, A. (1928) *Epicuri et Epicureorum scripta*, Berlin.

Volk, K. (2002) *The Poetics of Latin Didactic*, Oxford.

Wardy, R. (1988) 'Eleatic Pluralism', *Archiv für Geschichte der Philosophie* 70: 125–46.

Warren, J. (2000a) 'Epicurean immortality', *Oxford Studies in Ancient Philosophy* 18: 231–61.

(2000b) 'Diogenes *Epikourios*: keep taking the tablets', *Journal of Hellenic Studies* 120: 144–8.

(2001a) 'Epicurus and the pleasures of the future', *Oxford Studies in Ancient Philosophy* 21: 135–79.

(2001b) 'Lucretian *palingenesis* recycled', *Classical Quarterly* 51: 499–508.

(2002a) *Epicurus and Democritean Ethics: An Archaeology of Ataraxia*, Cambridge.

(2002b) 'Democritus, the Epicureans, death, and dying', *Classical Quarterly* 52: 193–206.

(2004a) *Facing Death. Epicurus and his Critics*, Oxford.

(2004b) 'Ancient atomists on the plurality of worlds', *Classical Quarterly* 54: 354–65.

(2006) 'Epicureans and the present past', *Phronesis* 51: 362–87.
(2007a) 'L'éthique', in *Lire Épicure et les Épicuriens*, ed. A. Gigandet and P.-M. Morel, Paris: 117–43.
(2007b) 'Lucretius and Greek philosophy', in Gillespie and Hardie (eds.), pp. 19–32.
(forthcoming) 'The harm of death in Cicero's first *Tusculan disputation*', in *Death: Ethics and Metaphysics*, ed. J.S. Taylor.
Wasserstein, A. (1978) 'Epicurean science', *Hermes* 106: 484–94.
Wegner, D. (2002) *The Illusion of Conscious Will*, Cambridge, Mass.
Wendlandt, L. and D. Baltzly (2004) 'Knowing freedom: Epicurean philosophy beyond atomism and the swerve', *Phronesis* 49: 41–71.
Westmann, R. (1955) *Plutarch gegen Kolotes. Seine Schrift 'Adversus Colotem' als philosophiegeschichtliche Quelle*, Helsinki.
Williams, B. (1973) 'The Makropulos case: reflections of the tedium of immortality', in his *Problems of the Self*, Cambridge: 82–100.
Wilson, C. (2008) *Epicureanism at the Origins of Modernity*, Oxford.
Winiarczyk, M. (1990) 'Methodisches zum antiken Atheismun', *Rheinisches Museum* 133: 1–15.
Woolf, R. (tr.) (2001) Cicero, *On Moral Ends* (with notes by J. Annas), Cambridge.
(2004) 'What kind of hedonist was Epicurus?' *Phronesis* 49: 303–22.
Wycherley, R.E. (1959) 'The garden of Epicurus', *Phoenix* 13: 73–77.
Yates, F. (1966) *The Art of Memory*, Chicago.
Zacher, K. (1982) *Plutarchs Kritik an der Lustlehre Epikurs. Ein Kommentar zu 'non posse suaviter vivi secundum Epicurum', Kap. 1–8* (BKP 124). Königstein.

USEFUL ONLINE RESOURCES

Centro Internazionale per lo studio dei papiri ercolanesi (CISPE)	www.cispegigante.it/
Epicurus Wiki	http://wiki.epicurus.info/
Friends of Herculaneum Society	www.herculaneum.ox.ac.uk

ABBREVIATIONS TO ANCIENT WORKS CITED AND INDEX LOCORUM

* For works preserved on the Herculaneum papyri readers should refer to the list of editions maintained by the Friends of Herculaneum Society on their website. See: www.herculaneum.ox.ac.uk/books.html.
They also maintain a list of works by papyrus number:
See: www.herculaneum.ox.ac.uk/editions.html.
References are given to the more recent available editions and use the numbering and referencing format from that edition.

GENERAL INDEX

OTHER VOLUMES IN THE SERIES OF CAMBRIDGE COMPANIONS

ABELARD *Edited by* JEFFREY E. BROWER *and* KEVIN GUILFOY

ADORNO *Edited by* THOMAS HUHN

ANSELM *Edited by* BRIAN DAVIES *and* BRIAN LEFTOW

AQUINAS *Edited by* NORMAN KRETZMANN *and* ELEONORE STUMP

ARABIC PHILOSOPHY *Edited by* PETER ADAMSON *and* RICHARD C. TAYLOR

HANNAH ARENDT *Edited by* DANA VILLA

ARISTOTLE *Edited by* JONATHAN BARNES

ATHEISM *Edited by* MICHAEL MARTIN

AUGUSTINE *Edited by* ELEONORE STUMP *and* NORMAN KRETZMANN

BACON *Edited by* MARKKU PELTONEN

BERKELEY *Edited by* KENNETH P. WINKLER

BRENTANO *Edited by* DALE JACQUETTE

CARNAP *Edited by* MICHAEL FRIEDMAN

CRITICAL THEORY *Edited by* FRED RUSH

DARWIN *Edited by* JONATHAN HODGE *and* GREGORY RADICK

SIMONE DE BEAUVOIR *Edited by* CLAUDIA CARD

DESCARTES *Edited by* JOHN COTTINGHAM

DUNS SCOTUS *Edited by* THOMAS WILLIAMS

EARLY GREEK PHILOSOPHY *Edited by* A.A. LONG

EARLY MODERN PHILOSOPHY *Edited by* MICHAEL RUTHERFORD

FEMINISM IN PHILOSOPHY *Edited by* MIRANDA FRICKER *and* JENNIFER HORNSBY

FOUCAULT 2nd edition *Edited by* GARY GUTTING

FREUD *Edited by* JEROME NEU

GADAMER *Edited by* ROBERT J. DOSTAL

GALEN *Edited by* R.J. HANKINSON

GALILEO *Edited by* PETER MACHAMER

GERMAN IDEALISM *Edited by* KARL AMERIKS

GREEK AND ROMAN PHILOSOPHY *Edited by* DAVID SEDLEY

HABERMAS *Edited by* STEPHEN K. WHITE

HAYEK *Edited by* EDWARD FESER
HEGEL *Edited by* FREDERICK BEISER
HEIDEGGER 2nd edition *Edited by* CHARLES GUIGNON
HOBBES *Edited by* TOM SORELL
HOBBES' 'LEVIATHAN' *Edited by* PATRICIA SPRINGBORG
HUME *Edited by* DAVID FATE NORTON
HUSSERL *Edited by* BARRY SMITH *and* DAVID WOODRUFF SMITH
WILLIAM JAMES *Edited by* RUTH ANNA PUTNAM
KANT *Edited by* PAUL GUYER
KANT AND MODERN PHILOSOPHY *Edited by* PAUL GUYER
KEYNES ROGER E. BACKHOUSE *and* BRADLEY W. BATEMAN
KIERKEGAARD *Edited by* ALASTAIR HANNAY *and* GORDON MARINO
LEIBNIZ *Edited by* NICHOLAS JOLLEY
LEVINAS *Edited by* SIMON CRITCHLEY *and* ROBERT BERNASCONI
LOCKE *Edited by* VERE CHAPPELL
LOCKE'S 'ESSAY CONCERNING HUMAN UNDERSTANDING' *Edited by* LEX NEWMAN
LOGICAL EMPIRICISM *Edited by* ALAN RICHARDSON *and* THOMAS UEBEL
MAIMONIDES *Edited by* KENNETH SEESKIN
MALEBRANCHE *Edited by* STEVEN NADLER
MARX *Edited by* TERRELL CARVER
MEDIEVAL JEWISH PHILOSOPHY *Edited by* DANIEL H. FRANK *and* OLIVER LEAMAN
MEDIEVAL PHILOSOPHY *Edited by* A.S. MCGRADE
MERLEAU-PONTY *Edited by* TAYLOR CARMAN *and* MARK B.N. HANSEN
MILL *Edited by* JOHN SKORUPSKI
MONTAIGNE *Edited by* ULLRICH LANGER
NEWTON *Edited by* I. BERNARD COHEN *and* GEORGE E. SMITH
NIETZSCHE *Edited by* BERND MAGNUS *and* KATHLEEN HIGGINS

OCKHAM *Edited by* PAUL VINCENT SPADE
PASCAL *Edited by* NICHOLAS HAMMOND
PEIRCE *Edited by* CHERYL MISAK
THE PHILOSOPHY OF BIOLOGY *Edited by* DAVID L. HULL *and* MICHAEL RUSE
PICO DELLA MIRANDOLA: NEW ESSAYS *Edited by* M.V. DOUGHERTY
PLATO *Edited by* RICHARD KRAUT
PLATO'S 'REPUBLIC' *Edited by* G.R.F. FERRARI
PLOTINUS *Edited by* LLOYD P. GERSON
QUINE *Edited by* ROGER F. GIBSON JR.
RAWLS *Edited by* SAMUEL FREEMAN
THOMAS REID *Edited by* TERENCE CUNEO *and* RENE VAN WOUDENBERG
RENAISSANCE PHILOSOPHY *Edited by* JAMES HANKINS
ROUSSEAU *Edited by* PATRICK RILEY
BERTRAND RUSSELL *Edited by* NICHOLAS GRIFFIN
SARTRE *Edited by* CHRISTINA HOWELLS
SCHOPENHAUER *Edited by* CHRISTOPHER JANAWAY
THE SCOTTISH ENLIGHTENMENT *Edited by* ALEXANDER BROADIE
ADAM SMITH *Edited by* KNUD HAAKONSSEN
SPINOZA *Edited by* DON GARRETT
THE STOICS *Edited by* BRAD INWOOD
TOCQUEVILLE *Edited by* CHERYL B. WELCH
WITTGENSTEIN *Edited by* HANS SLUGA *and* DAVID STERN